The Catholic Church

Saint Mary's Press
Christian Brothers Publications
Winona, Minnesota

The Catholic Church

Our Mission in History

by Alphonsus Pluth, FSC
with Carl Koch, FSC

Nihil Obstat: Rev. Msgr. William T. Magee
           Censor Deputatus
           10 February 1985
Imprimatur: †Loras J. Watters, DD
           Bishop of Winona
           10 February 1985

The publishing team for this course book included Stephan Nagel, Robert Smith, FSC,
Rev. Robert Stamschror, and Thomas Zanzig,
consulting editors; Nancy Campbell, manuscript
editor; Mary Kraemer, production editor; and
Carolyn Thomas, designer and illustrator.

The acknowledgments continue on page 335.

Printed in the United States of America

Printing: 11 10 9

Year: 1995 94 93

ISBN 0-88489-161-5

Contents

1
Why Study Church History?

Why Study History at All?

Several years ago, the national news media focused on a Florida woman in her twenties who had been found wandering around near a highway; she had suffered severe bodily injuries from unknown causes. The reason the story got national attention was because the woman suffered from nearly total amnesia—that is, loss of memory. Her history had almost been totally wiped away. She did not know where she was or how she got there. So severe was her memory loss that she had to relearn elementary actions: how to dress herself, how to tie her shoes, how to eat properly. She had also forgotten basic skills such as reading and writing. In other words, she had to learn dozens of things that we take for granted. In addition, Jane Doe, as she was called, knew no one. In effect, she had no family or friends—no one to depend on in a world that was unknown to her.

She had to begin the slow process of building relationships. This meant gradually learning about others. During this long process, she suffered a sense of loneliness. Even if she had come from a family filled with difficulties, at least she might have depended on them for some help. On a very practical level, she would have had a name, an address, and an identifiable parentage. Without this information, she could not register for a driver's license, open a bank account, request school transcripts, or fill out an application for a job. Jane Doe, in many real ways, had to begin life again.

Our Memories Are
Our Identities

Clearly, for all of us, our memories and histories are very important. And on a much more profound level, without a family and all the information they give us about ourselves over the years, we would have no recognition of our talents, our attractiveness, our humor, our intelligence. In short, we would not have a personality—an identity.

We learn our identities from the interactions we have with many others. For instance, if you feel that being "athletic" is a trait you possess, it is probably because in grade school your dad and mom—and maybe some neighbors and coaches—said things like, "You can really shoot and dribble well." The more this aspect of your identity is reinforced by others saying the same sorts of things, the more your identity as "athlete" becomes a part of who you are.

As an amnesiac, of course, this understanding of yourself would be totally lost, and you would have to discover it all over again. Until you relearned your personality traits, you would be unsure of how to act or what to do. You would not have a memory that would automatically, unconsciously, give you the confidence that comes with knowing who you are. Not having a sense of our personal histories is to live in a prison of ignorance.

Knowing our personal histories can help us make better choices. If I know that I am sharp in mathematics, and have a history of success in math courses, I can make a better choice of a college major. If I have been dating someone and know a lot about him or her, I can make a better decision about whether or not to continue the relationship. An amnesiac has no history and no identity. Such a person is isolated and has little chance of coping with the real world.

The Problem
of Group Amnesia

If the amnesiac as an individual has problems coping with the world, imagine the dreadful consequences of whole groups of people forgetting their history. Whenever this happens, we have to relearn terrifying lessons. For instance, during the many centuries of Christianity, people have often forgotten that, in fact, Jesus was a Jew and that the roots of Christian faith are in Judaism. Thus, there is no way to hate Jews without hating Jesus.

One recent result of forgetting this historical fact was the holocaust during World War II, in which millions of Jews were murdered by the German Nazis. Adolf Hitler, the German chancellor, played on his people's mistaken notion that the Jews had killed Jesus. Hitler's many lies about Jews were accepted. The Jews became scapegoats for all of the problems of Germany, which was still recovering from the humiliating defeat of the First World War. A stronger sense of history might have weakened the power of a man like Hitler and have prevented the slaughter of millions of people.

Another example: Two of the most important deterrents against nuclear war are the stories of Hiroshima and Nagasaki. The memories of the agonizing deaths of the thousands who were burned in the blast or crushed under collapsed buildings make us more hesitant to repeat the use of atomic weapons. If we ever forget what hell is caused by nuclear weapons, we will be one step closer to using them again.

However, when we do look back and draw on our history, we can find more encouraging examples. Centuries ago, Greek dramatists wrote plays to inspire, challenge, and enlighten their audiences. Aristophanes, Sophocles, and Aeschylus set the patterns for structuring plays that would be used by Shakespeare, as well as all modern playwrights. In fact, in learning to write scripts for the stage, movies, or TV, authors study great writers from the past. From them, new writers learn what touches the human spirit, what makes us laugh or cry. Thus, in this positive way, history is invaluable.

Few Mistakes, More Choices

The job of the historian is to keep the story of humankind always available to us. With the lessons of history clearly in mind, we can avoid the mistakes of the past and plan for a better world. A keen awareness of history can thus be liberating.

The records of historians also enable us to see possibilities of action and, thus, to make better choices. For instance, medical researchers need to know the uses of various drugs in order to put together new curative compounds. Medical journals and textbooks record the history of pharmaceutical research. They also report on recent findings of scientists all over the world. So, if a researcher in India has uncovered certain uses of a substance, her fellow researcher in Holland will not have to duplicate the same tests. He can instead do new explorations based on these earlier findings. Thus, time is saved, and even more important, lives may be saved. History—in this case, the story of medical findings—can be liberating because it opens up new possibilities.

So why study history? Because it gives us a sense of our personal and cultural identity. Because knowledge of the story of humankind can free us from making the mistakes of the past. Because history helps us make informed choices so that we can see more options.

Why Study *Church* History?

Christianity is a historical religion. That is, it is based on the life of a historical person—Jesus Christ. The Gospels give us a record of who Jesus was during his life on earth. Likewise, the histories of the Church provide a perspective on how Christians have lived out the gospel message over the centuries.

As our understanding of the Church's history grows, our identities as Catholic Christians deepen. We can see ourselves as members of a great religious movement that began two thousand years ago. What began in a small and remote country with twelve disciples continues today with the over seven hundred million Catholic Christians who live throughout the entire planet.

A person's identity as "athlete" comes from actual performance and from other people's praise of his or her abilities. Our identities as Catholic Christians develop in the same ways. First, our parents, teachers, and friends identify us as Catholics. We then study our religious heritage to find out what it means to be Catholic. Eventually "Catholic" becomes part of our identity. As we become rooted in this aspect of who we are, we act out Catholic behaviors.

Being Catholic, Knowing How It Changes

During the 1960s, many Catholic Christians were shocked when the altars were turned around and the priest celebrated Mass facing the people. More shocking for some was that the language used was not Latin, but the local language. Instead of a choir singing Latin chants, the congregation was supposed to join in the music—sung in the language of the congregation, accompanied by guitars, drums, flutes, and other instruments. In some cases the names of the sacraments changed too. Instead of Penance, we now had the Sacrament of Reconciliation. Extreme Unction became the Rite of Anointing and Pastoral Care of the Sick.

In addition to the alterations in the sacraments, other new and sometimes disturbing developments were going on in the Catholic Church. Priests and religious adopted what had been considered secular dress. Women began lobbying for ordination. Married deacons started serving in parishes and preaching at Sunday Mass. The idea of a married clergy was talked about more frequently and by greater numbers. These changes were terribly upsetting for those Catholics who thought that the Church was unchanging, permanent, infallible—a rock in the midst of the revolving world.

Unfortunately many Catholics had little sense of the rich history of the Catholic Church. If they had, they would not have been so distressed by these changes, and their identities as Catholic Christians would not have been threatened. They would have known, for instance, that for many centuries Latin was the most commonly understood language of Europeans. Yet the Apostles probably celebrated the Eucharist in Aramaic (ar-uh-*may*-ik)—not in Latin. And Saint Paul broke the bread and wrote his Epistles in Greek. What was essential was not the language in which the Mass was celebrated, but the celebration itself—including the reading of the Word of God and the Communion of the People of God. Similarly, for many centuries there had been married deacons working in the Church. In fact, up until about the year 1200, many priests were married men. Also, in the early Christian communities women participated in electing the bishop of Rome. Thus, knowing church history can give us insights about what is essential and/or changeable in the practice of our faith.

Saint Peter's Basilica

Church History and the Future

Understanding church history can be as liberating as knowing our personal histories and our world history. When we have a solid historical sense, we are less shocked by developments in our community. Also, we can participate more fully in the unfolding plan of God in history; we can choose ways of responding to the world, enlightened by a sense of our tradition. We have our role to play in the grand sweep of church history—a history that is not accidental but that is moved by the Spirit of God. We have been shaped by this history, and we will shape its future.

We shape history by who we are to and for others. For instance, if you are an honest used-car salesperson, you can influence your customers' futures by letting them know the defects and good points of a car. By knowing the quality of the car, they can anticipate repairs and not suffer disappointment and anger about the car. Consequently their attitude toward all humans might be more positive. After all, your customers have met an honest person in their history—a person who was in a position to cheat them, but who did not. On the other hand, if all the people you deal with take advantage of you, most likely you will develop a negative attitude about people. Simply put, we do make a difference in other people's lives; we do shape personal histories, world history, and church history.

Studying History Is Like Forming a Relationship

Perhaps the best way to approach the study of church history is to think of the effort as similar to building a relationship with someone. In fact, learning about the Church is learning about the presence of Jesus Christ throughout history. Christ acts through and in the Church's people; he lives in people's hearts and is seen in the actions of those who work in his name. Clearly not all the actions of the Church's members are Christlike—after all, the Church is composed of regular human beings. However, these same people have at times been the signs of the Lord's presence. Thus, knowing the Church is knowing the work of Jesus through his people.

Ordinarily, where does a relationship begin? First, it starts with becoming acquainted. Reflect on the questions you ask strangers whom you would like to know better—for example, new classmates who have just transferred from another city. Probably you ask their names, where they moved from, what subjects they are taking, where they live. As you spend more time with these new persons, you may begin to ask more personal questions: how do they feel about various issues; who are they going out with; what are their families like?

Besides conversing with these persons, you also have a chance to see them in action. This tells you a lot too. You can judge how trustworthy they are, how studious, how helpful. With all of this information about other persons, you can understand them better—and appreciate them better. Eventually you will make some choices about what your relationship is going to be with them. Do I want to discuss this problem with them? Can they be

trusted to help with a student council project? Is the help they will give me going to improve my math grades? What can I help them with?

Without adequate knowledge of other people, our decisions about them will be unfair or unreasonable. We may cut off persons who could have been loyal, caring, helpful friends. We may end up trusting people who are liars or gossips. People are not all good or all bad; they have both talents and failings. But without knowledge of persons, we cannot know what they have as gifts and what they cannot do.

As you read the history of Catholic Christians, you will in a very real way be learning about people—people who have shaped the way the world is today and the way the Church community is today. Some parts of church history may disturb you. Many parts may inspire you. Just remember that as in friendships, we need to know both the bad and the good.

Where Does the Church Begin?

The Church began with the group of people that gathered around Jesus: the Apostles and the disciples. The beliefs that united them came from Judaism. They believed that a Savior, or Messiah, would come to redeem Israel. Accordingly, when the Apostles and disciples heard Jesus speak, saw his miraculously loving deeds of healing, and were invited to join him, they became convinced that he was the Messiah, the Christ. Thus, church history began—the story of Jesus and his believers—a story that continues now.

The First Among the Faithful

The most prominent of these followers was **Simon Peter**. When Jesus first called him from his fishing business in Galilee, Simon Peter certainly would have laughed if anyone had told him how his life would change. Oddly enough, this illiterate, hot-tempered, married fisherman was to be the rock on which Jesus built the Church. Jesus called and Peter was among the first to listen: "As [Jesus] was walking along by the Sea of Galilee he saw Simon and his brother Andrew casting a net in the lake—for they were fishermen. And Jesus said to them, 'Follow me and I will make you into fishers of men.' And at once they left their nets and followed him" (Mark 1:16–18). Simon Peter could be said to be the first member of Jesus' band. Why a person like Peter was chosen is a mystery only Jesus could fully explain.

Part of the answer may lie in Peter's blunt honesty, in his great enthusiasm, and (after betraying Jesus and failing him) in Peter's complete dependence on Jesus' love. In any case, Jesus certainly made it clear that Peter was to be central to the new group of believers once he was gone: "You are Peter and on this rock I will build my Church. And the gates of the underworld can never hold out against it. I will give you the keys of the kingdom of heaven: whatever you bind on earth shall be considered bound in heaven; whatever you loose on earth shall be considered loosed in heaven" (Matthew 16:18–19). Jesus knew Peter and loved him "warts and all"—including his ignorance, angry moods, betrayals, and so on. After all, Jesus had come to save the sinners; Peter was clearly one.

As Jesus marched triumphantly into Jerusalem, the crowds who acclaimed him Messiah were huge. But crowds do not necessarily make up a Church of genuine believers. So, the night before he died, Jesus gathered only the twelve Apostles together to celebrate the Passover. Even one of those present—Judas—was not a believer. At the Last Supper, Jesus showed the Apostles how the Church should share the Word of God and the meal in remembrance of him. This was the Church.

In the garden of Gethsemane, Peter and the others disappointed Jesus. Instead of keeping vigil with him, they all went to sleep —abandoning their leader to lonely agony. After the soldiers came and took Jesus away, Peter and maybe some of the others followed after, but Peter then denied him. The Apostles were probably at the Crucifixion, but we are sure only of John's presence there.

In the Gospels, we have a picture of the Apostles, scared and worried, huddled together when Mary of Magdala came rushing back from the empty tomb to announce Jesus' Resurrection. Peter "went running to the tomb. He bent down and saw the binding cloths but nothing else; he then went back home, amazed at what had happened" (Luke 24:12). Later, Jesus appeared to his followers on the road to Emmaus, and he appeared again in a room where they were staying— the place where "doubting Thomas" insisted on touching Jesus' wounds.

Perhaps the most amusing story about the Apostles seeing Jesus after the Resurrection comes from John's Gospel. Peter and some of the Apostles had gone to the Sea of Tiberias. Characteristically, Peter said, "I'm going fishing." The other Apostles joined him. Then Jesus appeared on the shore. He called out, "Have you caught anything, friends?" Evidently nothing was biting. Typical of the Jesus they knew, he said, "Throw the net out to starboard and you'll find something." The Apostles did as he instructed, and the nets filled up until they were bursting. The story ends as we might expect: "The disciple Jesus loved said to Peter, 'It is the Lord.' At these words, 'It is the Lord,' Simon Peter, who had practically nothing on, wrapped his cloak round him and jumped into the water [in his eagerness to be with Jesus]. The other disciples came on in the boat, towing the net and the fish" (John 21:4–8). This seems very undignified behavior for one who was to lead the Church, but it was Peter as we know him. And this is an example of Jesus as we know him, touching the daily lives of the ordinary people who are the Church.

The Resurrection was the most important event in Jesus' life. Without it, the Apostles would have certainly disbanded, and Jesus would be a forgotten religious fanatic who was executed for rebellion. After the Resurrection, the Apostles were united in their belief with many others whose lives had been touched by Jesus.

Pentecost

The next major event in the founding of the Church was **Pentecost** (*pent*-i-kawst)—the coming of the Holy Spirit. For two months, between the Resurrection and Pentecost, the Apostles had drifted like boats that have lost their rudders. These disciples and Mary gathered to celebrate the traditional Jewish feast of Pentecost, to thank God for the year's harvests. "When Pentecost day came round, they had all met in one room, when suddenly they heard what sounded like a powerful wind from heaven, . . . and something appeared to them that seemed like tongues of fire; these separated and came to rest on the head of each of them. They were all filled with the Holy Spirit, and began to speak foreign languages as the Spirit gave them the gift of speech" (Acts 2:1–4). Everyone who heard these previously ignorant and frightened men speak in different languages was amazed, to say the least.

Saint Peter, an artist's depiction of Peter's remorse following his denial of Jesus

Peter:
An Unlikely Church Leader

We know that he was a fisherman from Bethsaida on the Sea of Galilee. Originally his name was Simon, but Jesus named him Peter (*Cephas* in Aramaic). When Jesus called him, he was living in Capernaum with his wife, mother-in-law, and probably his brother. Nevertheless, when Jesus called, Peter followed. No one has reported what his wife and mother-in-law said about Peter picking up and leaving. It is likely that he was illiterate and rather crude. After all, fishing in Peter's time was a grueling affair: men in small boats, throwing out nets by hand; grappling with the heavy, full nets (if they were lucky); and then cleaning the fish by hand. Without sonar fish detectors and the sophisticated nets and pulleys that fishers have today, it must have been difficult work. All this was hardly the preparation we would expect for the "rock" on which Jesus would build his Church.

Nevertheless, Peter was the first to call Jesus "the Messiah"; he knew that Jesus was the Chosen One who would save the world. Peter's name is always listed first among the Apostles. His name appears 114 times in the Gospels and 57 times in the Acts of the Apostles—far more times than anyone else's except Jesus. Peter was the first Apostle to see the Risen Jesus. Later, he initiated the selection of the replacement for Judas. After Pentecost, Peter preached the great sermon that reportedly converted three thousand. Peter led the Christian community in Jerusalem and later traveled to Rome where he was crucified.

Peter had an impulsive streak. When the soldiers came to capture Jesus, Peter whipped out his sword to protect Jesus and managed to cut off a servant's ear. When Jesus appeared on shore after the Resurrection, instead of rowing the boat to shore, Peter jumped in the water just so he could get to Jesus first. Peter was also rash when he said that he would never deny Jesus; ultimately he denied Jesus three times.

So, why did Jesus choose Peter as the first of the Apostles? Have you ever wanted to do an imaginary interview with someone long deceased, just to find out what it was really like "back then"? Maybe an interview with Peter would have gone something like this:

Interviewer: Why did you follow Jesus?
Peter: I've never been able to figure it all out. Who can? There were lots of folks who thought that Jesus was the Messiah, but who refused to go along. They were too high and mighty. A fisherman like me sometimes really hated the Pharisees and Sadducees because they were so snobby and self-righteous. When I saw what they did to Jesus and yet were forgiven by him—well, I felt awful. It's hard to love like he did, even with his example right there. Jesus was so special. When he called me, my heart and mind burned. Sorry, that probably doesn't answer your question.

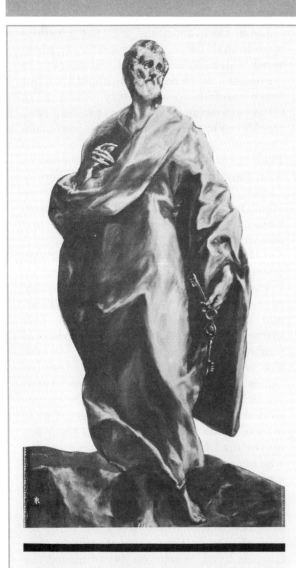

of course what happened. People thought we were drunk at Pentecost because they could not believe that an illiterate clod like me could speak so powerfully.

Interviewer: So he chose you because of your incompetence and illiteracy?

Peter: Well, not exactly. Everybody else would have used their own ideas—not his. I had to hope he would put words in my mouth and faith in my heart. Of course, I had to believe he would. He never let me down. He loved me—bad eyes from the sun, arthritic knees and back from fishing, hot temper, thick skull, and all. I put myself down maybe too much because I'm so grateful for what Jesus brought out in me—a sensitivity I never would've admitted, courage that had never been tested, leadership qualities that a fisherman never gets a chance to use. Mine was an amazing life that my mother-in-law would hardly have predicted.

Interviewer: Thank you, Peter. May I have your blessing?

Peter: Sure. Lord, keep blessing this young person here. Let her love and hope and trust in you. Amen. I keep the words short because God knows anyway. See you.

Interviewer: What was it like to be selected leader of the Apostles?

Peter: I couldn't believe that either. I kept wondering if Jesus had been out in the sun too long. It scared the wits out of me. All of us were so dumb. We had Jesus right there with us: eating with us, sleeping on the ground near us, listening to us argue and swear, gently caring for us, talking to us in simple stories that even we should have been able to understand. Yet we doubted right up to the Resurrection. But to try to answer your question, I guess Jesus knew that I would be so witless and frightened that I would throw myself into his care, and that's

Even more shocking was the powerful speech that Peter gave immediately afterward: "Men of Judaea, and you who live in Jerusalem, make no mistake about this, but listen carefully to what I say" (Acts 2:14). After convincing his audience that Jesus was the Messiah, the audience was eager to join the small Christian community. The words Peter spoke next have been used ever since with those who wish to become followers of Christ: "You must repent . . . and every one of you must be baptised in the name of Jesus Christ for the forgiveness of your sins, and you will receive the gift of the Holy Spirit." So "that very day about three thousand were added to their number" (Acts 2:38–41).

The rest of this course outlines the history of the Church that was formed on Pentecost and that continues in the present. Our history is exciting; the Word has spread in hundreds of languages throughout the world. The work of Jesus and the Apostles continues. In studying the history of the Church you will become "friends" with the people who are the Church. You will meet, for instance, saints who were burned at the stake by the mad Nero, people of humble origins who became famous, people of noble parentage who became humble. Our history is full of heretics and holy people, mystics and mercenaries. Through it all, the Word is preached, the sick ministered to, the homeless sheltered, the ignorant taught—the Gospels lived. When you have finished the course, the hope is that you will have found your place in this history.

Review Questions and Activities

1) Explain what it would be like for you not to remember your personal history.

2) Why is it important to have a sense of world history? Can you think of some recent events that have changed our ways of living?

3) Why does the author state that knowing history can be liberating? Do you agree?

4) Why is it important for Catholic Christians to study church history?

5) How is learning history somewhat like developing a relationship or friendship?

6) What was Peter's role in the formation of the Church?

7) Why did Jesus pick Peter to be the "rock" on which to build the Church? Do you agree with the reasons given in the imaginary interview with Peter (see pages 16–17)?

8) Why was Pentecost such a key event for Peter?

Personal Reflection Exercise

In order to get more in touch with your own personal history, to remind you of key events in your own story, you might find this exercise enriching. On a sheet of paper, list in random order as many important events from your life as you can remember. These key events may not seem important to others, but they are to you. Leave several lines between the events on your list. Then, answer the following questions:

- Who was there with you?
- Where did the event take place?
- What exactly happened?
- When did it happen?

After you have answered these questions, try to list and describe the causes for and effects of one very early event that you listed. Usually our lives are marked by these key events, so dig deeply into your memory. From this exercise you could probably write an autobiography—which is a kind of history.

Now, on a different sheet of paper, write the name of one of your closest friends. Then, list five very important times in this relationship: conversations, joint projects, trips, other things done together. After you have made your list, write a brief summary of why each event was so important to your relationship. Consider the effects of the events. Afterward, answer the following question: How important has it been to me to know a lot about my friend?

2
Five Ways of Seeing the Church

People are mysteries. Just when we think that we know them, they surprise us. Most of us have had the experience of being shocked by our friends—people we think we know. Perhaps you find out one day during a walk with someone that he is fatally allergic to stinging insects. Or maybe one day at school a friend is very upset, and in a moment of real trust, she tells you that her father and mother are going to get a divorce. Or think of someone you have not seen for a long time. Maybe the last time you saw him, he was dressed very conservatively, never spoke up in a group, and was scared to go anywhere on his own. When you met him recently, he was clad in the latest fashions, obnoxiously loud, and disturbingly aggressive. Granted that such changes are rare, everyone develops in new and often unexpected ways. Consequently they are mysterious; we never totally know them.

If people are mysteries, so is the Church. The Church is a mystery that we will never completely understand. No single description of the Church is possible. Pope Paul VI made this clear in his statement at Vatican Council II: "The Church is a mystery. It is a reality filled with the hidden presence of God. It lies, therefore, within the very nature of the Church to be always open to new and ever greater exploration." Just as friendships are exciting because we are always learning more about our friends, so exploring the Church's life can be fascinating because we learn more about God and people. We can study the Church knowing that it is so full of God's presence that we will never thoroughly know it.

An interior of Saint Peter's Basilica

Although we can never completely know the Church, there are ways of studying the Church that will aid our appreciation of it. One way is to explore its history. Most of this course is about the story of the Church, including the events and characters that compose that story. Another way of examining the Church is to look at various forms the Church takes—to examine, that is, "models" of the Church.

When architects are planning a new building, they make small-scale models of the ways it will look. They use these models to provide visual representations of the finished product. Blueprints are hard to understand for the average person; physical or material models are much more effective because one can actually see them. Aircraft designers make models of new planes. Then they put the models in a wind tunnel to see how they perform with resistance. The model plane helps them see the real thing better. We can also understand the Church better if we look at some visible, physical models of it.

Model 1: The Body of Christ, or the People of God

In the Christian Scriptures, the Church is often described as the Body of Christ. The community of believers—professing its faith, caring for one another, celebrating the Eucharist together, serving the poor—becomes the physical expression of Jesus on earth. Perhaps the best way to understand the Body of Christ is to look at Saint Paul's explanation in First Corinthians:

Just as the human body, though it is made up of many parts, is a single unit because all these parts, though many, make one body, so it is with Christ. In the one Spirit we were all baptised, . . . and one Spirit was given to us all to drink.

Nor is the body to be identified with any one of its many parts. If the foot were to say, "I am not a hand and so I do not belong to the body," would that mean that it stopped being part of the body? If the ear were to say, "I am not an eye, and so I do not belong to the body," would that mean that it was not part of the body? If your whole body was just one eye, how would you hear anything? If it was one ear, how would you smell anything?

Instead of that, God put all the separate parts into the body on purpose. If all the parts were the same, how could it be a body? As it is, the parts are many but the body is one. They cannot say to the hand, "I do not need you," nor can the head say to the feet, "I do not need you."

Now you together are Christ's body; but each of you is a different part of it. (1 Corinthians 12:12–21,27)

From this passage we see that all of us are important to the Body of Christ, the Church. Therefore, just as we would care for our own bodies, we must take care of one another because other people make up the Body of Christ with us.

In addition to the Body of Christ, the Church as a community goes by another name—the People of God. In the Hebrew Scriptures, the people of Israel were called the Chosen People. Jesus called all people to his Father's love. Thus, those who believe become the People of God:

You are a chosen race, a royal priesthood, a consecrated nation, a people set apart to sing the praises of God who called you out of the darkness into his wonderful light. Once you were not a people at all and now you are the People of God; once you were outside the mercy and now you have been given mercy. (1 Peter 2:9–10)

If we accept Jesus, then we become the People of God and the Body of Christ. This model of the Church should help us realize that God has not abandoned us but instead has given us a part in his presence on earth in the Church.

Model 2: The Institution

Whenever a group of people gather together for some common purpose, they usually become institutions after a certain period of time. Institutions are not just buildings, but any group of persons organized for a similar purpose. A school band, for example, is an institution. Its common purpose is to play music and march together. Usually it has a band leader who gives directions. A drum major is chosen to provide leadership when the band is marching and sometimes to act as mediator between the members and the band director. Most of the time certain rules are followed so that some discipline is maintained. Without all these structures, the common purpose would not be fulfilled.

As another example, India received its independence after a long struggle with Great Britain. In his efforts toward achieving India's independence, Mohandas Gandhi had organized the Congress Party to systematically lead the people in nonviolent demonstrations, strikes, and confrontations. After independence was gained, other institutions were needed to make policies, take care of the needy and handicapped, and mediate disputes. Thus, a parliament, a president, and a prime minister were elected.

The Church is an institution too. In fact, the model of the Church as Institution is probably the one most familiar to us. The word *church* has come to mean both a building for worship and a particular denomination. Actually the Church began very simply with common ideals and goals. Its "constitution" was the Gospels and Epistles. The leader was Jesus Christ. The first "president" was Peter. Peter's "parliament" was the group of Apostles and disciples living in Jerusalem. The Church even had initiation rites: Baptism, Confirmation, and Eucharist. However, several centuries passed before the Church had impressive buildings where the Christians could meet for worship. And Jesus' first followers would not have thought of themselves as an institution; they were a small group, and formal structures were not necessary.

Like any institutional leader, Peter did have authority. After all, Jesus said: "I will give you the keys of the kingdom of heaven: whatever you bind on earth shall be considered bound in heaven; whatever you loose on earth shall be considered loosed in heaven" (Matthew 16:19). With this authority Peter called councils of the community of Jerusalem to settle disputes that sometimes arose—as we shall see in the next chapters.

The institutional aspect of the Church also emerged when the Apostles were first commissioned by Jesus to go out into the whole world and preach the Good News. Commissioning is an act of passing on authority to another. Later, the Apostles would formally commission others to go out and preach. The Twelve also selected "seven men of good reputation, filled with the Spirit and with wisdom" whose duty it was to look after the material welfare of the Christian community's needy—especially widows (Acts 6:3–6). These deacons are even named for us: Stephen, Philip, Prochorus, Nicanor, Timon, Parmenas, and Nicolaus of Antioch. We shall hear more of Stephen later. Eventually the roles of bishops and, finally, of priests were established as the number of Christians grew throughout the Roman Empire. Structures had to be set up to ensure that the Word was preached, the needy were cared for, worship was conducted, and the community was nurtured.

The Apostles never dreamed that the Church as Institution would become so huge and visible. It is difficult to imagine the old fisherman Peter feeling very comfortable being carried through Vatican Square cheered by thousands of devoted Catholic Christians. But then again, Gandhi would never have dreamed that India would have sophisticated fighter airplanes in its army and tumultuous arguments in parliament. And George Washington probably never dreamed that there would be fifty states, billions of dollars of national deficit, U.S. troops all over the world, and monumental tensions with the Soviet Union. In short, institutions, even the Church founded by Jesus, have the tendency to grow and to become more and more complex. The structures may all be necessary. The danger for the Church is that its structures—and especially the people who work in them—become ends in themselves and not means for service, preaching, and worship.

Model 3:
The Sacrament

Jesus was a physical sign of God acting in the world. Through Jesus' death and Resurrection, God saved humankind. The Church continues being a sign of God's presence among us. Therefore, the Church is a sacrament: that is, a physical sign of God's saving love. When the people of the Church worship, serve, and preach, God's saving power is revealed as present. They remember what Jesus was all about when he was on earth. So the third model of the Church is Sacrament.

The Church through its very presence in the world is a sign. In Jerusalem, for example, when Peter and John preached as witnesses of the Resurrection of Jesus, they were harassed because they obviously reminded people about Jesus. They were living signs of him. Later, while Saint Paul and Saint Barnabas were living in Antioch, the pagans around them realized that this new

Cardinals meeting in the Sistine Chapel

Church was a reminder, a sign, of Christ. They began to call members of this group Christians. As the Church spread, it became an increasingly visible sign that Christ—even though crucified as a common criminal—was still present in the world. Consequently the persecutions of the first Christians were attempts to stamp out Christ's presence in the Roman world.

The most recent church council, Vatican Council II, concluded in the *Dogmatic Constitution on the Church:* "The Church is a kind of sacrament of intimate union with God and of the unity of all mankind; that is, she is a sign and instrument of such union and unity." We see this unifying action of the Church most clearly through the celebration of the seven sacraments. For instance, at the Eucharist, in sharing the body and blood of Christ, we testify to one another about our faith and our commitment to the Christian community. In the Sacrament of Reconciliation, we are reunited with the Body of Christ through admission of our failings and expression of our desire to be more Christlike. In each of the sacraments the unity of the People of God is revealed.

The Eucharist is also the Christian community celebrating its salvation together. This means that first we are a Christian community—real people at a specific place and time, expressing our identity through activities we do in unison. Just as a volleyball team cannot be identified as a team unless it plays games regularly together, the Christian community maintains its identity through its liturgical celebrations.

The unity of all Christians is required so that the Church can be one sign of Christ. The more Christians are divided, arguing, or unloving, the less Christ can be seen in the world. As the lives of the members of the Church are transformed in hope, joy, love, and peace, the Church becomes more and more the sign of Christ's presence—a Sacrament.

The Structure of the Catholic Church Administration

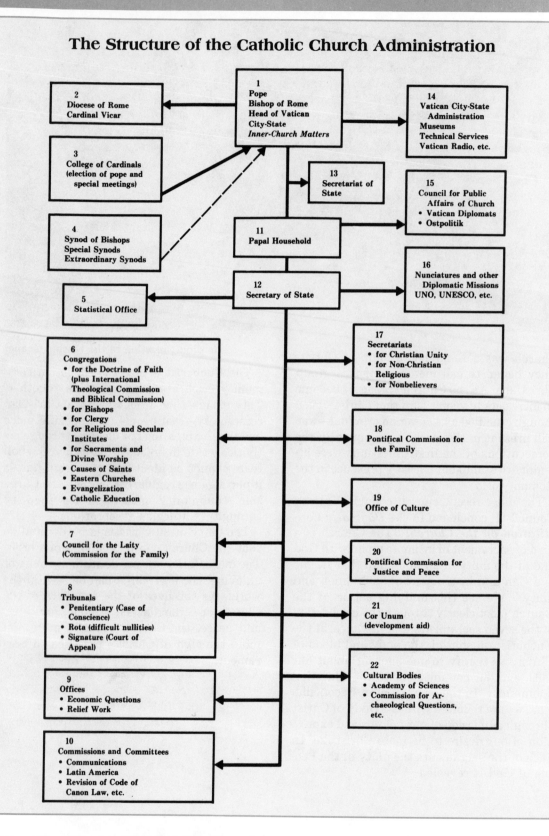

1
Pope
Bishop of Rome
Head of Vatican
City-State
Inner-Church Matters

2
Diocese of Rome
Cardinal Vicar

3
College of Cardinals
(election of pope and
special meetings)

4
Synod of Bishops
Special Synods
Extraordinary Synods

5
Statistical Office

6
Congregations
• for the Doctrine of Faith
  (plus International
  Theological Commission
  and Biblical Commission)
• for Bishops
• for Clergy
• for Religious and Secular
  Institutes
• for Sacraments and
  Divine Worship
• Causes of Saints
• Eastern Churches
• Evangelization
• Catholic Education

7
Council for the Laity
(Commission for the Family)

8
Tribunals
• Penitentiary (Case of
  Conscience)
• Rota (difficult nullities)
• Signature (Court of
  Appeal)

9
Offices
• Economic Questions
• Relief Work

10
Commissions and Committees
• Communications
• Latin America
• Revision of Code of
  Canon Law, etc.

11
Papal Household

12
Secretary of State

13
Secretariat of
State

14
Vatican City-State
  Administration
  Museums
  Technical Services
  Vatican Radio, etc.

15
Council for Public
  Affairs of Church
• Vatican Diplomats
• Ostpolitik

16
Nunciatures and other
  Diplomatic Missions
  UNO, UNESCO, etc.

17
Secretariats
• for Christian Unity
• for Non-Christian
  Religious
• for Nonbelievers

18
Pontifical Commission for
the Family

19
Office of Culture

20
Pontifical Commission for
Justice and Peace

21
Cor Unum
(development aid)

22
Cultural Bodies
• Academy of Sciences
• Commission for Ar-
  chaeological Questions,
  etc.

Church Structure Today

Every day the institutions of the Church are at work. We are most familiar with our local diocesan institutions: parishes, schools, hospitals, retreat centers, social service agencies. These same institutions function throughout the world. We may not be as familiar with the central administration of the Church residing in Rome. The diagram below outlines the various offices, congregations, and secretariats that operate out of the Vatican.

Brief explanations follow for the headings in each box:

1) *Pope: Bishop of Rome, Head of Vatican City-State.* In the traditions of the Church, the pope is the successor of Saint Peter as head of the Church. He is also bishop of Rome. Since the Vatican is also an independent, though very small, country, the pope also heads the Vatican City-State.

The institutional structures on the left side of the diagram take care of inner-church matters.

2) *Cardinal Vicar—Diocese of Rome.* A cardinal vicar bishop is appointed to help the pope oversee the Diocese of Rome.

3) *College of Cardinals.* While the title *cardinal* is a great honor, the single real duty of a cardinal is to vote in the election of a new pope.

4) *Synod of Bishops. Synod* means "an assembly." Since the bishops are leaders of the world's dioceses, they meet to share common concerns.

5) *Statistical Office.* This small office collects the data any organization needs: number of members (783,660,000 approximately), parishes (206,503), and so on.

6) *Congregations.* These very important offices oversee church practice in various areas. For example, the Congregation for Sacraments and Divine Worship makes sure that the administration of the sacraments throughout the world stays within the traditions of the Church.

7) *Council for the Laity.* This rather new group studies matters about the lay members of the Church.

8) *Tribunals.* Disputes occur within the Christian community. The tribunals attempt to settle these arguments. The largest of these tribunals arbitrates when couples seek marriage annulments.

9) *Offices.* The Church must be financed; so, the office for economics sees to this. The other office coordinates the massive relief work sponsored by the Vatican.

10) *Commissions and Committees.* These are set up to deal with specific topics that come up; they are not permanent. When the Code of Canon Law is distributed worldwide, the commission will most likely cease to function.

11) *Papal Household.* The pope lives in the huge Vatican household and needs lots of help managing it.

The next list contains institutions that look after the relations between the Church and the world.

12) *Secretary of State.* This cardinal must try to create smooth relations between the Church and the governments of the world.

13) *Secretariat of State.* This office aids the secretary of state.

14) *Vatican City-State Administration.* This office looks after the day-to-day management of the city.

15) *Council for Public Affairs of the Church.* When possible, the pope tries to bring the Christian message to bear on public policy. Many governments look for moral leadership from the Church. Thus, this council, working with *nunciatures* all over the world, makes friendly ties with governments.

16) *Nunciatures.* A nuncio is like an ambassador. He represents the Vatican and maintains correspondence between the Vatican and local churches and governments.

17) *Secretariats.* Constant work is being done by these agencies to develop better understandings with those not in the Catholic tradition.

18) *Pontifical Commission for the Family.* Initiated in 1981, this commission seeks ways to promote pastoral ministry to families. Christian education within the family is of special concern to this commission.

19) *Office of Culture.* This is another recently formed office that deals with studying the interaction between Catholic Christianity and the many cultures in which the Gospel is preached.

20) *Pontifical Commission for Justice and Peace.* This commission is charged with educating Catholics to the call of the Gospels for justice and peace among all of humankind.

21) *Cor Unum.* This office coordinates Catholic aid services and human development organizations throughout the world.

22) *Cultural Bodies.* These groups study pertinent issues in science, archaeology, art, and so on, and transmit their findings through journals and conferences.

You may be surprised by the number of offices in the Vatican, but remember that these offices service an institution of over 700 million members worldwide.

Model 4:
The Herald
of God's Word

The Church is the Body of Christ, an Institution, a Sacrament. It is also a Herald, the fourth model. What is a herald? You may have seen movies about medieval European castles, towns, and the people who lived in them. When the king wanted to send an official message to the people, he sent out a herald. This herald would blow a horn, ring a bell, or just yell really loud to call people together. Often heralds wore special clothes so that the crowd would know that they came from the king and were commissioned to speak for him. When the mob was quiet, the herald delivered his message. Usually it was a message for everyone to hear, and it was considered very important. A modern equivalent to the king's herald might be a president's or prime minister's press secretary. When they call a press conference, we know that they probably have something important to say to everyone in the country. Instead of gathering in the town square, citizens gather around the TV set to watch and listen.

The Church is the Herald of Jesus Christ. It is the official messenger to proclaim the Word of God to all people everywhere. John and Peter were speaking as heralds when they told the authorities in Jerusalem: "We cannot promise to stop proclaiming what we have seen and heard" (Acts 4:20). They had been commissioned by Jesus to go out and preach: " 'Go out to the whole world; proclaim the Good News to all creation. He who believes and is baptised will be saved.' . . . they, going out, preached everywhere, the Lord working with them and confirming the word by the signs that accompanied it" (Mark 16:15–16,20). The first church members, especially the Apostles, spread the Word of God.

Belief comes from hearing the Word of God. We cannot believe in something about which we know nothing. We must hear first, then believe, then celebrate. The Church is joined in a common belief in Jesus and then becomes a Sacrament. The role of Herald is essential to hearing the Word.

Words in themselves have power. Also important is our trust in the speaker of the words. For instance, if you tell someone you love him or her, but you are laughing at the same time, the word *love* will have little power. However, if you have been going out with a person for a long time, if you have gotten very close and have gradually made a commitment to each other, it becomes obvious that you do in fact love each other. So when you finally tell the other person that you love him or her, the word *love* will have great power. In short, the speaker's credibility helps give words their power.

Since the death and Resurrection of Jesus, the Church has been a Herald of the Good News. Yet if the Church is to continue fulfilling its mission as Herald, its members must live the lives to which the Word of God calls them. If the Church's life is **not** consistent with the words proclaimed, obviously the listeners will have a difficult time believing the Word of God.

The Church acts as Herald in several ways. Jesus said, "where two or three meet in my name, I shall be there with them" (Matthew 18:20). Thus, on a very simple level, any gathering at which Christians read the Word of God or pray together is a sign of the Church as Herald. During the liturgy of the Word at Mass, for example, the Church is Herald. Many church publications herald the

Word, as do TV and radio programs. Missionaries still preach the Gospels to people who have not heard the Word. Finally, our actions are heralds. And since actions do indeed speak louder than words, our lives become important ways of heralding the Word of God.

Model 5: The Servant

The fifth and final model of the Church is Church as Servant. Many times in the Christian Scriptures, Jesus is referred to as a servant. The word had a special meaning to the people of Israel. *Servant* meant "slave of the king." High officials often addressed the king starting with the expression "your servant has come here to report." Moses, David, Elijah, and other prophets and kings used the term *servant* in the Hebrew Scriptures to refer to themselves when they talked to Yahweh. Consequently, when Jesus is referred to as servant, he is placing himself at the service of God—the King of all creation.

In the Hebrew Scriptures, the prophet Isaiah said the Messiah was a servant who would suffer for the people in order to redeem them. Jesus even paraphrased well-known passages from Isaiah that picture the Messiah as a servant: "The spirit of the Lord has been given to me, for he has anointed me. He has sent me to bring the good news to the poor, to proclaim liberty to captives and to the blind new sight, to set the downtrodden free, to proclaim the Lord's year of favour" (Luke 4:18–19; see also Isaiah 61). Jesus' whole life was one of service—even to his death on the cross.

In many places in the Christian Scriptures, Jesus is referred to as the Good Shepherd. A shepherd has to watch out for the wolves that attack his sheep. Jesus himself says: "I am the good shepherd: the good shepherd is one who lays down his life for his sheep. . . . No one takes it from me; I lay it down of my own free will" (John 10:11,18). The night before Jesus did lay down his life, he gave the Apostles an example of how to serve—he washed their feet. During Jesus' lifetime, this was a ritual of service for guests coming into a Jewish home. Most people went about on foot, walking dusty roads in sandals or barefoot. So, washing of feet was a welcome relief for the weary, dusty traveler. After Jesus had washed the Apostles' feet, over Peter's strong objections, he concluded: "If I, then, the Lord and Master, have washed your feet, you should wash each other's feet. I have given you an example so that you may copy what I have done to you" (John 13: 14–15). Following this, Jesus broke the bread and gave it to the Apostles saying, "This is my body." We not only remember Christ through the Eucharist, but also through the service we do.

Jesus made clear what sort of services Christians should give. These services are direct. Jesus did not want to load people down with more duties than they could do. In a sermon to his followers, Jesus pointed out how people would be judged at the end of time:

The King will say to those on his right hand, "Come you whom my Father has blessed, take for your heritage the kingdom prepared for you since the foundation of the world. For I was hungry and you gave me food; I was thirsty and you gave me drink; I was a stranger and you made me welcome, naked and you clothed me, sick and you visited me, in prison and you came to see me." Then the virtuous will say to him in reply, "Lord, when did we see you hungry and feed you; or thirsty and give you drink? When did we see you a stranger and make you welcome; naked and clothed you; sick or in prison and go to see you?" And the King will answer, "I tell you solemnly, in so far as you did this to one of the least of these brothers of mine, you did it to me." (Matthew 25:34–40)

Jesus did not want us to simply wait around for community-wide efforts: Christmas food drives for the poor, clothing drives run by the Catholic Charities Office, or service programs that are part of religion classes. All these group projects are good, but charity is also the day-to-day way of life for individual Christians.

The ways in which we become servants may vary a lot. We all have different talents, positions, and circumstances. It is not proper to say that someone is not serving God's people if they are not serving as we are. For instance, a professor in an Ivy League university may not be working with the poor directly. However, she may be studying the effects

The Church as Servant Today

The Church has set up many service organizations. Church groups, frequently religious orders, sponsor the following services worldwide:

75,000 Primary schools with 21,000,000 students
30,000 Secondary schools with 11,000,000 students
2,100,000 Students study in Catholic colleges and universities
6,500 Hospitals
12,000 Dispensaries
750 Leprosaria
10,000 Homes for the aged, chronically ill, handicapped
6,200 Orphanages
5,800 Nurseries

Clearly, this is not a complete list of all the services sponsored by the Catholic Church. The Church also runs literacy programs, agricultural development projects, publishing houses, and so on. At one time, when slavery was common, there were religious orders dedicated to freeing those in bondage. As needs arise in the world, the Church seeks to meet these needs. While an individual's service is at the center of the Church as Servant, the Church provides channels for individual service.

of certain pollutants on the human body. Based on the findings of this lone researcher, agencies can protect the people from harm. In the long run, more people may be helped by her research than if this professor were working in some direct service capacity—like dishing out food in a soup kitchen. In short, we need to look at our abilities realistically and use whatever talents we possess in the best ways for the greatest good. We all have something to give; each of us can render some special service. **We make our marks on history most often through the service we render to humankind.**

Church History and the Models

As we study the history of the Catholic Christian Church, we will use the models as ways of seeing different aspects of the Church's role in history. This course will trace the ways the Church has been and still is the Body of Christ, Institution, Sacrament, Herald, and Servant. The concluding section of each of the following chapters will summarize changes in the models that occurred during the time span discussed in the chapter. You will find that over the centuries the Church has developed in different ways. For instance, as the Church grew, the institutional dimension became much more obvious. At other times, the missionary activities of the Church highlighted the Church's role as Herald. All in all the Church's alterations through history have mostly been made so that it could be a more effective Body of Christ, Institution, Sacrament, Herald, and Servant. Yet it is important to keep in mind that the Church is more than the sum of its parts—more than all the models put together. Ultimately the Church remains a fascinating mystery.

Review Questions and Activities

1) Why do we say that the Church is ultimately a mystery?

2) What are the benefits of using models to discuss the Church?

3) Why does Saint Paul compare the Church to the human body? What unifies the Body of Christ? What must we do to help the Body of Christ survive and grow?

4) What are the advantages of having structures in the Church?

5) Write a brief essay on the ways in which your school helps build the Church.

6) Explain how the Church is a Sacrament. What activities of the Church show that it is a Sacrament? Why is unity so important in making the Church a Sacrament?

7) Why is the model of Church as Herald so important? What church activities illustrate this role?

8) What are the origins of the model of the Church as Servant?

9) Some examples are given in this chapter about Jesus as Servant. Find some other examples of Jesus as Servant in the Christian Scriptures.

Personal Reflection Exercises

1) Complete the following statements: Today, in my activities,

I can be the mouth of Christ by . . .
I can be the hands of Christ by . . .
I can be the eyes of Jesus when I . . .
I can be the ears of the Lord by . . .

2) The more we are familiar with the Gospels and Epistles, the more we can participate in the Church as Herald of the Word of God. Find a short passage from the Christian Scriptures that interests or touches you. Spend some time reflecting on the passage you chose. What is God telling you about your life? After some close reflection, write a response to God that discusses two topics: (a) what the passage seems to be telling you about yourself, (b) how you will change in light of the passage. You may wish to write your reflections in the form of an imaginary dialogue with God (see the interview with Peter in chapter 1, pages 16–17, as an example).

3
A Church of Conversion: The Case of Saul

Jesus founded the Church, and Peter was its first leader. But in a real sense the story of the Church is written through the lives of the first converts—those who had not seen Jesus but still believed. Indeed the Christian Church was originally a Church of converts. The Acts of the Apostles (that is, of the twelve Apostles and Saint Paul) gives an accounting of the early Church.

The first Christians were mostly Jews who lived in Jerusalem and worshiped at its Temple. In a short time, Christianity spread far beyond Jerusalem's gates. Yet those who spread the Word usually continued by preaching in synagogues because the Jewish communities could understand the prophecies about the Messiah. Thus, Jesus came first to the Jews, the Chosen People.

Saul, whom we know as *Saint Paul,* was a devout Jew and also knowledgeable about Greek and Roman ways. He is typical of many of the first converts; like Saul these converts were Jews living outside Jerusalem who had not known Jesus but who were waiting for the Messiah. And, like Saul, these first Christians were immersed in Judaism but coped with life in a pagan world. On the other hand, Saul was certainly exceptional. He would first be a persecutor of the Christians and then, through a dramatic conversion, become the single most effective preacher of the Word of God.

Through Saul's eyes we can see where and how the Church's story began. Peter was the rock of foundation for the Church, but Saul is the one who really made the Church "Catholic," that is, universal. His story is amazing because of the scope and hardships of his travels and the fantastic results of his preaching. But let's begin at the beginning of Saul's story—in Tarsus.

Coming of Age in Tarsus

Growing up in Tarsus was an exciting experience for Saul. People came there from all directions to buy and sell. Through the passes in the high mountains right behind Tarsus came rugged mountain people bringing with them the heavy goat's haircloth. From as far east as Persia, caravans came with donkeys and camels loaded with sacks of spices, perfumes, and jewelry. Up the river from the blue Mediterranean, small ships came powered by oarsmen and by bright sails when the wind was right. And, of course, there were always Roman foot soldiers and cavalry on the roads. These Romans were easily recognized by their plumed helmets, long spears, sharp swords, and emblazoned shields.

Saul lived in the Jewish neighborhood in Tarsus. The Jews lived together to maintain their identity as followers of the one God in a city of pagans—people who worshiped many gods. The Jewish neighborhood was clustered around a simple meeting hall, the synagogue (sin-uh-gahg). Synagogues were roughly equivalent to our modern parish churches: small, local groups of people who come together to pray, to help the poor, and to discuss religious matters. Saul studied

Aramaic, the language of his Jewish ancestors. For everyday use he spoke Greek, the language of Tarsus.

In the synagogue Saul joined his family and friends in listening to the readings of the Hebrew Scriptures, which had been translated into Greek. Then the people discussed the passages' meanings and prayed together. Following the meeting each person left something at the door of the synagogue for the poor of the community.

Beyond Saul's neighborhood was the marketplace of Tarsus. It was a different world. In the marketplace Jews and Gentiles bought, sold, and talked politics. The word *gentile* in Greek means "the nations" or "the others" and was used by the Jewish people to refer to all non-Jews. Around the market area stood statues of Mars, the Roman god of war; Venus, the goddess of love; and Neptune, the god of the sea. Tarsus had an open-air theater with seats built into the hillside and a long stadium for track events. Then

The ruins of a synagogue at Capernaum

CILICIA

Adana

Tarsus

Issus

Seleucia Tracheotis

(Birthplace of
Saint Paul)

Antioch

Seleucia

Laodicea ad Mare

CYPRUS

Salamis

Emesa

Aradus

Tripolis

PHOENICIA

SYRIA

MEDITERRANEAN SEA

Heliopolis

Byblos

Berytus

Damascus

Sidon

Tyre

Caesarea Philippi

Ptolemais

Sea of Galilee

Tiberias

DECAPOLIS

Caesarea

Jordan River

Jaffa

SAMARIA

Jericho

Jerusalem

ARABIA

there was the gymnasium where men and boys ran, wrestled, boxed, and threw the javelin. Also, the gymnasium had baths and rooms for the study of music and literature.

About three hundred years before the time of Saul, Alexander the Great, a Greek, conquered the known world. Since that time, Greek culture had produced great writers and scholars, sculptors and architects, musicians and philosophers. Yet, to a well-bred young Jew like Saul, Greek culture was not enough; it did not include what was most important in life—knowledge of the one true God. Because of this, Jewish parents kept their sons away from the gymnasium.

Saul, like other Jewish boys, learned a trade. He was an apprentice weaver of tents and cloaks in his father's shop. Nevertheless, when Saul was about age fifteen, his family decided to send him to Jerusalem to study with Gamaliel (guh-*may*-lee-uhl), one of the greatest teachers of the time. After three weeks of walking, Saul caught his first glimpse of Jerusalem on top of one of the distant hills. With renewed enthusiasm, he must have hurried forward. The city on the hill was protected by thick walls, high towers, and heavy gates in arched openings. The narrow streets were jammed with people bartering, donkeys carrying packs, and sheep being led to the Temple for sacrifice. Tarsus was quite large, but nothing like this city.

The Temple and the Law

Perched on the east edge of Mount Moriah and having its own high walls, the Temple was like a city within a city. Inside the walls was an open space usually filled with people. Beyond the crowd was the Temple itself, looming more than a hundred feet into the clear sky.

The Temple was built in five levels. Each level was reserved for a special group. Gentiles were allowed only on the first level; under penalty of death, they could go no further. Women were permitted on the second level, but only men could go to the third level.

On the fourth level priests sacrificed animals. Above, on the final level, stood the most sacred part of the Temple where there were the seven-branched candlestick and, deep in the darkness, the holy of holies. The holy of holies stood empty, but it was regarded as the most sacred room in the Temple. Once the ark of the covenant, which contained the tablets upon which Moses had written the commandments given by God, had been preserved in this room. By the time of Saul, the ark had disappeared—taken during one of the invasions of Jerusalem. Nevertheless, the holy of holies was still considered to be specially blessed with God's presence.

Saul was in awe of the Temple. Soon he would be joining the small groups of students sitting cross-legged on the paved floors. He would listen attentively to the teachers who sat on low stools under the long porches. Saul was well prepared for his studies in Jerusalem. As we know, from his childhood he had read the Hebrew Scriptures, and on the Sabbath he heard them explained in the synagogue. Now in Jerusalem, he began to study the Law in both its written and oral forms.

For Saul and his people, the Law was the covenant in which God made a promise to be faithful to the Jews. This covenant implied a special relationship that God formed with the Jewish people making them the "Chosen People." To follow the Law did not mean simply keeping a set of rules. The Law meant that one lived a lifestyle that showed love and respect to the God who saved Israel.

As Saul studied the written Law in the Hebrew Scriptures, he was fascinated by the long history of his people since the first call of Abraham, two thousand years before. He realized that it would be impossible for a small nation like Israel to have escaped from Egyptian slavery and have come to the Promised Land (1259 B.C.) without some special help. During their flight from Egypt, God made a covenant with the Hebrews at Mount Horeb in the Sinai Peninsula. He would be their God, and they would be his people. King David made Israel a strong nation (1000 B.C.). But then the people of Israel abandoned the covenant and the Law. Subsequently, in 586 B.C., they were beaten in war and taken into slavery in Babylon (*bab*-eh-luhn). After being freed by God's power, they came home to Palestine. They sinned again and were conquered by the Greeks, by the Syrians, and finally by the Romans. And so they waited for a leader to make them independent again. In Aramaic this leader was called the **Messiah,** the one chosen by God. All this history and the Law of God were contained in the **Torah,** the first five books of the Hebrew Scriptures in the Bible.

The oral Law that Saul studied is a collection of explanations of the written Law. For example, from the Hebrew Scriptures they knew the law about keeping the Sabbath, but, as times changed, they needed to know what was the kind of work forbidden by the written Law. The oral Law described in detail the proper observance of the Sabbath.

The **scribes** (from the word meaning "to write") studied and taught both written and oral Law. The best scribes were deeply religious men who not only knew the Law but made it part of their everyday lives. Saul's teacher Gamaliel, a scribe, was admired for his knowledge and understanding of people. The more he studied, the more Saul realized that the Law made the Jews different from their Gentile neighbors. He also began to see that there were politics connected with religion.

The **Sanhedrin** (san-*hed*-ruhn), the supreme council of the Jews, had its assembly hall near the Temple. There were two parties in the Sanhedrin. The **Sadducees** (*sad*-yuh-seez) generally included priests who served in the Temple as well as rich and powerful men who collaborated with the Romans. The **Pharisees** (*far*-uh-seez) were more in touch with the common people and were opposed to Roman

The Temple in Jerusalem

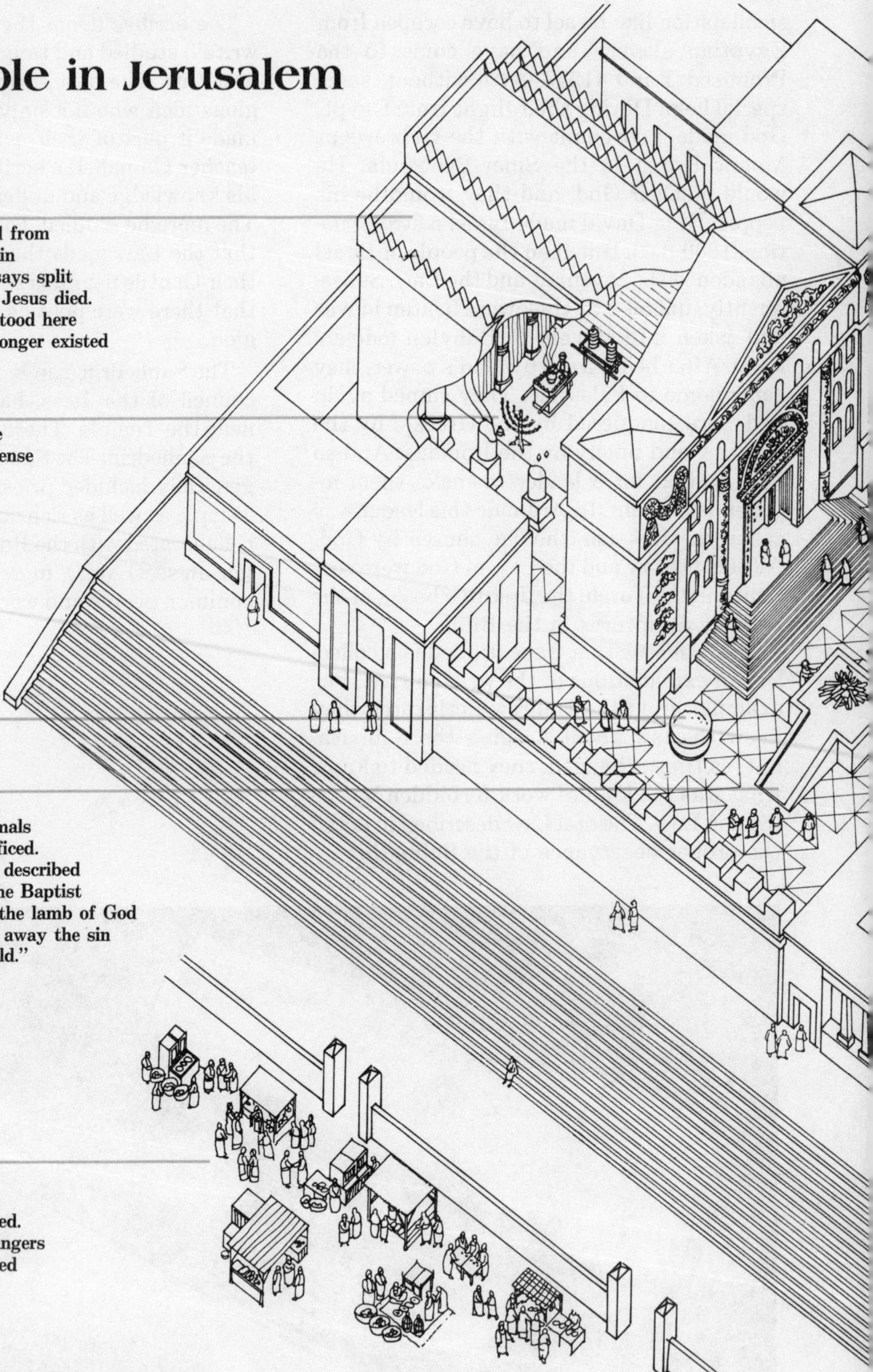

The holy of holies, divided from
the Holy Place by a curtain
which Matthew's Gospel says split
from top to bottom when Jesus died.
The ark of the covenant stood here
in Solomon's day but no longer existed
in Jesus' time.

The Holy Place, where the
priests regularly burnt incense

A bowl
for ritual
washings

The altar
where animals
were sacrificed.
Jesus was described
by John the Baptist
as being "the lamb of God
that takes away the sin
of the world."

The court of the Gentiles.
This was the only part in
which non-Jews were allowed.
The traders and money-changers
worked here and were turned
out by Jesus.

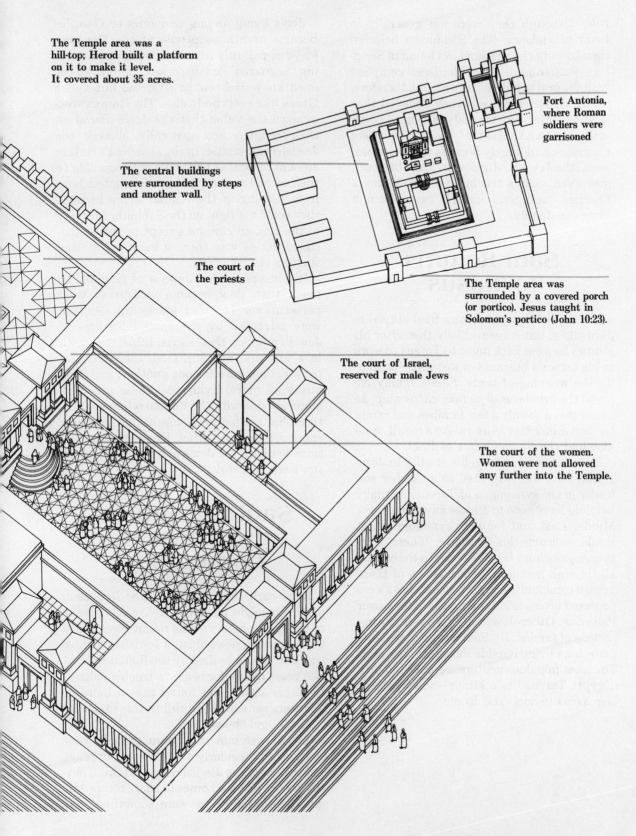

The Temple area was a hill-top; Herod built a platform on it to make it level. It covered about 35 acres.

The central buildings were surrounded by steps and another wall.

The court of the priests

The court of Israel, reserved for male Jews

Fort Antonia, where Roman soldiers were garrisoned

The Temple area was surrounded by a covered porch (or portico). Jesus taught in Solomon's portico (John 10:23).

The court of the women. Women were not allowed any further into the Temple.

rule—although they were not generally in favor of violence. The Sadducees believed that keeping the written laws found in Scripture was enough. The Pharisees complied with the oral traditions as well and, therefore, led much stricter lives. They believed that the Law—both written and oral—must be exactly observed. Most of the scribes were Pharisees, and largely because of the scribes' work, the Jewish religious heritage has been preserved. Saul's teacher, Gamaliel, was a Pharisee, and Saul himself came from a Pharisaic family.

Saul Returns to Tarsus

We do not know how long Saul stayed in Jerusalem, but it seems likely that after his studies he went back home to Tarsus to work in his father's business of weaving—primarily the weaving of tents. Saul's family enjoyed the privileges of Roman citizenship, an honor given to only a few families and rarely to such minorities as Jews. As a result, Saul also had the Roman name of Paul.

Having returned from his studies in Jerusalem, Saul was respected as a teacher and leader in the synagogue of Tarsus. Actually he could have gone to almost any town in the Middle East and found a synagogue that would welcome his learning. There were synagogues from Iran and Iraq to Rome, and all through northern Africa. Some of these Jewish communities grew because Jews were deported after various conquerors took over Palestine. Other Jews left Palestine during periods of famine. By Saul's time there were more Jews living outside Palestine than in it. The most populous centers were Alexandria (Egypt), Tarsus (Asia Minor—now Turkey), Damascus (Syria), and Rome.

Jews living among non-Jews or Gentiles became known as people of the **Diaspora** (deye-*as*-puh-ruh) from the Greek word meaning "scattered" or "dispersed." Many did not even know Hebrew or Aramaic but spoke Greek like everybody else. The Romans recognized the value that the Jews placed on their religion and generally allowed the Jewish communities of the Diaspora a certain amount of local self-government according to their own laws. The Romans exempted Jews from serving in the regular army because they could not fight on the Sabbath. Nowhere in the Roman Empire except in the Jewish communities was there a weekly holy day such as the Sabbath.

In some places the Jews were resented so much that they became victims of local persecutions. In other places the Gentiles were attracted by the special features of Jewish practice: their sacred Bible, their faith in a just and merciful God, their habit of prayer, their care for one another, and their stress on moral living. All these practices stood at odds with the Roman religious practices that tended to change each time a new emperor came into office. Evidently the relations between the Jews and Gentiles in Tarsus were peaceful.

Saul Encounters the Christian Community

In his early thirties, Saul visited Jerusalem again. He might have wanted to celebrate one of the major feasts, or he might have heard the disturbing news about a Jewish carpenter who had been crucified by the Romans about two years before for being "a troublemaker." In either case, Saul found that a band of followers remained faithful to this executed Galilean (gal-eh-*lee*-uhn).

As a Jewish minority group, the followers of Jesus met regularly at the Temple to pray, and they kept the Jewish religious laws. They also met in private homes to share meals and special prayers. They were sometimes harassed by the authorities. What upset the authorities was that the leaders of the group, especially the fisherman Peter and a fellow named John, kept telling everyone who would listen that Jesus of Nazareth was alive, that they had seen and talked with him, even eaten with him—all this after everyone knew that he had been executed and buried. They also claimed that he was the Messiah sent by God to give freedom to the Chosen People. In addition, the followers of this Jesus were able to cure the sick. The cures could not be denied because there were too many eyewitnesses.

Because of this trouble with the Jewish authorities, the Apostles were in and out of jail a number of times. Finally the Pharisee Gamaliel, Saul's former teacher, urged the Sanhedrin to let them alone (Acts 5:34–42). If Jesus was the Messiah, he said, the Sanhedrin could not do anything about it as they would be fighting against God. On the other hand, if Jesus was not the Messiah, his followers would disband and die. As Saul learned, the group was not dying but growing every day.

The followers of Jesus in Jerusalem belonged to two groups: some were Jews born in Palestine and others were Jews born in communities of the Diaspora. Many of the Jews from Jerusalem had heard and seen Jesus while he was alive. Yet some Jews of the Diaspora became Jesus' followers after the unusual events during the celebration of the Jewish feast of Pentecost. Saul, on his visit two years after this first Christian Pentecost, heard a lot of talk about this new sect. What he heard disturbed him deeply.

Saul may have been present at one of the synagogues to listen to the deacon Stephen speak. Stephen, a formidable Christian preacher, "was filled with grace and power and began to work miracles and great signs among the people. . . . They found they could not get the better of him because of his wisdom, and because it was the Spirit that

prompted what he said" (Acts 6:8,10). Devout Jews thought that Stephen was a blasphemer because he claimed that Jesus had divine qualities and because he cured people in the name of Jesus. They were especially angry when Stephen claimed that the Temple was no longer necessary for worship. And this in Jerusalem! Stephen had to be stopped, so the people hauled him before the Sanhedrin.

In a long speech outlining how all of Jewish history had led to the coming of Jesus the Messiah, Stephen tried to persuade the Sanhedrin to believe. His main point was that if Jesus was the Messiah, the Temple became unnecessary for worship: "the Most High does not live in a house that human hands have built" (Acts 7:48). The ending of his speech sealed Stephen's fate with the Sanhedrin; he concluded: "You stubborn people, with your pagan hearts and pagan ears. You are always resisting the Holy Spirit, just as your ancestors used to do" (Acts 7:51). This accusation was too much for the Sanhedrin who "stopped their ears with their hands; then they all rushed at him, sent him out of the city and stoned him" (Acts 7:57–58). Stephen, in effect, had accused his Jewish listeners of resisting God's revelation, of being like pagans and not the Chosen People at all. Devout Jews considered this a blasphemy.

A Church of Conversion 43

Stephen's Martyrdom Is Repeated Today

Stephen, the deacon, is considered the first Christian martyr. His belief in Jesus as the Messiah and his active practice as Servant and Herald led to his being killed by those who saw him as a threat to their beliefs and lifestyles. Through the centuries there have been thousands of martyrs—some recognized and honored by the Church and others unknown except to God. While we may think that martyrdom was a phenomenon of the past, it does continue now. Many contemporary women and men are giving their lives because they preach the Word, because they serve the poor and oppressed, and because they are the Sacrament of Christ present in the world. Here is a very short list of some recent martyrs and of some instances where people are suffering for their faith:

March 1980—Archbishop Oscar Romero of San Salvador was shot to death by an unknown sniper while preaching at a memorial Mass. Romero was a strong opponent of political violence in El Salvador and a courageous advocate for justice and the rights of the poor.

April 1980—Amnesty International said that in 1979 at least twenty-five Ukranian (Russian) Catholics and about ten Jehovah's Witnesses were believed to have been imprisoned because of their religious activities.

May 1980—In Guatemala, Father Walter Voordeckers was machine-gunned to death at his parish, and Father Conrado de la Cruz and a catechist were kidnapped; it was thought they were victims of a far-right terrorist group. Miguel Albizures, head of the National Labor Center, said they "are being killed because they are involved with the poor."

August 1981—Raoul Leger, a Canadian lay missionary, was killed in an explosion when Guatemalan security forces attacked a private home. The government accused him of being a guerrilla leader.

Also, in Lithuania, Father Leonas Mazeika was "fatally wounded" by unknown assailants. It was reported that he had signed a letter to officials of the communist government asking for an end to religious repression.

February 1982—Brother James Miller, a Christian Brother, was shot to death by masked men while repairing a window at the Indian Center in Huehuetenango, Guatemala. It was thought that he was murdered because of his identification and work with the poor as a teacher and director of a vocational farm project.

Who Are the Deacons?

When we think of those who function officially for the Church, we most often think of bishops, priests, and the pope. In the first days of the Church, however, two roles were most often referred to: the Apostles, who were roughly equivalent to the first bishops, and the deacons, who were appointed by the Apostles. Later, when the communities of Christians got much larger and more numerous so that bishops could not handle all the liturgical functions, priests were appointed to help preach and administer the sacraments. During the early years, however, the deacons had an extremely essential role in church life.

What did deacons do? First, it is necessary to understand that the early Church lived in much closer community than parishes do now. This community was described beautifully in the Acts of the Apostles (4:32–35):

> The whole group of believers was united, heart and soul; no one claimed for his own use anything that he had, as everything they owned was held in common.
>
> The apostles continued to testify to the resurrection of the Lord Jesus with great power, and they were all given great respect.
>
> None of their members was ever in want, as all those who owned land or houses would sell them, and bring the money from them, to present it to the apostles; it was then distributed to any members who might be in need.

Evidently, despite the close bonds in the community, some disputes arose over distribution of goods. The Apostles settled the problem by appointing deacons to look after the welfare of the Christian community. Again, turning to the Acts, we get an idea of what happened: the "widows were being overlooked. So the Twelve called a full meeting of the disciples and addressed them, 'It would not be right for us to neglect the word of God so as to give out food; you, brothers, must select from among yourselves seven men of good reputation, filled with the Spirit and with wisdom; we will hand over this duty to them, and continue to devote ourselves to prayer and to the service of the word' " (Acts 6:1–4). Thus, the deacons took charge of the charitable works in the community.

After some centuries, the practice of appointing deacons in each parish seemed to die out. Instead, the diaconate (deye-*ak*-eh-nuht) was looked upon as just one step on the way to becoming a priest. However, in recent years, the permanent diaconate has been restored in many dioceses. Men of good reputation are trained in theology, in preaching, and in the practice of ministry. They are then given assignments in the dioceses to do work similar to the early deacons. Most deacons are married men; most have full-time jobs. Deacons might be airline pilots, executives, carpenters, or engineers. In addition, they devote considerable time to the community of Christians. The same Spirit of God that moved the Apostles to appoint deacons almost two thousand years ago has moved the Church of today to reinstitute the role of deacon.

Saul was at the stoning of Stephen. In fact, the witnesses "put down their clothes at the feet of a young man called Saul" who "entirely approved of the killing" (Acts 7:58; 8:1). He was so convinced of the need to stamp out the followers of Jesus of Nazareth that Saul joined in the persecution that gathered force after Stephen's stoning: "Saul then worked for the total destruction of the Church; he went from house to house arresting both men and women and sending them to prison" (Acts 8:3). Saul considered the followers of Jesus as enemies of everything he held most important in life. Saul even got warrants from the Sanhedrin to go north beyond Galilee into Syria; he was authorized to arrest any refugees he could find in Damascus, a city in which there had been a Jewish community for as long as five hundred years.

The Apostles stayed on in Jerusalem, but most of the Christians fled into the countryside until the persecution died down. For those of us reading this history twenty centuries later, it is important to realize that the followers of Jesus had no notion of starting a new religion. On the contrary, they believed that Jesus, as the Messiah promised in the Jewish Bible, came to complete their Jewish faith. In Jerusalem, they were known as "the Way"—a particular way of being religious Jews (Acts 9:2; 22:4). Consequently the persecution must have been shocking to people who considered themselves conscientious Jews.

A Dramatic Conversion

With warrants for the arrest of any Christians, Saul journeyed on the high road east of the Jordan toward Damascus, a city at the meeting of three major trade routes leading from Asia Minor, Palestine, and Egypt. Just outside the walls of this ancient city, Saul was knocked off his feet. In the Acts of the Apostles, Saul tells about his experience:

I was on that journey and nearly at Damascus when about midday, a bright light from heaven suddenly shone around me. I fell to the ground and heard a voice saying, "Saul, Saul, why are you persecuting me?" I answered: Who are you, Lord? and he said to me, "I am Jesus the Nazarene, and you are persecuting me." The people with me saw the light but did not hear his voice as he spoke to me. I said: What am I to do, Lord? The Lord answered, "Stand up and go into Damascus, and there you will be told what you have been appointed to do." The light had been so dazzling that I was blind and my companions had to take me by the hand; and so I came to Damascus. (Acts 22:6–11)

Saul was in a state of shock, blind and unable to eat or drink anything. His old world had come to an end. He had been doing what he thought was right—protecting his religious heritage. With the startling experience on the road, his thoughts must have gone around in circles always ending with Jesus. Jesus really was alive. Now what?

After three days of mental and physical blindness, a man named Ananias came to visit Saul; Ananias claimed that the Lord had sent him. Saul felt the man's hands on his face, and suddenly he could see again. Not only could he see the physical world, but a spiritual insight was given to him. Acknowledging Jesus as Lord, he received Baptism from Ananias.

When he was well again, cared for by the people whom he had come to harm, Saul needed time to rebuild his life. In his letter to the Galatians, which he wrote years after his conversion, he says that he left Damascus and went to Arabia—the desert area east and south of the city. He does not say what he did there, but very likely he went back to work as a tentmaker. He must have spent much time reading, again and again, what the prophets had to say in the Bible about the Messiah. Above all, he must have prayed and reflected deeply on his experience at Damascus.

Saul was a vigorous, determined, dynamic person. When he came out of the desert after having studied and prayed, all the energy he had put into persecuting the followers of Jesus was now directed toward the spread of the Word of God. Saul's whole fate was changed. He would not be the successful Jewish tentmaker in Tarsus but instead would travel ten thousand dangerous miles mostly on foot to spread the Good News that had knocked him off his feet on the road to Damascus.

Gentile Converts: A Cause for Controversy

While Saul was living in the quiet desert country, unexpected things were happening elsewhere among the People of the Way. After the execution of Stephen, many of the followers of Jesus had to get out of Jerusalem to stay alive. Persecution continued there. Some escaped as far north as Damascus. Along the way they spoke of Jesus to whoever would listen. Philip, for example, stopped in Samaria. For centuries the Jews and Samaritans (suh-*mar*-eht-nz) had been enemies, but now the Samaritans listened to Philip's Good News about Jesus. Many asked to be baptized. Peter and John were sent by the Jerusalem community to find out what was going on there. They saw the great belief the Samaritans had in Jesus. Spurred by the success of the Good News, Philip went west to the towns on the Mediterranean coast, speaking to both Jews and Gentiles.

Later, following in Philip's footsteps, Peter taught and healed the sick. At Jaffa, near what is now Tel Aviv–Jaffa, Peter brought back to life a woman named Tabitha (Acts 9:36–43). At Caesarea (see-zuh-*ree*-uh), the Roman capital of Judaea (joo-*dee*-uh), he baptized some Gentiles, as well as the Roman commander Cornelius and his whole family (Acts 10). Amazingly these Gentiles then received the Holy Spirit and began speaking in foreign tongues just like the Apostles did on Pentecost.

When he got back to Jerusalem, there was turmoil in the community. How could Peter baptize Gentiles—non-Jews? They were not the Chosen People. Jesus came to the Jews. Besides, didn't Peter break the Jewish Law by visiting Gentiles and eating with them?

Peter defended his actions by telling them that he had had a vision in which he was told that no food was forbidden him and that he was to go to the Roman's house. Peter was convinced that while Jesus came to the Jews first, his gift of salvation was for all people—

The Wailing Wall in Jerusalem, a small remaining portion of the original wall of Solomon's Temple

not just for the Jews. He reminded the Jerusalem community that Jesus ate with sinners, tax collectors, and Samaritans; and that he had commissioned the Apostles to go out to the whole world. These reminders probably stung the Jerusalem community. While they were followers of Jesus, they still thought of themselves as religious Jews, not as members of a new religion. Peter's explanation calmed the group for a while, but the problem did not end here.

Focus on the Models

Clearly, Saul experienced the Church as Sacrament. The Christians' community reminded everyone of Jesus—they were a sign of his continuing presence. In fact, they were so dynamic that Saul felt he must persecute them. Just as clearly, the Church acted as Herald in these years immediately after Christ's Resurrection. Peter and Stephen are both seen preaching the Word of God. And when the oppression began in Jerusalem, the fleeing Christians spread the Word to towns throughout Palestine and beyond its boundaries.

The Church as Servant was certainly modeled in the work of the deacons like Stephen. And, one of the most impressive signs that the Apostles had power from God was their ability to cure. The People of God were regularly gathered at the Temple, but they had their own meals and prayers together that were special to them. While they had no buildings, Peter was acknowledged as head of the community. In the next phase of Saul's story, these aspects of the Church take on new dynamism.

Review Questions and Activities

1) Describe what it was like for Saul to grow up in Tarsus—that is, as a Jew in a pagan city.

2) Trace on the map (see page 37) Saul's trip to Jerusalem and home, and from Jerusalem to Damascus.

3) Why was Jerusalem so important to Saul?

4) What is meant by the Law? Why did the Jews think that the study of the Law was so important?

5) Like any human organization, Judaism was split into religious and political parties. What were these groups? How did they differ?

6) What was life like for Jews of the Diaspora?

7) Why did the early Christians seem to pose such a threat to a devout Jew like Saul?

8) What was life like for the early Christians in Jerusalem?

9) Why was Stephen considered a blasphemer?

10) In Scripture, we are often reminded that God's ways are not the ways of humans. How is this made obvious in Saul's conversion?

11) Why did the Christian converts from Judaism object to Gentiles' being converted? How did Peter handle their objections?

12) How were the models of the Church reflected in the events of this chapter?

Personal Reflection Exercise

Reflect on the following two cases. While the names have been changed, the events are real. Try to put yourself in each situation described. Keep in mind what you know of the early Christian community. Outline your response to the problems posed.

a) "Fire Destroys Tenement Block"

Bridgetown is a very poor neighborhood, consisting mostly of old houses that were converted into numerous apartments. Some have been condemned, and the rest probably should have been. Two factories have moved out of the area, so conditions are worse than ever. Unemployment is very high. A small parish, Saint Angela's, has managed to stay open, but has only one priest. One very cold night a raging fire sweeps through a block of tenement apartments. Quickly fifteen families are made homeless, and most have lost their few possessions. You are one of a group of parish lay leaders. You meet late at night to decide what the parish should do to help. Since the need is immediate, you must draw up a plan of action very swiftly—if you are going to help at all. What will you do? If you decide to help, draw up very specific plans. Try to outline the reasons for your decision.

b) "The Murdered Missionary"

Your high school is run by a religious order. You like your school and admire the religious who teach there. One day, your religion teacher tells the class that a member of the order was shot down in cold blood in a small Latin American village in which the order ran a school for poor children. The class is asked to pray for the souls of the slain religious and the two students who were also killed. In your social studies class you read that the government of your country supports the Latin American regime that was responsible for the death of the religious, who that regime claimed was a guerrilla sympathizer. Finally, after several days have passed, the religion department asks for donations of money to send down to the mission school to support the work of the religious. You wonder what to do and whom to believe. What would you do—contribute or not? Outline the issues involved.

4
Paul's New Community

The Word of God was spreading because the persecutions in Jerusalem had dispersed enthusiastic Christians into the lands of the Diaspora—that is, Palestine, Asia Minor, and other areas of the Roman Empire. Both Jews and Gentiles began to accept the Way. While this was a cause for rejoicing, the conversions of Gentiles brought the young Church to a crisis, as we will see. The successful resolution of this crisis would give Saint Paul, formerly called Saul, a mandate to preach to all who would listen. And so, Paul, the Apostle to the Gentiles, began the travels that would be the hallmark of his Christian life. In this chapter, we will also see how charity was practiced in the early Church. Social service and collections for the needy are not twentieth-century phenomena. On the contrary, they are rooted in the practice of the very earliest Christian community.

Paul Begins His Mission

Paul came out of the Arabian Desert and immediately caused trouble in Damascus. His preaching was so powerful that some people complained to the governor. Paul's friends warned him that a guard was posted at the city gates with instructions to arrest him on sight. They managed to lower him over the high city walls in a large basket ordinarily used to carry fruits and vegetables. In the darkness, he headed south to Jerusalem. Paul, who had persecuted others for preaching about Jesus, was now a marked man himself (Acts 9:23–25).

Paul spent two weeks with Peter and James (Galatians 1:18–19). Undoubtedly they told him many things about Jesus as they remembered him. Above all, the three men must have talked about their greatest experience: encountering Jesus after his Resurrection. About twenty years later Paul recalled these conversations in a letter to the people of Corinth: The Lord "appeared first to Cephas [Peter] and secondly to the Twelve. Next he appeared to more than five hundred of the brothers at the same time, most of whom are still alive, though some have died; then he appeared to James, and then to all the apostles; and last of all he appeared to me too; it was as though I was born when no one expected it" (1 Corinthians 15:5–8).

While in Jerusalem, Paul got himself in trouble again by preaching in public. Christian friends heard of a plot against Paul and smuggled him out of town, taking him to Caesarea on the coast. From there he got safely back home to Tarsus.

A mosaic depicting Paul's escape from Damascus

Antioch

Some of the Christian refugees from Jerusalem had gone to Antioch (*ant*-ee-ahk), the third largest city in the Roman Empire. Situated on a river not far from the Mediterranean, Antioch was beautiful and impressive. The city had a mixed population of Gentiles and Jews. Evidently they got along well together. Some of the Gentiles attended the synagogue with the Jews, but they did not usually become converts since they felt that the Jewish Law was too difficult to observe. When the Christian refugees from Jerusalem arrived at Antioch, they spoke of Jesus to this mixed Jewish-Gentile audience in the synagogue. Consequently those asking for Baptism included people from both groups. The Christian community in Jerusalem was upset when they heard about this. Barnabas was sent to make inquiries (Acts 11:19–26).

Barnabas saw that clearly the Jews and Gentiles were united in their faith in Jesus. He was glad; in fact, he decided to stay in Antioch to teach the people and to encourage them in their new way of life. As the community grew, Romans and other outsiders remarked about how different this group was compared to the Jewish community. So to distinguish them from the Jews, the general population began to call this community *Christians,* that is, "followers of Christ." This was the first time the term was used.

When the Gentiles heard about Jesus from Jewish Christians, they were convinced that he really did show them God's goodness by the way he preached, by the way he helped the needy, and by the special power he had. The Gentiles could know and love God through Jesus. So they became his followers. They had faith in Jesus the anointed one, the Messiah, the Christ. It was natural to call them "Christians."

Barnabas, who had gone to investigate the large number of conversions of Gentiles and who had ended up staying in Antioch, soon found the work too much for a lone person. Paul was the first person he called on for help. Barnabas made the 150-mile trip to Tarsus to find him. In about ten days, he was knocking on the door of Paul's home. Little persuasion was needed. Paul was willing to come with him, and only a few days later the two men were on the road to Antioch.

A Visit of Charity

Paul and Barnabas had been working together at Antioch for about a year when a traveler from Jerusalem told them about a crop failure in the south. As the Christian community in Jerusalem was in danger of starvation, the Christians at Antioch took up a collection for them and sent Paul and Barnabas to deliver the money (Acts 11:27–30).

This visit of charity must have been encouraging to the community in Jerusalem. They were saved from starvation. A new wave of persecution was brewing, however. The Jewish king, Herod Agrippa I, had arrested the Apostle James and had him beheaded. Because many people in Jerusalem approved of this, Herod next arrested Peter.

Peter escaped from jail miraculously, as can be seen from the story in the Acts of the Apostles:

> On the night before Herod was to try him, Peter was sleeping between two soldiers, fastened with double chains, while guards kept watch at the main entrance to the prison. Then suddenly the angel of the Lord stood there, and the cell was filled with light. He tapped Peter on the side and woke him. "Get up!" he said "Hurry!"—and the chains fell from his hands. . . . "Wrap your cloak round you and follow me." Peter followed him, but had no idea that what the angel did was all happening in reality; he thought

he was seeing a vision. They passed through two guard posts one after the other, and reached the iron gate leading to the city. This opened of its own accord; they went through it and had walked the whole length of one street when suddenly the angel left him. It was only then that Peter came to himself. "Now I know it is all true," he said. (Acts 12:6–11)

When Peter came back to where he was residing, the people there would not let him in at first because they could not believe he had escaped. After telling his story and appointing James, a relative of Jesus, as head of the Jerusalem community, Peter escaped from the city under the cover of darkness.

Paul's First Journey

Having returned to Antioch for a brief period, Paul and Barnabas were satisfied that the community there was solidly established. After praying about what to do next, they decided to leave Antioch to preach in other cities. This was going to be a new challenge. Up until now, they had been working in familiar territory where people were Jewish or Syrian. From here on Paul and Barnabas would be preaching to mixed populations: Greeks, Romans, and people from distant lands. Nevertheless, in many places, they would find Jewish congregations with whom they could stay.

Travelers in the first century had an advantage in that the whole Mediterranean region was ruled by the Romans. There was peace and order in most places; there were good roads between larger cities; the sea was generally clear of pirates; and almost everyone spoke the common language, Greek. The greatest problem facing Paul and Barnabas was to find people who would listen to their message.

Logically they decided to reach out first to the Jewish communities and then to the Gentiles. They chose to work close to home, in Barnabas's birthplace, Cyprus. Their work met with success.

Encouraged, they went farther afield, sailing northwest on a merchant ship to the southern coast of Asia Minor (modern Turkey). They worked their way through the seaside towns, staying in each place for several months. Then they pushed north over the rugged mountains to the plateau prairie lands. The summers were scorching, the winters dreadfully cold. The climate was not the worst of their problems though.

Paul and Barnabas's plan was first to preach in the synagogues on the Sabbath. They spoke to the people about Jesus as the one sent by God to them as Messiah. Some Jews accepted Jesus; many did not. Jesus was not the Messiah many of them expected. Many Jews expected the Messiah to be someone who would lead a rebellion against the Romans. How could the Messiah die on a cross like a common thief or murderer? Those who rejected Paul's teaching ignored him or forbade him to speak in the synagogues again. Others, usually a small minority, became violent. Years later, Paul wrote in his letters, or Epistles, of being driven out of towns, of being beaten, and of once being stoned and left for dead. Somehow he survived all this.

The Gentiles who accepted Jesus were relieved that they did not also have to accept the many laws that their Jewish neighbors followed. Both Jewish and Gentile Christians formed new communities, distinct from the synagogues. Paul and Barnabas would stay in each town for a while—teaching, praying, and counseling the new Christians. Paul often paid his way by working as a tentmaker so that he would not have to depend on the hospitality of the local community.

Eventually Paul and Barnabas decided that they had traveled enough for a while. Instead of heading directly home to Tarsus, they went back through the towns in which they had established communities. In each respective town they preached and taught for a short time, and then they worked out any difficulties that might have come up. At last, they returned to the Mediterranean coast and sailed east to Antioch. They told the community there that God "had opened the door of faith to the pagans" (Acts 14:27). This was welcome news to the Christians at Antioch.

Crisis over the Jewish Law

Peter, after his escape from Herod, seems to have visited Antioch several times in the course of his work. There he became embroiled in two issues that almost tore the young Church apart (Acts 15:1–35).

At Antioch, the Gentiles ate foods forbidden by Judaic Law; the Jewish Christians could not accept this as proper religious practice. In the first century, much more so than today, meals were considered very important in human relations. People who ate together shared their lives as they shared food at the table. Thus, meals were signs of unity. The small Christian community of Antioch enjoyed having meals together. Peter joined them. As had happened earlier, a group of Jewish Christians from Jerusalem reprimanded Peter for eating with a group that included Gentiles. He was breaking the law forbidding Jews to eat with non-Jews. This was a serious charge against the man designated as leader of the Apostles.

Even more upsetting to the Gentile men of Antioch was the insistence by the Jerusalem delegation that they be circumcised. All Christians, in the view of the Jerusalem group, had to observe the **entire** Jewish Law. Shock ran through the Antioch community. In fifteen years of existence as a Christian community, no one had made this demand. In effect, they were being told that biblical laws were even more important than the faith. The implications of this conflict were tremendous, and Peter must have immediately grasped the gravity of the situation.

If the Gentiles were required to observe the Jewish Laws, they would probably be less likely to accept Jesus as the Christ. The work of Peter, Paul, Barnabas, Philip, and all the other missionaries to the Diaspora would be destroyed. Most importantly, didn't Jesus come to save all of those who believed—even if they did not follow the Judaic Law? The issue had to be settled once and for all.

It probably would not have been hard for Paul to imagine what the Gentile Christians might have been thinking—especially those at Antioch: "Peter doesn't come to eat with us any more. Since we're not born Jews, we're being treated like second-class Christians. It's hard to take this, to be discriminated against by Peter whom we love as a special friend of Jesus. And our Jewish friends, who believe in Jesus as we do, are now snubbing us by staying away from our dinners. This includes even Barnabas, who never comes to eat with us anymore."

Peter also had a problem. Indeed, he might have been thinking the following: "From the vision I had at Jaffa, I know that all food is allowed us by God. One day Jesus himself said that evil is not in food but in our hearts, our thoughts, our likes and dislikes. I don't think it's wrong to eat with my Gentile Christian brothers and sisters. However, the Jewish Christians are putting pressure on me, saying that I'm embarrassing them in Jerusalem, that they can't talk to their Jewish friends about Jesus because of the way I'm acting. So I've quit eating with my own Christian friends here."

Certainly Paul was upset; he might have reasoned: "This is all wrong. For most of my life, like a good Pharisee among my Jewish people, I believed that I was obeying my Father in heaven, God himself, by keeping the Law I was taught as a child. Jesus was the only one who was able to obey his Father with perfect love, as he proved by dying on the cross for us. God accepted his love by raising Jesus from the dead, and Jesus sent us the Spirit who alone is able to change us inside where it counts. Everywhere on my travels I've seen thousands of Gentiles begin to love Jesus and change their lives. It just doesn't matter so much whether Peter or I keep all the Jewish customs or not. Parts of the Law are valid and binding—like loving God and our neighbors—but not each and every custom, especially the dietary laws. What matters is that we have faith in Jesus, that we give ourselves to him and try to live as he showed us. Peter is splitting our Christian community by refusing to eat with our Gentile sisters and brothers. We have to work this out."

To What Jewish Laws Did the Gentiles Object?

The Law of Moses contained two sets of guidelines—those written and those orally transmitted. The written Law is contained in the book of Leviticus from the Hebrew Scriptures. There are hundreds of laws governing what may be eaten, what one should wear, what to do on the Sabbath, what feasts to celebrate, and exactly how they should be celebrated. Understandably a Gentile Christian might have found these laws terribly perplexing and incomprehensible, but a serious Jewish Christian who had practiced the Law from childhood would have found the laws reassuring. A faithful follower of the Law felt secure about his or her relationship with God.

Some of the laws from Leviticus are listed here. If you were not a Jew and were a convert to this new Christian faith, would you have objections to these laws?

You may eat any animal that has a cloven hoof, divided into two parts, and that is a ruminant. The following, which either chew the cud or have a cloven hoof, are the ones that you may not eat: . . . the hare must be held unclean, because though it is ruminant, it has not a cloven hoof; the pig must be held unclean, because though it has a cloven hoof, divided into two parts, it is not ruminant. (11:3–8)

Anything that has fins and scales, and lives in the water, whether in sea or river, you may eat. But anything in sea or river that has not fins or scales, of all the small water-creatures and all the living things found there, must be held detestable. . . . you are not to eat their flesh and you must avoid their carcases. (11:9–11)

If a woman conceives and gives birth to a boy, she is to be unclean for seven days, just as she is unclean during her monthly periods. On the eighth day the child's foreskin must be circumcised, and she must wait another thirty-three days for her blood to be purified. She must not touch anything

consecrated nor go to the sanctuary until the time of her purification is over. (12:2–4)

You must eat nothing with blood in it. You must not practise divination or magic. You are not to round off your hair at the edges nor trim the edges of your beard. You are not to gash your bodies when someone dies, and you are not to tattoo yourselves. (19:26–28)

While some of the laws of Leviticus seem odd to us today, many were very helpful because they protected the Jewish people from unsanitary practices. Other laws prevented the Jews from acting like the pagans who lived around them. Along with these very practical laws, Leviticus also contains profound moral laws such as "You must not exact vengeance, nor must you bear a grudge against the children of your people. You must love your neighbor as yourself" (Leviticus 19:18). This law is one of the two great commandments given by Jesus to his followers; it is taken from the Hebrew Scriptures. Thus, when the early community rejected some of the Jewish Law, they did not turn away from the most important parts of it.

Paul was a man of action. He lost no time in bringing the issue before the whole Christian community in Antioch. As might have been expected, the Jerusalem group turned against Paul, and arguments followed. However, little was accomplished. Finally the Antioch Christians commissioned Paul and Barnabas as their representatives to go to Jerusalem and to talk to the leaders about the problem.

The Council of Jerusalem

In Jerusalem a meeting, later considered the first council of the Church, was called. Paul and Barnabas described their work among the Gentiles, stressing especially the enthusiasm and faith of these people who had turned away from their idols and now believed in Jesus and the one true God. But a group of Pharisaic Christians in Jerusalem insisted that everybody, including Gentile converts, had to keep the Law of Moses. After lengthy discussion, Peter stood up and addressed the council:

> "You know perfectly well that in the early days God made his choice among you: the pagans were to learn the Good News from me and so become believers. In fact God, who can read everyone's heart, showed his approval of them by giving the Holy Spirit to them just as he had to us. God made no distinction between them and us, since he purified their hearts by faith. . . . Remember, we believe that we are saved in the same way as they are: through the grace of the Lord Jesus."

This silenced the entire assembly, and they listened to Barnabas and Paul describing all the signs and wonders God had worked through them among the pagans. (Acts 15:7–12)

James, the head of the Jerusalem community, supported Peter and proposed a solution that was accepted by the assembly. Two men from the Jerusalem community were chosen to go with Paul and Barnabas to Antioch to deliver a letter telling what had been decided upon.

The letter stated that the earlier Jerusalem delegation, which started the trouble at Antioch, was not authorized by the leaders. It assured the Christians of Antioch, Syria, and Asia Minor that they had to do only what was essential for the followers of Jesus. They did not have to observe the complete Jewish Law; for instance, circumcision was not required. Since the communities included both Jews and Gentiles, however, the latter were asked to act in a way that would make it possible for the Christians to live together in peace. Thus, "It has been decided by the Holy Spirit and by ourselves not to saddle you with any burden beyond these essentials: you are to abstain from food sacrificed to idols, from blood, from the meat of strangled animals and from fornication. Avoid these, and you will do what is right" (Acts 15:28–29). The Gentiles gladly accepted these conditions and "were delighted with the encouragement it gave them" (Acts 15:31).

The decision resulting from the meeting in Jerusalem directly concerned only Gentile Christians; it did not say whether or not Jewish Christians had to observe all of Jewish Law. It seems that at least some of the Christian converts from Judaism continued to keep the Law. The Christian communities allowed free choice in this matter so long as all agreed that they were saved by Jesus and not by the Jewish Law.

Opening of the Last Council:
A Tradition Continues

The most recent council, Vatican Council II, convened on 11 October 1962; it met for the next three years. Like the Council of Jerusalem, Vatican Council II set policies, formulated new insights into the Word of God, and deliberated on problems facing the Church. Here are Pope John XXIII's opening words:

Mother Church rejoices that, by the singular gift of Divine Providence, the longed-for day has finally dawned when—under the auspices of the virgin Mother of God, whose maternal dignity is commemorated on this feast—the Second Vatican Ecumenical Council is being solemnly opened here beside Saint Peter's tomb.

The Councils—both the twenty ecumenical ones and the numberless others, also important, of a provincial or regional character which have been held down through the years—all prove clearly the vigor of the Catholic Church and are recorded as shining lights in her annals. . . .

It is but natural that in opening this Universal Council we should like to look to the past and to listen to its voices, whose echo we like to hear in the memories and the merits of the more recent and ancient Pontiffs, our predecessors. . . . They are voices which proclaim in perennial fervor the triumph of that divine and human institution, the Church of Christ, which from Jesus takes its name, its grace, and its meaning.

Side by side with these motives for spiritual joy, however, there has also been for more than nineteen centuries a cloud of sorrows and of trials. . . . The great problem facing the world after almost two thousand years remains unchanged. Christ is ever resplendent as the center of history and of life. Men are either with Him and His Church, and they enjoy light, goodness, order, and peace. Or else they are without Him, or against Him, and deliberately opposed to His Church, and then they give rise to confusion, to bitterness in human relations, and to the constant danger of fratricidal wars.

Ecumenical councils, whenever they are assembled, are a solemn celebration of the union of Christ and His Church, and hence lead to the universal radiation of truth, to the proper guidance of individuals in domestic and social life, to the strengthening of spiritual energies for a perennial uplift toward real and everlasting goodness.

In effect, the councils are the People of God working together to discern the will of God so that the Church can be the Sacrament of Christ really present in the world.

Temple ruins at Philippi

Paul was now completely free to speak about Jesus to Gentiles everywhere. Soon there were more Gentiles than Jews in the Christian communities. Naturally not all Christians accepted the decision formed at the Council of Jerusalem. Whether Jewish Christians should obey the Law was to remain a bothersome issue for Paul and the whole Christian community. Though they had received many blessings from the Jews—the Bible, community worship, high moral values—the Christian congregations began to develop their own non-Jewish identities. Mainly they were different because of their faith in Jesus, who came for both Jews and Gentiles. Saint Paul summed up this view in a letter saying that through Baptism "there are no more distinctions between Jew and Greek, slave and free, male and female, but all of you are one in Christ Jesus" (Galatians 3:28).

Paul's Second Journey

After things settled down at Antioch—the community there having been restored to unity by the decision at Jerusalem—Paul elected to go on the road again to visit the Christian communities that he and Barnabas had started in Asia Minor on their first journey. To accompany him on this second trip, Paul chose Silas, a Christian from Jerusalem. Along the trade route through Asia Minor, Paul recruited Timothy, a young man of Greek-Jewish parents, who became a valuable assistant and lifelong companion. Also, about this time, Luke, who later wrote the Acts of the Apostles, seems to have joined Paul, Silas, and Timothy in spreading the Good News about Jesus (Acts 15:36—16:5).

Paul had intended to cover the western part of Asia Minor. But he began having doubts. One night in a dream Paul saw a man from Macedonia (mas-eh-*doh*-nyuh) urgently begging him to come across the sea to his country. Following the Holy Spirit's promptings, Paul and his companions sailed two days across the Aegean and landed at Philippi (*fil*-eh-peye) in Macedonia. For the first time, the Good News was to be preached in Europe. Until now, Christian communities existed only in Asia—Palestine, Syria, and Asia Minor.

Macedonia was the home of Alexander the Great, and Philippi had been named after his father. Philippi, although located in Greece, was a western Roman colony with Roman architecture, Roman government officials, Latin as a common language, and a large number of Roman soldiers. Indeed, Latin, not Greek, was the common language for the western part of the empire as well as the official language for imperial documents. Another unusual reality in Greek Philippi was the presence of many retired Roman soldiers who had been given land throughout the empire as pensions for their years of service.

Soon after his arrival, Paul met the Jewish minority of the town on the riverbank, for they were too small to have a synagogue. Immediate success was forthcoming, as Luke narrates:

> We sat down and preached to the women who had come to the meeting. One of these women was called Lydia, a devout woman from the town of Thyatira who was in the purple-dye trade. She listened to us, and the Lord opened her heart to accept what Paul was saying. After she and her household had been baptised she sent us an invitation: "If you really think me a true believer in the Lord," she said, "come and stay with us"; and she would take no refusal. (Acts 16:13–15)

In accepting the offer he could not refuse, Paul broke precedent. Usually, as he traveled from place to place, he made his living by tentmaking. Evidently the Philippians were too impressed with Paul's preaching to let him spend his time at his trade.

Inevitably Paul and Silas landed in jail once again. And again their crime was being too charitable. Luke tells the story vividly because he was there:

> One day as we were going to prayer, we met a slave-girl who was a soothsayer and made a lot of money for her masters by telling fortunes. This girl started following Paul and the rest of us and shouting, "Here are the servants of the Most High God; they have come to tell you how to be saved!" She did this every day afterwards until Paul lost his temper one day and turned round and said to the spirit, "I order you in the name of Jesus Christ to leave that woman." The spirit went out of her there and then. (Acts 16:16–18)

Being released from the evil spirit was good for the girl, but it was a financial loss for her owner. So Paul and Silas were charged with "causing a disturbance." They were flogged and shoved into a cell, and their feet were fastened in chains.

A violent earthquake occurred in the middle of their first night in jail. Right after the quake when the poor jailer saw the doors burst open, he drew his sword and was on the point of suicide when Paul stopped him. The compassionate reassurance that Paul gave to the distraught guard made one more convert to the Lord. That night the guard and his family were baptized. The Roman officials were so scared by the event that they released Paul and Silas early the next morning. Free again, Paul spent a few more days at Philippi with the new community before moving on.

Traveling southward, Paul and his friends stopped in Thessalonika (thes-uh-luh-*nee*-kuh), a coastal city with a busy harbor. The mostly Greek population was ruled by a Roman governor, but there was a large Jewish minority. Far from accepting the teachings of Paul that Jesus was the Messiah, the Jewish leaders here went so far as to bring charges of treason against him. They said that he was trying to substitute worship of Jesus for worship of the Roman emperor. Violence was brewing. Consequently Paul and Silas were smuggled out of town in the night's darkness. When Paul preached in Berea (buh-*ree*-uh) near Thessalonika, Jews came and stirred up a riot. Paul somehow escaped on a ship bound for Athens, the most famous city of Greece.

Despite having seen a lot in his travels, Paul could not help but be impressed with Athens. This was a special city filled with ancient temples and majestic buildings. In many ways, Athens was the home of Western philosophy and what we now know as democracy. The center of the city was the **agora,** or marketplace, where the men of Athens met each day to hold discussions about all sorts of topics. Athenians loved to debate and discuss. Even in government assemblies, citizens had a right to speak in their own names—not just through representatives. Paul began telling these people who worshiped many gods about the one and only living God who created the world. Day after day Paul walked around in the marketplace, unafraid to argue even with the learned Greeks he met there.

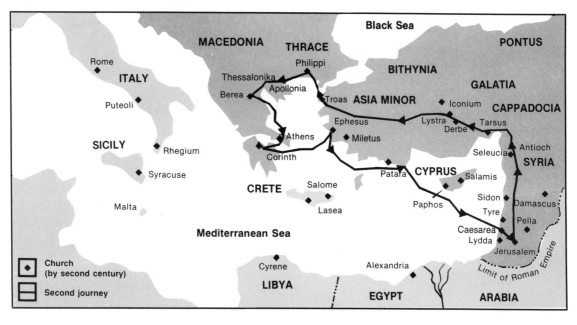

Paul's unusual ideas created so much interest that he was invited to speak in the council hall called the Areopagus: "The one amusement the Athenians and the foreigners living there seem to have, apart from discussing the latest ideas, is listening to lectures about them" (Acts 17:21). All went well until Paul began to tell about the Resurrection of Jesus. When his audience heard this, "some of them burst out laughing" (Acts 17:32). This ended the meeting.

The Greek philosopher Aristotle had taught that all knowledge comes through the senses. Since the Greeks had never seen such an event as the Resurrection, they would not believe in such a seemingly bizarre notion. However, Luke records that other Athenians did say, "We would like to hear you talk about this again" (Acts 17:32). Even in Athens, there were a few believers. In a short time, Paul and his faithful companions left Athens for Corinth.

Corinth was another important Roman city with many Roman army veterans living there. Like most seaports, it was a vice-ridden place. Prostitution, gambling, heavy drinking, and brawling all flourished. But it was a prosperous town because of the active trade in items needed by the empire. Paul began his mission in Corinth with the Jewish congregation. When they rejected him, he preached to the Gentiles, especially the poorer people. After eighteen months there, the community had grown quite large. During his time in Corinth, Paul took up his old trade as tentmaker in the shop of Aquila and Priscilla. This couple followed Paul when he returned to Antioch; they were not only converts but became missionaries with him (Acts 18:1–4,18,24–26).

Paul finished this second journey by sailing back to Caesarea, visiting the Church in Jerusalem, and finally returning to his home base in Antioch. He had been on the road for four years.

The acropolis at Athens

Focus on the Models

The most obvious facet of the Church's work during this time was the Church as Herald. The discussions in Jerusalem about following the Jewish Law were important because they freed Paul and the other Christians to spread the Word to more and more people all over the empire. Also, by clearing up the matter of what Gentiles could eat, the communities could celebrate their Sacrament of Eucharist with clear consciences. After all, the table of the Lord should be a sacrament of unity; if disputes broke this unity, then the Church could not be a sign of Jesus' presence among humankind.

The collection that Paul took up in Antioch to pay for food needed by the hungry Jerusalem community models the service that Christians are called upon to do. "Love your neighbor as yourself" is the central moral principle of the Gospels. While collections at Sunday Mass may seem nuisances, financial aid to the needy is clearly a tradition from the earliest days of the Church. Finally, the institutional part of the Church was seen functioning in the Council of Jerusalem. At this council, critical, divisive matters were discussed, debated, and resolved.

In the following chapters, other councils will play an important role in defining the nature of Christian life and practice. Councils are a way of gathering together the community's leaders and, under the guidance of the Holy Spirit, of providing the direction that the Church needs in order to deal with its complex difficulties. No one council could ever solve all the problems facing Christians. As we shall see in chapter 5, the Council of Jerusalem may have helped the Gentiles, but many questions about the relationship between Judaism and Christianity still tugged at the unity of the early Church.

Review Questions and Activities

1) Why was Antioch such an important city in the Roman Empire?

2) Why did Paul and Barnabas make the trip to Jerusalem from Antioch? Why would this act be so significant in light of later events with the Antioch community?

3) Describe Paul's first missionary journey with Barnabas.

4) What was the overall strategy that Paul used in preaching the Word of God? Why did he adopt this approach?

5) Why did the Gentiles object to the Jewish laws? Were their objections justified? Why did the Jewish Christians insist on following the Law? What did it mean to them?

6) Why did the conversion of Gentiles pose such a critical problem for the early Church? What were the motives of the Jewish Christians? How was the controversy finally solved?

7) What was Peter's position in the controversy that arose in Antioch? What did he do to bring the matter to a peaceful settlement? What pattern did his actions set for the Church that lasts up until today?

8) Did Jesus really reject the Jewish Law? What was his attitude toward it?

9) What significant events happened to Paul in Philippi? Why did he have to leave the city? What pattern does this seem to establish for Paul and his companions?

10) What charges were brought against Paul in Thessalonika? How would this same accusation be used later as a cause for persecuting the Christians?

11) What made Athens such an important city? Why did the Christian message fail to stir most of the Athenians?

12) In the events of this chapter, how did you see the Church as Herald? Servant? Institution? Sacrament? Mystical Body?

Personal Reflection Exercises

1) How do you really feel about collections at Mass? Do you feel that people support and encourage you to give money in the collections? Write a list of names of people who encourage you to give. Then, formulate a prayer of thanksgiving for them.

2) Read again and reflect on Paul's thoughts about the Antioch situation. Realizing that what he says about Jesus is as true today as it was then, try to describe how you would see your life if you did not have some faith in and/or knowledge about Jesus. Would you be different? How?

3) In any group of people there is always the temptation for some people to reject others because of things such as the way these others dress, where they are from, what they look like, their color, religion, or sex. In short, we find ourselves rejecting people because of externals —very often these are people we hardly know. Make a list of people whom you have rejected in some way—mostly because they were different from you. Next to the name, write down what it was or is that causes you problems about the person. Clearly we cannot be "best friends" with everyone, but are your reasons valid for rejecting these people? Then, make up a prayer for those whom you have rejected.

The Parthenon in Athens

5
The Lasting Legacy
of the Apostles

The fire of the Holy Spirit was too strong in Paul to allow him to settle comfortably in Antioch. This chapter takes us on the road again with Saint Paul as he preached his way through much of the Roman Empire. The hazards were constant and enormous. And while he made many converts, Paul's message made enemies too. God kept reaffirming Paul's efforts, but Paul knew that someday he might have to pay with his life for going against both Jewish and pagan beliefs and customs. The letters Paul wrote during this period are a precious legacy of Christian faith and wisdom to which the followers of Jesus still turn for guidance in the Way of the Lord. The apostolic era was fading, but the young Church was beginning to grow up, healthy and dynamic.

Many of the particular events of the years between A.D. 67 and 100 have escaped being recorded. However, there were two major developments that had far-reaching consequences. First, the Gospels and other Epistles were written and circulated during this period. Second, the relationship between Jews and Christians changed quite dramatically. What had been a mutual, although sometimes uneasy, toleration became in many cases overt hostility. Both of these developments caused the Christian communities to become more unified in their identity as Christians.

Paul's Letters: Our Epistles

During Paul's second journey an important event took place in Corinth. In about A.D. 51, when he wrote his Epistle (that is, letter) to the Christian community in Thessalonika, he was composing the first material that would eventually be included in the Christian Scriptures. Paul's only intention was to give advice to the community there. He did not have time to travel back to Thessalonika again; a letter would have to suffice. He wanted to moderate their enthusiasm about what they thought would be the immediate second coming of Jesus. They thought that Jesus would come to earth again very soon and would bring his followers with him to heaven. Consequently some of them had quit working and had lost interest in the world around them. Paul wanted to affirm the Christian belief that Jesus is coming; however, he realized that we don't know exactly when. Therefore, he urged the Thessalonians to go about their business, living as Christians but not ignoring daily concerns.

A few weeks after he had written to the Thessalonians the first time, Paul found it necessary to write to them again to clarify his earlier message. He certainly would have been shocked if someone had told him that he was writing part of the Bible. The only Bible he knew was the Hebrew Scriptures.

The letters of Paul—as well as those of Peter, James, John, and Jude—were treasured by the Christian communities. Copies were made by hand and circulated year after year. Letters were rarely received in those times; ones from important people like the Apostles would have been especially cherished. About a century and a half after Paul began to write—about the year A.D. 200—the Christian people agreed that certain writings were so valuable for Christian living that they really were God's Word, equal in value to the Hebrew Scriptures. Accordingly they gathered these writings together to form the Christian Scriptures. While Paul was alive, however, there were no Gospels. The first of the Gospels, written by Mark, was composed after Paul had died as a martyr in Rome, between the years A.D. 65 and 70.

Only a minority of the population of the Roman Empire could read and write. For letters, most of the people in the first century went to professional scribes—scholars who specialized in beautiful handwriting. Because experts today find several different styles in Paul's letters, they believe that he, of necessity, used varying methods for his writing. In some cases he seems to have dictated slowly, word for word. In other instances, he probably had ideas coming so fast that the secretary recorded only the general thought from Paul and then later put it into words of his own. Finally some of the Epistles that we credit to Paul were possibly written by his followers, perhaps after his death. These writers knew Paul's thinking, and they felt that they should put his name on the teachings they learned from him years earlier. They believed that they were recording Paul's teaching, not their own.

When the Christian communities received Paul's letters, they were read during community prayers and at the times of the Eucharist. Copies were circulated to neighboring communities. As a result, one hundred and fifty years after he wrote them there was a sizable collection of Paul's letters in circulation throughout the Mediterranean cities.

Paul's Third Missionary Journey

Paul rested from his journeys only a short time before he was on the road again. He had promised the people of Ephesus (ef-eh-suhs) that he would be back. Also he wanted to see how the communities in Asia Minor were doing. So, for the third time in about eight years, he was walking west on the caravan trail. Paul was now in his fifties. While he seems to have been

What Did Nonbelievers Think of the Christians?

The following excerpts from an anonymous letter to Diognetus, dating possibly from the second century, clearly state the somewhat mixed feelings that nonbelievers had about this new group called Christians:

They live in both Greek and foreign cities, wherever chance has put them. They follow local customs in clothing, food and the other aspects of life. But at the same time, they demonstrate to us the wonderful and certainly unusual form of their own citizenship.

They live in their own native lands, but as aliens; as citizens, they share all things with others; but like aliens, suffer all things. . . .

They marry and have children just like every one else; but they do not kill unwanted babies. They offer a shared table, but not a shared bed. They are at present "in the flesh" but they do not live "according to the flesh." They are passing their days on earth, but are citizens of heaven. They obey the appointed laws, and go beyond the laws in their own lives.

They love every one, but are persecuted by all. They are unknown and condemned; they are put to death and gain life. They are poor and yet make many rich. . . . They are dishonoured and yet gain glory through dishonour. . . .

They are attacked by Jews as aliens, and are persecuted by Greeks; yet those who hate them cannot give any reason for their hostility.

To put it simply—the soul is to the body as Christians are to the world. The soul is spread through all parts of the body and Christians through all the cities of the world The soul is in the body but is not of the body; Christians are in the world but not of the world.

Was it this wonderment about Christians that brought them new converts? Would this same writer say these things about Christians today?

A statue of the goddess Diana

Paul's preaching at Ephesus made a strong impression on the whole province of Asia because his words would be spread by the many travelers coming to and going from the city. What he said was illustrated by what he did. His acts of healing the sick caught immediate attention and created envy among the magicians who lived in Ephesus. These magicians were healers and religious leaders for the Gentiles. When the magicians saw what Paul was doing, some burned their own books and scrolls containing magical secrets; others wanted to force him out of town. Evidently Paul got into even worse trouble with the Ephesian silversmiths.

Many citizens began to abandon the worship of Diana, goddess of fertility. The silversmiths, who made a good living by making statues of the goddess, held an angry protest meeting against Paul (Acts 19:23–41). Sadly he had to leave the Christian community of Ephesus and head off for Macedonia. While in Ephesus, he wrote two very important letters to the Corinthians, and one letter to the community in Galatia.

About this time, Paul was told that the Christian community at Corinth was becoming split into several factions. He wrote to the Corinthians perhaps his most eloquent letter about love and the Lord's Supper. His reminders, however, about the charity that should characterize Christian communities evidently did little to improve the situation. Paul then traveled to Corinth personally. The troublemakers rejected his help, so he left. Then he sent Titus, one of his young coworkers, to Corinth. Shortly, Titus reported that the community had settled down and that they were ready to listen to Paul again. In his second letter to the Corinthians, Paul expressed his happiness over the renewed spirit of community.

in reasonably good health, he probably wondered if he would ever see Antioch or Tarsus again. Fifty was old age for persons then, and Paul's life was far from easy.

He stayed in Ephesus, the capital of the Roman province of Asia, for almost three years—probably because of the city's importance. Ephesus was a meeting place for eastern and western travelers and traders. It was also a warehouse center for brass, iron, marble, spices, and wheat. Among its impressive buildings was an outdoor theater that seated twenty-three thousand spectators. Ephesus was, moreover, the center for the worship of the Greek goddess Diana.

After visiting different communities in Macedonia, Paul stayed some days in Troas (*troh*-as). One incident in Troas shows that even Saint Paul's sermons went on far too long:

> We met to break bread. Paul was due to leave the next day, and he preached a sermon that went on till the middle of the night. A number of lamps were lit in the upstairs room where we were assembled, and as Paul went on and on, a young man called Eutychus [*yoo*-tee-kuhs] who was sitting on the window-sill grew drowsy and was overcome by sleep and fell to the ground three floors below. He was picked up dead. Paul went down and stooped to clasp the boy to him. "There is no need to worry," he said, "there is still life in him." Then he went back upstairs where he broke bread and ate and carried on talking till he left at daybreak. They took the boy away alive, and were greatly encouraged. (Acts 20:7–12)

The scene above also gives us a picture of how the small communities gathered in homes to worship. Christians formed close-knit groups and were clearly interested in the Good News of Jesus the Christ.

In this third journey, Paul observed groups of Jewish Christians who were agitating for the observance of the Jewish Law by all Jewish Christians. The Gentiles had been freed from Mosaic Law by the earlier Council of Jerusalem. Apparently many "Judaizers" still wanted Jewish Christians to abide by the old Law. Thus, they were causing friction everywhere. Most of the Christians in Asia Minor were converts from Judaism.

The strong interest in the Jewish Law at this time was largely caused by political factors. Many Jews were restless under Roman rule. To set aside the close observance of Jewish Law was a sign of disloyalty to the people of Israel. In Paul's thinking, there was danger that the Christian communities, with both Jews and Gentiles as members, would be divided. The matter of whether or not Jewish Christians should follow the Jewish Law had to be settled once and for all.

Paul journeyed to Jerusalem to help resolve both this matter and one other. Paul had pledged that the Christian communities would help one another—indeed, this was an essential part of the Way. The people of Jerusalem were now once again suffering from famine. Christian Gentiles in Greece and Asia Minor contributed generously to a fund for the community in Jerusalem. Thus, accompanied by Gentile representatives from various communities and carrying the contributions, he set sail.

Paul's Return to Jerusalem

Paul knew that there was trouble ahead for him in Jerusalem. As he told the people of Ephesus when he was leaving them:

> I am on my way to Jerusalem, but have no idea what will happen to me there, except that the Holy Spirit, in town after town, has made it clear enough that imprisonment and persecution await me. But life to me is not a thing to waste words on, provided that when I finish my race I have carried out the mission the Lord Jesus gave me—and that was to bear witness to the Good News of God's grace. (Acts 20:22–24)

As he sailed to Jerusalem and stopped at various communities, Paul seemed to be saying farewell for the last time. Luke writes that the communities were deeply moved: "When he had finished speaking he knelt down with them all and prayed. By now they were all in tears; they put their arms round Paul's neck and kissed him; what saddened them most was his saying they would never see his face again" (Acts 20:37). The person who had brought them hope, love, meaning, and faith in Jesus

Paul's Third and Fourth Journeys

was leaving them. These new communities would now have to continue the struggle to become the Church without Paul.

Luke says that Paul and his band were given "a very warm welcome" by the Jerusalem community (Acts 21:17). Undoubtedly the contributions that Paul delivered were the cause of much thanks, but many of the community were also probably glad to see someone who could help settle the dispute over Jewish Law. Unfortunately Paul never had the opportunity to deal with this.

On the advice of James and other leaders of the community, Paul took part in one of the services in the Temple to show that he respected the Law. Some Jews from Asia saw him and began shouting their protests. Before he realized what was happening, Paul was being dragged outside the Temple gates by the mob. Alerted by the noise, the Roman military unit stationed in the fortress near the Temple came charging into the crowd and carried Paul away from a sure death. Though he was badly bruised and his clothes were torn, he asked the commanding officer to allow him to speak to the mob outside. His speech went well until he said that he was sent to preach to the Gentiles. Rioting broke out all over again.

Paul spent the night in prison; the next day his remarks before the Sanhedrin stirred up another violent disturbance. Since Paul was a Roman citizen and protected by Roman law, he was sent to Caesarea, the Roman capital of Palestine. During the night and with an escort of well over two hundred men, Paul made the trip safely. The escort was necessary because forty Jewish men had taken a vow to kill Paul. Paul, by saying that converts to Christianity need not adhere to the Jewish Law, was viewed as an enemy and a collaborator with the Roman oppressors.

The high priest arrived from Jerusalem to accuse Paul of stirring up trouble among the Jews. However, Felix, the Roman governor, made no decision because the high priest failed to bring witnesses against Paul. Under custody in the governor's palace, Paul was "free from restriction" and could receive visitors. For an active man like Paul, however, this had to be frustrating. He was under house arrest for approximately two years—from A.D. 58 to 60. Then a new governor named Festus was appointed.

Festus soon offered Paul a chance to defend himself before the Sanhedrin in Jerusalem. Yet, realizing that he could never have a fair trial before judges who were also his enemies, Paul did a bold thing: he told the governor that he wanted his case heard in Rome, this being the right of every Roman citizen. Festus had to grant Paul's request. "You have appealed to Caesar; to Caesar shall you go" (Acts 25:12).

The Final Years in Rome

A short time later Paul was placed on board a merchant ship carrying cargo, including a group of prisoners, bound for Rome. This was certainly no pleasure cruise. The small craft was tossed furiously by several winter storms, and eventually Paul and the others were shipwrecked on the island of Malta. Finally, Paul did arrive at Rome, where he was unexpectedly met and escorted through the city by a group of Roman Christians. He saw that Rome, the largest and grandest city of the empire, also had its share of dingy, crowded slums.

At an army camp, a soldier was assigned to guard Paul. However, Paul was allowed to live in a rented house, and he was allowed to have visitors. Within three days of his arrival in Rome, Paul invited the local Jewish leaders to his house. Most of them rejected his news about Jesus the Messiah. Nevertheless, Paul's house soon became a very busy place, as he welcomed everybody, Jews and Gentiles. His most regular visitors were from the Roman Christian community.

The first Roman Christians were probably Jews who had converted in Jerusalem soon after Pentecost. It is quite likely that Peter had organized them into a community. In any case, Paul was able to help this community grow.

We don't know much about what happened to Paul after he came to Rome. Luke ends his account abruptly: "Paul spent the whole of the two years [from about 61 to 63] in his own rented lodging. He welcomed all who came to visit him, proclaiming the kingdom of God and teaching the truth about the Lord Jesus Christ with complete freedom and without hindrance from anyone" (Acts 28:30–31). Possibly Paul's case was dismissed by a Roman judge. In any event, Paul seems to have been freed at this time and to have visited some Christian communities in Greece and Asia Minor.

Probably soon after Paul had left Rome, a raging fire spread through about two-thirds of the city, destroying the small shops, most of the slums—even the palace of the Emperor Nero. No one seemed to know how the fire began, but someone had to be blamed. Though Nero was not in Rome that July night in the year 64, the people suspected that he had arranged for the fire to be started—perhaps so that he could rebuild the city the way he wanted it. To squelch the rumor about himself, Nero accused the Christians—who clearly lived differently from Romans and were a small group. Many Christians were arrested and quickly executed. This inaugurated the era of Roman persecution of Christians.

A second outbreak of persecution started three years later. Despite all the dangers, many Romans had converted to Christianity. They avoided the pagan religious ceremonies honoring the many gods; yet attending these ceremonies was considered the patriotic duty of every Roman citizen. Consequently, Roman Christians were viewed as treasonous. Further, Nero—regarded by historians as possibly insane at this time—still needed to blame someone for the deteriorating conditions in Rome. In A.D. 67, Nero ordered the mass execution of Christians.

Paul and Peter both died in Nero's persecutions. According to legend, Peter, because he was a Roman subject and not a citizen, was crucified. Paul, a Roman citizen, was beheaded. Luke, of course, was not there to record Paul's

Nero's Persecution of the Christians

This passage, written by the Roman historian Tacitus, illustrates why Christians were easy targets for persecution by the mad Emperor Nero:

To kill the rumours [that Nero started the fires that destroyed much of Rome], Nero charged and tortured some people hated for their evil practices—the group popularly known as "Christians." The founder of this sect, Christ, had been put to death by the governor of Judea, Pontius Pilate, when Tiberius was Emperor. Their deadly superstition had been suppressed temporarily, but was beginning to spring up again—not now just in Judea but even in Rome itself where all kinds of sordid and shameful activities are attracted and catch on.

First those who confessed to being Christians were arrested. Then, on information obtained from them, hundreds were convicted, more for their anti-social beliefs than for fire-raising. In their deaths they were made a mockery. They were covered in the

skins of wild animals, torn to death by dogs, crucified or set on fire—so that when darkness fell they burned like torches in the night. Nero opened up his own gardens for this spectacle and gave a show in the arena, where he mixed with the crowd or stood dressed as a charioteer on a chariot. As a result, although they were guilty of being Christians and deserved death, people began to feel sorry for them. For they realized that they were being massacred not for the public good but to satisfy one man's mania. (*Annals*, 15.44)

The Colosseum in Rome (top) was the site of the
death of many Christians.

Christians hid from their persecutors in the
catacombs—underground passageways (left).

An early Christian symbol (right).

The Lasting Legacy of the Apostles   77

words and actions. But we know Paul's attitude toward death. Several years earlier he had written to his friends at Philippi: "Life to me, of course, is Christ, but then death would bring me something more" (Philippians 1:21). His faith gave him confidence that now at last he would see Jesus face-to-face forever. There could be no greater source of hope for Paul or Peter.

The Way Is Now the Church

Forty years had passed since Jesus had been executed on a Jerusalem hill and had risen from the dead. The number of Christians around the Mediterranean, especially on its northern shores, had been steadily growing. Nevertheless, they were still only a very small minority in the huge Roman Empire. People wondered about them. On the one hand, they were ordinary people who worked, ate, laughed, and cried like everyone else. On the other hand, they seemed to have great self-confidence, hope, and meaning—different from their neighbors. Why?

Paul suggests a reason for the Christian difference in the salutations he uses in his letters: "From Paul . . . to the church of God at Corinth" (2 Corinthians 1:1) or "From Paul to the churches of Galatia" (Galatians 1:1). Paul's word *church,* in Greek, meant "assembly," that is, the meeting of citizens in the civic center of town for the purpose of deciding matters of government. Paul used this word to refer to the assembly of people who believe in Jesus the Christ, the Christian community. For Paul, Church was not a building for worship because Christians worshiped wherever it was convenient, usually in private homes. Nor was the Church a powerful international institution with well-known leaders and a system of laws. Christians of the first century saw themselves primarily as people gathered in an assembly to express their belief in the Good News about Jesus Christ and to break the bread and to say the prayers together. As

Church in this sense, they were definitely different from their neighbors, and Paul would have rejoiced had he seen the Church's faith in the centuries to come.

The Gospels Emerge

During the last third of the first century, after the deaths of Peter and Paul, Christians in various churches began to put into a new written form what they believed and taught about Jesus Christ. Eventually these writings became known as **gospels**, literally meaning "Good News." Soon these writings were considered to be as important as Paul's Epistles.

Composing the Gospels was a long process (they were not completed until about A.D. 100). People wrote down the Good News for two compelling reasons. One of the reasons was that only a few of the people who had known Jesus personally were still living. If the firsthand experiences about Jesus were to be preserved accurately, they had to be written down. Also, like Paul's letters, the Good News in written form could reach many people throughout the Roman Empire.

In the first century there were no printing presses and, of course, no newspapers. Radio and television were probably not even dreamed of. Books were written by hand and were very expensive. For ordinary people they might as well not have existed. And, as we saw with Paul's Epistles, even letters were rare treats.

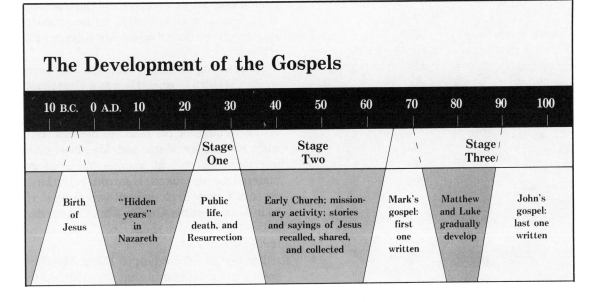

The Development of the Gospels

10 B.C.	0 A.D.	10	20	30	40	50	60	70	80	90	100

| | | Stage One | | Stage Two | | | | | Stage Three | | |

| Birth of Jesus | "Hidden years" in Nazareth | Public life, death, and Resurrection | Early Church; missionary activity; stories and sayings of Jesus recalled, shared, and collected | Mark's gospel: first one written | Matthew and Luke gradually develop | John's gospel: last one written |

Many stories about Jesus had been kept alive in the Christian communities by public recitations. Indeed, talking and storytelling was one of the most important sources of entertainment and information before the advent of printing presses—not to mention TV, radio, and videogames. In the process, the people of these early times developed unbelievable memories. They remembered things much better than we do—they had to. Of course, the storytellers frequently added their own unique twists or interpretations to the original tales. The interpretation presented by the storyteller frequently depended on their audiences.

Eventually in some particular communities people began to write down certain incidents in the life of Jesus that they considered most important. Very likely they first wrote about the sufferings of Jesus, his death on the cross, and his Resurrection. Christians also described some of his healings and recorded many of the things that he said. All these were just bits and pieces—nothing like a full scroll or book. However, they were useful to the communities, especially in the liturgy when these notes were read, discussed, and prayed about.

The Four Evangelists

The first person to organize these scraps of writings and to combine them with the oral tradition of the community was **Mark.** Mark probably was the companion of Barnabas and Paul on their first journey and was later in Rome with Peter. There he undoubtedly heard many things about Jesus from the leader of the Apostles. Mark wrote his Gospel in Rome after Peter's death, probably in the mid-sixties. He wrote particularly for the Gentiles who had become Christians.

The second Gospel, that of **Matthew,** was written in the early seventies. The author seems to have belonged to the community at Antioch. Since this community was composed of both Jews and Gentiles, Matthew speaks of things that interested people of Palestine, such as the meaning of the Law and the coming of the Messiah. Matthew used Mark's Gospel as

a reference, but he kept in mind the traditions of his Antioch community. So he produced what might be described as a Jewish-Christian Gospel.

Luke, a companion of Paul in the later years, wrote the third Gospel. He was a Gentile and probably a doctor. The style of his writing shows that Luke was a gentle person careful of the feelings of his readers. Besides using such sources as Mark and Matthew, Luke interviewed people at various places to get material for his Gospel. He wrote in the latter seventies, very likely in southern Greece. He wanted to help his Gentile Christian readers understand that Jesus came to save everyone, regardless of race.

The Gospels according to Mark, Matthew, and Luke are similar in that they express the same general understanding about Jesus. The Gospel of **John** is different from the others even though it is based on the same events in the life of Jesus. This fourth Gospel was the last to be written, just at the end of the first century. Many scholars believe that it is based on the teaching of the Apostle John—a fisherman like Peter who was prominent in the Jerusalem Church in the early days. Very likely this Gospel was put into final form by John's followers after his death. In any case, the author was writing as an eyewitness to the deeds of Jesus. The purpose of the Gospel was to help people believe in Jesus. John's Gospel talks more about the mystery of Jesus being God made flesh. The miracles were signs of Jesus' godly power.

After each of the four Gospels was written, copies were made by hand and distributed to various churches in the Roman Empire. Other accounts of the life and teachings of Jesus were written later. However, only the Gospels according to Mark, Matthew, Luke, and John—all written in Greek during the first century—were accepted by all the churches. In time these Gospels came to be appreciated as inspired by the Holy Spirit. With the letters of Paul, the Gospels form most of the Christian Scriptures.

A representation of Saint Mark (top)
A papyrus of the Epistle to the Hebrews (bottom)

Sunday in the Early Church

Sundays began early. Christian worship started before sunrise. The community would meet in someone's house; the location would vary because persecutions occurred occasionally. When all the believers were gathered, the leader of the assembly would read the sacred writings—letters of Paul, parts of the Good News from Mark, Matthew, Luke, or the most recent Gospel by John—sometimes called the memoirs of the Apostles. Then the leader would explain the meaning of the texts. Prayers for all the people followed. The first part of the worship might include singing too. The pace was unhurried, and people sometimes joined into the discussion of the readings. At this point, those who had not been baptized left the celebration and were given instruction in the Christian life; these uninitiated persons were called *catechumens*.

The second part of the worship service of early Christians is described by Justin, a martyr who died in the second-century persecutions:

At the end of the prayers, we greet one another with a kiss. Then the president of the brethren is brought bread and a cup of wine mixed with water; and he takes them, and offers up praise and glory to the Father of the universe, through the name of the Son and of the Holy Ghost, and gives thanks at considerable length for our being counted worthy to receive these things at his hands. When he has concluded the prayers and thanksgivings, all the people present express their joyful assent by saying Amen.... Then those whom we call deacons give to each of those present the bread and wine mixed with water over which the thanksgiving was pronounced, and carry away a portion to those who are absent.

We call this food "Eucharist," which no one is allowed to share unless he or she believes that the things which we teach are true, and has been washed with the washing that is for remission of sins and unto a second birth, and is living as Christ has commanded. For we do not receive them as common bread and common drink; but as Jesus Christ our Saviour.... For the apostles, in the memoirs called Gospels composed by them, have thus delivered unto us what was enjoined upon them; that Jesus took bread, and when he had given thanks, said, "This do in remembrance of me, this is my body"; and that, in a similar way, having taken the cup and given thanks, he said, "This is my blood"; and he gave it to them alone. (*Apology,* 65–66)

Sometimes the worship service was followed by another meal called the *agape.* Here the community ate together, talked, and generally had a good time being with people of similar faith. These meals were chances to support one another too—for the times were quite threatening to these new, small communities. The persecutions of the Christians by Nero, in which Paul and Peter died, were moderate compared to the troubles that lay ahead.

The Church and Judaism

The latter half of the first century saw a dramatic alteration in the relationship between Christianity and Judaism. The causes for the increasing hostility will be described here, but the effects have far overshadowed these causes, which have for the most part been forgotten. Many of the persecutions of the Jews, even in our century, were rooted in misunderstandings beginning in the first century.

Jesus was a Jew. While he was growing up, his parents taught him to speak the language (Aramaic) used by the Jewish people, to read the Jewish Scriptures, and to say Jewish prayers. He was at home in the great Temple in Jerusalem. The professional Jewish teachers admired him for his learning. Though he criticized hypocrites and those overly strict about keeping religious rules, he himself kept the Jewish Law, the Torah.

The friends of Jesus were all Jews. So were his earliest followers. The Jewish Christians in Jerusalem continued to live as Jews. The Christians in Jerusalem, for the most part, lived peacefully as a minority. Most Jews, however, did not believe that Jesus was the Messiah. But as long as the Jewish Christians kept the Torah, their belief about Jesus as the Messiah did not divide them from their fellow Jews.

Separation between Jewish Christians and the majority of the population in Jerusalem began in the year 62 when James, the leader of the Christians there, was arrested by the high priest for blasphemy, thrown from the roof of the Temple, and then stoned to death. During the next four years many Christians left their Jerusalem homes, crossed the Jordan, and settled in Pella, a Gentile town about six-ty miles away. Meanwhile, strong rebellious feelings against Rome were swelling in the Jewish capital.

In A.D. 66 an official act of rebellion was committed in the Temple when the daily sacrifice for Nero, the Roman emperor, was discontinued. Shortly, Jerusalem was attacked by the strongest Roman army of the time. For four years Jerusalem held out; but finally, in the year 70, the Temple was destroyed and the city taken. With the center of Judaism gone and thousands killed or imprisoned, it seemed that Israel as a nation would disappear forever.

Before the revolt against the Romans there was a variety of ways in which Jews could practice their religion. As we have seen, there were Pharisees, Sadducees, and priests; but there were also some groups who were like monks. The first Christians formed another sect within Judaism, and so they were tolerated. However, with the defeat of Israel, many Jews felt that Judaism was being destroyed. If it were to be saved, it had to be unified. Conformity of belief was required.

Within a few years after the fall of Jerusalem, Christians were no longer welcome in the synagogues. The Jewish Christians who had followed the Law all their lives were hurt and angered by this rejection. As a result, by at least the year 90, Christianity and Judaism were definitely separated. And—as often happens when people who were once close begin to exclude one another—distrust, some bitterness, and even hatred often took the place of love.

Writing before the separation of the Jewish Christians from Judaism, Paul reflects little of the later antagonism toward the Jews. As we saw, Paul was persecuted several times by different Jewish communities. Yet his criticism of Jews does not become a general rejection of all Jews and Judaism. He expresses his disappointment in his fellow Jews because many could not accept Jesus. Nevertheless, they were still the Chosen People, and God had not broken off the covenant with them. Paul even goes further. He encourages the Gentile Christians to maintain unity with the Jews because of faith in the one God.

In excluding the Christians from Jewish communities, the Jews were trying to maintain their identity as a people. As the number of Christians increased, some of them began to think that the Jews were no longer God's people. Even more erroneously, some Christians began to blame the Jews for Jesus' death. As a result, in many places, especially in Europe, the Jews were persecuted by Christians. As late as 1965, Vatican Council II saw that it was necessary to remind Christians that they are united with the Jews as brothers and sisters in a common God. A proper understanding of the Gospels will never give anyone a reason for prejudice against the Jews. However, this first-century separation generated many centuries of misunderstanding and intermittent persecution.

The interior of the church at Cappadocia, one of the first Christian church buildings

The exterior of same church (next page)

Focus on the Models

The followers of Jesus were now identified as *Christians.* They got this name because they were living out the values Jesus taught. In short, they were the Body of Christ, the People of God. While a few questions about following the original Jewish Law still remained when Paul returned to Jerusalem, these seem, for the most part, to have been settled. The sacramental life of the Church was still somewhat simple; people were baptized, listened to the Word of God, broke bread together, and prayed. Heralding the Word was most obvious during the travels of Paul, but clearly many other Christians were spreading the Good News because the Church was growing. The written copies of the Gospels and Epistles also greatly aided all the congregations in remaining faithful to Jesus. The practice of service to other Christian communities was firmly established. To strengthen the Church as Institution, the Apostles who had led the Church left bishops in charge of local congregations. Deacons were serving each community too. We know little about the Church after the deaths of Peter and Paul until the year 100. Local congregations must have flourished—due to their faith and to the communal structures that gave them continuity of leadership—because by the year 100, the People of God were steadfast, growing to the point where they were seen as a threat to the Roman Empire. The fledgling Church had all the means necessary to enter into the second and third centuries—centuries that would test the Church in fires of persecution.

Artist's depiction of a funeral in the catacombs

Review Questions and Activities

1) Why did Paul write his two letters to the Christians in Thessalonika?

2) Why did the communities of Christians who received letters from Paul—as well as Peter, James, John, and Jude—cherish them, copy them, and exchange them with others?

3) Describe the ways in which Paul wrote his letters.

4) On Paul's third journey, he spent a good deal of time in Ephesus. Why?

5) The silversmiths in Ephesus almost killed Paul. Why? Does their reaction seem typical of people's reactions to new religions or to ideas that challenge old beliefs? Can you think of some examples to support your position?

6) What unresolved problem still caused some division in the Church? Why was this problem more complicated than just another religious dispute?

7) What attitude did Paul have about returning to Jerusalem? What external motivations existed that caused him to go there?

8) Why was Paul protected by the Romans? Why were the Jews so determined to kill him?

9) Why did Nero persecute the Christians? If you are not familiar with the word *scapegoat,* look it up in a dictionary. Have any groups of people recently been put into the position in which Nero put the Christians? If so, were any of the reasons for making them scapegoats similar to Nero's reasons for persecuting the Christians?

10) What really made the Christians different from their neighbors? Explain.

11) According to Luke's account in the Acts of the Apostles, Paul gave at least thirteen years of his life to difficult and dangerous travel in order to tell people the Good News, the Gospel of Jesus the Christ. As a good storyteller, Luke gives some very interesting details about Paul's experiences. To appreciate this, read the following passages in Acts and then write a newspaper headline summarizing each episode:

a) **The first journey:**
Acts 14:1–7
Acts 14:8–20

b) **The second journey:**
Acts 16:16–40

c) **The third journey:**
Acts 19:23–41
Acts 20:7–12

12) Why were the Gospels composed? How were they used by the early Church?

13) How did the communities in which the authors lived influence the writing of the Gospels? Why is the Gospel of John so different

from the other three? To get a sense of the difference, read the introduction to John's Gospel and the introduction to Matthew's. How are they different in tone and content?

14) What is similar and what seems different about the liturgy of A.D. 100 and the liturgy you attend at your parish? What do you think accounts for the differences?

15) Why is it important for Christians to remember that Jesus was a Jew?

16) What were the causes of both the split and the later mutual distrust between Christians and Jews?

17) How did the events of the first century of Christianity prepare the communities for the second century?

Personal Reflection Exercises

1) Paul wrote letters to his friends in Corinth, Galatia, and the other places where Christian communities depended on him for encouragement. Write a letter to someone you know who could use some encouragement or just a greeting from you. Try to let them know how important they are to you and how much you care about them. Mail this letter.

2) Reread the letter to Diognetus (see p. 71). If you were writing to a friend of yours and you wanted to describe contemporary Christians, what would you say? Try to view today's Christians as if you were an outsider. Use the topics mentioned in the letter to Diognetus as suggestions of points to consider. Then, write your reflections down as the outline of a letter.

3) Choose one of the narratives given in question 11 above and, putting yourself in Paul's place, write briefly how you feel about what happened.

4) Write an imaginary dialogue with a first-century martyr. What sort of questions would you ask, and how do you think he or she would respond?

5) What sort of stereotypes exist today about Jews? Try to list and describe as many of these as you can. What stereotypes do non-Catholics have about Catholics? List and describe these. How do you feel about these stereotypes? Do they apply to all Catholics? Do they apply to you? Do the stereotypes listed about Jews apply to all Jews? How do you feel about stereotyping? Is stereotyping a helpful process in arriving at a just view of the world?

6
Gold Tested in Fire

Peter and Paul were executed by Nero. In addition, all over the Roman Empire many other Christians suffered at the hands of their neighbors. Yet these first persecutions were minor—especially when compared to the general suppression that was ordered by a series of emperors in the years from 100 to 312. Nonetheless, the resulting executions of thousands of Christians actually caused the conversion of thousands of other people. The Church grew because the spectators at the public massacres saw people filled with courage, faith, hope, and love. The Roman Empire was crumbling from within and being attacked from without. People needed something in which to place their trust, and Christianity withstood the test. Then in A.D. 312 the situation of the Church changed dramatically: the new emperor was converted to Christianity. Suddenly the Church became the dominant force in the Roman Empire; the history of Europe and the world was permanently altered from this point on.

Christians
in the Roman Empire

In the year A.D. 100, Christians really had to contend with three groups of people: the Jews, who by this time were at odds with the Christians; the Romans, both government and people, who were suspicious of this new group; and the barbarians, or nomadic tribes, who lived beyond the frontiers of the empire but were gathering strength to attack Roman lands. **Barbarian** comes from the Greek word meaning "hairy ones"; it came to mean any non-Roman who spoke an unfamiliar language and who was unshaven.

Small communities of Christians were scattered throughout the empire, especially after the destruction of Jerusalem. These communities were identified as being Christian because they believed in one God, they studied the writings of the Apostles, they practiced a morality different from their non-Christian neighbors, and they celebrated the breaking of the bread on Sundays. Much of this tradition came from Jewish practice. Also part of their Jewish heritage was the calendar that they followed, which included one day set aside for worship of their God and for the building of relationships in the community and family.

Another aspect of Christian life that held them together was the organizational structures that had evolved by this time. Each community selected one of its members to be a **bishop** (from the Greek word for "supervisor"). The bishop led the community's worship, and, as the Greek meaning implies, supervised the life of the Christian congregation. Since the communities were small and all the members could meet at one location for the Eucharist, each city only needed one bishop. Thus, the position of priest did not develop for many years. Assisting the bishop were deacons. Like Stephen, the first martyr, deacons attended to the welfare of the community's poor, widowed, orphaned, and sick persons. The bishops and deacons were not full-time ministers; in most cases, they continued to support themselves through their own labor.

Another development was the increasing importance of the bishop of Rome. Of course, before the fall of Jerusalem, the bishop of Jerusalem was considered most important. After Jerusalem's fall, because Peter had died in Rome and because Rome was the imperial capital, the bishop of Rome was looked upon more and more as a central figure in the Church. Most significantly, the bishop of Rome was considered to be Peter's successor. Since Peter had been appointed by Jesus as head of the Church, his successor was head also.

The Peace of Rome

For most citizens, life in the Roman world from approximately A.D. 100 to 200 was peaceful enough. Prosperous cities ringed the Mediterranean, the various ethnic groups were held together by Roman law, a single currency was used in the empire, and roads led everywhere. Thus traders were able to bring their goods to all the cities. In addition, the shipping lanes of the Mediterranean were filled with cargo vessels.

Indeed, commerce flowed throughout the empire. Egypt supplied grain from its Nile farmlands and also the papyrus that everyone needed for writing. Iron, copper, and zinc were mined in northern Gaul (*gawl*). Western North Africa, southern Spain, Greece, and Italy supplied the olive oil essential for cooking. Asia Minor exported wool. Italy was the center for winemaking, weapons and other metalware, pottery, and glass; it shipped these products to Illyria (il-*ir*-ee-uh) across the Adriatic (ay-dree-*at*-ik) Sea, north to Gaul, west to Spain, and even to faraway Britain. Silk and spices from distant China were obtainable, if only for the rich.

During the second century, Rome was ruled by five "good emperors," as they came to be known. They were good because they kept out the barbarians and the Persians. Of the two

Aqueduct arches, built by Romans in 30 B.C. in Provence, France

threats, the nomadic tribes were by far the worse threat. They lived on the northern frontier formed by the Rhine and Danube rivers. The Romans built forts and walled cities to protect the northern border. Beyond the border roamed the barbaric tribes. Sometimes the Romans hired these tribes to help guard the frontier. Later on, barbarians were recruited for the imperial army. Most barbarians, however, lived free of control and liked to make quick raids across the borders into Roman lands. As we will see later, the Church would suffer deeply from barbarian attacks as the Roman Empire began to crumble.

Centuries of Martyrdom

While outright persecution was limited to specific periods of time, the Christians were continually looked upon with suspicion. Small in number, but well known, the Christians were not content to stay quiet about their beliefs. They preached to the whole Roman world, inviting everyone to join them as followers of Jesus. This brought both visibility and trouble.

Christian communities took root not only in Syria and Asia Minor, but also in Greece, Italy, Gaul, Spain, and later on the coast of Africa. For refusing to take part with their neighbors in the public sacrifices to the Roman gods, Christians were accused of atheism—that is, not believing in God. For refusing to put a few grains of incense into the flame burning before the statue of the emperor, they were accused of disloyalty to Rome. The Roman citizens believed that the gods sent blessings on them only if they offered sacrifices. They

The Trial and Execution of Polycarp

[Polycarp steps toward the proconsul—his judge.]

Proconsul: Are you Polycarp of Smyrna?

Polycarp: I am.

Proconsul: You have been charged with being a Christian; you can quickly deny this and save your life. Respect your years! You have not grown old to die as a criminal but as a respected citizen of the empire. Swear by Caesar's fortune; change your attitude; say: Away with the godless!

Polycarp: [face set, looks at the crowd in the stadium, waving his hand toward them; then sighs, while looking up to heaven]: Away with the godless!

Proconsul: Swear, and I will set you free: deny Christ!

Polycarp: For eighty-six years, I have been his servant, and he has never done me wrong: how can I blaspheme my king who saved me?

Proconsul: I have wild beasts. I shall throw you to them if you don't change your attitude.

Polycarp [firmly]: Call them. We cannot change our attitude if it means a change from better to worse. But it is a splendid thing to change from cruelty to justice.

Proconsul: If you make light of the beasts, I'll have you destroyed by fire, unless you change your attitude.

Polycarp: The fire you threaten burns for a time and is soon extinguished: there is a fire you know nothing about—the fire of the judgment to come and of eternal punishment, the fire reserved for the ungodly. But why do you hesitate? Do what you want.

[Proconsul sends the crier to middle of arena.]

Crier: [repeats three times]: Polycarp has confessed that he is a Christian.

Crowd: Burn him alive! Burn him!

[The crowd rushes to collect logs and sticks from workshops and the public baths; a pyre is built.]

Polycarp [after he is tied to the stake]: O Father of your beloved and blessed Son, Jesus Christ, through whom we have come to know you, the God of angels and powers and all creation, and of the whole family of the righteous who live in your presence; I bless you for counting me worthy of this day and hour, that in the number of the martyrs I may partake of Christ's cup, to the resurrection of eternal life of both soul and body in the imperishability that is the gift of the Holy Spirit. Amen.

[Men light the fire; great flames shoot up.]

Adapted from Eusebius,
History of the Church IV, 15

feared that the gods would curse them for tolerating the Christians' refusal to sacrifice. Consequently, starting during the reign of Nero, A.D. 54–68, persons could be arrested simply on the suspicion of being Christians. While this law remained in effect for two centuries, it was enforced only periodically. But Christians never knew when someone might turn them in or when the next persecution would come. Sometimes the persecutions were carried out in just a few provinces. Still, despite the frightening tensions under which they lived, Christianity spread. The blood of the martyrs was described as watering the seeds of new conversions.

Among the early martyrs was **Ignatius** (ig-*nay*-shee-uhs), bishop of Antioch, who was taken to Rome to be eaten by lions in the amphitheater for the amusement of the crowds at the circus. Not concerned about himself, Ignatius wrote letters to the Christians of each of the seven towns at which they stopped en route to Rome, encouraging them to be united with their own bishop. Ignatius at one point wrote: "Now at last I am beginning to be a disciple. . . . The Devil may inflict his ugly penalties on me—fire, the cross, wild beasts in hordes; he may tear me to pieces, quarter me, dislocate my bones, crush every part of my body—if only I can come at Jesus Christ." At Smyrna (*smuhr*-nuh), on the west coast of Asia Minor, he wrote to Polycarp, the young bishop there. Many years later, Polycarp, nearly ninety, was himself condemned to die and then burned at the stake.

The Apologists

In spite of the risks involved in being a Christian, some members of the community did not hesitate to speak out publicly in defense of their faith. These were well-educated people who knew Greek philosophy and could debate with non-Christians on an equal basis. One of the most important **apologists**, or "defenders of the faith," was **Justin**. Born of pagan parents, he had studied all kinds of philosophies in his search for the meaning of life. He found his answers in Christianity. After living in various parts of the empire, Justin came to Rome and started a school of philosophy. Because his active ministry was so well known to the public, he was arrested for being a Christian. Justin and six of his students defied a judge's order to sacrifice to an idol. They were all executed. Through his teaching and writing, Justin gave his life to building a bridge between pagan philosophy and Christianity.

Other apologists lived, taught, and wrote important commentaries on Christian faith and practice in the newer parts of the Roman Empire. For example, **Irenaeus** (eye-ree-*nee*-uhs) was a Syrian Christian who moved west and spent most of his life in Gaul, where he learned the language of the Celts. As bishop of Lyons, he taught that Christians must continue the original teachings of the Apostles. He particularly opposed the **Gnostics** (*nahs*-tiks)—one of the many splinter groups in Christianity who challenged the beliefs of the majority of church members.

The Gnostics believed that all material things, including human bodies, were evil. But they claimed that Gnostics had a special divine spark deep inside them that made them different; salvation depended on recognizing that divine spark, on having secret knowledge (gnō-sis) of one's spiritual nature—which would be released from the prison of the body at one's death. In short, salvation was not the gift of Jesus to all persons, but the special privilege of the Gnostics, who recognized their spiritual destiny. Clearly their beliefs were contrary to the Gospels and the Epistles. Gnostics were considered to be heretics by the Church. **Heretics** are people who, while considering themselves Christian, clearly deny a truth that is an essential part of the faith.

From these early days on, there never seemed to be a shortage of people in the Church who were eager to advance their own views. Challenges to Christian belief caused turmoil, but also led to clarity and unity. For instance, in facing the case of Gnosticism, members of the Christian community who valued their faith had to state very clearly what they believed in, what they accepted as truths about God. As a result, by the year 200, Christians had formulated a statement of faith—the Apostles' Creed. This creed became part of Christian worship. Candidates for Baptism had to understand it and accept it publicly before they could join the Church.

The Decline into Chaos

The years from A.D. 100 to 200 had seen persecutions of Christians, but the next hundred years saw the emergence of worse emperors, crueler persecutions, and a sharp decline in the power of the Roman Empire. When Emperor Marcus Aurelius died in A.D. 180, he had not named a successor. His son took the throne but was so tyrannical that he was assassinated after twelve years of rule. The next emperor actually bought the office. In protest, Lucius Septimius Severus, the officer in charge of the Roman legions on the Danube, marched to Rome and took the throne himself. Severus

was efficient, but his main concern was to strengthen and enlarge the army and to increase the army's pay. So higher taxes were heaped on the people. Severus died in Britain in 211 while fighting the invading Scots. His sons ruled in turn for the next twenty-four years. They were weak men. The last of them was killed by his own soldiers for offering the barbarians a bribe rather than fighting them.

For the next fifty years the army set up and deposed twenty-six emperors in all. Due to this governmental chaos, the economy was a mess. Taxes were so high that many farmers lost their lands. Unemployment was rampant because workers could not compete with slave labor. Only the army prospered—of course, at the expense of the people. The empire was rotting from the inside, and on the outside the nomadic tribes were sharpening their swords.

Corrupt as it was, the government demanded complete loyalty from all citizens. In 250 the Emperor Decius required each citizen to carry a certificate showing that he or she had sacrificed to the gods. Because Christians refused to take part in the pagan rites, Decius ordered a general persecution of Christians. The bishops of Rome, Antioch, and Jerusalem were martyred. Among others, Bishop Cyprian of Carthage in north Africa went into hiding. Other periods of persecution followed that of Decius.

Besides mourning for martyred or enslaved families and friends, Christians had to face a new problem resulting from the persecutions. What should they do with Christians who had sacrificed to the idols? Should they be allowed to reenter the Christian communities? Most of those who had sacrificed to idols in order to save their lives wanted to repent and return to the Church. These **apostates** (uh-*pahs*-tayts), who had renounced their faith, now wanted to renew their loyalty. Some bishops said that their sin of denial could not be forgiven. Other bishops disagreed—including Stephen, the bishop of Rome. There was sharp debate about this issue for many years, but the decision of the bishop of Rome was generally accepted. Apostates could be reunited with the Christian communities after repentance. The public penance and ritual were the first forms of the Sacrament of Reconciliation. Meetings of bishops to discuss issues—like what to do with repentant apostates—were and are called **synods** (*sin*-uhds). There were four synods from 100 to 312 at Rome, Antioch, Alexandria, and Carthage.

Diocletian's Persecution

As the 200s came to an end, the empire finally had a competent ruler. Diocletian (deye-uh-*klee*-shuhn), a general born in Illyricum across the Adriatic Sea from Italy, thought that the gods had chosen him to rule. So he demanded complete conformity to his will. He managed to hold off the barbarians' invasions—something his immediate predecessors had failed to do. He reorganized the government, moving from military to civilian administration. He divided the government duties among four men: he ruled the eastern part of the empire with a co-emperor in the West, and each had an assistant who was eventually to become a co-emperor. Next, he grouped provinces together into dioceses for better management. The changes were good, but the cost of making them was enormous. Taxes increased again, and people were frozen in their jobs. For example, sons were commanded to do the same kind of work their fathers did—so that the government could be assured of taxing them similarly. Diocletian even tried to fix prices paid for food and other products, but this only produced a "black market" in which goods were sold secretly at higher prices. Discontent began to simmer.

In his drive for conformity—which he mistakenly thought would bring unity—Diocletian eventually turned his attention to the Christians. In his last two years of rule, he ordered churches destroyed, sacred books burned, and leaders executed. The persecutions were especially horrible in north Africa and in the East;

Gaul, Spain, and Britain suffered less. Ironically some of Diocletian's own relatives were Christians.

In 305, Diocletian unexpectedly resigned and retired to his native Illyricum. Some of his successors harassed the Christians, but only in isolated instances. By now the Church had endured, even thrived, during three centuries of persecution. The suffering had tested the convictions of anyone who wanted to be a Christian; to become a Christian was like signing a death warrant for oneself that could be carried out at any time. Yet, while there was still some disagreement about accepting apostates back into the Church, the persecutions had for the most part united Christian communities. Little did the early Christians realize that in the year 312 they would change from a Church of martyrs to a Church that would dominate the culture and the politics of Europe for many centuries.

A statue of the Roman emperor Diocletian

Priscilla's Thoughts About Her Christian Initiation

Easter Monday, A.D. 239, Ostia, Italy. Today is the happiest day of my life, when I think how a new life has just started for me. Most people I know lead lives of anxiety, hate, anger, jealousy; I did too and thought I was trapped in that for the rest of my life. When I was at the lowest point in my life—my husband, Lucius, was frequenting a brothel and my children were gone, Antoninus with the army in Gaul, Sylvia married to that drunk Paulus—I met Sylvester and his wife Agatha. That was a wonderful time because I found two people who really cared for me. When I first found out that they were Christians, I was shocked and afraid. As I listened more to what they said, I knew that I too could pull out of the hopelessness I was in. So three years ago I enrolled in the catechumenate. They were so cautious with new people because any one of us could have turned them in to the government; spies are all over. In those years I learned about the memoirs of the Apostles, how to pray, and what was expected of Christians. It seemed a terribly long period. I couldn't take part in the liturgy after the readings. Sometimes I resented this. Not knowing what happened kept me curious, I must admit.

Eight weeks ago, a dramatic event happened. We stood before the bishop and requested Baptism. He sat on a large raised chair. One by one each of us came in front of him with our sponsors; Agatha was holding my hand because I was so nervous. As I stood

there, the bishop asked my neighbors if I drank too much, if I was faithful to my husband, if I was trustworthy, if I was sincere in my learning about Jesus. I felt all right about this because I didn't have the serious faults anyway. Everyone was so nice. Finally the bishop wrote my name in the "book of life." At this point, I knew there was no turning back because if any Roman authority got ahold of that book we could all be executed. I was thrilled but scared too. All of us had heard about the community in Carthage that had been slaughtered in the circus when the book had been sold to the proconsul by a spy. Anyway, I knew I had to become part of the community; somehow courage seemed to flow from these people.

During the rest of Lent, we were asked every day if we rejected the Devil. We had heard the story of the temptations of Jesus during readings on the first Sunday of Lent. This made clear to me that I had to turn away from my old way of life, even though I was not too bad. We also learned the Our Father and the Creed—in fact, we had to memorize them. Agatha helped me with this; I hate memorizing generally. Since I was attending the liturgies every day, some of my friends and slaves got suspicious. My husband didn't seem to care what I was doing; I found this terribly depressing but learned years ago to put up with his neglect.

Holy Thursday arrived. All of the catechumens were told to take a ritual bath as a sign of purifying our bodies for the last days before Baptism. On Good Friday and Holy Saturday we fasted and prayed. Saturday was terrible for me. My husband had the habit of going out at night—usually to drink and go to the fancy brothel with his friends. But he hung around the house later than usual. I had to be ready for the service at ten o'clock. I prayed hard that he would leave although I hated where he was going. At last Agatha came about half past nine. When Lucius saw I had a visitor, he decided to leave. Agatha and I hurried.

We joined the other women catechumens with their sponsors and the deaconesses. We all faced west as a group. The west signified darkness, sin. The sun sets there and darkness enters. We raised our arms toward the west and proclaimed together: "I detach myself from you, Satan, from your pomp, your worship, and your angels." No more going to the games and making sacrifices to the gods for me. Then we turned to the east, raised our arms, stretching them to the light, and said: "I attach myself to you, O Christ." The light comes from the east every morning bringing hope and growth. Even though the room was still fairly dark, I felt incredibly excited and light in my heart. Now the bishop came among us and anointed us with oil.

My heart pounded when we all moved into separate rooms next to the baptistry—men in one, women in another. Here we took off our clothes. This made me nervous, not from embarrassment—I always went to the women's public baths—but because this meant I had taken off the old life that I led. In my nakedness, I was like the innocent Adam and Eve. Funny, I got so wrapped up thinking about all this that I was startled when the deaconess anointed me with oil from my head to my toes. This oil was a sign that I was cured from the sickness of my past life.

Next we lined up in the baptistry itself. I could see the pool, with its steps going down one side and coming up on the other side. It was round like a tomb or a womb. This certainly would be a new birth for me. Since I was first in line, the deaconess beckoned for me to walk into the waters. When I reached the middle, I stopped as I had been instructed. The water was up to my chest. The deaconess

knelt, put her gentle hand on my head; I ducked my head under water for a few seconds. She asked me quietly, first if I believed in the Father, then the Son, and finally the Holy Spirit. My answers were yes. Agatha kidded me today that I nearly shouted the yesses. Then the deaconess said: "Priscilla is baptized in the name of the Father, and the Son, and the Holy Spirit."

When I came out of the water and dried off, I was anointed with oil on all my five senses while a prayer was said that I receive the Holy Spirit. Agatha helped me put on my white linen robe, and then she gave me my lighted candle, along with a wonderful hug that everyone calls the "kiss of peace." Things seemed to be happening in a daze for me, but it was wonderful. Tears were streaming down both our faces as we walked into the banquet hall for the Eucharist—my first time. The community applauded and cheered when we came in to join them. I was still teary-eyed, but then so were they. Our destinies were bound up together from now on; I could never be the same again.

It's a day after now. As I sit here spinning, I know that the world seems different to me now. I even smiled at the scullery maid who has been so lazy. I don't know what my new life will mean for Lucius and me, but I can pray and hope now. And I do at last have people to turn to. I can only wonder how this new life began.

Constantine's Conversion: Changes in the Church

After Diocletian there were many people grasping for the imperial throne. The Christians could hardly have cared that, upon the death of the general commanding the Roman army in Britain, the troops chose his son **Constantine** to be emperor. His mother Helena was Christian; but Constantine, like his father, belonged to the educated class of pagans who had lost interest in the many Roman gods. Instead, they worshiped only one god, the unconquerable sun.

To establish his claim to power, Constantine invaded Italy with a small army. While he was completely successful in his battles on the way to Rome, there he faced the superior forces of the rival emperor. Before the battle Constantine had a dream or vision that told him that he would conquer through a special sign, the sign of Christ. Trusting this message, Constantine had his soldiers put the first two Greek letters of Christ's name—**XP**—on their banners and shields. When the forces joined in battle, Constantine's smaller army emerged victorious. Constantine now ruled the western part of the empire. The Roman senate erected a triumphal arch to Constantine attributing the victory to the sun god; Constantine shocked them by honoring the Son of God instead.

Within the following year, Constantine defeated another rival and claimed the throne. Then he made an agreement to share imperial power with a general named Licinius who would be emperor of the East. In June of 313 Constantine and Licinius issued the **Edict of Milan** granting freedom of worship to Christians in the Roman Empire. Christians could no longer be punished by law for practicing or preaching their religion.

Further privileges followed. As emperor of the West, Constantine exempted Christian clergy from taxation and built many churches, especially in Rome and Palestine. His mother Helena was particularly interested in having churches in Bethlehem and Jerusalem in order to honor the birth and death of Jesus.

For his part, Constantine followed the custom of putting off his own Baptism until shortly before he died in 337. Since the Sacrament of Reconciliation had not developed at this time, Christians generally believed that forgiveness of sins was given only at Baptism. Therefore, people waited until the last hours of life to be baptized.

In 324, Constantine quarreled with and defeated Licinius. He then unified the empire and became sole ruler. Problems still plagued the empire. Taxes remained high—for it was expensive to maintain an army sufficient to keep the barbarians out. Rome itself was run-down; many people lived in crumbling slums. As a result, Constantine felt that a fresh start was needed. He decided to move to a new capital in the eastern part of the empire, closer to the centers of population. For the site he chose a little town called Byzantium (beh-*zan*-shee-uhm) near the southwest shore of the Black Sea. It had a huge safe harbor and was separated from Asia Minor by only a narrow channel. Being in the center of the empire, Constantine could communicate more efficiently with local governors. In addition, the Danube frontier was nearby so that Constantine could keep a close eye on the nomadic tribes. He named his city New Rome. Indeed, he modeled the public buildings after Roman structures. **Constantinople,** as it came to be called, became the center of the empire.

Having turned from paganism, Constantine treasured the Christian faith. However, like emperors before him he saw religion as a way of unifying the people from various cultures

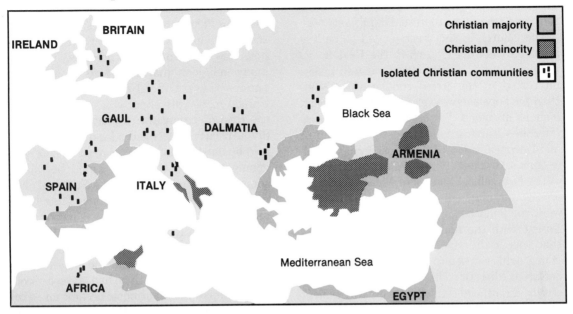

A bust of Constantine the Great

who were now under Roman domination. Thus, although dioceses had been set up under bishops and the Church had its own structure, Constantine began to interfere in Church matters. His predecessors had dominated the Roman religions; so Constantine was following a precedent by trying to run the Church. A year after he became sole ruler, Constantine called the bishops together in a council to discuss a problem that was dividing Christians and was especially troublesome in the East. The problem had to do with the teachings of an Alexandrian priest named Arius (*ar*-ee-uhs) who denied that Jesus is divine.

Arianism

Bishops came to the council from Egypt, Palestine, Syria, Greece, and Asia Minor. They gathered at Nicaea (nih-*see*-uh), a small town across the water from Constantinople. More than two hundred bishops came, mostly from the East. Christians from the East seemed highly interested in theological debates. Naturally, because of the great number of participants and because of the varied cultural backgrounds, disagreements and some disharmony occurred. Sylvester, the bishop of Rome, sent two priests to represent him.

The Church in the West tended to be less involved than the Church in the East in developing concepts about Jesus—as well as less interested in the Arian controversy. Other than the pope's representatives, five European bishops attended. Important to remember is that the Church was still mostly made up of non-Europeans: North Africans, Syrians, Palestinians, residents of Asia Minor and Greece.

The Ecumenical Council of Nicaea (I) met in 325. After much discussion, Arius's beliefs were condemned as wrong. They were inconsistent with the understanding about Jesus that was traditional in the Church at large. When Arius refused to alter his stand, he was declared a heretic. The bishops also wrote a creed, an official statement of the beliefs handed down from the Apostles. The **Nicene Creed** is still recited at Mass in many countries. The part of the creed that Arius rejected states that Jesus is "the only Son of God . . . one in Being with the Father." Of course, even with the council's decision, the Arian problem did not just suddenly disappear. Arianism had many followers for years to come.

There are several things to remember about a heresy such as Arianism. First, most heretics are not simply troublemakers; they are often sincerely committed to their beliefs. In many instances, these beliefs had been thought out carefully and had become deeply ingrained convictions. Second, heresy is not just a simple mistake about theology. A heresy must go against a belief that is held as an official teaching of the Church. Often, as in the case of Arianism, someone will start teaching a partial truth that blocks out or denies the whole

truth. Debate will follow among church leaders. Eventually a decision is made about the official teaching. Then the teachers of the contrary theory will have a chance to retract; if they do not, they are considered heretics. Third, in many religious matters there is room for various views. Official church teachings are usually made only about what is essential. In the case of Arianism, to deny that Jesus is divine clearly challenged a fundamental belief held by most Christians. Yet most Arians were genuinely afraid that they would be taking something away from God the Father if they were to say that Jesus is divine. Their belief may have been sincere, but it was inconsistent with the traditions of the Christian Church.

After the Council of Nicaea some of the bishops from the East had second thoughts about the creed that they had agreed upon. The bishop of Constantinople became an Arian and even put Arian bishops in charge of Eastern dioceses. In some places there were two rival bishops claiming authority over the same diocese. Sometimes a bishop was brought in or thrown out by military force, particularly when some of Constantine's successors favored Arianism. What had started out as a theological matter became a political football. For instance, if an emperor favored Arianism, the Arian dioceses would ask his help to kick orthodox bishops out of their dioceses. The opposite was true too; orthodox emperors would restore orthodox bishops to dioceses having Arian bishops.

This close involvement of the emperors in church affairs seems odd today. However, "separation of church and state" is a modern notion only accepted by a minority of countries even today. From ancient times to the present, governments have seen religion as a primary unifying factor. The moral teachings of a religion help bring stability to a country. If all citizens pray to the same god, the god is more likely to bless the country. Consequently, the government provides buildings for worship and subsidies for priests. Yet, inevitably, when church and state work hand in hand, the church is the loser.

Thus, while Constantine's conversion saved the Church from the horrors of persecution, a new era began when the Church was intimately connected with worldly power and, too often, with the corruption of power. By the mid-300s Christian bishops ranked high in public life, some of them holding civil positions as judges. For them it was not easy to keep free from pressures and influence. The Church was also given lands, and the revenues from these properties were to be used for the upkeep of the Church. However, the accumulation of property sometimes led to greed. The Church in 350 was a far cry from the band of Apostles that wandered with Jesus, having no place to lay their heads.

Athanasius

Nevertheless, much of the early enthusiasm for Jesus remained. Great saints emerged in the Church, and Christianity gave many people hope and purpose. One of the great persons to emerge was **Athanasius**, bishop of Alexandria in Egypt. As a young deacon present at the Council of Nicaea, he impressed everyone with his knowledge of theology. When he was chosen bishop, he was constantly harassed by Arian bishops in the East. To force him out of office, they brought all sorts of accusations against him that had nothing to do with his teachings—accusations such as theft of sacred vessels, murder of a bishop (who was known to be alive), and even holding up grain shipments bound for Constantinople.

As a result of such plotting by the Arians, Athanasius was removed from office five times—the last time at the age of seventy—by four emperors in turn. In all he spent seventeen years of his life in exile, sometimes safely hidden by people in the city, other times escaping to the Egyptian desert. During the last seven years of his life, he was able to bring peace to the Church in Alexandria. His efforts and those of people like Bishop Basil in Asia Minor helped bring about the end of Arianism's strength. His story is a good example of what can happen when religious leaders depend on government authorities to solve religious disputes. The government tends to use force—hardly the way Jesus, Peter, and Paul would have done things.

In 380 a man who had been born in Spain succeeded to the imperial power in the East. **Theodosius I,** as a Westerner, believed in the divinity of Jesus and made this belief part of his policy. He called the Council of Constantinople in 381 to reaffirm the Nicene Creed. He appointed a new bishop for Constantinople, the first in more than fifty years who was not an Arian. In 388, Theodosius outlawed Arianism within the empire and declared paganism illegal. Arianism continued to grow outside the empire among the Goths who had been taught by missionaries sent from Constantinople years before. But within the empire, by the end of Theodosius's reign in 395, what we now call the Catholic faith was the official religion of the Roman Empire.

Women in the Early Church

Christians in the early Church did not escape the prejudices of their culture any more than Christians do today. Consequently, in the few documents that we have from those early centuries, few women make appearances. Saint Paul mentions the good work done by Evodia and Syntyche in Philippi: "These women were a help to me when I was fighting to defend the Good News. . . . Their names are written in the book of life" (Philippians 4:3). "A true believer named Lydia" invited Paul to come and stay at her house while he was in Philippi, and "she would take no refusal." Clearly, then, women did spread the Word. Agatha and Cecilia were two among many women martyrs honored by the Church. We know too that there were deaconesses who had the same responsibilities as deacons. Women were almost certainly part of the deliberations in the Jerusalem community, and as members of congregations they had their voice in the selection of bishops.

However, as the Church accepted more and more Gentiles into membership, they brought with them some attitudes that changed what seems to have been a brief period of more equal relationships between men and women. For most periods of Western history, women were kept illiterate and skilled only at homemaking. Their purpose in life was to please their husbands; this often meant being subservient, obedient, and the mother of sons. Consequently women appear infrequently in the histories of those times, and when they do, often their most important claim to fame is pictured as being the mother or wife of some famous man. In short, in recorded histories, it has been a man's world. This has been no less true in church history. We know very, very little about what women thought, felt, or did during much of church history.

When women do appear, they are often being preached at about their place in the scheme of things. The belief that Eve was responsible for original sin and that women were the sources of temptations—especially sexual temptations—for men, led many early Christian writers to urge women to wear chaste dress, to assume quiet ways, and to keep orderly houses for their men. There is a good example of this in an essay written by Tertullian, a theologian who died about A.D. 230. Here are a few things that he has to say about female dress:

Very many women . . . have the boldness so to walk in public as though chastity consisted only in the bare integrity of the flesh and in the avoidance of fornication. . . . In their gait they display the same outward appearance as Gentile women, in whom the sense of true chastity is lacking. . . .

The desire to please by outward charms, which we know naturally invite lust, does not spring from a sound conscience. Why should you rouse an evil passion? Why invite that to which you profess yourself a stranger? . . .

That other [a male tempted by a woman], as soon as he has lusted after your beauty and in his mind committed the lustful act, perishes; and you have been made the sword of his destruction. . . .

A holy woman may be beautiful by the gift of nature, but she must not give occasion to lust. If beauty be hers, so far from setting it off she ought rather to obscure it.

You must not overstep the line to which simple and sufficient elegance limits its desires, the line which is pleasing to God. Against Him those women sin who torment their skin with potions, stain their cheeks with rouge, and extend the line of their eyes with black coloring. Doubtless they are dissatisfied with God's plastic skill. . . . I see that some women change the color of their hair with saffron dye. They are ashamed even of their own nation, ashamed that they were not born in Germany or Gaul; and so by changing their hair they change their country. Evil, most evil, is the omen of those flame-coloured heads, a defilement imagined to be a charm....

Such delicacies, then, which can by their softness and effeminacy unman the manliness of faith, must be discarded. The arm that has been wont to wear a bracelet will scarce endure to be benumbed to the rigor of a prisoner's chain.... I fear that the neck on which coils of pearls and emeralds have rested will never give a place to the executioner's sword....[Delicacies will make women unwilling to be martyrs for the faith.]

Draw your whiteness from simplicity, your rosy hues from chastity. Paint your eyes with modesty and your lips with silence. Fix in your ears the words of God and fasten on your necks the yoke of Christ. Bow your heads before your husbands, and you will be sufficiently adorned. Busy your hands with wool; keep your feet at home; and then you will please more than if you were arrayed in gold.

Tertullian is pointing out that all too often non-Christian women were treated simply as sex objects by men, and that our bodies are created by God and should be treated that way. However, typical of the men of his time, he blames women for men's lust, and relegates women to the home and the commands of their husbands.

Tertullian was a product of his times; we are products of ours. In the following chapters, the most prominent figures in church history are men, with a few very remarkable exceptions. This does not mean that women were not active in and essential to church life; it simply illustrates that the recorded history of the Church was written by men, primarily for men, in a world where public deeds (wars, governmental proclamations, and so on) were performed by men.

A biblical illustration by Gustave Doré picturing the women's clothing style and demeanor that Tertullian advocated

A stone relief celebrating a military victory by the emperor Marcus Aurelius

Focus on the Models

The three centuries from 100 to 400 were filled with dramatic changes for the Church. As an institution, the Church of the year 100 consisted of small scattered communities led by bishops and helped by deacons. There was some communication among congregations, and the Word was preached—but the frequent persecutions made the communities rather secretive. By 400, Christianity was the official religion of the empire, and other religions were barely tolerated. Councils met. Creeds were written. Lands were given to the Church, and buildings were constructed for Christian worship. The Church took on the status of an institution, and perhaps the community emphasis was weakened by the change.

As a legal, institutionalized religion, Christianity accepted new members who were more committed to being on the right side of the government than to being firmly committed to their faith. The Church grew so rapidly that training for preachers of the Word was hasty and often far from adequate. The careful, three-year preparation of candidates for admission to the Church gave way to speedy Baptisms.

During the persecutions, the Christians were united closely for their very survival, and they had little time to engage in theological arguments. As the People of God became increasingly larger, their unity became more difficult to maintain; there were language and cultural differences, political and theological disagreements. The change in the Church's status ended the executions of Christians by nonbelievers but also began an era when internal struggles would emerge. As Servant, the Church now had lands and revenues from those lands with which to help the needy. In essence, the official status of the Church changed during these three eventful centuries. While the years of living in fear were ended, a new phase in church life began, filled with new challenges to Christian living.

Review Questions and Activities

1) Describe the three groups with whom the Christian community had to contend.

2) What helped hold the Christian communities together during the years A.D. 100–312?

3) Why were the Christians persecuted? Try to put yourself in the shoes of the Roman emperors. Why did the Christians stand out?

4) Who were the apologists? What service did they perform for the Church?

5) Explain the problems encountered with the Gnostics.

6) After A.D. 200, what was beginning to happen to the Roman Empire?

7) Who were the apostates, and what dilemma did they pose for the early Church? Who was important in settling this issue?

8) Describe how Constantine's conversion altered the future of Christianity. What positive changes followed his conversion? What negative results occurred?

9) Arianism represented the most serious threat to the Church in its history to that point. Why? How was Arianism dealt with?

10) What is heresy? What are its positive and negative results?

11) How does Athanasius represent the positive and negative effects of religion's becoming institutionalized in a country?

Personal Reflection Exercises

1) Try to think of some examples from everyday life of what your life would be like today if you could be sent to prison for being a Christian. How would this threat influence your emotions and your actions?

2) Reflect on what was said about women's place in the Church as seen in the history of the Church. Read Ephesians 5:21–33. Would Jesus agree with the way in which women have been treated in the Church? What changes might take place in the status of women in the Church during your lifetime? How do you think women should best participate in the Church?

3) There is a sort of daily martyrdom that takes place in many of our lives. Think about the events in your life during this last week. Have your beliefs in Christianity caused you to suffer in any way? Did the suffering enrich your life in any way?

7
Building the City of God

The fourth and fifth centuries were far from peaceful times in European history. Nevertheless, important developments were afoot in the Church that would set the course of theology and church structure for centuries to come. For instance, a new style of missionary came on the scene in the person of Saint Patrick. And deep in the deserts of Egypt and Syria, men and women were fashioning a lifestyle that was to give spiritual sustenance to the Church. Monasticism, as conceived by Saint Antony, also influenced the way Christians thought about prayer, possessions, fasting, and living in the world. From about 350 to 470, dynamic people were shaping the Church in new ways.

A People Who Step Apart: Monasticism

Beginning in the 300s, **monasticism** affected the entire Church and also influenced European culture, theology, agricultural methods, art, music, and architecture.

Why did men and women go into the deserts to fast, pray, study the Scriptures, and spend hours in silent meditation—isolated from the outside world? There is no single reason. It is true that the ending of the period of martyrdom made many Christians more complacent about Christian living. Moreover, clergy, during and after the reign of Constantine, were given positions of prestige and power. In short, women and men found that life in the cities in the fourth and fifth centuries easily distracted them from being dedicated to becoming Christlike. For these reasons and others, some Christians left the cities in search of a different challenge—finding it in the wilderness alone with their God.

Among the most important figures in early monastic development was **Saint Antony** of Egypt (about 251–356), who in his twenties went to live in the desert. He stayed wherever he found shelter, usually in a cave. He spent his time in prayer and fasting, living on bread and water and occasionally vegetables. As much as possible, Antony wanted to simplify his lifestyle, so that he would rely completely on God's grace. He visited the city of Alexandria on two occasions: once to encourage Christians while the persecutions were still going on, and once to support Bishop Athanasius in his struggle with Arianism—the heresy that denied Jesus' divinity. During his long life many people, including one emperor, came searching for Antony in the desert in order to ask his advice. Athanasius, who had fled to the desert for safety from Arian persecutors, was so impressed with Antony that he wrote his biography. In time others became hermits in the desert as Antony did. Some lived in small communities; others lived alone.

Bishop Basil of Asia Minor, who lived a short distance north of Tarsus, followed up on Antony's new ideas. Up to the age of thirty, Basil had studied at Constantinople and Athens to become a teacher. After teaching for a few years, he left his post and became a hermit. Soon other young men joined him in this new kind of Christian lifestyle. Basil decided to form them into a religious community. He developed a rule of life stressing simple living—own almost nothing, eat only the bare essentials, and obey the bishops. The monks were to help the poor and care for the sick—although these were not their main tasks. Their main work was to seek God in their hearts by listening in the silence of prayer. Basil's rule has been observed for centuries, especially in the East—that is, in Greece, Palestine, and Egypt.

The Spread of Monasticism

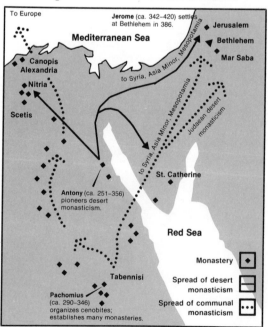

To Europe

Jerome (ca. 342–420) settles at Bethlehem in 386.

Mediterranean Sea

Jerusalem
Bethlehem
Mar Saba

Canopis
Alexandria

to Syria, Asia Minor, Mesopotamia

Nitria

to Syria, Asia Minor, Mesopotamia

Judaean desert monasticism

Scetis

St. Catherine

Antony (ca. 251–356) pioneers desert monasticism.

Red Sea

Tabennisi

Pachomius (ca. 290–346) organizes cenobites; establishes many monasteries.

Monastery

Spread of desert monasticism

Spread of communal monasticism

Church Scholars: Recording the Tradition

Ambrose: A Scholar and Pastor

Saint Ambrose (339–397), bishop of Milan, bridges the time immediately after Constantine's death and the end of the rule of Theodosius. In his thirties Ambrose was the Roman governor of northern Italy with his headquarters in Milan. When the Western emperor decided that an Arian should succeed the bishop of Milan who had just died, the people protested. Ambrose went with his military guard to the cathedral where a large, angry mob was milling around. He succeeded in calming the crowd. When the people began shouting, "Ambrose for bishop! Ambrose for bishop!" he was naturally shocked—for he was not even baptized yet. Nonetheless, he was the people's choice.

He fled the scene and hid, thinking the people might rethink their decision. It was no use; they found him and persuaded him to accept the office of bishop. In great haste, he was baptized, confirmed, given the Eucharist, and ordained bishop. Ambrose, however, realized that his career as lawyer and governor was not an ideal preparation for his new role as spiritual leader. Thus he began what was to be a lifelong study of Christianity. He learned quickly. In the midst of a busy life, he managed to write numerous books on theology that rank as some of the most important works written for the Church. As a scholar and writer, Ambrose helped people to understand their relationship to Jesus and to the Church.

A monk at a Greek monastery

Bishop Ambrose was not only a scholar; he was a pastor as well. Times were hard; famines were frequent; barbarian tribes were becoming bolder. At one time, Ambrose sold the gold and jewels given to his church so that he could ransom people held captive by the Goths. He also had problems with the Arians. The new emperor was just a boy, so his mother ruled for him. When she demanded that Ambrose turn over one of the churches in Milan to the Arians, he flatly refused. To support Ambrose, his people crowded into the church, occupying it day and night—praying, singing hymns, and listening to Ambrose speak about the Holy Trinity. The emperor had to back down.

On several other occasions Ambrose showed his courage in the face of imperial power. For instance, the emperor Theodosius had ordered several thousand people killed in Thessalonika in Greece, because one of his generals had been murdered there. Hearing this, Ambrose refused to offer Mass in the church that the emperor attended until the emperor repented in public. Theodosius, knowing Ambrose's high standing with the people, did several weeks of public penance—a humiliating experience for an emperor. Clearly the Church had become a force to be reckoned with, for even emperors obeyed it. At Christmas, Ambrose gave the emperor Communion, to the great joy of the huge crowd gathered in Milan's cathedral. Citizens felt insecure when the Church and Rome were at odds. Some time later, Theodosius left his two sons under the care of Ambrose; these boys were to become emperors—one of the West and one of the East—a situation that would last into the next century.

Jerome: A Monk and Bible Scholar

Just a few years younger than Ambrose, **Saint Jerome** (about 345–420) was another famous scholar of the Church in the fourth century. Except for their religious dedication, two men could hardly have been less alike. Jerome was not a bishop but a monk. For most of his life he worked day and night in a cave, studying and writing. As a boy growing up in northern Italy, Jerome was sent to Rome to be educated in Latin and Greek by some of the best pagan teachers of the time. However, more and more people were converting to Christianity. After serious study he decided to follow the footsteps of his mother who had been baptized—it was common at this time for the father to remain non-Christian if he had been raised that way.

At age eighteen Jerome joined the Church. In the 300s, most people were baptized in adulthood—it would be nearly a century before infants were commonly baptized. Jerome traveled and studied, first in Gaul, then at home and at Antioch. Instead of staying in the city of Paul and Barnabas, he went into the desert

An artist's representation of Saint Jerome, including a lion from whose paw he was said to have drawn a thorn

where as a hermit he prayed, fasted, and began the study of Hebrew. Next he went to Constantinople for more study and eventually to Rome where he served as the pope's secretary.

Pope Damasus I encouraged Jerome to make a Latin translation of the Christian Scriptures and the Psalms, a project that led Jerome to begin teaching the Bible to interested noble Roman women. Jerome, a monk at heart, encouraged the women to form a contemplative convent. This caused considerable opposition from the nobles. When Pope Damasus died, Jerome thought it best to go east again. Within a year he began a new life in Bethlehem where he built a monastery for religious men and several convents for the women who followed him from Rome.

In Bethlehem, Jerome and his students continued the translation of the Bible into Latin

King Alaric, who conquered Rome in A.D. 410

from the original Hebrew and Greek. In his struggles with Hebrew, as well as Aramaic, Jerome received help from Jewish rabbis living nearby. This Latin version, which took fifteen years of daily work to finish, became known as the **Vulgate,** the version in the common language of the people of the West. More than a thousand years later the Council of Trent (1545–63) made Jerome's Latin Bible the official version for the Catholic Church. Jerome's translation is still valued as an important help in understanding the Word of God. Jerome wrote many tracts and scholarly works as well. It was fortunate that Jerome did this translating and writing in Bethlehem, because sad news was coming from the West: Rome was beginning to fall.

By the end of the 300s, large groups of barbarians had been allowed to settle inside the frontiers of the Western empire in order to help defend it. In fact, many officers on the frontiers were themselves barbarians. Among the dominant groups of barbarians were the Goths under King Alaric. The time came when the

Goths wanted the empire to give them land in northern Italy as their own, but they found they had to fight the Romans to get it. The Romans were too weak to defend the land; their army in Italy had become lazy and corrupt. In 410, Alaric's Goths broke through the walls of Rome, and they looted and burned the city. After centuries of dominion over the Western world, as well as most of the Middle East and North Africa, Rome had fallen to an uncouth, savage enemy.

Jerome must have been horrified at the stories he heard from refugees who managed to escape to Bethlehem. At about age seventy-five he died. He is remembered not as a popular saint but as a hermit working in his cave to give the people a Bible in their own language—a treasure cherished for fifteen hundred years.

Augustine: A Scholar in Search of Direction

Best known and most influential among those who are called "fathers of the Church" was **Saint Augustine.** He was born in North Africa. This region was often called Roman Africa because, separated from the rest of Africa by the Sahara Desert, it was home for people whose everyday language was Latin and who loved Roman customs as much as anyone living in Rome itself. Augustine's father, Patricius, was a local Roman official and a pagan until shortly before he died. Augustine's mother, Monica, was a Christian.

From the time he started going to school Augustine easily led his class. He was brilliant. Yet at sixteen he had to leave school because his father could not pay his tuition; heavy taxes at this time made it impossible. During this year of idleness Augustine acquired habits for which he would later repent. With wild friends, he visited prostitutes, drank, gambled, and led a purposeless life. When he returned to school, he studied to be a lawyer; and, finishing his studies at age eighteen, he became a teacher. He also took a mistress. This was not uncommon among non-Christians of the time, but Monica had tried to raise Augustine as a Christian.

Augustine next became a **Manichaean** (man-eh-*kee*-uhn), believing that because there was one god who created good and another god who created evil, no one was responsible for his or her sins. Monica could only pray for her son's conversion; he was too brilliant and stubborn to be influenced easily. Then, without telling anyone, Augustine moved to Rome with his mistress and their young son. A year later he went to teach in Milan. Two strong influences came into his life in Milan: his study of Plato and his meeting Bishop Ambrose.

Manichaeism was dissatisfying. Plato was not. Plato claimed that there is a world beyond what we see, that there is a spiritual part in human beings beyond their bodies, and that God is a spirit. Once convinced that there was a single God and that humans have a spiritual side, Augustine was ripe for his meeting with Ambrose. Monica had followed Augustine to Milan; the two would sometimes visit Ambrose at his house. In addition, Augustine began attending Sunday Mass just to hear Ambrose preach.

Slowly Augustine, through the truth of Ambrose's message and the influence of his mother's love, began trying to reform his life. For one thing, he decided to marry and then to be baptized. However, the legal waiting period before marriage was too much of a test for Augustine; instead he took another mistress. (His first mistress had already returned to North Africa because Augustine was going to marry someone else.) In any case, the marriage plans were broken. Augustine was at a low point in his life: he wanted to reform, but his "lust"—as he said—was too much for him.

Augustine's Conversion

Augustine continued his studies and teaching but was dissatisfied. At last, though, he was converted. In *The Confessions,* Augustine says that he was sitting on a bench in his backyard one day when he heard a group of neighborhood children chanting over and over a little song: "Take and read, take and read." Almost without thinking, he picked up the Bible lying next to him on the bench and opened it at random. Saint Paul's advice to the Romans stood out on the page: "Let us live decently as people do in the daytime: no drunken orgies, no promiscuity or licentiousness, and no wrangling or jealousy. Let your armour be the Lord Jesus Christ; forget about satisfying your bodies with all their cravings. If a person's faith is not strong enough, welcome him all the same without starting an argument" (Romans 13:13—14:1). This passage struck him as the solution to his confusion. He could turn his great love to something wonderful by loving God and serving his neighbors.

At the age of thirty-three he was baptized by Ambrose. After Monica died he left Italy for his hometown of Tagaste in North Africa. He organized a small monastery. Soon the people of the town urged him to become a priest. Although most priests were still married during this period, Augustine decided to remain single. Later he wrote, "I was caught and made a priest." Four years later, he was elected bishop of Hippo by the congregation of that city.

Augustine as Minister and Teacher

Augustine must have been a very effective minister to his people. An interesting description is given of his homilies on Sunday; they were more like dialogues. He sat and the congregation stood for the sermon. The audience would sometimes interrupt with shouts of agreement or questions. Augustine is reported to have enjoyed this give-and-take, yelling back: "I'm glad you shouted, for it shows you know the Scriptures!" After some more shouting: "I see by your acclaim that you have run ahead of me. Your shouts show you know what I am going to say." Sometimes he would ask them questions to check that they understood what he was saying. Once, while talking about a long psalm, he must have realized he had been speaking too long; for he said: "Go out and take some refreshment, not for your spirits which appear tireless, but go out and give some little refreshment to your bodies; and when you are refreshed, then come back to your real food."

Augustine was all too human, but his weaknesses made him perhaps more sensitive to others. Scripture was his main source: "I meditate on the Law of God, not indeed day and night like the psalmist, but during the brief moments I can snatch; and lest I forget the ideas that come to me I pin them down with my pen." Over and above his work as a bishop, Augustine turned his great learning into writings that challenged three different erring Christian groups.

Augustine had no trouble convincing his people that the beliefs of the first group, the Manichaeans, were faulty since he himself had been a Manichaean for ten years. The second group were the **Donatists**, Christians who had their own churches in Africa for almost a hundred years. Their separation was a result of the terrible Roman persecutions. As we saw in the last chapter, some Christians denied their faith in the face of torture or execution. The Donatists maintained that such a denial could never be forgiven, that priests who had been disloyal could never again give real Baptism. The Donatists held on to their ideas for years, even though most bishops, including the bishop of Rome, had said that forgiveness of sinners was one of the main purposes of the Church and that the sacraments are actions of Christ coming to us through human beings who are liable to sin. Partly because of Augustine's influence and partly because of the workings of time, the Donatists started to die out.

A third group of Christians against whom Augustine argued were the **Pelagians**, who said that a person could get to heaven without the special help of God—help that we call **grace**. This was contrary to the belief held by the large majority of Christians from the Apostles' time onward. Augustine wrote detailed discussions of grace, arguing that without God's grace there would even be more sin and injustice: war, crime, dishonesty, greed, lust, and all the rest.

Augustine and Thomas Merton: Two Dramatic Conversions

Augustine led a directionless and irresponsible life before his conversion. He wrote *The Confessions* in order to explain his change in life and to show people that God's grace is there for all.

Thomas Merton lived from 1915 to 1968. Much like Augustine's, his youth was spent without clear purpose. He did his share of wild living, and like Augustine fathered a son out of wedlock. He was equally brilliant. Finally, after periods of depression about where his life was going, Merton began a serious study of Christianity and began the process of conversion. Eventually he entered the Trappist monastery at Gethsemani, Kentucky. For over twenty years as a monk, he wrote some of the most influential books on Christian living of the twentieth century. In all he wrote dozens of books and scores of articles. Merton died in Bangkok, Thailand, while visiting Buddhist monasteries in an effort to discover the parallels between Buddhist and Christian monasticism. Like Augustine, Father Louis (Merton's religious name) wrote about his conversion—in a work entitled *The Seven Storey Mountain*.

Below are passages from *The Confessions* of Saint Augustine and *The Seven Storey Mountain* by Thomas Merton that show rough comparisons between these two great Christians; they show mostly that God's grace can turn sinners into great saints.

From *The Confessions:*

I propose to now set down my past wickedness and the carnal corruptions of my soul, not for love of them but that I may love Thee, O my God. I do it for love of Thy love, passing again in the bitterness of remembrance over my most evil ways that Thou mayest thereby grow ever lovelier to me....

My one delight was to love and to be loved. But in this I did not keep the measure of mind to mind, which is the luminous line of friendship; but from the muddy concupiscence of the flesh and the hot imagination of puberty I could not distinguish the white light of love from the fog of lust. Both love and lust boiled within me, and swept my youthful immaturity over the precipice of evil desires to leave me half drowned in a whirlpool of abominable sins.... I departed further from You, and You left me to myself: and I was tossed about and wasted and poured out and boiling over in my fornications.... I, arrogant and depressed,

From *The Seven Storey Mountain:*

Three or four nights a week my fraternity brothers and I would go flying down in the black and roaring subway to 52nd Street, where we would crawl around the tiny, noisy and expensive nightclubs that had flowered on the sites of the old speakeasies in the cellars of those dirty brownstone houses. There we would sit, for hours, packed in those dark rooms, shoulder to shoulder with a lot of surly strangers and their girls, while the whole place rocked and surged with storms of jazz. ...If you moved your arm to get your drink you nearly knocked the next man off his stool....

It was not that we got drunk.... It was a strange, animal travesty of mysticism, sitting in those booming rooms, with the noise pouring through you, and the rhythm jumping and throbbing in the marrow of your bones. You couldn't call any of that, *per se,* a mortal sin.... If we got hangovers the next day, it was more because of the smoking and nervous exhaustion than anything else....

weary and restless, wandered further and further from You into more and more sins which could bear no fruit save sorrows.

My family took no care to save me from this moral destruction by marriage: their only concern was that I should learn to make as fine and persuasive speeches as possible. I came to Carthage, where a cauldron of illicit loves leapt and boiled about me. I was not yet in love, but I was in love with love, and from the very depth of my need hated myself for not more keenly feeling the need. I sought some object to love.... Within I was hungry, all for the want of that spiritual food which is Thyself, my God.

Thus I polluted the stream of friendship with the filth of unclean desires and sullied its limpidity with the hell of lust. And vile and unclean as I was, so great was my vanity that I was bent upon passing for clean and courtly.

... There is nothing so dismal as the Flushing bus station.... There were always at least one or two of those same characters whose prototypes I had seen dead in the morgue.... Among all these I stood, weary and ready to fall, lighting the fortieth or fiftieth cigarette of the day—the one that took the last shreds of lining off my throat.

The thing that depressed me most of all was the shame and despair that invaded my whole nature when the sun came up, and all the laborers were going to work: men healthy and awake and quiet, with their eyes clear and some rational purpose before them. This humiliation and sense of my own misery and of the fruitlessness of what I had done was the nearest I could get to contrition. It was the reaction of nature. It proved nothing except that I was still, at least, morally alive.... The term "morally alive" might obscure the fact that I was spiritually dead. I had been that long since! ...

[*Because of this despair, Merton began reading Christian authors; time passed.*]

Sometime in August, I finally answered an impulse that had been working on me for a long time. Every Sunday, I had been going out

[Years pass; Augustine is in Milan.]

She with whom I had lived so long was torn from my side as a hindrance to my forthcoming marriage. My heart which had held her very dear was broken and wounded and shed blood. She went back to Africa, swearing that she would never know another man, and left with me the natural son I had had of her. But I in my unhappiness could not, for all my manhood, imitate her resolve. I was unable to bear the delay of two years which must pass before I was to get the girl I had asked for in marriage. In fact it was not really marriage that I wanted. I was simply a slave to lust. So I took another woman.

[Augustine continued to study with Ambrose; the moment of his conversion finally came.]

And I continued my miserable complaining: "How long, how long shall I go on saying tomorrow and again tomorrow? Why not now, why not have an end to my uncleanness this very hour?" Suddenly I heard a voice from some nearby house, a boy's voice or a girl's voice, I do not know; but it was a sort of singsong, repeated again and again, "Take and read, take and read." . . . [I interpreted] the incident as quite certainly a divine command to open my book of Scripture and read the passage at which I should open.

[As we learn, Augustine then read the passages from Romans, repented his way of life, became a priest, bishop, writer, and saint.]

on Long Island to spend the day with the same girl. But every week, as Sunday came around, I was filled with a growing desire to stay in the city and go to some kind of church. . . .

. . . with the work I was doing in the library, a stronger desire began to assert itself, and I was drawn much more imperatively to the Catholic Church. . . .

[More time passed; his studies continued.]

I took up the book about Gerard Manley Hopkins. The chapter told of Hopkins at Balliol, at Oxford. He was thinking of becoming a Catholic. . . .

All of a sudden, something began to stir within me, something began to push me, to prompt me. It was a movement that spoke like a voice.

"What are you waiting for?" it said. "Why are you sitting here? Why do you still hesitate? You know what you ought to do. Why don't you do it?" . . .

I got up and walked restlessly around the room. . . .

. . . I could bear it no longer. I put down the book, and got into my raincoat, and started down the stairs. I went out into the street. . . .

And then everything inside me began to sing—to sing with peace, to sing with strength, and to sing with conviction.

. . . Then I turned the corner of 121st Street, and the brick church and presbytery were before me. I stood in the doorway and rang the bell. . . .

. . . "Father, I want to become a Catholic."

The "City of God"

Besides opposing these three groups, Augustine also challenged the pagans. Many pagans charged that the barbarians were stronger because Christianity's God did not protect the empire like the old pagan gods had done. Augustine answered with *The City of God.* Written over a period of twelve years, it remains regularly in print today and is considered to be one of the most important books ever written in the West. Its major point is that evils always exist in the world. This is always the case in the "City of Man" where people look out only for their own selfish interests. The "City of God" will come only in the next life; in this city everything will be purely good. However, at the present time, we must prepare for the "City of God," especially through the Christian Church, which helps people live in the love of God and neighbor. In this way, people prepare themselves to be citizens of the "City of God" in eternity.

Desire for such a "City of God" became more real as various barbarian groups continued their invasions. Not only did the nomadic tribes steal, rape, and pillage, but they even set up separate kingdoms inside the boundaries of the empire itself. The Franks were in northwest Gaul, the Goths in southern Gaul. The Vandals (from whose name we get our modern word for destructive groups) plundered as they pleased through Spain, then crossed over into North Africa and began their siege of Hippo when Augustine himself was nearing death. *The City of God* helped Christians see that they were building something

good, that their story had a purpose. Augustine's book was treasured by later generations, first in handwritten copies and then, within the first fifty years of printing in the 1400s, in twenty-four different printed editions. Augustine's influence is still pervasive in Christian thinking.

A New Kind of Missionary

At the same time that the Vandals were sweeping through North Africa around the year 430, a new hope for the Church was being established—just beyond the northwest corner of the Roman Empire. **Saint Patrick** (about 389–461) was bringing Christianity to the people of Ireland.

Called **Celts** (*selts*), the Irish belonged to a people who had lived for a long time in central Europe and then had migrated westward into Gaul and Spain and still later into Britain, Scotland, and Ireland. They were skilled ironworkers who tended to move a good deal and who built temporary settlements of thatched houses. Celts disdained the soft clothing of the Romans; they wove good wool into practical garments. Their intricate jewelry, bronze mirrors, and decorated shields are greatly admired today.

About fifty years before Jesus was born, Julius Caesar conquered the Celts in Gaul. Then he invaded Britain, and the Celts there became part of the empire. The Romans built towns, such as London and York, and laid out roads. And in the north near the Scottish border, in 122, Emperor Hadrian built a long wall across the island to defend the frontier. By about the year 350, a few years after the death of Constantine, most of Britain as far north as Hadrian's Wall was Roman and Christian.

Patrick grew up on his father's small farm near the western coast of Britain just south of Hadrian's Wall. His father was a deacon in the Church and a government magistrate. His grandfather had been a Christian priest in Britain (priests could still marry at this time). The Roman legions had mostly departed from the country; they were needed to fight the barbarians on the Continent. One day, when he was about sixteen, pirate ships from Ireland landed, and Patrick was taken captive. For the next six years he was a slave in Ireland, tending sheep. He worked long hours, was separated from his family and friends, and had to live among his enemies. Living in a kind of isolation, he had time to think; and according to legends he prayed fervently for rescue.

Gradually Patrick learned the Celtic language of the Irish. He also learned that they worshiped gods of the sea and forest. The oak was their sacred tree, especially when covered with mistletoe. The **Druids** were pagan priests who also served as judges, teachers, and advisers to tribal kings. The Druids spent many years memorizing the legends of the Celts.

At the end of six years of slavery, Patrick escaped. He was twenty-two and knew something about the country. One night he quietly left his master's farm and began the long journey that brought him to the southern shore of Ireland. He managed to sail to Gaul and eventually returned home. After a short time, he decided to enter a monastery in Gaul.

After twenty years as a monk, Patrick answered a call to return to Ireland. In 432, when he was in his mid-forties, Patrick was made a bishop and was sent to the Celts to preach the Good News. Another bishop had preceded him but had died after only a year. Nevertheless, a handful of converts gave Patrick a place to begin. And Patrick initiated a new approach to spreading the faith: he established monasteries all over the island. He brought monks first from Gaul. Gradually Irish monks swelled their numbers and more monasteries were built. The monks taught the local people to read and write Latin first and later Celtic. Monks and nuns also copied books (rare treasures in those days before printing) and embellished them with elaborate decorations called **illuminations**. In time the Irish monasteries became the roots from which Christianity spread not only within Ireland but later to Scotland, Germany, Switzerland, and northern France.

Without a doubt, the driving force behind the missionary work was Patrick. Legends about him abound. If all were believed, he would be a combination of saint and superman. He is pictured as driving throughout Ireland in his chariot, matching magical powers with the Druids. Supposedly the Druids could turn the noontime into night, but Patrick could bring out the sun. The Druids could produce a snowstorm, but only Patrick could make the snow melt. Whatever the truth of the legends, after twenty-five years of work, Patrick could rightly claim that Ireland was Christian.

The Church, Pope Leo, and the Invaders

While Patrick was becoming the source of fables in the northwest corner of the Roman Empire, another great man was solidifying the role of the bishop of Rome. Leo the Great, or Leo I as he was known during his life, became pope in the year 440. Leo was intelligent, tough, and courageous; he had to be all of these and more to face the challenges of his times. Rome was being attacked from all sides and from within. The faith too was under attack.

Leo came to his job as pope with impressive credentials as a mediator and a leader. Early in his career he had been called to settle a dispute between a Roman general and the Roman governor of Gaul. He was famous for his short but eloquent sermons that would pack churches. The Church needed such a capable person because the role of pope was becoming more complicated; he was expected to be a statesman, spiritual leader, administrator, scholar, and saint. Indeed, the bishop of Rome began to use the title *Pontifex Maximus*—a title previously used by the Roman emperors to indicate their role as high priests in Roman religion. This title now indicated Leo's power in the Western empire particularly. The earlier title *pope* came from the Greek *papas,* a respectful but affectionate term for "father." The title pope came into use when the community in Rome was small and the bishop was a well-known, friendly figure leading the persecuted local church there. Clearly, when "papa" or Pope Leo also became Pontifex Maximus, there was a change of understanding in the nature of the office of the bishop of Rome. Leo was a spiritual father and also a powerful state official.

One problem that divided the Church, and consequently the empire, was the question of the Incarnation: the nature of Jesus as God and man. The Arians had tried to say that

S. LÉON LE GRAND

Jesus was not divine. Now a group in the East led by an aged monk from Constantinople, **Eutyches** (*yoot*-i-keez), taught that Jesus had a divine nature but not a real human nature; the divine somehow absorbed the human part of Jesus as he grew up. A council of bishops met to decide the matter. Led by Archbishop Flavian, patriarch of Constantinople, the council condemned the teachings of Eutyches.

Eutyches appealed to Pope Leo. Meanwhile the Eastern emperor called another council. A mob of monks showed up to defend Eutyches. A riot ensued in which Flavian was injured; he died three days later. At the council Leo's delegates, who did not speak Greek, were not even allowed to deliver the pope's *Tome*—his statement of doctrine. When Pope Leo heard what happened, he called the council a "gang of robbers" and ruled it invalid. Meanwhile the Eastern emperor, Theodosius II, who supported Eutyches, died from a fall from his horse. Pope Leo was free to call a new council.

The Council of Chalcedon

In 451 more than five hundred bishops assembled at Chalcedon (*kal*-seh-dahn), a town across the sea from Constantinople. The bishops rejected Eutyches's teachings and stated that Jesus has two natures—human and divine; he is the real Son of God and he is a real human. Leo's position paper was influential in the deliberations. Nevertheless, all the bishops did not agree. Following the lead of the Egyptian bishops, some of the Christian leaders of Syria and Ethiopia split from the main body of Christians. They formed separate churches, the Jacobite Church and the Coptic Church—which still exist in these respective countries.

One decision of the Council of Chalcedon, which Leo disagreed with, would have far-reaching effects over the next six centuries. The bishops declared that the bishop of Rome was preeminent among all Christian bishops and that second in authority was the patriarch of Constantinople. This represented a change because the bishops of Antioch and Alexandria had long been considered the two highest authorities next to the bishop of Rome. Constantinople was not even founded until the Church was three hundred years old. Leo objected because the decision to move Constantinople up in prestige was motivated by politics. Giving Constantinople greater authority would mean that the Roman emperor living there could interfere more with religious matters. There was little Leo could do, but this change from tradition would lead to five centuries of disputes between the Christians in the West led by the bishop of Rome and the Christians in the East led by the patriarch of Constantinople.

The Pope Stops Attila

Pope Leo's next challenge came the following year when, at the request of the beleaguered Western emperor, he and two senators traveled more than two hundred miles north to a military camp on the shores of a mountain lake, not far from the city of Milan. There he stood face-to-face with Attila the Hun, a short, powerfully built man with fierce black eyes.

Attila had a huge and ferocious army behind him. The Huns were wanderers living in tents and moving whenever the food supply ran short. They burned and looted towns in their path, taking people as slaves or killing as they pleased. Attila's warriors were archers, skilled at fighting from horseback. Behind these warriors roamed a mob of camp followers and Germanic barbarians from various areas—eager to get a share of whatever spoils came their way in the aftermaths of the Hun's battles.

The Huns had come into the grasslands of Europe from Asia, from as far east as China. About thirty years after Constantine, the Huns first camped in what is now southern Russia, between the Black and Caspian seas. They threatened Constantinople, but Attila spared the city when he was bribed with masses of gold by the Eastern emperor. The dynamics of power now reversed: the great Roman Empire, instead of receiving tribute from its subject peoples, was now paying barbarians for its own safety. Attila stormed westward and was only stopped when the Romans and Goths joined forces and defeated him on a battlefield south of what is now Paris. Soon after this, Attila decided to march into weakly defended Italy.

The Western emperor did not have enough troops to stop Attila. So he asked Leo to negotiate a peace. Leo approached Attila unarmed. We have no record of what Leo and Attila said to one another, but the fact of history is that the Huns turned back. Rome was saved. Soon after that, Attila was unexpectedly found dead —possibly murdered by his wife.

Pope Leo witnessed history repeat itself within ten years. The Western emperor was murdered, and an army of Vandals hurled across the Mediterranean from North Africa to sack Rome. No emperor or army opposed them. Leo faced the enemy virtually alone. While Leo could not prevent the Vandals from looting and taking some Romans as slaves, they did agree not to kill people unless attacked. The Vandals pillaged surrounding areas of Italy, then sailed back to Africa. Pope Leo's service on both of these occasions— turning back Attila the Hun and minimizing the destruction to Rome by the Vandals— clearly showed that the empire in the West was unable to face its enemies. From this point on, the pope became one of the key figures in almost all government matters within the Western empire.

An artist's depiction of Attila the Hun

Focus on the Models

Using Patrick as an example, it is clear that missionary work was constantly going on. The heralding of the Word could take place more freely now that the Church was legally recognized in the Roman Empire. Also, a new structure was forming during this period: the monastery. It would play an important role in heralding the Word in places like Ireland as well as in studying the Word. Most of the scholarship concerning the Bible and other religious matters was undertaken in monasteries. The Church was more and more a sign of Christ in the world. In fact, the Church was beginning to be called *catholic*—a word meaning "universal."

Between 350 and 470, perhaps the most significant aspect of the Church that changed was its institutional structure. Since the Church had grown enormously, one bishop in each city was insufficient to perform the sacramental duties required. Consequently, during the fourth and fifth centuries, more and more **presbyters**, that is, priests, were appointed to assist the bishops in their sacramental roles. Also, with the spread of Christianity to the countrysides, priests were needed in small towns and villages. Besides bishops and priests, deacons and even subdeacons served in parishes. Each role became more clearly defined; bishops and priests were full-time ministers and most were married. Gone were the days when those spreading the Word had, like Saint Paul, to labor with their own hands. Starting with Constantine, the Church was given lands from which it derived its support.

Finally, another important institutional development occurred when the bishop of Rome became recognized as the highest authority in the Church. However, the councils could still overrule the pope on some matters, and bishops maintained a large amount of freedom of action. Many of the Roman bishops would now have to use this power to protect what was left of the Western empire from total destruction.

Review Questions and Activities

1) What motivated people to become monks or cloistered nuns? What developments in the Roman Empire contributed to the growth of monastic life?

2) How have monasteries been part of the Church as Servant?

3) How were bishops selected during the fourth and fifth centuries? What is your reaction to the way in which Ambrose was made bishop of Milan? Could good bishops be selected this way now?

4) Using Ambrose's life as a bishop as a guideline, write a job description of a bishop. Then, list as many characteristics as you can for a good bishop.

5) What kind of relationship between church and state do you see developing in this chapter? Give examples that describe this relationship.

6) Why is Jerome's work as a religious scholar so important even to our time? Why are religious scholars important people in the life of the Church?

7) Why was Alaric's sacking of Rome such a shocking event?

8) In your own words, describe the conversion of Augustine. What was it about his personality that made him first a great sinner and then a great saint?

9) You have read some passages from Saint Augustine's *The Confessions* and Thomas Merton's *The Seven Storey Mountain.* Why would these two very great Christians write about their reckless young adulthoods and their mysterious conversions? What elements are similar in their processes of conversion?

10) What were Augustine's homilies like? Why is there such little interaction between the priest and the congregation during homilies today?

11) Describe the three groups that Augustine opposed. What beliefs did they hold that were contrary to Augustine's belief?

12) Why did Augustine write *The City of God?*

13) Who were the Celts? How were they different from people living in the Roman world?

14) What approach did Patrick take to missionary work among the Irish?

15) Many legends abound about Patrick. Why do people create fables about saints or heroes? What positive values do legends have—even if they are not literally true?

16) How did Leo I influence the role of the bishop of Rome? What do the titles "pope" and "Pontifex Maximus" mean? How did the changes in the pope's position come about? What were the forces that altered his role?

17) What issues did Eutyches's teachings raise? How were these problems settled?

18) Based on the decisions of the Council of Chalcedon, describe the authority of the pope at this time.

19) Why were Leo's confrontations with Attila and then the Vandals so important?

20) Why did priests become more numerous in the fourth and fifth centuries?

Personal Reflection Exercise

Both Saint Augustine and Thomas Merton describe times when they felt helpless to change their lives—times when they felt sinful, alone, directionless—times of searching. Think back in your own life to a time when you were feeling helpless. Describe where you were, who was with you, what you were doing, and what had most recently happened to you. What helped you come out of this feeling? What place did God have in your experience?

8
Church Growth in a Crumbling Empire: 400-700

The years A.D. 400 to 700 saw the complete disintegration of the Western Roman Empire. All of what is now Europe was divided into areas ruled by local kings who often warred with their neighbors. The Eastern empire held firm, but was gradually weakening too. Consequently the Church was the one stable element in the lives of most people. Previously pagan princes accepted Christianity and brought their subjects into the Church with them. The Church grew in numbers. However, when people converted because their leaders did, the firmness of their commitment was hard to gauge. Nevertheless, the Church provided a means for warring kings to negotiate with their enemies, supported monasteries that preserved (in the libraries) the learning of the ancients, and offered spiritual guidance to people whose lives were short and hard. Yet, despite the strength of the Church in these times, a new religious force rose out of the deserts of Arabia that would threaten Christianity's very existence.

Greek East and Latin West

The emperors ruling from Constantinople were generally capable, and there were few disturbances when power changed hands through succession. The East's economy was solidly based on trade and on a stable currency. Importantly the Eastern emperors had money to pay their troops. The Church and the Roman Empire in the East worked closely together. In fact, the emperor there became a kind of "super-bishop," and the clergy seemed to belong to a department of the government.

In the West, invasions and poor leadership caused the economy to slide. When the Vandals in North Africa developed a navy and pirated ships that carried food and goods across the Mediterranean, the situation grew even worse. Trade was blocked, farmers and merchants were unpaid, and prices soared. Taxes to maintain the army were enormous.

Added to all this was the violence caused by the movement of the barbarian Germanic tribes into the western part of the empire. Small kingdoms were being set up by the Franks in northern Gaul, and by the Goths in other parts of Gaul and Spain.

By the mid-400s the Angles and Saxons from northern Europe were landing on the shores of the British Isles, pushing the Celtic Romans westward. Italy, where an incompetent central government was still located, had been invaded several times, although the barbarians never tried to settle there. However Italy could not hold out forever. Its final defeat came at the hands of a revolt by the Roman army, now composed mostly of Germanic soldiers—the army of true Romans had nearly disappeared by this time; even the commander in chief, Odovacar (*ohd*-uh-vay-kuhr), came from one of the Germanic tribes.

A stone relief portraying the first Baptism of the Goths

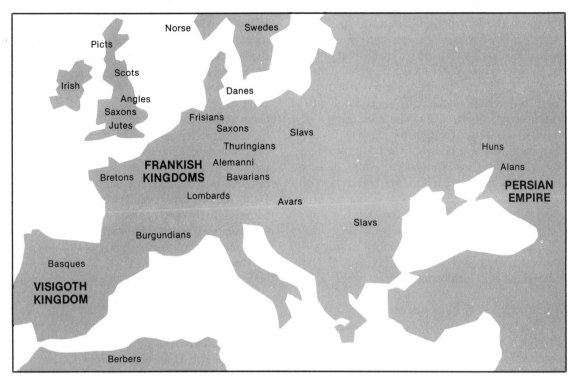

Disgusted with Rome's weakness, Odovacar, as king of the Goths, deposed the Western emperor in 476. He sent the royal seal and robe to Constantinople, saying that there was no need for a second emperor in the West. Thus, after 476 there was never again a Roman emperor in the West. Odovacar became the actual ruler in the West, although he governed in the name of the Eastern emperor to whom he pledged his loyalty. He ruled for seventeen years but was killed by **Theodoric** (thee-*ahd*-eh-rik), the king of the eastern Goths (a tribe from the region that is now Czechoslovakia, Hungary, and Yugoslavia). Theodoric then took over.

In 493, Theodoric began his thirty-six-year rule of Italy. He gave his retiring soldiers land in Italy, and so they settled alongside the Romans. Theodoric managed to keep peace among the two groups despite their mutual dislike and different customs. One important difference concerned religious belief: the Romans were allied to the Church of Rome; the Goths, including Theodoric, were Arians (remember that Arians denied the divinity of

Jesus). Even so, Theodoric granted religious freedom to all. He realized that in Italy the Church alone had the organization needed to keep a large body of people peaceful. Even as an Arian, he did not hesitate to ask Catholic bishops to help him solve the empire's problems. During his long reign Theodoric ruled justly. Thus Italy and the Church experienced some years of relative peace.

Clovis: King of the Franks

Ruling at roughly the same time as Theodoric was **Clovis**, king of the Franks. A pagan tribe, the Franks lived north of the Rhine River in an area that would now include parts of Germany, Holland, Belgium, and France. To unite the small groups of Franks, Clovis defeated the other Frankish kings. He then crossed the Rhine to subdue several Germanic tribes. Next he marched south into Gaul, defeating the Roman army of Goths. This victory added the northern third of modern France to his kingdom. In five years his power had swelled.

In 496, Clovis was baptized by Bishop Remy at Rheims. Three years earlier Clovis had married a Christian princess, from whom he learned much about the faith. As an intelligent ruler, Clovis also realized the advantages of having the same religion as his newly conquered subjects. Following the custom of the times, about three thousand of his soldiers received Baptism with him. The conversion of the Franks as a nation was a much longer process but was inevitable once the king was baptized. Among all the nomadic tribes along the Rhine, the Franks were the only Catholics—the rest were still Arians. Clovis used the Church to help him bring stability to his subjects; it gave them a common moral code and a unifying set of religious rituals.

About ten years later, Clovis expanded Frankish power by defeating the Goths in southern Gaul. He made the small town of Paris his capital. Modern France received its name from its conquerors—the Franks. Catholic Christianity spread now throughout the tribes that had been Arians. Consequently Arianism began to die out in the western part of the empire.

As the year 500 approached, people in the West continued to hope for some peace and order. For many years, marauding tribes had brought death and destruction with them into the Roman world. Conditions improved somewhat under Clovis in Gaul and under Theodoric in Italy, but no one knew when danger would again arise. The Church had problems too. Disagreements arose between the bishop of Rome and the patriarch of Constantinople, who was allied to the Eastern emperor. In order to settle some of the theological questions and matters of liturgical practice, during his papacy (492–496) Gelasius (je-*lay*-shee-uhs) assigned a number of projects to a very capable monk named **Denis the Short** —one of the few scholars who knew both Latin and Greek.

Denis collected the teachings of the various synods and councils that had been held in the West. He then combined these with the documents of the great councils of the East—first translating them into Latin. This collection of decisions was the beginning of **canon law** or **church law**. Denis also reviewed the lists of saints honored in the Church and shortened them according to the pope's directions. Finally he started a new calendar to replace the one that had been used in the Roman Empire for more than a thousand years. Instead of counting the years from the founding of Rome, Denis began the dating from the year of Christ's birth—the system we still use today. Christians accepted this new calendar as a daily reminder that Jesus Christ is the center of all time.

Benedict

While Clovis was building the kingdom of the Franks in Gaul and while Theodoric the Goth was ruling Italy, a young man named **Benedict** was studying law in Rome. Before he finished his studies, at about age twenty, Benedict became disgusted with the sin, crime, and confusion that seemed to exist everywhere. Like Antony and the monks before him, Benedict wanted to seek God in the silence of the countryside. So he left Rome and joined a religious group living about thirty miles from the city. A short time later, he took another step and became a hermit—living alone in a mountain cave. At last, he had the solitude he desired.

His lone existence did not last long. People began to come to Benedict seeking his advice and prayers. Eventually a group of monks came to ask him to be their superior. They wanted to be good monks but found it hard to order their lives in such a way that they could balance prayer, meditation, work, and service. Unfortunately this first group was insincere, and within a short time resented Benedict's attempts to give them direction. Soon he was back in his cave alone with God. Before long, another group came to seek his guidance. This group followed Benedict's advice and became the nucleus of his first monastery.

In the year 530 on the top of Monte Cassino—about halfway between Rome and Naples—Benedict and his monks built the center of Western monasticism. The community was composed of ordinary people, converted Goths and Romans. Benedict taught them how to read so that they could understand the Scriptures and the prayers said each day. Their lives were simple and well ordered, balanced between "prayer and work"—in Latin, *ora et labora.* The community within the monastery at Monte Cassino was nearly a complete economic unit, supplying itself with food, clothing, and shelter. In its quiet scriptorium, monks copied sacred books and preserved secular books containing the writings of famous authors. At Monte Cassino, Benedict wrote what came to be called the **Benedictine Rule**—which eventually became the basic guide for religious life and discipline in communities throughout the Western world.

Though the points of the Rule came from his own experience and immense common sense, Benedict realized that he was building on a tradition that was centuries old—a tradition begun by Antony, the hermit living in the deserts of Egypt. He may also have contemplated the sample rule written by Basil for the monks in Asia Minor. Jerome had lived as a monk in Bethlehem and had organized several monasteries. Even Augustine had written a short set of guidelines for the religious community that he began in his North African hometown. Patrick too had established monasteries in Ireland. Nonetheless, Benedict's Rule became recognized as the most inspired description of monastic life.

The monastery at Monte Cassino

Selections from
Saint Benedict's Rule

- A monastery ought, if possible, to be so constructed as to contain within it all necessaries—that is, water, mill, garden, and places for the various crafts . . . so that there will be no occasion for monks to wander abroad.
- A mattress, a coverlet, a pillow are to suffice for bedding.
- There [should] be at all seasons of the year [two] cooked dishes, so that he who happens not to be able to eat of the one may make his meal of the other. . . . "Take heed to yourselves lest perhaps your hearts be overcharged with [indulgence]."
- Although we read that "wine is not the drink of monks at all," yet, since in our day they cannot be persuaded of this, let us at least agree not to drink to excess but sparingly. A pint of wine a day is sufficient for anyone.
- When the brothers rise for the Divine Office, let them gently encourage one another, because of the excuses made by those who are drowsy.
- Let all guests who come be received as Christ would be. . . . As soon, therefore, as a guest is announced let him be met by the prior or the brethren, with all marks of charity. . . . Let special care be taken of the poor and pilgrims, because in them Christ is more truly received. . . .
- Let there be stationed at the gate of the monastery some wise old man who knows how to give and receive an answer, and whose age will not allow him to wander from his post. . . . As soon as any one shall knock, or some poor man shall call for help, let him reply, "Thanks be to God," or invoke a blessing.

The Monk's Day at Monte Cassino—Prayer and Work

Quietly a robed figure moves about a chilly dormitory filled with sleeping men; the sound of a bell is heard as this monk summons his brothers to Nocturns—the first of seven periods of prayer each day. It is 2:00 A.M. The monks rub the sleep from their eyes, silently gather themselves together and file into the chapel. The monks meditate while waiting for the leader to intone the start of Nocturns. The simple melodies of the chant flow through the stone church. When Nocturns is completed, the monks make their way back to their wooden cots for another hour or so of sleep. Before six, with the sun, they are back in chapel for Lauds. Leaving chapel, they spend some time in private reading and meditation before meeting back in chapel for Prime. A simple breakfast is eaten just before a period of morning work. Each brother has jobs to do according to his ability and the needs of the monastery. These men do not mind; most of them are simple men from the countryside— if they were laymen, most would be farmers or do some other kind of hard labor. Besides, to them prayer and work are one. At 9:00 A.M. Terce is sung, and the monks celebrate the Eucharist. All join in the singing because "he who sings prays twice."

Mass done, another period of manual labor follows. Right before noon, Sext is chanted, and lunch is eaten. It is a plain meal of vegetables and bread, accompanied by a little ordinary wine. By this time the monks are ready for a brief siesta or nap. At 3:00 P.M. they are gathered in chapel for None. After this they head for the fields to tend the crops, for the tailor shop to sew new robes, for the scriptorium to copy books, or for the bakery to prepare the sturdy bread for the monks and the frequent beggars and pilgrims who appear at their gate; there are numerous jobs to be done if the monastery is to sustain itself. At 6:00 P.M. they are once more chanting the Psalms and listening to the Word of God during Vespers; the light meal they have just had has a chance to digest. They are content in this period before the close of their day. Like most of their lives, the short time for private reading and meditation is spent silently in the presence of God. Compline is sung right before they head to the dormitory and their much-deserved rest.

The followers of Saint Benedict have worked about six hours, slept about eight hours and prayed together about three hours. The rest of the day is spent in spiritual reading and meditation; even meals are eaten silently while inspirational texts are read by a brother monk. They have praised God with their heads, hearts, and hands. Some might call it a hard life, but not these men. The only hard life for them would be life away from the presence of God so apparent in Monte Cassino.

Justinian: The Last Strong Emperor

At the age of forty-five, the **Emperor Justinian** succeeded to the throne of the Eastern empire. He was intelligent, hardworking, and known to the people as "the emperor who never sleeps." He is important for being the last really strong Eastern emperor, for setting up a code of law uniform throughout the empire, and for building one of the most grand Christian churches of all time—the **Hagia Sophia** (*hah*-gee-uh soh-*fee*-uh)—in Constantinople. During his rule from 527 to 565, the Church reached a pinnacle of influence in the East, ruling over the regions of Syria, Greece, Iraq, Lebanon, Jordan, Egypt, Albania, Turkey, and southern Russia.

Much of Justinian's time was taken up with war. For about half of his reign the Romans fought the powerful Persian Empire, which covered most of the territory from Syria eastward to the boundary with India. Because of Justinian's selection of able generals and through the use of innovative techniques and improved armor, Justinian's troops managed to keep the Eastern empire intact. Justinian also won back North Africa and Italy. The costs in human life and in money were frightful.

Yet Justinian's greatest achievement was not in war but in reform of the law. Most of the laws used in the empire had been written in pre-Christian times and did not reflect Christian values. For seven years, a committee appointed by Justinian worked to revise the legal code. The result was the **Justinian Code,** a collection of laws stated clearly in Latin that later became the basis of European law. When a summary of this material was completed for law students, the emperor closed all law schools except those at Constantinople and Beirut. In this way, all young lawyers would be trained properly in the new system.

An ivory relief depicting Justinian (right)

Hagia Sophia (next page) as it is today, decorated as a mosque

The new legal system did manifest a more Christian orientation. For example, Justinian's law took away much of the power that a man had over his wife and children. The father could no longer send his children into slavery to pay his debts. Women and children could now hold property in their own names. Marriage was protected from easy divorces. Admittedly, some of the punishments were dreadful, such as the cutting off of hands and ears for certain crimes. Yet, like all laws, they were based on the conditions of life at that time. As late as three hundred years ago the laws of England allowed criminals to be mutilated. Some Islamic countries still chop off the hands of thieves. In short, Justinian's Code, despite its problems, better reflected the new Christian ethics taught by the Church.

While Justinian's Code was a great advance over earlier laws, he still reflected a belief that was held by the Roman emperors in pre-Christian times. That is, he thought that he was responsible for the salvation of all his subjects.

Since he believed in Christianity, everyone else should too. Thus all would go to heaven. As a consequence, Justinian persecuted non-Christians, Jews, and heretics, depriving them of their rights as citizens. In addition, Justinian tried to rule the Church in some matters. Once he even kept the pope under arrest in Constantinople. Justinian made regulations for the election of bishops who had to serve as government officials in supervising public works projects, in enforcing laws related to morals, and in taking care of orphans. In some districts, the bishops had more authority than the governors.

Justinian will be remembered, perhaps foremost, for rebuilding the Hagia Sophia church. After the original Hagia Sophia (that is, "Holy Wisdom") church was destroyed by fire in the riots of 532, he built the present church, St. Sophia, with a labor force of ten thousand people working more than five years. The cost has been estimated at about $150 million. Materials were brought from all over the empire. When it was to be dedicated, Justinian entered through the heavy doors covered with silver and bronze; he raised his arms to heaven and cried out: "Glory to God, who has thought me worthy of doing something so great. O Solomon! I have beaten you."

After Justinian's death in 565, his good work was undone. His successors on the imperial throne were weak. New barbarian invasions began in the West. The Lombards took over large areas of Italy. Other nomadic tribes moved into unprotected lands. The Western empire had crumbled some years before; now the East began to disintegrate too.

Gregory I: Bishop of Rome

With the demise of imperial power, the people once again looked to the Church for leadership and mediation. Fortunately a strong pope was elected. In some ways Gregory was a surprise as pope. As a young man he was prefect of Rome—serving as governor, chief of police, and chief justice. Despite his efforts and because of the huge war debts, Rome was in shambles. Even the aqueducts were broken, making drinking water scarce. People had moved away, looking for better places to live. Moreover, Rome was only part of Gregory's responsibilities. In charge of a large part of southern Italy, he became an expert in organizing the distribution of grain and generally in taking care of the poor.

Yet Gregory was not entirely happy with the success of his public office. When his father died, he resigned his position and started giving away much of his money and land. He turned the family mansion into a monastery and lived there as a monk. Refusing to be **abbot**—the director of a monastery—he followed the lifestyle of the rest of the monks. This quiet life was broken by a command from the pope that he go to Constantinople to keep the emperor informed about the needs of impoverished Rome. After seven years at the corrupt court, he gladly returned to Rome. Following a few more years as a monk, he became secretary to the pope.

Conditions in Rome degenerated further when the Tiber River flooded the city, destroying food supplies and homes, and breeding fatal sickness. When the pope himself died from the plague, the people of Rome elected Gregory, trusting that with his experience and abilities he would save them. Not wanting the job, he hid out for three days, hoping that the people would choose someone else. They did not. So at age fifty, Gregory became pope. The year was 590.

The life of a pope during Gregory's time was far from easy; he was expected to fill many different roles. He had to be a servant of the poor; the Church was the only welfare agency in existence. Using the profits from the farms owned by the Church, Gregory fed as many of the poor as he could. Profits from the farms also helped him to rebuild crumbling churches and to build new ones. As spiritual leader, he was expected to preach on Sundays and to tend to the religious matters of his growing flock. Concerned about the ill-educated clergy of his time, Gregory encouraged bishops to open schools for young men wanting to become priests. In turn, he expected that the priests would open church schools for children. These church schools were the only sources of education. Gregory wrote many letters covering topics such as the Bible, the duties of pastors, and the proper way to celebrate the liturgy. Nine hundred of his letters are still preserved in libraries. Gregory was social worker, pastor, theologian, educator, administrator, farmer, and builder. He was a rare person because he could ably function in all of these roles.

Gregory the Diplomat

The Lombards, another nomadic tribe, had settled in large areas of Italy. The emperor was too busy warring in the East to worry about the West. In effect, the pope had to represent the Roman government. Accordingly, Gregory negotiated with the Lombards, paying ransoms for the release of people captured in raids. Soon after these negotiations, he sent missionaries to convert the Lombards. Gregory knew that the Roman Empire was finished. These marauding groups of nomads could eventually dominate Europe. If the Church were to be a force for peace, justice, and hope, and if the message of Christ were to be spread, the still non-Christian tribal groups including the Lombards, Goths, and Vandals must be converted.

Pope Gregory encouraged the Franks to continue their efforts for the conversion of the eastern part of their kingdom, in what is today central Europe. He also helped the Christian king of Spain to find ways of living peacefully with the Visigoths in his country. But Gregory's most distinctive work in spreading the Gospel was his mission to Britain.

The Mission to England

One hundred years previously, the Angles and Saxons from present-day Denmark and northern Germany had stormed into Britain. To escape these tough new tribes, the romanized Christian Britons fled westward into Wales. The invaders eventually set up seven kingdoms in the south and east of Britain. There was little communication between the western Christians and the seven kingdoms. Consequently Pope Gregory sent forty monks from his own monastery to Britain. Their abbot, Augustine, was in charge. Their only protection was a large crucifix. As they passed through Gaul, they heard hair-raising tales about the tribes in Britain. Gregory sent the monks letters urging them to make the crossing. In 597, Augustine and his fellow monks landed in Britain.

The Benedictine historian, Venerable Bede, who will be discussed in the next chapter, described the conversion of the Anglo-Saxon King Ethelbert:

> After some days, the king came to the island and, sitting down in the open air, summoned Augustine and his companions to an audience. But he took precautions that they should not approach him in a house; for he held an ancient superstition that, if they were practisers of magical arts, they might have opportunity to deceive and master him. But the monks were endowed with power from God, not from the Devil, and approached the king carrying a silver cross as

Gregorian Chant

One of Pope Gregory's greatest contributions to the celebration of the liturgy and to our culture was his emphasis on the recording of music in written scores. Before Gregory, hymns were learned by heart, but little sheet music existed to record melodies for future generations and for wide distribution. Gregory ordered that church music be systematized and recorded. While the following introductory hymn does not look like music today, the notes could be followed to produce a wonderful chant to celebrate Easter—the Resurrection of Jesus the Christ.

Many years later, the notes were placed on staffs to produce sheet music more familiar to us; this is the same piece of music, but in the newer Gregorian chant.

Intr. 4

REsur-réxi, * et adhuc técum sum, al- le- lú- ia: po- su- í-sti su- per me má- num tú- am, al- le- lú- ia: mi-rá- bi-lis fá- cta est sci én- ti- a tú- a, alle- lú-ia, al- le- lú- ia. Ps. Dó- mine, probásti me, et cognovísti me : * tu cognovísti ses- si- ónem mé- am, et resurrecti- ó-nem mé- am. Gló-ri- a Pátri, et Fí-li- o, et Spi-rí-tu- i Sáncto. * Sic-ut e-rat in princípi- o, et nunc, et semper, et in saécula saecu-ló- rum. Amen.

their standard and the likeness of our Lord and Saviour painted on a board. First of all they offered prayer to God. . . . And when, at the king's command, they had sat down and preached the word of life to the king and his court, the king said: "Your words and promises are fair indeed. . . ."

In the spring of that year, at Pentecost, King Ethelbert was converted. Bede continues his story:

At length the king himself, among others, edified by the pure lives of these holy men and their gladdening promises, the truth of which they confirmed by many miracles, believed and was baptized. Thenceforth great numbers gathered each day to hear the word of God. . . . It is said that . . . [Ethelbert] would not compel anyone to accept Christianity; for he had learned . . . that the service of Christ must be accepted freely and not under compulsion.

In spite of this early success, a hundred years passed before the whole of Britain was again Christian.

The Meaning of Christianity

What did it mean to be a Christian at this period in history? First, people accepted the same beliefs we do today; they heard the Word of God from the monks and believed. While the rituals of the sacraments were a bit different from ours today, there was general acceptance of seven sacraments. The rite of Reconciliation, for instance, was performed for the most part publicly and only in cases of the most serious of sins. The penances were quite severe by our standards. People went to Mass on Sundays and observed the feast days of their favorite saints. They had a strong sense of God's power and also of the Devil's presence.

In the sixth century, people had little control over disease, climate, and, in general, their fate. Most people did not live past age forty-five, and they had to scrape for their food day by day. Moving to a higher position in society was almost unheard of. Consequently people had a strong sense that God ruled creation; clearly they did not. They identified with the suffering Jesus and hoped to go to heaven because life often seemed like hell. Certainly sixth-century people also laughed, fell in love, cherished their children, and shared in all the other normal activities of life. They believed that God "looked down"—protecting and blessing the good or punishing and cursing the wrongdoers.

Worship was central to Christian life—especially the eucharistic worship. The form of the Mass was fairly standardized by this time for both the West and the East. In the West, the Mass was much like we have it today, except that the language used was Latin. In the East, there were some differences. In Eastern churches—like the Hagia Sophia, for example —curtains and decorated wall panels separated the sanctuary from the congregation. The liturgy of the Word was celebrated in front of the panels, but the eucharistic celebration took place behind the panels. This added to the sense of mystery surrounding the rite. The language used in the Eastern churches was generally Greek, although other languages were used depending on the place.

An important feature of the liturgy was music. In the first centuries, the Church inherited Jewish forms of sacred songs. Gradually Greek and Roman hymns were composed, some adapted from the music of the day. Gregory organized all this musical material into a system that covered the liturgy of all feast days as well as the Psalms and hymns sung each day in the monasteries. This music, called **Gregorian chant**, was used for centuries in Catholic churches of the West.

Another increasingly important part of worship was the veneration of saints—especially martyrs. By A.D. 600 many saints were called upon in prayer and remembered during the liturgy. The relics of saints, which might be particles of their bones or even small pieces from their clothes, were treasured.

From the fifth century to the beginning of the seventh century, qualifications for the priesthood gradually became more standardized. During the papacy of Innocent I (401–417), the minimum requirements for priests were, if married, to have married a virgin and not be married to a twice-married woman or widow; not to have done public penance in one's lifetime; not to have served in the army since the time of Baptism; not to have paid for public games; and not to have been a pagan priest. Nearly a century later Gelasius, who was pope from 492 to 496, expanded the list: no illiterate person, proven criminal, physically deformed man, or woman could be a priest.

These regulations may seem very odd to us today, but in these centuries, priests were often chosen by the local people or by the ruler of the neighborhood castle; thus these guidelines for choice, though clearly limited, were helpful. However, enforcement of the qualifications by the bishops was frequently weak because communications were poor. During Gregory's papacy (590–604), the training of priests improved somewhat, and celibacy (staying unmarried) was encouraged, although not required.

Gregory's contributions to the Church were incredible. Many of his acts solidified the Church in a time of tremendous calamity. Yet he saw himself as simply "Servant of the Servants of God," a title that all of his successors have adopted. Most of Gregory's efforts were expended on the Western Church because it was the most strife-torn from nomadic invasions, widespread disease, and a babble of languages that prevented communication. (Latin was now virtually unknown by the common people; dialects were developing that later became Italian, Spanish, French, and German.) The Church in the East was more stable because the Eastern empire—while weakened—still had a stronger economy, a more hospitable climate, and a common language—Greek. But even the East's relative stability would be shattered in a few short years.

Muhammad and Islam

An irresistible force was driving westward out of the desert beyond the Red Sea. A young caravan leader named **Muhammad** (moh-*ham*-uhd) was telling his fellow Arabs that the angel Gabriel had revealed a new religion to him. As his caravans traveled up and down the shores of the Red Sea, Muhammad (570–632) had learned elements of both the Jewish and Christian Scriptures. He recognized these writings as inspired by God; aspects of Jewish and Christian teachings appear in his own writings, which became the Islamic Scriptures called the **Koran**. The followers of Muhammad became known as *Muslims* and the religion itself as *Islam*—both terms referring to a "submission to God." The most important teachings of Islam are belief in one God, in a life after death that is full of delights, in a strict moral life, in praying five times each day, and in periods of fasting. Jesus is respected as a prophet, along with the Jewish prophets, but Muslims do not believe in the Trinity. In Islam there is only one God, and Allah is his name.

Muhammad taught that Muslims honor Allah by spreading Islam everywhere. Mounted on swift horses, Arab warriors rode northward to Damascus and easily conquered Syria, Palestine, and Egypt. At Alexandria they took over a ready-made navy, so that they were able to hurtle westward along the North African coast of the Mediterranean—by both land and

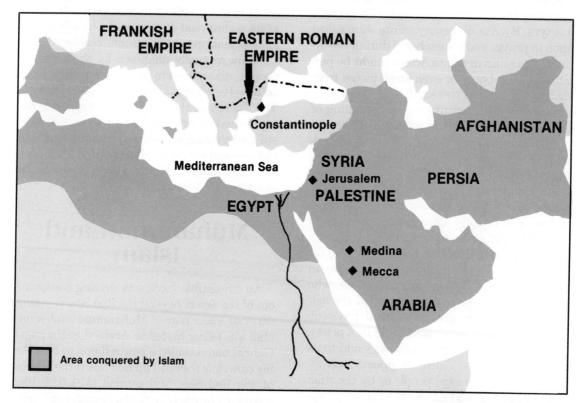

FRANKISH EMPIRE

EASTERN ROMAN EMPIRE

Constantinople

AFGHANISTAN

Mediterranean Sea

SYRIA

Jerusalem

PALESTINE

PERSIA

EGYPT

Medina

Mecca

ARABIA

☐ Area conquered by Islam

sea. In these early days conversions were sometimes made at the point of a sword, but generally the Muslim conquerors did not force anyone to accept Islam. However, they collected annual taxes from the **infidels**—those who refused to convert to Islam. Thus, many Christians in the East converted to Islam, weakening the Church in the East.

Shortly before the year 700, the Muslims began an attack on Constantinople itself; it lasted five years. The navy of the Eastern empire finally routed the Muslims with a weapon called "Greek fire," a mixture of chemicals shot out of flamethrowers that was able to burn even on water. Constantinople was saved for a while, but the Muslims had control of the southern and eastern shores of the Mediterranean. Only Asia Minor, Greece, and a few coastal strips here and there were still ruled

by Constantinople. Muslim ships destroyed trade between the West and Constantinople. The Mediterranean was no longer Roman. Worse still, people began to fear that the Muslims would conquer Europe. In 711 it seemed that this was likely to happen.

Europe Divided

In 711, Muslim raiders, mostly Moors from North Africa, landed for the first time on European shores at Gibraltar, where Spain and Africa almost touch. The Muslims, it seems, came by invitation. The people of Spain had been badly divided. For over a hundred years, the Roman population of Spain had been under the rule of the Goths. Now the Goths were grouped into a number of rival parties, each eager to claim the throne that had just been vacated by the death of the old king. One of the factions had sought the help of the Muslims. As the raiding party of Moors found it easy to advance from one town to another,

African Muslims at prayer

Second, Spain was divided into many small groups—similar to the one that invited the Muslims into the country. As a result, the Muslims met no united opposition in Spain. As the Muslims marched north, panic spread in Gaul because conditions there were much the same as in Spain. Since the death of Clovis, Gaul had been poorly governed. His sons and then his grandsons had divided and subdivided the kingdom until there was virtually no central government left. Lawlessness coupled with relentless poverty made Gaul a hard place in which to live. When the Muslims took control of the Mediterranean, trade in the West was cut off. Money became scarce, and people had to return to barter—exchanging such things as wine from the south for furs from the north. The only thing that was worth much was the land.

The Franks possessed improved methods of farming, such as a plow on wheels that was pulled by a team of oxen. Each family was given a small piece of land by the local lord along with the right to cut wood in the local forest. Yet there were frequent crop failures, and wandering gangs often would destroy the fields. In desperation a poor man would go to one of the rich landowning lords and ask to become his vassal, or servant, probably for life. If accepted, the vassal would work the lord's land and, when necessary, fight in the lord's small army. The lord would, in turn, give the vassal and his family necessary food, clothing, and a small house to live in. Eventually most people in Gaul were either lords or vassals. This arrangement was the basis for the political organization called **feudalism**, which prevailed later during the ninth through fifteenth centuries. This system of many small

they decided to stay and take over the country for Islam. In a few years, Spain was under the rule of the Muslim caliph of Damascus. Eventually the Moors found their way through the mountain passes of the Pyrenees, northward into Gaul.

Two other factors aided the Moors in taking over so readily. First, the Jewish minority desired a change from the Goths. The Jews had long been harassed because the kings wanted the profits that the Jewish merchants made by monopolizing trade in the southern seaports. At times the Jews were forced to choose between Baptism and loss of their homes and businesses. Since the Muslims controlled much of the Mediterranean, some Jews thought that cooperation with the Moors might open up trade again.

local lords and their vassals had a serious disadvantage—how could the people unite to fight a common foe like the Muslims?

Fortunately for the Franks, by the 700s Gaul was being led by a kind of prime minister called "the mayor of the palace." The most ambitious of these mayors was **Charles Martel** (mahr-*tel*), who not only fought the new nomadic tribes east of the Rhine but also defeated the western Franks in a battle near Paris. Martel chose a new king for the Franks. To gain his power in Gaul, Martel did what lords and kings had been doing for many years: he gave land to vassals. Sometimes he even took land from the Church and monasteries to give to his vassals.

In spite of his injustice to the Church, Martel did a great service to Christian Gaul when he met and defeated the Muslims who were invading Gaul. After being defeated at Tours (*tuer*), southwest of Paris, the Muslims were forced to retreat over the mountains back into Spain. This was in 732. During the next few years Martel had to fight them several more times, but he lived up to his name—Martel means "the Hammer." His victories prevented Islam from spreading over Europe.

Focus on the Models

From 400 to 700, the work of the Church as Servant greatly expanded. In fact, the Church became almost the sole recourse of the poor, as we saw in Pope Gregory's work. Similarly monasteries and some church schools were just about the only sources for education. The role of the institutional Church expanded too. During this period, it was the only force that could mediate between the warring factions of Europe. The pope's roles increased dramatically. The Church's holdings in land and property grew enormously, even considering the loss of properties in North Africa and the Middle East due to Muslim takeover.

Heralding the Word of God continued through monks like Augustine and his followers. Huge groups converted in the West when their leaders decided to become Christian. And in the confines of monasteries, theology was being written. Most people in Europe considered themselves Christian, but gone was the notion of earlier days that close, caring communities characterized Christianity. Most individuals had a keen sense of a divine being who controlled life. The Church mediated between God and the individual; saints, especially Mary, were honored and prayed to for special favors. Christian values did influence laws and customs as seen in the Justinian Code. Nevertheless, the sheer size of the Church and the enormous diversity of people who called themselves Christian made the Mystical Body more difficult to experience, especially at times when two supposedly Christian lords were fighting each other. The Church in the East was almost surrounded by Muslim armies. Without communication with Rome, some of the differences between the Church in the West and the Church in the East that had developed in theology and practice were to become more strongly marked. The time was coming when a radical split would divide the People of God.

Review Questions and Activities

1) What were the main differences between conditions in the Western and Eastern empires? How did these differences influence the roles that the Church played during this period?

2) What services did the Church in the West provide in the West? Why was the Church's position so central to life during this period?

3) How was the conversion of Clovis an important event in the spread of the faith? What custom and what larger process were set into motion when Clovis converted? What problems did the conversion of the Franks cause the Church?

4) What creations of Denis the Short are still important to us today? Why would a pope command Denis to work on these projects?

5) Why was Benedict's Rule so essential to monastic life?

6) The Justinian Code illustrates another way in which the Church influenced the lives of people in this period. Explain.

7) What other contributions did Justinian make to the Church? In what ways did he cause problems for the Church?

8) How did Gregory demonstrate the changes that had taken place in the roles that a pope was supposed to fill?

9) What was life like for the average Christian during these centuries from 400 to 700? How did the Church help make life meaningful?

10) Describe some of the difficulties in the selection and training of priests.

11) How did the Muslims change the course of church history? How did Muslim control of the Mediterranean Sea exaggerate the differences between the Western Church and the Eastern Church?

12) Why was it so easy for the Muslims to conquer so much territory? Why was Spain particularly vulnerable?

13) Describe the system of land ownership later called feudalism. What were the advantages and disadvantages of this system?

14) How did the Church model itself as Servant? Sacrament? Herald? Institution? People of God? Which model of the Church seemed to suffer most because of the enormous growth of the Church?

Personal Reflection Exercise

There has been much discussion in this chapter about the role of monks in the Church. Monks and nuns who lead a contemplative life spend most of their lives silently praying and meditating on God's presence. This very focused type of existence may, at first or even second glance, seem terribly boring or maybe even meaningless. Nevertheless many women and men today are entering monasteries all over the world.

Reflect on your own life during the last couple of weeks. Try to list some times when you just wanted time to think—time to be silent with yourself. Did you find the silence you wanted? Were you tempted to turn on the radio, TV, or stereo to drive away the silence? If so, why did you want to distract yourself? What did you think you would find in the stillness? Would you and/or people around you be better off if they had some time or took some time to meditate, pray silently, or think quietly?

9
New Challenges, New Solutions: 700–1000

By the year 700, the Church had lost to Islam many of its numbers in the East. Nevertheless, missionaries were undeterred; the hazardous and lonely journeys of brave monks continued into new areas. Other monks worked diligently in monasteries—writing histories, copying church teachings, praying for people in a dangerous world. Amidst all of these activities, the Church had to cope with new invasions by nomads like the Vikings. To protect Rome, the Church allied itself with a new Holy Roman emperor—a relationship that dramatically restructured society for centuries. Feudalism became a rigid social system. Finally, despite the invasions of the Vikings from Scandinavia, Christianity also became rooted in eastern Europe and Russia.

The Irish Missionaries

While much of the Eastern Church was overwhelmed by Islam, missionaries continued their work of spreading the Gospel. This spread can be traced, in large part, to the monks and nuns in Irish monasteries who were preparing themselves to preach in distant, often hostile, lands. Saint Patrick had converted Ireland in the first place by establishing monasteries. By the 500s, Irish missionaries were working in Scotland. Others went into Gaul where there were still non-Christian Germanic people, not only in what is now France but also in areas of Switzerland and northern Italy.

What developed throughout Europe was a common Christian faith, yet Christian practices varied depending on what group did the converting and who the converts were. After all, communications were poor, and so standard practice in many matters was difficult to establish. For instance, Christians in southern England celebrated Easter on one date, while in Scotland and Ireland, it was celebrated at a different time. At the Synod of Whitby in northern England in 664, the bishops of the English Church decided to ally themselves with Rome, especially regarding the date for the observance of Easter. Matters like this would be settled in time as the Church became more and more the one religion common to all Europeans.

Bede

Some years after the Synod of Whitby a little boy was born in northern England and given the Anglo-Saxon name of **Bede** (*beed*). As a child he was taught by monks in a nearby monastery. After he grew up, Bede himself became a monk and spent his entire life in the same monastery—studying, teaching, and writing. He seems never to have traveled and was probably never heard of by anyone outside his little village; yet his name is still remembered today. The library of his monastery contained immensely valuable books from Gaul, Spain, Rome, and the rest of the ancient empire. By studying these works, Bede was acquainted with the great minds of Europe. He wrote explanations of the Scriptures, as well as sermons on religious topics. Clearly his greatest work is the history of the English people, which is still read today though Bede finished writing it in about 731. Careful and accurate in his historical writing, Bede gives real-life pictures of the people of his time.

Bede's work points to the important role that the monasteries had in fostering the very limited scholarship that went on during these violent times in the West. While Muslim scholars were making great strides in mathematics, in astronomy, in architecture, and in translating the ancient Greek writers, learning was extremely hampered in the West and relied heavily on the work going on in the monasteries. Not only did the monks teach children to read and write; they also hand-copied important manuscripts. Then, too, there was a small group of monks like the Venerable Bede who wrote history, theology, and philosophy. We might ask if the great books from ancient times would have survived the violence of this era in the West without the contributions of these silently persistent monks.

Venerable Bede's Account of a Miracle at the Tomb of Saint Oswald

People in the early medieval period had a strong faith that miracles could and often did happen. Often miracles were performed through the works of saints interceding in heaven. Naturally the historian Bede would wish to inspire his readers with accounts of miracles taking place through the intercession of English saints. What follows is one such account from Bede's *A History of the English Church and People,* chapter 12, entitled "A Little Boy Is Cured of Ague at Saint Oswald's Tomb":

Some while after this, there was a little boy in the monastery who had been seriously troubled by ague.* One day he was anxiously awaiting the hour of an attack, when one of the brothers came in to him and said: "My boy, shall I tell you how you may be cured of this complaint? Get up, and go to Oswald's tomb in the church. Remain there quietly and mind you don't stir from it until the time that your fever is due to leave you. Then I will come and fetch you." The boy did as the brother advised, and while he sat by the saint's tomb the fever dared not touch him: furthermore, it was so completely scared that it never recurred, either on the second or the third day, or ever after. A brother of that monastery who told me this story added that the boy who had been so miraculously cured was by then a young man and still living in the monastery. But it need cause no surprise that the prayers of this king [Oswald], who now reigns with God, should be acceptable to him, since when he was a king on earth he always used to work and pray fervently for the eternal kingdom.

It is said that Oswald often remained in prayer from the early hour of Lauds until dawn, and that through his practice of constant prayer and thanksgiving to God he always sat with his hands palm upwards on his knees. It is also said, and has become proverbial, that his life even closed in prayer; for when he saw the enemy forces surrounding him and knew that his end was near, he prayed for the souls of his soldiers. "God have mercy on their souls, said Oswald as he fell" is now a proverb. As I have already mentioned, his bones were taken up and buried in the Abbey of Bardney; but the king who slew him ordered that his head and hands with the forearms be hacked off and fixed on stakes. The following year, Oswald's successor Oswy came to the place with his army and removed them, placing the head in the church at Lindisfarne, and the hands and arms in his own royal city of Bamburgh.

---

*Ague is a sickness characterized by chills and then severe fever and sweating.

Boniface

Born about the same time as Bede, another English monk did much to build up the Church in Europe, mostly in the area that is today Germany, but also in western Gaul—contemporary France. This missionary was Winfrid, renamed **Boniface** (675–754) and known in history as the "Apostle of Germany." After spending his first thirty-five years in southwest England, Boniface left his monastery for Friesland, the lowland off the North Sea—today's Holland. After two years of his hard work there, the people would still have no part of Christianity. Discouraged, Boniface went to Rome to see the pope, who sent him to preach in the Germanic regions that were non-Christian. There he met success.

Four years later, Boniface was again in Rome, called there by the pope who made him bishop. Charles Martel, leader of the Franks, supported Boniface's work because he thought Christianity could bring peace between the northern tribes and the Franks. Boniface first went to England, recruiting monks and nuns to work with him in Germany. Then, like Patrick, Boniface built monasteries and used them as centers for evangelizing. Soon there were several dioceses in German lands.

Boniface was able to work as a missionary for twenty more years, becoming a sort of wandering bishop with a few monks for company. They lived a hard life, always on the move, preaching where there were no priests, visiting the small congregations and their pastors. This life made Boniface rugged physically—but then it also took a rugged soul to lead such a life. One instance of his boldness and courage was recorded when he chopped down a sacred oak that the pagans worshiped as the tree of Thor, their principal god. Seeing that this English monk was not instantly struck down by Thor and admiring Boniface's great courage, many people asked for Baptism. Boniface became a legend because of his success at bringing people to understand and accept Christianity.

Boniface's influence grew too. When Charles Martel died, his two sons succeeded him as mayors of the Frankish palace. Eventually the second brother, **Pepin the Short,** was the sole mayor. After ten years as mayor, Pepin decided that since he was doing the work of the king he should also have the title. The pope approved. In 751 Boniface, acting as Pope Zachary's legate, crowned Pepin as king of the Franks. Boniface and Pepin worked together to reorganize the Church in western Gaul; they did this through a series of councils called by Pepin. By this time Boniface was an old man. Wanting to finish his days preaching the Word and not administering an archdiocese, Boniface resigned and, with a few monks, started northward toward the flatlands of the Rhine. Soon after starting his work with the Frisians (a tribe living in Holland), Boniface and his companions were killed by pagans while they were preparing some of their converts for Confirmation.

Boniface's work stretched across the terms of four popes. He succeeded in uniting the Christians in the German provinces east of the Rhine, in lands that were beyond the boundaries of the old Roman Empire.

Boniface's acts would have far-reaching effects that he could not dream of at the time of crowning Pepin king. About three years before Boniface's death, the pope and Rome were threatened with being overrun by the Lombards. Though by now they were nominally Christian, the Lombards' lust for power and plunder was stronger than their commitment to a religion many did not really understand. When the pope asked the Byzantine emperor for help (the area around Rome was still part of the empire), there was no response except a note of protest that was sent directly to the Lombards. In desperation Pope Stephen II gathered a group of horsemen and started north, crossing the Swiss Alps at the Saint Bernard Pass, then going northwest into Gaul where Pepin was staying at the time. Since the pope recognized Pepin as king of the Franks, in return he expected and received Pepin's assurance that the Franks would protect Rome from the Lombards.

Three years later, in 756, Pepin came down through the Alps to drive off the Lombards who had begun to march on Rome. After his victory Pepin decided that the pope needed some way of protecting Rome himself; so he gave the pope a section of Italy, about a fifth of it, in the middle of the Italian boot. This territory became known as the Papal States, with the pope as ruler or king. The Papal States remained an independent country under the rule of the popes for more than eleven hundred years. While the Papal States did provide money to cover the expenses of running the Church, feeding the poor of Rome, and paying the clergy of the Vatican, and while they were not won in war or expanded through theft of other lands, they did create serious dilemmas for the Church over the centuries—as we will see.

Charlemagne

Following the custom of Germanic kings, Pepin willed his kingdom to his two sons. One of them died three years after his father. The other, Charles, took over his brother's share and began to organize a good part of western Europe into a huge Frankish kingdom. Charles himself became known as **Charlemagne** (*shahr-luh-mayn*) or "Charles the Great." First he conquered the tough Saxons living in the north. After defeating them, Charlemagne forced the Saxons to receive Baptism under penalty of death. Obviously this sort of conversion did not create committed Christians. But Charlemagne saw it as a way of strengthening his kingdom and, at the same time, increasing the membership of the Church. Forced conversion was a traditional way of unifying a kingdom. As we already discussed, the Roman emperors persecuted the early Christians because they did not worship the ancient gods. Constantine's successors also used pressure to convert pagans to Christianity. Likewise, as we have seen, Muslims occasionally converted by the sword—to create a unified Islamic world.

Charlemagne led his cavalry through the passes of the southern Alps into Italy, that is, into Lombard territory. For some time the Lombards had again been threatening to invade Rome. In 788, Charlemagne defeated them and extended his Frankish rule into the northern half of Italy. Like his father Pepin, Charlemagne gave land to the pope and assured him of protection. Toward the end of the 700s, he brought Bavaria, on the eastern border, under his rule. In order to keep his huge kingdom in peace and order, Charlemagne became a king constantly on the move. He lived in the saddle except during the coldest months of winter.

Image Breakers in the Eastern Church

While Charlemagne ruled most of Christianized Europe, events in the Eastern Church had effects on the entire Christian Church. About fifty years before Charlemagne's time, the Byzantine emperor Leo III issued an order banning icons—that is, crucifixes, statues, and paintings—from all church buildings. **Iconoclasts**, or "image breakers," tore down gorgeous religious artworks and even plastered over intricate mosaics. A partial reason for the emperor's attitude was the fact that Byzantine Christians often overstressed these images, seeming to make them into idols—just as the pagan Romans and Greeks had done long before. At the same time, the large Muslim and Jewish populations believed that the first of the Ten Commandments forbade the making of religious images. Their rejection of images was one reason that they did not accept Christianity.

So concerned was the Eastern emperor about images that he once sent his fleet to Italy to force the pope in Rome to obey his orders to remove images from the churches. However, the ships were wrecked in a storm in the Adriatic Sea, and the orders were never carried out. Later emperors, with some exceptions, were also iconoclasts; some even ordered the mutilation of Christians who possessed images by blinding them or cutting off their ears, noses, or hands.

Finally in 787, after sixty years of iconoclasm in the East, a council of bishops was allowed to meet in Nicaea. The council reinstated the Church's teaching that images, if used properly, can help Christians worship God. Although iconoclasm did not die out immediately in the East, the teaching of the Church was clear. Eventually this teaching made it possible for the Greek churches to use religious images again.

In the West the people had long prayed before statues and mosaics as sources of inspiration. However, a problem related to this developed at the Council of Frankfort. This council, called by Charlemagne and approved by the pope, received from Constantinople a copy of the statement of the Council of Nicaea (II) translated into Latin from the original Greek. Though the Ecumenical Council of Nicaea condemned the image breakers, the Latin translation seemed to say just the opposite. So bad was the translation that the bishops at Frankfort, representing not only Charlemagne's kingdom but also England and Italy, refused to accept the statement as the true teaching of the Church. This was an unfortunate situation. The two main parts of the Church, speaking different languages, were beginning to have trouble understanding each other.

Ties Loosen Between East and West

In the year 800 an event occurred in Rome that was another sign that East and West were beginning to pull apart. At the Christmas Mass, Pope Leo III unexpectedly crowned Charlemagne emperor of the Romans. For more than three hundred years there had been no emperor in the West. During that time it was understood that the Byzantine ruler living at Constantinople was emperor of both West and East, and that the pope was a subject of the Eastern emperor. Clearly the pope's crowning of Charlemagne signaled a break away from the East by the pope. At protecting and aiding the West, the Eastern emperor had been ineffectual at best, an obstacle at worst. Most of the barbarians who had overrun the Roman Empire were now citizens of it. It was Charlemagne who had succeeded in uniting most of the West after almost five hundred years of trouble. Consequently it seemed right that, although he was one of the former invaders—the Franks—he was now himself emperor of the Romans.

As emperor, Charlemagne was greatly interested in governing according to Roman traditions of law. He could read Latin, and he appointed educated men of his time—mostly priests, monks, and bishops—to government positions. He centered the empire in the Frankish capital, Aachen (*ah*-kuhn), near the Rhine River.

At Aachen, Charlemagne started a palace school, bringing the best teachers from all parts of the empire. The head of the school was **Alcuin**, an Anglo-Saxon monk who had been a pupil of Bede. The books used in the palace school were the work of many generations of monks who had spent years copying the writings of learned people. Valuing the work of the monks in education, Charlemagne encouraged the building of Benedictine monasteries throughout the empire. And his interest in scholarship brought large numbers of monks from beyond the empire, particularly the Irish, who were eager to share their own heritage of learning.

Charlemagne also felt a strong responsibility for the religious life of his Christian subjects. He promoted the adoption of the liturgy used in Rome. He had his scholars search for the best copies of the Bible available in Latin. Sometimes his interest in religion carried him too far, as when he tried to make decisions for the church councils. Yet his interference was rather minimal, and the protection he afforded the Church in the West was welcome relief from the long periods of being vulnerable to invading forces.

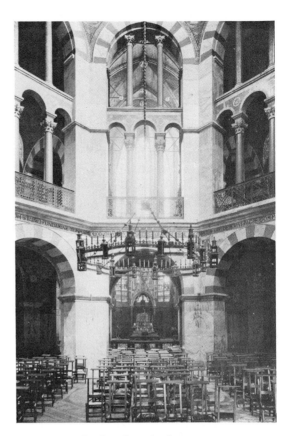

Charlemagne's chapel at Aachen

Feudalism: The Way of Life for the Middle Ages

Charlemagne's great Frankish Empire, which people thought of as the Roman Empire, disappeared within less than a hundred years after his death in 814. After Charlemagne's son and successor Louis the Pious died, his sons inherited and divided the empire according to Frankish custom. By 870 the empire was split into two parts, with Louis the German ruling the eastern part and Charles the Bald the western section. Centuries later these territories became modern France and Germany.

Louis and Charles were weak rulers, unable to protect the people in times of danger. The people of Paris realized that their king could not help them when forty thousand Vikings began attacking their city. The *Vikings* (the word means "sea rovers") swooped down from Scandinavia in their long, narrow boats. The Parisian leader Count Odo and his troops held off the invaders for ten months. When the king finally arrived in Paris, all he could do was bribe the Vikings to spare the city. He gave them gold and allowed them to go up the Seine River to plunder inland territories. If the local forces had not been strong enough, the people of Paris would have died waiting for their king to come.

This system of local government and defense, which was a part of **feudalism** mentioned earlier, had really begun developing in the 600s. By the late 800s it was an entrenched way of life. Under feudalism a local leader protected the people of his area in return for their service to him. This **lord** rented land to his **vassals** in return for their military service in his small army of fighting horsemen. The lord and his vassals had **serfs** who worked the land in return for their food and housing.

Feudal lords belonged to two classes of society: **counts,** who were the richest men in an area about the size of a county; and **churchmen,** such as bishops or abbots of monasteries. The churchmen owned land, but their vassals were not slaves and were not treated as such. Bishops and abbots, if they were living up to their Christian faith, respected vassals as people redeemed by Jesus Christ. The counts and other secular lords usually respected their vassals' rights, because they needed them for battle. The most important right a vassal had was the right to be judged by peers, that is, one's equals.

The serfs were the lowest class in the feudal system. They were not soldiers in the lord's army but rather were farmers or servants in the manor. Serfs generally lived on the same piece of land all their lives. Knowing that his serfs had to be kept strong and healthy if they were to serve him well, the lord or the master usually took fairly good care of them—although serfs generally lived only a bit better than the lord's horses. Clearly, living conditions during the early feudal times were hard, as can be seen by the fact that the population in Europe in A.D. 900 was at its lowest since the end of the Roman Empire in the West. Hard work, unsanitary living conditions, primitive health care, scarce food, and frequent warfare accounted for many deaths at an early age.

Lords and wealthy vassals lived in castles. In the tenth century, castles were simple stone structures, but eventually they became more elaborate. With the lord would live his lady, their children, some knights who had no land of their own yet, the personal servants of the family, and maybe a priest. The serfs lived in huts usually located near the castle, so that they could hide there in case of attack. Everyone at the castle rose with the sun, said a brief prayer, ate a simple breakfast of bread and diluted wine. There was much work to do; life was not luxurious. The lord supervised all operations on his land: farming, making lumber, shepherding, and so on. After all, the manor—the entire estate of the lord—was a self-sufficient unit that could not depend on financial aid from any central government. The manor was involved in a political unit larger

Baptism and Reconciliation

Poor communications accounted for many of the problems in having a common liturgical practice during the Middle Ages. Nevertheless, several major developments were going on concerning the practices and beliefs about Baptism and Reconciliation.

Infant Baptism was common practice now. As the nomadic tribes were converted, whole families would be baptized together. Eventually most Europeans were Christian and were used to the notion that Baptism was celebrated for infants. Sometimes midwives baptized children who were only minutes old. Confirmation was separated from the rite of Baptism because it seemed appropriate only for adults. Frequently people went through their entire lives without being confirmed.

Another factor prompting the Baptism of infants was the high mortality rate among children. Fearing for the souls of their children, parents sought early Baptism. Gradually a theology of "original sin" was used to explain the necessity of infant Baptism. Saint Augustine had taught that all persons are born with the original sin of Adam on their souls. This belief was based on the story from Genesis of the fall of Adam and Eve. They and all their descendants were banished from the Garden of Eden because of their sin. Consequently their descendants inherited the guilt from the first sin and needed to be cleansed of it by Baptism.

Since infants now received Baptism, how would adults be absolved from their sins? Remember that for the early Christians, Reconciliation was reserved for one time in a person's life—usually right before death. The traditional penances had been extremely harsh, were done in public, and were called for only in cases of the most serious of sins—murder, for example. In response to the change in circumstances, the Irish monks had developed the practice of private confessions. In this manner, adults could return repeatedly to be reconciled from their sins and be given spiritual direction. The rite of Reconciliation was now administered for even minor sins as people tried to make their lives better. By the 900s, even though public confessions and penance were still the official means of reconciliation in the Church, private confessions had almost completely erased this practice.

Unfortunately, the private rite of Reconciliation was symbolic of a loss of the sense of community that had existed earlier in a smaller Church. In addition, an attitude developed that frequent confessions could substitute for a virtuous life. The private rite also gave rise to the development of the penitential books. These books guided the priest in his selection of the proper penance for each sin. Most priests found it difficult to select suitable penances. And the penitent might be the castle lord who fed and clothed the priest; thus, the priest needed some outside authority for his penances. In the books the sins were listed on one side of the page and penalties on the other. For instance, if a person were gluttonous, he or she had to do one day's penance. Most of the penalties were strict but seemed lighter than the old public penances. More importantly, people in this time span saw their lives as a struggle toward God and away from the Devil; so the stakes in this struggle were high, and the penalties for sin should be just as high.

than itself only in times of war when a king, his lords, and their vassals would band together for mutual protection.

The Church had its place in the feudal system. On the local level, most manors had a resident priest who looked after the spiritual welfare of the lord, the lord's family, and everyone who lived on the landholding. The **chaplain** had a status far above that of a serf, but perhaps equivalent to that of the master of the horses or the falconer—depending on the interests of the lord. Most secular priests were literate but not well educated. If they wanted a peaceful life, they stayed in their place and out of politics.

Some monasteries, on the other hand, had large landholdings—usually given to them by lords or kings over long periods of time. The abbot became, in status, a lord. The monastery had vassals who actually looked after most of the property, while the monks spent their time

A Day in the Life of a Christian Lady of the Manor

At 5:00 A.M., the rooster's crowing and the noise from servants became too much for Lady Anna. She rose quickly, as did her husband, the lord of the castle. While the manor's monk chanted matins outside her chamber, the lady was helped into her warm apparel by her ladies-in-waiting. While walking down the steep stairs to the chapel, she listed in her mind the good deeds that her spiritual adviser had indicated for her to do. Mass took but a short time. Most of the family were there, and several ladies-in-waiting—although it usually annoyed Lady Anna when Jeanine dozed off. After chapel the lady and her lord talked a bit as they waited for a breakfast of bread and watered-down wine. The lord had to be gone for a few days to see the king. Lady Anna would be in charge, but then she was used to this because her husband was frequently called to arms by the king and was gone for months at a time.

Nevertheless, today she did not have to worry about the three hundred people who lived outside the castle: the butchers, herdsmen, foresters, and their families. Her husband's orders had gone out; that should suffice to keep everyone busy for some days. She could concentrate on preparing the wool that would be made into the coarse cloth needed for new garments for all the inhabitants of the fief. The wool had to be cleaned, carded, woven, cut, and sewn. Then, too, she had to oversee the dozens of servants who cleaned the castle, preserved the newly processed pork, dried vegetables, and stocked the larders for winter. In the middle of all this she could expect to have to mend a serf's cut hand or leg—she was the closest thing to a doctor, and during harvest time serious cuts were all too frequent. By the big meal at 10:00 A.M., she was feeling the hectic pace. Of course, being pregnant with her eighth child did not help matters. She reflected cheerfully on her four healthy children, who would some-

day inherit the manor, and considered herself blessed that she had lost only three little ones —one at birth and two from illnesses.

In the afternoon, Lady Anna supervised work on the vegetable gardens—a few things were still growing. And she had to send out two of the servants for some medicinal herbs; already she was in short supply of certain herbs, and winter was coming. Luckily there were no visitors today. Usually she had to entertain some travelers. Yesterday their guests were two monks returning to Cluny and a young boy with his manservant who was going to a neighboring lord to begin service as a page.

Soon darkness called an end to work. Tonight she would not have to entertain but could have a leisurely meal with the inhabitants of the castle. Lady Anna might play the lute and sing—even though some people thought this beneath her. After seeing her children off to bed, Lady Anna went to her own bed chamber and said her prayers, begging God to look after her husband—to protect him from robbers who lurked in the forests or from a chance meeting with a Viking band. She also prayed for the safe delivery of her baby and for her other children; word had reached her ears of a new and deadly disease that had broken out about 100 kilometers away. While she kept this news to herself, she pleaded with God that it might spare her family, the serfs, and herself. Lady Anna crawled into bed exhausted but knowing that she was very fortunate too. Most people were far worse off than she.

praying, studying, and educating. Many monasteries were small, and in these the monks continued the tradition of work and prayer. But again, the monastery had to be a self-sufficient unit—both to feed and clothe its members and to ensure its protection too.

Certainly even in this era there were traveling merchants who peddled goods such as grindstones, iron utensils and tools, salt, and spices. However, these items were not plentiful. The roads were mere paths, and travelers were frequently held up by robbers. Many lords demanded payment of tolls from people passing through their lands. Then, too, the seacoasts, areas near rivers, and border territories were being invaded by a new wave of barbarians.

The Vikings in the West

The new barbarians of the 800s were the Vikings, who appeared suddenly on the seacoasts. Their boats were long and narrow, able to float on the rivers as well as on the oceans, propelled by oars and by one tall, squarish sail. The Vikings were the best sailors in Europe. As they rowed, they had their shields lined up on each side of the boat and their sharp iron axes handy. The first Vikings came as pirates —attacking swiftly, looting, and then quickly disappearing. Later Vikings came to stay.

Scandinavia spawned these fierce tribes of Vikings. Their homelands were rocky. The summers were short. The sea was their main source of food, and fishing voyages prompted exploration. The Norwegian Vikings discovered islands to the west of them and sailed as far as Iceland, possibly even to the North American coast. Eventually they landed in Scotland and England. Attracted by the large, prosperous-looking churches, monasteries, and castles, they began to raid and carry away rich loot. Other sea rovers landed in Ireland and, after typically bloody battles, settled in large enough numbers to set up a Norwegian kingdom in Dublin that lasted about two hundred years. As they intermarried with the Irish, they began adopting some of the local customs—including religion. By about 950 the Norsemen ("men from the North") held large areas of Ireland in their control.

At the same time other Vikings, usually identified as Danes, landed on the east coast of England in the Anglo-Saxon kingdoms. Soon the Vikings controlled about half the island. They built strategic forts along the eastern coasts that served as bases of operations. The Christian Anglo-Saxons were divided into small kingdoms with very little unity among them. By the same token, the average man—the serf—having little or no skill as a soldier, was no match for the fierce Norsemen. Even the walled towns were inadequate protection against the Vikings. As the Danes advanced each year, they took control of one kingdom after another; and then, after a few

A woodcarving of a dragon's head, like the ones that decorated bows of the sleek Viking ships

years, these rugged seamen settled down to farming. By the time Alfred succeeded to the throne of Wessex, which included a long strip on the south coast of England, the invaders held a large part of eastern England known as the Danelaw.

Alfred the Great spent more than half of his thirty-year reign fighting the Danes. He was the only Anglo-Saxon king able to stop them. Alfred made a treaty with the Danes that allowed the Danes to continue governing the territories they possessed but forbade them to go beyond the Danelaw. As usual, the treaty also included acceptance of Christian Baptism by the Viking king. Even after the treaty there were battles. Eventually Alfred took London from the Danes and was proclaimed king of the English for this deed.

Other Vikings explored the channel and northern shores of the western Frankish kingdom, present-day France. Soon they controlled a large area that is today called Normandy, derived from the names by which the Vikings were known—Northmen, Norsemen, or Normans. Once they had settled into this territory, Rollo, their leader, made a treaty with the Frankish king; the Normans agreed to adopt the Christian religion and the French language of the people around them. Within relatively few years the Normans were building churches instead of destroying them. In fact, a distinctive church architecture of the period is known as Norman.

The Vikings in the East

During the years when Norwegian and Danish Vikings were taking over seacoast areas in western Europe, Vikings from Sweden discovered a trade route to Constantinople. They traveled eastern Europe from top to bottom, about a thousand miles each way, using the north-south rivers between the Baltic and the Black Seas. Portaging their boats using log rollers, they brought furs and walrus tusks south to Greek and Muslim traders. Though outnumbered by the Slavs in this region of eastern Europe, the Vikings soon controlled towns such as Novgorod and Kiev. As elsewhere, they settled among the people living there—the Rus—giving their own Viking names to various events, places, and people. After more than a thousand years this region is still known as Russia.

The sea-roving Vikings encountered Christianity in Ireland, Britain, and France. Word of the different religion spread back home. Soon after the Vikings had invaded these areas, some daring missionaries voyaged to Scandinavia. The kings of Denmark and Sweden gave such missionaries as **Ansgar** their royal support. Ansgar, who was bishop of northern German areas near Denmark, built the first Christian church in Sweden. Though other Viking leaders later brought back the old religions for a time, eventually all of the Scandinavian countries became Christian.

While the Vikings who invaded western Europe found settled Christian people living a feudal existence, those who traveled the rivers of eastern Europe had a different experience. Eastern Europe was populated by the Slavs, whose name comes from their word *slava,* meaning "glory." They are the ancestors of today's Czechoslovakians, Croatians, Serbians, Bulgarians, Poles, and Russians. Since they had no written language and little if any contact with the Roman Empire, not much is known of their early history. During the 400s and later, the small villages of the Slavs in east central Europe were attacked by the Huns. Consequently the Slavs began to move westward into the lands abandoned by the Germanic tribes that were breaking into the crumbling Roman Empire.

The Slavs were farmers, hunters, and fishermen who had little skill at warfare. When attacks came, they tended to abandon their villages and wait in the forests until the marauders were gone. However, during the 800s a Slav state called Greater Moravia did develop. Accordingly missionaries started arriving—first from the Latin Church of the Frankish kingdom and then from the Greek Church of the Byzantine Empire.

The German-speaking missionaries who first came to Moravia had very little success since they did not know the Slavic language. The Slavic duke, leader of the Moravians, realizing the language problem of the Frankish monks, asked the emperor at Constantinople for help.

Cyril and Methodius

The emperor sent to the Moravians two brothers, **Cyril** and **Methodius**, sons of a Greek family. They were well qualified to work in Moravia because some years earlier they had lived with the Slavs who had their homes on the north shore of the Black Sea. They learned the basic Slavic language. Cyril and Methodius then devised a Slavic alphabet because there was no written Slavic language. Subsequently they translated the Gospels into the newly developed written Slavonic.

With the help of these two missionaries, the Slavs in Moravia soon heard the Good News preached. Conversions followed, and soon congregations of Slavs were worshiping in their own language. When some German bishops heard about this, they raised objections to the pope. The bishops argued that Catholics for many years had celebrated Mass either in Greek, the first language used, or in Latin, but never in Slavonic. Cyril and Methodius were called to Rome to explain what they were doing. After some hesitation the pope agreed that the Slavs in Moravia could continue celebrating the Mass and the sacraments in their own language.

Cyril suddenly died in Rome, but Methodius, now a bishop, returned to Moravia. When the Slavic duke of Moravia was defeated and

forced from power by the German Frankish king, Methodius was imprisoned for almost three years—finally to be released only by order of the pope. Because the new duke of Moravia was under the power of German advisers, he asked the pope to remove the Slavic missionaries. Consequently, Methodius's followers went south to Bulgaria where they had great success under the protection of the Greek Church.

The Bulgarians were originally a warrior people who had invaded the Slavic tribes living just west of the Black Sea, near the Balkan Mountains. They settled among the Slavs, intermarried, and adopted the local language. For many years they had periodic skirmishes with the Byzantine Empire to the south. Eventually peace developed between the Bulgarians and the Byzantines. The Bulgarians converted to Christianity about the year 870 when their leader Czar Boris I put himself under the authority of the Greek Church.

Also during the 800s another army of warriors galloped out of Asia and conquered a large part of Moravia north of the Danube River. The Magyars (*mahg*-yahrz), who were ancestors of the Hungarians, raided northern Italy, central France, and Germany. The German emperor, Otto I, stopped them in 955. The Magyars settled down in the area of present-day Hungary, establishing themselves as a nation. When their king Stephen I converted, the slow process of Christianization began throughout the whole country. The pope crowned Stephen king of Hungary and recognized him for his dedication to the Church; eventually he was acknowledged as a saint.

The Poles, like the Hungarians, were a new, independent nation, and they wanted to stay free from the Germans. King Boleslaw the Brave worked to strengthen Christian faith in Poland—a faith brought by Bohemian missionaries. Making Poland a vassal state of the pope, he thus protected it from the German emperor. Poland and Hungary received missionaries from the West and formed the eastern boundary of the Latin Church.

Russia became part of the Eastern Church. Vladimir I, the Russian ruler, brought Christian teachers from Constantinople. He married the daughter of the Byzantine emperor and through her began learning about Christianity. He was baptized in 989. Vladimir encouraged the missionaries, at least in part because they taught people how to read and write in the newly developed Slavic language.

By the year 1000 most of the Slavs in Europe were Christians. To the Latin Church belonged the Croatians, Czechoslovakians, Moravians, and Poles (as well as the non-Slavic Hungarians); to the Greek Church belonged the Russians, Bulgarians, and Serbians. At this time there were three official languages in which Christians celebrated the liturgy: Latin in western Europe, from Ireland to Poland; Slavonic in east-central Europe; and Greek in the northern coastal countries of the Mediterranean.

Problems of Church and State

The rulers in both East and West treated the Church as a department of their governments. In the East the Byzantine emperors controlled the patriarch of Constantinople to such an extent that they sometimes decided on what should be taught as part of the Christian message. This kind of interference led to misunderstandings between the eastern and western parts of the Church that continued off and on through several centuries.

One of the most serious problems between the East and the West occurred in the later 800s when the patriarch Ignatius refused Communion to an important official of the Byzantine government. The Eastern emperor replaced Ignatius with a layman named Photius who became an instant patriarch by receiving all the orders from acolyte to bishop within a few days. When the pope ruled that Photius was not a legitimate patriarch, the emperor called a council at Constantinople and excommunicated the pope—in effect throwing him out of the Church, at least as far as the Eastern emperor was concerned. A few years later a new emperor put Ignatius back into office; Rome and Constantinople became friendly again.

In the West the civil rulers at various levels usually had the final word in the appointments of bishops, but they seldom interfered with church teachings. Under the feudal system, bishops and abbots often served as government officials because they were educated and in charge of church lands. Local dukes or counts were naturally interested in putting loyal supporters in as bishops. And a bishop chosen for his ability to manage a farm or to lead an army would not be expected to be especially concerned about preaching the Gospel. Worse, a rich man could buy himself the office of bishop, even though the Church condemned this as the sin of **simony** (named after Simon the Magician who tried to buy from Saint Peter the power of healing). Some bishops passed on their religious offices to relatives, regardless of whether or not they were fit for the work.

The pope's control of far-flung churches was limited by the information he had about them. Messages took months to reach Rome—if they got there at all. Also, during the 900s especially, the popes had many of the same problems —maybe even worse ones—in Rome itself. Local barons of the Roman area, who were supposedly vassals of the pope, wanted to control the appointment of the pope. They disregarded the fact that the pope was more than a feudal lord, that he was primarily head of the Church. As a result, the rich Roman families did more harm to the Church than outside enemies ever did. In their family feuds they did not hesitate to use force to get their candidates on the papal throne. They disregarded the Roman people and clergy who had been electing popes since the time of Peter. On one occasion the losers opened the gates of Rome to allow the Saracens to come into the city and rob the sacred places—even the tombs of Peter and Paul. In the period from 896 to 900, there were six different popes. One of these was strangled, and another's body was thrown into the Tiber by his enemies who had dug up the corpse from its proper grave.

The only way to end this feuding over the papal office seemed to be to call on the power of the German emperor. In 962, Pope John XII, rated by some historians as the most unworthy pope of all time, called on King Otto I of Germany for help against the Roman nobles. When Otto arrived in Rome with his army, John crowned him Roman emperor, and the pope and nobles pledged him loyalty. No sooner had Otto marched north again than John joined a conspiracy against him. Otto came back and called a meeting of bishops to depose John and to elect one of his own assistants as bishop of Rome. For almost a hundred years after this, the popes were usually chosen by the German emperors. Most of the popes were improvements over the past, but few were suitable spiritual leaders. Only a couple were genuine saints. In any case, the control of the papacy by a secular head of state was in itself an interference with the freedom of the people in the Church to govern themselves.

Cluny

After the year 900 an event occurred that was eventually a powerful help toward bringing back a renewed Christian spirit to the Church. In east-central France a small group of Benedictine monks was given land for a new monastery. This gift from Duke William was nothing unusual because many local leaders built monasteries as signs of their faith. However, this new monastery at Cluny was different. It was independent of any control by the local lord. The monks selected their abbot, who only answered to the pope. The monks at Cluny lived simply, prayed long and devoutly, gave food to the poor, and generally inspired others to take the message of Jesus seriously.

Soon other monasteries adopted the Cluny reforms and asked to be governed, through their own superiors, by the abbot of Cluny. Enthusiasm for a better Christian life spread outside the monastery especially through those students who attended school there and eventually became priests or bishops. Cluny's influence on the spiritual life of Europe lasted almost two hundred years. All this was possible because Cluny was free from feudalism. It was not governed by an outsider but by a monk. While feudalism as a system did protect local areas and became the standard social system of Europe, it did not prove to be the proper organization for the Church of Jesus.

Focus on the Models

The period from 700 to 1000 saw the Word of God heralded throughout huge tracts of land, to people speaking completely different languages. Two missionaries, Cyril and Methodius, even had to create a written language for the Slavs. While many Baptisms resulted from allegiance to a newly converted king, the seed of faith was planted and the monks and nuns would water it. Christians did perceive themselves as belonging to a People of God; they had a strong sense of divine power and hoped for final mercy. For the average man or woman—especially the serfs—a happy afterlife in heaven was a source of hope in a world of bloody invasions, rampant disease, and unjust overseers. Despite extremely poor communications, the sacramental life of the Church was becoming more systematized and common.

Even so, three languages were used—Latin, Greek, and Slavonic—and the language groups did celebrate in somewhat different fashions.

The Church was the Sacrament of Jesus present in the world. Even though the Church at Rome was in chaos and under the thumbs of a succession of greedy Roman nobles and German kings, all over the rest of Europe—especially with the reforms from the abbey of Cluny—the Church gave spiritual nourishment to the people. It was a Servant too. Monasteries built into their rules service to the poor and education for the ignorant. As in any age, unknown Christians served their neighbors; some charitable souls were sainted, but most lived their lives trying to be good, do good, and survive.

As Institution the Church went through a disastrous three centuries. Feudalism divided Europe into small landholdings. Local churches relied on local lords and were often subject to the whims of those lords. Priests were poorly educated in general and were appointed by the lords. Add to this set of problems poor communication, and the Church was almost impossible to unite institutionally. While most paid lip service to the notion that the pope was the leader of the Church, he was often in no position to provide consistent guidance for the faithful because popes were easily and often replaced by secular rulers. At this time in the Church, primarily the sustained faith and devoted practice of the common people kept the spiritual life of the Church a reality.

Review Questions and Activities

1) Why was the work of Bede so significant, especially in light of what was happening all over Europe?

2) Veneration of saints is still common today but less so than in this period from 700 to 1000. Why do you think that people today are skeptical about miracles happening?

3) What were the major contributions of Saint Boniface? Try to imagine what it would have been like for him to cross from Amsterdam to Munich in those times. How many miles would he have traveled? Describe what the roads would have been like. Where would he have slept at night? What dangers would he face? If necessary, do some research about this period.

4) Why was Pepin such an important figure in the church history of this period? of later centuries?

5) Why did the crowning of Charlemagne as Holy Roman emperor by the pope change the relationship between the Eastern and Western empires and parts of the Church?

6) What is an iconoclast? How did the dispute over icons illustrate the splits that were growing in the Church?

7) Describe what feudalism was and how it operated. Why did this system of society emerge? What was the role of the Church in feudal society? Are there any societies today that are feudal? For instance, look into countries like El Salvador. How could they be considered feudal?

8) Why was it so difficult to have common practice of the sacraments during this time span? What developments took place in the celebration of Baptism? Reconciliation? Why did changes take place with these sacraments?

9) How did the Vikings aid the spread of Christianity?

10) Why was it that some central and eastern European countries used Latin, others Slavonic, and others Greek? How did politics, in part, determine the development of the Church in these areas?

11) What major contribution did Cyril and Methodius make toward the heralding of the Word to the Slavs?

12) Why did the Church have to rely so much on various kings and nobles? How did this reliance harm the Church and its ability to be the Sacrament of Christ present in the world?

13) Why did people welcome the reforms of Cluny?

Personal Reflection Exercise

People in the early Middle Ages had a real sense of their dependence on God. They knew that some Divine Being ruled the universe. God punished but also performed miracles. How would you describe people's reactions to the idea of miracles happening today? How do you react to the idea of miracles? Do you ever pray for something miraculous to happen? What would it say about someone's attitude toward God if he or she did not believe that miracles were possible? Do you think that there are miracles happening now right in front of you that you just are not seeing?

10
The High Middle Ages: 1000–1300

The years 1000 to 1300 are considered to be the High Middle Ages. There was less turmoil in the lives of the ordinary citizens of Europe compared to the previous two or three centuries. This is not to say that living conditions were a great deal better, but there were fewer invasions and the social structures were more stable. The Church was the center of life—almost every person in Europe belonged to it. Pockets of Christians survived in the Middle East, and Constantinople still held out against the armies of Islam.

Even though most Europeans were Christians, there were disagreements among them about some aspects of the faith. Internal arguments in the Church did encourage two positive developments: one was the rise of a new type of religious order and the other was the growth of theological scholarship.

The High Middle Ages saw the building of magnificent cathedrals in Chartres, Rheims, and York that still dazzle architects today. Then too, the Crusades, while seeming barbarous to us today, brought back new knowledge from the East. At this same time, great universities evolved from cathedral schools. In short, the events of these centuries laid the foundations for many cultural, artistic, literary, and scientific traditions. Most importantly, the impetus for these developments came from the Church.

An Urban Culture Develops

By A.D. 1000 much of the land able to be cultivated in Europe was the property of large landowners. The only new land being brought under the plow was in isolated areas, and the cultivators were groups of monks belonging to a new and strict order—the **Cistercians**. Founded in 1098, they were an offshoot of the Benedictines. The Cistercians emphasized manual work rather than running schools or pursuing scholarship. These monks sought solitude at the edges of Europe. And, since the lands they selected were difficult to farm, they developed new agricultural techniques—such as new ways of draining swamps and the use of crop rotation. Soon these techniques were being employed by farmers all over Europe. Increased agricultural output in turn improved the quality of life just enough so that the population began growing slightly too. In addition, since there was less war, the flow of goods throughout Europe increased too. These goods needed marketplaces.

Towns began springing up throughout Europe and provided jobs for those not needed in agriculture. Towns were markets for goods, and centers of administration for both Church and state. Most towns grew around castles or monasteries, others along the roads traveled by merchants. Skilled workers came to live and work where there were enough people to hire them or to buy the things they made—such as farming tools, shoes, the spinning wheels for weaving cloth, and swords. As the towns grew, these workmen formed **guilds,** or unions. The guilds regulated the training of young men learning a trade and, at the same time, got a fair price for their work. Guilds usually chose patron saints and took part in church liturgies with displays of banners and statues.

One of the chief employers of the guilds was the Church. In building the great cathedrals, the Church needed skilled workers—stonemasons, carpenters, glassmakers, and artists. Thus, the Church encouraged and supported these guilds—out of which a whole new class of free citizens evolved.

Merchants came regularly to the towns with goods to be sold, and at harvest times peasants brought in their surplus crops. A large town had a population of about ten thousand people. At these, there were fairs where a large number of merchants gathered, forming a kind of shopping center. The fairs were also places of entertainment with singers, jugglers, and acrobats. All this opened up the world for the townspeople as they saw things brought in from various parts of Europe and the East, sometimes at great risk.

Merchants' wagons moving at a walker's pace were easy prey for robbers. Shipping long distances on rivers was no easy task either. England sent wool across the channel to the north shores of France, Belgium, and Holland,

where it was woven into cloth. Some of the cloth eventually reached Venice where it was colored with dyes that the Italian ships brought from the East—usually Syria or Palestine. By about the year 1200 shipping improved with better use of sails and with a new invention called the compass. Harbors and lighthouses along the north Mediterranean coast improved, thus cutting down on sailing time and reducing the risk of losing valuable goods in the sea. While the threat of pirates still remained, the presence of strong Italian and Byzantine fleets reduced the danger considerably.

With the increase of trade in Europe, the supply of money began to increase, especially in the form of gold coins used by the Italian merchants of Venice and Florence. A simple banking system began to be employed for the exchange of coins from various countries. Christian law forbade Jews from owning land; this restriction led to their becoming merchants and bankers. Furthermore, since early Christian teaching had forbidden charging interest on loans of money, the result was that generally only Jewish merchants became bankers and moneylenders. Later, only the excessive charging of interest, called **usury,** was forbidden to Christians. That Jewish business people historically are connected with banking and loaning money is thus a result of Christian practice. Ironically, Jews would later be persecuted for being too successful in roles that they were pushed into by Christians.

The astrolabe as well as the compass were necessary instruments for medieval navigators. The astrolabe measures the altitude of planets and stars, from which the time and a ship's position can be calculated.

The Cathedrals: Sources of Solace and Inspiration

As the towns grew, new landmarks began to rise among the small wooden houses in which most people lived. These were the magnificent cathedrals, built mostly after A.D. 1000. The huge buildings of stone, with colorful stained-glass windows and many statues in arched recesses in the walls, were so well built that many of them are still standing today— over eight hundred years later. The cathedrals were the works of master craftsmen who knew how to carve images and designs in stone. They knew how to hoist huge blocks three or four hundred feet into the air and to fit them together to create beautiful pictures in three dimensions. They had no power tools or engines for cranes—but they did invent creative techniques for completing the cathedrals. Thus, the building of cathedrals made significant contributions to architecture and engineering. A long time was required to construct the cathedrals and even longer to furnish them completely. Money often ran out; new revenues had to be raised from the bishop, king, and lords. The common people contributed chickens or pigs to sustain the craftsmen.

The cathedrals were meant to be expressions of Christian faith, inspiring the people with the beauty of God. The cathedrals were used for worship of God in various ways. The front enclosure—the **choir** or **chancel**—was reserved for the priests and monks who sang and recited the divine office (the series of psalms and prayers organized for use during each liturgical season) several times each day. On the sides of the cathedral were small chapels for the Mass; in some of these chapels saints and kings were buried beneath the stone floors. The main room, called the **nave,** was used for the common people's Mass, and in a section of the nave was the font for Baptisms. Most cathedrals also had large pulpits where long Sunday sermons were given—one of the few sources of religious education for the people.

Romanesque and Gothic Cathedrals

Two rather distinct types of cathedrals—the *Romanesque* and the *Gothic*—were built during the years 1000–1300. The first type, named after the Roman style, employed massive pillars to hold up stone roofs that were used to replace the flammable wood beamed ceilings. Most Romanesque cathedrals have a more horizontal appearance than do the Gothic cathedrals. Frequently the pillars holding up the rounded arching ceiling would be decorated in styles similar to Roman buildings in pre-Christian times. Large mosaics decorated the spaces above the altars; statuary was not as abundant as in the Gothic churches. Romanesque cathedrals gave an aura of peace and solidity—perhaps this is the reason that many of the churches of monasteries were Romanesque. This style of architecture flourished in the eleventh century, but declined in use after 1150.

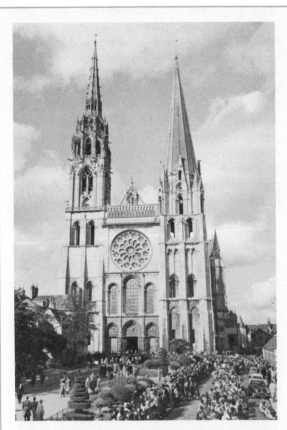

The Gothic style was followed from 1130 to 1250. These churches tended to be much taller and gave the appearance of lightness and delicacy. In order to employ more windows than the Romanesque churches, the walls were supported by flying buttresses. Instead of rounded or barrel arches, Gothic arches were pointed. They built tall towers reaching into the heavens: Notre Dame of Paris (right)—114 feet; Chartres (above)—123 feet; Beauvais—157 feet. When one considers that structural steel and cranes were unheard of, buildings of this height must have seemed miraculous to medieval men and women. The windows were stained-glass storybooks depicting scenes from the Bible or, sometimes, from nature. Statues stared out from all parts of the cathedrals—representing saints poised in prayer and sinners being cast into the fires of hell. Even the rainspouts were carved into grimacing gargoyles or giggling children.

Though the cathedrals were intended primarily for worship, the people, especially those belonging to the guilds, frequently used them for meeting places or hiring halls; often pilgrims and poor travelers slept on the floors. There was no disrespect in this. Indeed, using God's house in these ways helped people to see God as a loving parent. In addition, the cathedral was a pictorial Bible for the illiterate poor.

Wealthy people usually could read—although even they might possess only one or two books. But every poor peasant could visit the cathedral and see the carvings and windows that told stories from the Bible. Adam, Eve, and the serpent are pictured in Eden and after the Fall. Christ can be seen dying, rising, and enthroned in heaven. Mary is the frequent subject of cathedral art. In summary, the cathedrals instructed people in the faith and were sources of inspiration, expressions of belief, places of solace, and centers of worship for life in the Middle Ages.

The Rise of Kings

After the year 1000, as the kings grew stronger, there was a gradual change in the governments of Europe. Eventually this rise of kingly power would profoundly influence the Church. Though local nobles still held much power, feudalism was slowly being weakened. Kings became strongest in England and France, less so in Germany and Spain. When thinking of these places, by the way, remember that these countries are not exactly the same today as they were then—their modern-day boundaries are now quite different.

Shortly after 1000, England was a part of the Scandinavian Empire under King Knut (kuh-*noot*), who ruled not only his own Denmark but Norway and a strip of Sweden as well. Then in 1066 England was conquered by the Normans under Duke William, ruler of Normandy in northwest France across the English Channel. By this time the Normans (or Norsemen) had adopted French culture. When William began his rule, French became the language of the English government, although the common people still spoke Anglo-Saxon—what we call Old English. Naturally many French words became incorporated into the English we use today. In 1150, King Henry II of England became ruler of the western half of France, from Normandy down to Spain. He had married Eleanor of Aquitaine, a French princess. This ruling of a part of France by an English monarch set the stage for conflict between the two nations—a conflict that would cause strife between English and French Christians.

Like the English kings, the kings of France had gradually strengthened their authority. At first, they were rulers of only a small area around Paris called the "Island of France." Each king was crowned with great ceremony in the cathedral at Rheims. However, not having much land, the king of France also did not have much power. Philip Augustus changed all this by conquering small areas one at a time. Then, as the towns flourished, he made treaties with them by which he garnered both men and money. Oddly enough, King John of England became a vassal of King Philip Augustus. He was king of England, but also a vassal of Philip because of the lands John had in France. As John's lord, Philip Augustus disapproved of John's marriage to a French woman; their disagreement led to war. In 1214, John lost the war and, with it, England's French lands. In this way Philip got control of more land than any of his vassals, and his power over them increased.

While the kings of France and England were consolidating power, the rulers of German lands had special problems—some of them coming from their relationship with the pope. Since the mid-900s when the pope placed a crown on the head of the German emperor Otto I, the German leaders considered themselves the successors to Charlemagne. In fact, people began to think of the German state as the Holy Roman Empire—that is, as an empire continuing the old Roman Empire but something more—a "Holy" Christian empire. Around the year 1000 this empire included not only lands where various Germanic people lived but also Switzerland, a strip of eastern France, and at later times most of Italy. The barons in the eastern part of Germany encouraged the peasants to move eastward into Slavic lands, especially into Poland, Bohemia,

and Moravia. This movement made the barons richer and more independent of their lords.

Adding to the problems of the German king was the fact that as Holy Roman emperor he was expected to be the protector of the pope. A special difficulty arose when **Pope Gregory VII** ruled that in the future neither the emperor nor any other government official could appoint bishops. Gregory wanted the Church to be free of politics. Of course, the king of Germany, Emperor Henry IV, objected. The argument worsened until Gregory excommunicated Henry and declared that Henry's subjects did not need to obey him any longer. Knowing that the German nobles would take advantage of the situation, the emperor went to see the pope in the middle of the winter of 1077. He stood barefoot in the snow outside the castle where Gregory was staying until the pope was ready to see him. After this humiliation and his penance, Henry was pardoned.

Once in control again at home, Henry continued to oppose the pope. At one point, he set up an antipope and marched on Rome. Gregory called on the Normans in southern Italy for help. They rescued the pope and took him south with them where he died a short time later. For a number of years trouble continued between the German emperors and the popes, partly because of the Papal States, which were located between the two parts of Italy ruled by the emperors. The pope was himself a feudal lord, and his small states were in danger of being caught in a squeeze. Thus, while the papal lands were intended for good purposes, they created a conflict with kings and lords.

The pope, in spite of disputes with kings and emperors, was the leader of the Church. His control over the politics in the new kingdoms was weakened by the nationalism, but he still wielded considerable power. Just as Gregory VII made Henry IV back down, so Pope Urban II was able to rally Europe to mount **Crusades** against the Muslims. For more than two hundred years armies of knights rode out from their homelands to fight in the Middle East. Many knew they would never return; their bones would bleach on a foreign desert. Yet the popes called and they followed. The

First Crusade, which set out in 1097, while intending to help the Byzantine Church actually added to the problems that the Christians of the East had with the leadership of the pope at Rome.

The Church Splits into East and West

As was discussed in the last chapter, during the 800s a temporary break between the Greek-speaking and Latin-speaking parts of the Church occurred over the appointment of the patriarch of Constantinople. This break was healed, but over the centuries real and substantive differences had begun to divide the churches of the East and the West. There were differences in language, customs, and religious practices. In 1054 a serious break occurred. Michael Cerularius, the patriarch of Constantinople, publicly declared that the two churches could not be united because of these differences. The real issue was the authority of the pope. While the bishop of Rome was considered the successor of Peter, the church in the East believed that the pope had taken far too much power away from the patriarchs—especially the patriarch of Constantinople. In addition, there were interpretations of theological matters that were disputed between East and West.

To reach an understanding of the issues, **Pope Leo IX** sent his representative to meet with Patriarch Michael at Constantinople. Tragically, Cardinal Humbert, head of the papal delegation, and Patriarch Michael seemed more interested in proving the other party wrong than in working for unity. While the two groups were arguing, Pope Leo died. Even though he was now without authority, Humbert excommunicated Michael and left Constantinople. Michael called a synod to condemn the action of the pope's representative and to claim that he was in complete charge of the Byzantine Church. The year 1054 is recorded as the date when the Latin and Greek churches split; however, the situation was not really clear-cut at that time.

In fact, less than twenty years after the Byzantine break the emperor at Constantinople asked Pope Gregory VII for help against the Turkish Muslims who had invaded eastern Asia Minor, not far from Saint Paul's hometown. Though the pope was in no position to help at the time, a later request from the emperor to Pope Urban II brought results. Urban called for a Crusade that would free Byzantine territory from the Turks and then would go down to take Jerusalem and the Holy Land from the Saracens. What made the matter urgent was that the Muslim Turks harassed Christians who were making pilgrimages to Jerusalem. For centuries the Arab Muslims had allowed Christians freedom to make the pilgrimage, but now difficulties arose. Despite the break of 1054, the pope wanted Christian armies from the West to help the Byzantines. As we will see, the unity in battle was short-lived.

The Crusades

The Crusades were seen by most people of the time as a great act of Christian faith. After all, the Muslims did not believe that Jesus Christ is the Son of God, yet they now had control over Jerusalem. The only thing to do was to get it back, by force if necessary. It probably would not have mattered so much if pilgrimages were not such an important part of Christian life during the Middle Ages. Some Christians would travel for months under great hardships to visit the shrines of saints, and especially, the place where Jesus died. Pilgrimages were expensive, and a person had to take time off from work for weeks, sometimes even months.

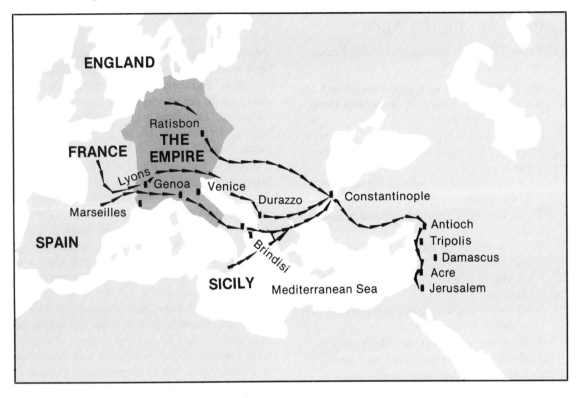

Much as the Crusades really did express the faith of Christians, they nevertheless showed the weakness of all human projects. Interested in grabbing power and wealth for themselves, the Crusade leaders often squabbled among themselves. The knights were frequently cruel in their victories. And, frequently, Crusades were even waged by Christians against other Christians.

In any case, with the blessings of Urban II, the First Crusade marched off. As a military action, it was successful. The Christian knights, most of them from France, recovered Byzantine territory from the Muslim Turks and then moved down the eastern shore of the Mediterranean. They captured Antioch from the Muslims and finally arrived at the walls of Jerusalem. A long siege followed. Finally in 1099 the knights broke through the walls. Crusaders massacred Jews and Muslims alike in a reign of terror that made the Muslims hate

the Christians for years to come. Four **Latin kingdoms** were set up along the coast of Syria and Palestine, and some Latin clergy and monks settled there.

The knights who returned from the First Crusade were honored as defenders of the faith; they also were granted **indulgences** by the Church—that is, all their sins were forgiven and they were remitted from all punishment for them. There were other more tangible rewards too. Most came back with loot to give their families. While they had been away, the Crusaders were immune from taxes. Their lands at home had been protected by the Church and the king. Those who stayed behind in the conquered territory could set up fiefs— or feudal estates—on land they never would have inherited back in France.

Two Attitudes About War from the Middle Ages

I. From "The Troubadour and Noble France," by Bertran de Born:

My heart is filled with gladness when I see
Strong castles besieged, stockades broken
  and overwhelmed,
Many vassals struck down
Horses of the dead and wounded roving at
  random.
And when battle is joined, let all men of
  good lineage
Think naught but the breaking of heads and
  arms,
For it is better to die than be vanquished
  and live.
I tell you I have no such joy as when I hear
  the shout
"On! On!" from both sides and the neighing
  of riderless steeds,
And groans of "Help me. Help me."
And when I see both great and small
Fall in the ditches and on the grass
And see the dead transfixed by spear
  shafts.
Lords, mortgage your domains, castles,
  cities,
But never give up war.

II. From the *Summa Theologica*, by Saint Thomas Aquinas (Part II–II, Q. 40, Art. 1)

Whether It Is Always Sinful to Wage War?

We proceed thus to the first Article:

Objection 1. It would seem that it is always sinful to wage war. Because punishment is not inflicted except for sin. Now those who wage war are threatened by Our Lord with punishment, according to Matth. xxvi. 52: *All that take the sword shall perish with the sword.* Therefore all wars are unlawful.

Obj. 2. Further, whatever is contrary to a Divine precept is a sin. But war is contrary to a Divine precept, for it is written (Matth. v. 39): *But I say to you not to resist evil;* and (Rom. xii. 19): *Not revenging yourselves, my dearly beloved, but give place unto wrath.* Therefore war is always sinful.

Obj. 3. Further, nothing, except sin, is contrary to an act of virtue. But war is contrary to peace. Therefore war is always a sin.

Obj. 4. Further, the exercise of a lawful thing is itself lawful, as is evident in scientific exercises. But warlike exercises which take place in tournaments are forbidden by the Church, since those who are slain in these trials are deprived of ecclesiastical burial. Therefore it seems that war is a sin in itself.

On the contrary, Augustine says in a sermon on the son of the centurion: *If the Christian Religion forbade war altogether, those who sought salutary advice in the Gospel would rather have been counselled to cast aside their arms, and to give up soldiering altogether. On the contrary, they were told: "Do violence to no man; . . . and be content with your pay." If he commanded them to be content with their pay, he did not forbid soldiering.*

I answer that, In order for a war to be just, three things are necessary. First, the authority of the sovereign by whose command the war is to be waged. For it is not the business of a private individual to declare war, because he can seek for redress of his rights from the tribunal of his superior. Moreover it is not the business of a private individual to summon together the people, which has to be done in wartime. And as the care of the common weal is committed to those who are in authority, it is their business to watch over the common weal of the city, kingdom or province subject to them. And just as it is lawful for them to have recourse to the sword in defending that common weal against internal disturbances, when they punish evil-doers, according to the words of the Apostle (Rom. xiii. 4): *He beareth not the sword in vain: for he is God's minister, an avenger to execute wrath upon him that doth evil;* so too, it is their business to have recourse to the sword of war in defending the common weal against external enemies. Hence it is said to those who are in authority (Ps. lxxxi. 4): *Rescue the poor: and deliver the needy out of the hand of the sinner;* and for this reason Augustine says (*Contra Faust.* xxii. 75): *The natural order conducive to peace among mortals demands that the power to declare and counsel war should be in the hands of those who hold the supreme authority.*

Secondly, a just cause is required, namely that those who are attacked, should be attacked because they deserve it on account of some fault. Wherefore Augustine says *(QQ. in Hept.,* qu. *x, super Jos.): A just war is wont to be described as one that avenges wrongs, when a nation or state has to be punished, for refusing to make amends for the wrongs inflicted by its subjects, or to restore what it has seized unjustly.*

Thirdly, it is necessary that the belligerents should have a rightful intention, so that they intend the advancement of good, or the avoidance of evil. Hence Augustine says (*De Verb. Dom.): True religion looks upon as peaceful those wars that are waged not for motives of aggrandizement, or cruelty, but with the object of securing peace, of punishing evil-doers, and of uplifting the good.* For it may happen that the war is declared by the legitimate authority, and for a just cause, and yet be rendered unlawful through a wicked intention. Hence Augustine says (*Contra Faust.* xxii. 74): *The passion for inflicting harm, the cruel thirst for vengeance, an unpacific and relentless spirit, the fever of revolt, the lust of power, and such like things, all these are rightly condemned in war.*

In 1133 Edessa, one of the four Latin kingdoms, fell to the Muslims. **Saint Bernard of Clairvaux**, the famous Cistercian, and other preachers prompted the kings of France and Germany to mount the Second Crusade to retake Edessa. It failed calamitously. By 1187 the brilliant Muslim commander Saladin had recaptured Jerusalem and all the other Crusader lands.

A Third Crusade was launched under the joint leadership of King Richard "the Lion-Hearted" of England and the kings of France and Germany. While they recovered a tiny strip of land on the coast of Palestine, it was hardly worth the devastating casualties they suffered—many of these inflicted by disease and by fighting among the Crusaders. Jerusalem remained in Saladin's hands. The original fervor of the First Crusade was lost; the Christian forces were quarreling among themselves, and many Crusaders were more concerned with booty than the fate of Jerusalem.

Inevitably there was a Fourth Crusade. **Pope Innocent III**, certainly one of the most powerful popes in history, was only able to rally a few French nobles to his call. The European kings were unwilling to invest money and manpower in what seemed like a lost cause. Pope Innocent's Crusaders decided to avoid the long march by land and to take the Mediterranean sea route instead. The Italian merchants of Venice agreed to transport the knights in their ships. While attempting to raise money to pay the Venetians, the Crusaders were approached by Alexius IV, son of a Byzantine emperor who had been deposed. Alexius offered to pay all the Crusaders' expenses if they would retrieve the throne for his father. Pinched for finances, they agreed.

The Fourth Crusade never even actually met the Muslim enemy. The Crusaders sailed southward around Greece, then up to Constantinople. After three days of attacks, they took the capital and began to loot and pillage it. They broke into churches and destroyed or stole precious shrines, even in Hagia Sophia. Christian knights vandalized the most beautiful Christian city in the world.

Back in Rome, Pope Innocent was in a rage with frustration; his army was out of control. The Crusaders went so far as to set up a Latin kingdom that included Constantinople, the eastern half of Greece, and parts of western Asia Minor. They appointed a Latin patriarch and imported Latin priests and monks. Naturally the Greek Christians were enraged more than ever against the Christians of Europe and the pope who led them. Though future leaders of the Byzantine Church were interested in reunion with the Western Church, the people themselves could not forget what their fellow Christians had done to their families, their homes, and their churches in the Fourth Crusade of 1204. Seventy years later, at the Council of Lyons, the patriarch of Constantinople accepted the pope as head of the Church, but when the news got back home, the Eastern bishops and people rejected this decision. The separation of the Christian Church into churches of the East and the West seemed irrevocable.

Some small Crusades followed. In 1212 the infamous Children's Crusade started out from France and Germany. A band of thousands of children marched toward the Mediterranean coast of Italy where they thought they would take boats to the Holy Land. Instead, when they got there, greedy slave traders captured them and sold them into bondage. Later, in the years 1228–29, Emperor Frederick II actually regained Jerusalem through negotiations with the Muslims, but the agreement was repudiated by the current pope because Frederick was under a ban of excommunication. The city reverted back to Muslim hands. King Louis IX of France mounted an assault on Jerusalem, but his Crusade, which lasted from 1248 to 1254, failed too. From this time on, the "Crusade fever" died. Europe had other, and even more serious, problems at home.

The Christian armies did not win back the Holy Land from the Muslims, and, much worse, they helped split the Church. As in most ventures, however, some good did come from the Crusades. For one thing, they opened up Europe to the East, even the Far East, especially China. Crusaders brought back to Europe silk, new spices, the compass, spaghetti, and all sorts of new and interesting goods and inventions. By their contacts with Muslim scholars, they learned of the advances being made in architecture, astronomy, mathematics, and science. In addition, they also returned with volumes of philosophy—especially that of the Greeks—which had been studied and preserved by the Islamic scholars. These discoveries would bring about profound changes that eventually led to the period in Western history called the **Renaissance,** which will be discussed later on.

Mendicant Friars: From the Monasteries to the Streets

Conditions of life in the Middle Ages inspired the emergence of two new religious orders: the **Order of Preachers** and the **Order of Friars Minor.** These two religious groups were different from the older orders whose members usually lived in large country monasteries. These **friars** (meaning "brothers") stayed on the move, teaching and preaching mostly in towns and living a simple life, dependent primarily on what people gave them for their efforts. Since they were, in effect, beggars, they came to be known as **mendicant** (meaning "begging") orders. They had no farms for food or large monasteries for housing—at least not originally.

The **Dominicans** (Order of Preachers) were founded by **Dominic de Guzman** (1170–1221). As a young priest he had been sent to convert the Albigensians (al-beh-*jen*-see-uhns)—a group of heretics living in the region of southeastern France known as Provence (preh-*vahns*). Frustrated that he had too little help in this task, Dominic gathered together a group of men who were willing to dedicate themselves to preaching. Soon his followers spread throughout Europe teaching and preaching. The Dominicans, or "Black Friars" (so-called because their habit was a white robe covered with a black cloak), lived in communal houses. They fostered fine scholarship, and consequently many of the great university teachers of the Middle Ages were Dominicans. They believed that through scholarship they would be better able to illustrate the truth of the Gospels and the wisdom of church traditions.

Selections from the Rule of Saint Francis of Assisi

1. This is the rule and way of life of the Brothers Minor: to observe the holy gospel of our Lord Jesus Christ, living in obedience, without personal belongings and in chastity....

2. ... And those who have now promised obedience shall have one gown with a hood and another, if they wish it, without a hood. And those who really need them may wear shoes. And all the brothers shall wear humble garments, and may repair them with sackcloth and other remnants, with God's blessing....

3. ... But I advise, warn and exhort my brothers in the Lord Jesus Christ that, when they go into the world, they shall not quarrel, nor contend with words, nor judge each other. But let them be gentle, peaceable, modest, merciful and humble, as is fitting. They ought not to ride, except when infirmity or necessity clearly compels them to do so....

6. The brothers shall possess nothing, neither a house, nor a place, nor anything. But, as pilgrims and strangers in this world, serving God in poverty and humility, they shall continually seek alms, and not be ashamed, for the Lord made himself poor in this world for us....

12. Whoever of the brothers by divine inspiration may wish to go among the Saracens and other infidels shall seek permission from their provincial ministers. But the ministers shall give permission to go to none but those whom they see to be fit for the mission....

The other great mendicant order was the Order of Friars Minor—the **Franciscans.** Their founder, **Saint Francis,** is certainly one of the most popular of all saints. He was born in 1182, the son of a wealthy silk merchant in Assisi, Italy. As a young man he was far from holy, becoming known as a spendthrift and occasionally fighting one of the small wars between his town and its neighbors. At the age of twenty-five he twice had visions of Christ. After a pilgrimage to Rome, he decided to live as a poor man and to take care of needy and sick people. His father angrily disapproved of such a life for his son, but Francis was unswerving in his decision and even publicly discarded the clothes on his back as a sign of putting off the old life. Francis declared that God was his only Father. Thus he began his life of wandering the countryside; repairing run-down churches; serving the lame, blind, poor, and even lepers.

With this living trust in God, Francis drew men and women to God. He also attracted followers. After much coaxing from them, he wrote a very simple rule of life for the first band of friars. Within ten years there were five thousand friars spreading out in Italy. Twice Francis tried to go to the Muslims to convert them, but in neither case did he arrive; the first time he was shipwrecked, and the second time he became seriously ill.

The severe poverty of lifestyle that Francis followed was not so easy for his friars. So there were times when Francis was at odds with some of his brothers. Likewise, his rejection of wealth as a source of corruption for the Christian—especially when there were so many poor in the world—did not sit well with some rich church officials. Nevertheless, the pope approved the Franciscan rule with its ideals of simple living and total trust in God.

Men were not the only ones attracted by Francis. Soon after he began his mendicant life, **Clare,** a rich young woman of Assisi, asked to join him. Women religious of the time only lived secluded in convents. Accordingly, Clare founded the first order of many that would try to follow the ideals of Francis. For more than twenty-five years after his death Clare kept the inspiration of Francis among her sisters. The **Poor Clares,** as they came to be known, depended on gifts from those outside their convent walls. They spent their lives in prayer and meditation, relying completely on God's providence. As the power of this kind of life became known, the order spread to several other countries in a short time. Confident that Clare's closeness to God gave her a clear vision of what should be done, bishops, and even a few popes, came to ask Clare's advice on important matters.

Today throughout the world there are over seven thousand Dominican priests and brothers, and dozens of congregations of Dominican sisters. Over thirty thousand Franciscan brothers and priests keep alive the spirit of their founder. In addition, just in the United States alone, there are two dozen convents of contemplative Poor Clares and nearly ninety religious orders of women who associate themselves with the Franciscan tradition and who work in schools, hospitals, orphanages, and other ministries.

The Roots of the Inquisition

One of the works to which the mendicant orders dedicated themselves—especially the Dominicans—was the suppression of heresy. Heresy, as mentioned earlier, is a belief that is contrary to the teaching of the Church. Sometimes heresies began as overreactions to abuses of church traditions. Eventually these overreactions evolved into distortions of church teachings. Usually a heretic goes public, openly opposing a doctrine that has been traditional. The Christians of Europe during the Middle Ages considered heresy a great evil.

Since the Church was recognized as the official religion of the European kingdoms and since uniformity of religious belief created a sense of stability in the state, anyone who would disrupt this harmonious relationship by introducing erroneous beliefs was looked upon as a traitor. So heresy was not just a religious error; it was treason.

Those dealing with heretics would attempt to persuade them to renounce their error. If that did not happen, the heresy was suppressed in order to protect the faithful. Sometimes protecting the faithful meant death for the heretics. As early as 1022, for example, King Robert II of France ordered some heretics put to death by fire at Orleans; in 1052 the German emperor Henry III hanged condemned heretics at Goslar; and in the early 1100s heretics were burned at Cologne. Until about 1150 all persons suspected of heresy were prosecuted by civil authorities. After that, church councils began to approve of the punishment of heretics, mainly by fines and prison sentences.

Near the end of the twelfth century, civil authorities began to utilize a practice called the **Inquisition**—a legal trial to determine whether or not a person accused of heresy was guilty. In the early 1200s King Philip Augustus of France and Emperor Frederick II supported the Inquisition in their lands and punished heretics. In 1215 the Lateran Council approved the practice of fines and prison sentences for those found guilty of heresy. This legislation was the result of a heresy mentioned earlier that had been developing for many years in Albi, France.

The Albigensians

The **Albigensians,** named after the town where they had their headquarters, were also called **Cathari,** "The Pure Ones." Their heresy saw all material things as bad, including the human body. (In this belief, they were similar to followers of Manichaeism in Augustine's time.) According to Albigensians, marriage was evil, as was the eating of meat. Some believed that suicide was the proper way of being freed from life, which was itself bad. Among the Albigensians was a small minority known as "The Perfect Ones," who took such beliefs seriously, living very strictly. Most Albigensians could live less carefully because they would be saved by "The Perfect Ones."

One of the reasons that the Albigensians grew in numbers was that in the south of France many of the Christian clergy were rich, living an easy life and neglecting the preaching of the Gospel; a few of these bishops and priests joined the heretics and took over several churches. Clearly, the Cathars began misleading the Christians of the area and eventually they might have destroyed Christian society by their teachings on marriage, suicide, and the value of life.

For more than fifty years church leaders tolerated or ignored the Albigensians. In the early 1200s Pope Innocent III began to act on the policy that had been long accepted in the Church: "Heretics are to be overcome by reasoning, not by force." He sent Cistercians, the leading religious order of the time, to preach in southern France and to explain the teaching of the Church in an attempt to convert the heretics. When very little came of this effort, Innocent sent Saint Dominic, who came wearing a peasant's cloak and walking barefoot. Saint Dominic and his friars, being mendicants who lived simply, thoroughly challenged the Cathars. Some of the heretics accepted Dominic's teaching but not many.

Pope Innocent III then sent his own special legate to southern France, but the legate was killed by a soldier; at that point the pope decided on drastic action. He called for a crusade against the Albigensians. He urged the king of France and his northern nobles to invade the area of France just north of the Spanish mountains and to drive out the heretics. However, there were to be no mass killings or taking of property.

Twenty years passed before the Albigensians were indeed pushed out of southern France. Even then, it was not the crusade that squelched the heresy—the heretics merely went underground. Determined to root out the remaining Cathars, the pope of the time, Gregory IX, decided to use the procedure already employed by civil authorities—the Inquisition.

The Inquisition in Operation

The word *inquisition* simply means "inquiry." Its purposes were to find out who the heretics were and to persuade them to give up their heresy. After the judges who were to hold an inquisition arrived in town, they called known heretics to come in, to confess their sins, and to receive a penance—such as the recitation of prayers, fasting, going on a pilgrimage, paying a fine, or being flogged. Then the public was invited to report any heretics they knew about. Two witnesses were sufficient to make a charge against an accused person, but the names of the witnesses were kept secret. The thinking was that this way the accused would have to answer the charges and not simply attack the credibility of the two witnesses. Inevitably some people would falsely accuse an enemy of heresy just to get him or her "out of the way"—often for political or financial reasons.

If the heretic refused to give up his or her beliefs, he or she faced severe punishments, such as life imprisonment or death by burning at the stake. The sentences were made publicly, as were the executions of the condemned parties. The cases were heard by church authorities; the execution of sentences was in the hands of civil authorities. The judges had to consult a board of advisers, composed of clergy and laymen, before bringing in the civil power. Sometimes such action was held back for as much as a year in the hopes that the heretic would have a change of heart and mind.

The Inquisition threw fear into the hearts of men and women, but they accepted it as a necessary evil. Fearing the effects of heresy on their lives they were willing to turn in a heretic for trial, and when it was over, they witnessed the punishments. Actually there were amazingly few actual executions during this age when a king or lord often condemned subjects to death for even trivial offenses. At least with the Inquisition a person came before a jury and had a chance to tell his or her side; this was not the case with many civil authorities. Bernard Gui, a judge of the Inquisition known for his severe punishments, presided over 930 trials. Only forty-two persons were turned over to civil authorities for punishment—fewer than 5 percent of the accused. Neither was the Inquisition a usual procedure everywhere. During this period it was used principally in southern France, northern Italy, and parts of northern Spain. It was held for only a short time in Germany, and not at all in England or Scandinavia. By the end of the thirteenth century, the Inquisition was discontinued except for occasional instances in particular countries—most notably Spain. Christians living today look with condemnation at the Inquisition, but this was not the attitude of most people of that period.

The Rise of the University

While the cathedrals were rising toward the sky and Crusades were being armed for battle and heretics were standing trial, another movement was just beginning that is still very alive today. This was the development of education, especially the founding of the first great universities.

By about 1200, with the growth of many towns, the schools attached to the cathedrals began to grow in numbers, surpassing the monastery schools in rural areas. In Italy and northern France teachers and students at the cathedral schools began to group together to study some of the classical subjects such as rhetoric, logic, literature, and mathematics, as well as theology, philosophy, law, and medicine. Such a group of students and teachers became known as a university, with an organization modeled on the guilds of craftsmen. Teachers earned a license, such as a master architect had; students were given "degrees" that recognized the steps they had reached in their studies.

At first, there was no campus for the university. At Paris, probably the most famous university in Europe at the time, the students and teachers overflowed from their rooms near the cathedral to the left bank of the Seine River, gathering wherever they could find a large enough space. Since Latin was the language of the University of Paris—as it was at every other university at the time—the left bank was soon known as the Latin Quarter (as it still is today).

Class schedules as we know them today were virtually nonexistent. A lecturer would announce a series of classes on a particular subject; students would come or not. If they came, they paid a fee to the tutor; if no students wanted to listen to the lecturer, he (most all were men) was out of a job. Books were very rare and expensive, as each had to be copied by hand. Teachers lectured and students listened, taking a few notes but depending mostly on their memories (paper was expensive too). Examinations were taken orally, each student being expected to give reasons for the acceptance or rejection of the teachers' statements about the subjects studied. Outside of study time, students were on their own and frequently ran into trouble with the citizens because of their rowdy behavior. Rather than trying to suppress the students, popes of that period made the universities responsible for their own affairs and, at the same time, freed them from the control of the local police and of the resident bishop.

While Paris was concentrating on the study of theology and philosophy, the University of Bologna, in central Italy, focused on law and medicine. The University of Oxford began when a group of students left Paris for England. Soon other universities were founded in Europe at Cambridge, Salerno, Prague, Cracow, Vienna, and Heidelberg. The Church supported the universities because most of the students were expected to become clerics. By the same token, knowledge gained in almost any field would increase people's understanding of God's creation.

At these centers of study, the main task of scholars was to try to gather together knowledge of all subjects, but particularly in theology and philosophy—especially Greek philosophy—from past centuries. A most unexpected source of help in this great work came from the Muslims. As it was forbidden to translate the Koran, the sacred book of Islam, all Muslims soon learned the Arabic language. Muslim scholars began using their common Arabic language to learn what their neighboring countries were thinking and learning.

From India, for example, Persian Muslims learned the use of simple numbers from one to nine, as well as zero. This was an incredible advance in mathematics, since Europe still had the Roman numeral system, which could not be used in even very simple computations. By the year 750 algebra was being developed by

Muslim mathematicians. Because Muslim merchants traded from one end of the Mediterranean to the other and because pilgrims to Mecca came from all directions, Muslims became experts in geography and mapmaking.

Syrian Christians, most of them no longer united with the Greek or Latin churches, gave Muslim scholars invaluable help by translating from Greek into Arabic the best ancient writings in philosophy, medicine, law, and natural sciences. At the time when Charlemagne was ruling his kingdom of the Franks (see chapter 9), the Muslim scholars of Baghdad were already more accomplished than any in Europe. By the 890s, when King Alfred was fighting the Danes in England, Persian Muslims added to their medical knowledge the best thinking of India and Assyria, and especially the discoveries of ancient Greek physicians.

Muslim scholars in Persia, and later in Spain, combined their knowledge of the great Greek philosophers with their own teachings of Islam. As Christians and Muslims lived side by side in southern Italy and in most of Spain, Europeans gradually learned of these Muslim writings. Soon translations were made by Western scholars from Arabic into Latin, the language of scholars everywhere in Europe.

Medieval European Universities

Later the teachers in the European universities went back to reading Aristotle in the original Greek and then making new Latin versions of his work. Saint Thomas Aquinas, one of the most influential Christian teachers of all time, used these versions for his theological writings, which have been studied in the Church for more than seven hundred years. By the 1200s scholars in the universities of Europe were learning how to put together the culture of the ancient Greeks, the special learning of the Muslims, and the understanding that their own Christian faith gave them. Often they were using Greek writings translated by Muslim scholars, preserved and retranslated by monks in the solitude of their monasteries.

Interestingly some of the greatest scholars in the universities during the 1200s are also canonized saints. **Albert the Great** was among the earliest. Born in Germany, he studied at the University of Padua, became a Dominican, and taught at both Cologne and Paris. Later he was a Dominican administrator and then a bishop. He studied Arabic writings and wrote books on theology and philosophy. He knew so much about the natural sciences—biology, chemistry, physics, astronomy, and geography—that he was sometimes accused of magic. He also defended the work of his most famous pupil, Thomas Aquinas, who after his death was attacked for trying to bring together Christian theology and the philosophy of Aristotle.

A woodcut picturing a lecturer at the University of Bologna in the fifteenth century

Thomas Aquinas

Saint Thomas Aquinas, the son of an Italian count, began his education at age five when he was sent to the Benedictine monastery at Monte Cassino. He finished his formal studies at the University of Naples and joined the Dominicans, in spite of the protests of his rich family. To force him to change his mind his father had kept him a prisoner in the family castle for more than a year. However, Thomas remained firm in his religious vocation and eventually went to Paris where Albert the Great was his teacher. Thomas taught at Paris and later at several Italian universities. Ironically the young man who was nicknamed the "Dumb Ox" because he was fat, slow moving, and serious became well known even in his own time.

Thomas had many new ideas—so much so that his bishop at Paris as well as some of the other professors at the university were opposed to his use of Greek and Arabic thinking in theology. However, Thomas was able to show that what God revealed is not contrary to reason, that in fact we can know some of these truths about God by using our minds, almost without depending on faith. He took his method from the Greek philosopher Aristotle but tried to base most all of his thinking on the Christian Scriptures.

While his writings were debated vigorously during his time and immediately after his death by the Council of Trent (1545–63), Thomas was the source of many of the official decrees coming from the Church. In 1879 the pope declared that Thomas's thinking was to be considered always valid. Certainly Thomas was a genius, but he was a simple person—a Dominican friar who never had any high positions outside the university. He composed poems and music for religious feasts. In a sense, he was the right person at the right time: that is, his genius brought together much of the scattered thinking from various sources and gave it method—philosophic reasoning.

Another scholar-saint of the 1200s was **Saint Bonaventure.** Born in Italy, he became a Franciscan and began his studies at the University of Paris. He taught there for about seven years until his work was interrupted by some of the teachers who objected to having friars on the faculty. Two years later he was elected superior general of his order, then made a bishop and a cardinal. He organized the Council of Lyons, especially the efforts to reunite the Greek and Latin churches. Bonaventure, using much of the same material as Albert and Thomas, was most interested in making theology serve as a guide for good Christian living. Thomas and Bonaventure certainly did not agree on everything, but both men contributed immensely to the scholarship of their day and to church tradition.

An engraving depicting Saint Thomas Aquinas at the school established by Albert the Great

Focus on the Models

If the Church is to be the Sacrament of Jesus' presence in the world, then the cathedrals were signs in stone and glass of the Church's presence in the world. Besides being beautiful buildings, to medieval people they were acts of praise in which the whole community was involved.

As Institution, this was an important period for the Church. The popes clearly became the sole and central powers in the Church. While this contributed to the break with the Eastern Church, papal power ensured unity of action on the part of the Church—a unity that the popes would need when facing kings who were more powerful than ever. The Church had become an institution encompassing all of Europe. To guarantee common practice, church laws or canon laws were being organized, written down, and studied by those becoming priests.

Another important institutional development was the establishment of the College of Cardinals in 1179 at the Third Lateran Council. Up to this time, the popes had been elected by the people of Rome—although too frequently the elections had been controlled by a king, emperor, or the noble Roman families. To protect the independence of the Church from outside forces, the cardinals would meet to elect the pope; whichever candidate received two-thirds of the votes became pope. This system

took a good many years to implement because the Romans objected, but it was a major step in freeing the Church from Roman control.

At the same time, many of the Vatican offices (listed on the chart in chapter 2, page 26) were begun during these centuries. At the Fourth Lateran Council of 1215, the Church forbade priests to marry. From this point on, a married clergy in the West disappeared. Priests were to have no secular occupations and had to be trained in the cathedral schools before ordination. While these decrees by the council were intended to reform an unhealthy situation among the clergy, many years would pass before they were fully followed.

Finally, preaching of the Word of God—the Church as Herald—gained new impetus with the founding of the mendicant orders. The Dominicans and Franciscans not only spread the Word in Europe but accompanied the Crusaders to convert the Muslims. At least two intrepid friars journeyed thousands of miles on foot and by mule to Cathay, or China as we know it today. Scholars at the universities and in the monasteries continued to study and explain the meaning of the Christian Scriptures. Built into the cathedrals were statues and windows that taught Bible stories to illiterate people. And, despite the disastrous Fourth Crusade and also the Children's Crusade, the attempts to reclaim the Holy Land for Christendom were motivated by a desire to proclaim that Christianity was the true faith that would lead to salvation.

In effect, the three centuries from 1000 to 1300 saw many crucial developments in the Church—most of which strengthened the Church's ability to become a clear sign of Christ's presence. The tragedies of some of the Crusades and of the Inquisition made it equally clear that fallible humans are still in need of conversion.

Review Questions and Activities

1) What role did the Church play in the development of towns? Why were towns important in medieval life?

2) How were the cathedrals symbolic of the Church's role in life of the Middle Ages? How is the Romanesque cathedral different from the Gothic cathedral? What purposes did the cathedrals have other than providing a place for worship?

3) What changes were happening to the governments of Europe after the year 1000? How did these developments influence the Church? Why were the German emperors particularly important to the Church?

4) What was the role of the papacy during this period?

5) In 1054, the Church was split in two. What were some of the causes for this division, and what event brought the final split?

6) Why were the Crusades initiated? How would you evaluate the effectiveness of the Crusades, in terms of their original purpose? What positive effects were there from the Crusades that were not part of the original intent?

7) Would present-day Christians rally around the pope and fight a Crusade today? Why or why not?

8) What attitudes about war made the Crusades acceptable to people in the Middle Ages?

9) In the Middle Ages, was the Christian attitude toward war really all that different from the Muslim attitude? What similarities and differences do you see between their attitudes toward war and our present-day attitudes?

10) How were the mendicant friars different from earlier religious orders? Why would the mendicant sort of life be attractive at this time in history?

11) What was the situation of women religious up to this time period? In what ways was Clare quite influential?

12) Why did civil authorities want to suppress heresy? What was the procedure used to find, try, and prosecute people considered heretics? Why were the Cathars, or Albigensians, heretics? Why were they seen as such a threat? From the medieval point of view, why was the Inquisition acceptable as a sort of necessary evil?

13) Describe the development of the universities. How were they different from today's universities? How was the development of the universities directly related to the Church?

14) What materials did the medieval scholars depend on to do their research?

15) Saint Thomas Aquinas contributed a whole new method to theology. What did he do differently? How did people react during his lifetime to these changes? How was Thomas Aquinas more than just a scholar?

16) The Third and Fourth Lateran Councils brought several changes to the Church as Institution. What were these changes? Why were they so important?

Personal Reflection Exercise

How did you react to Bertran de Born's declaration about war? If you said something similar in a conversation with friends, and you meant it, how would they react? Then, think about all the comments, scenes within movies and TV, words to songs, and so on that encourage or at least approve of violence, especially as a means of solving a problem or winning an argument. Try to list as many of these as you can from the last week or two. Take out a newspaper; look at the first section's stories. How many of these are about war or in defense of military spending? Finally, do you think modern people have a substantially different mentality about war than Bertran de Born? Describe any similarities and/or differences. What would you like your stand to be about war or the uses of violence?

11
Public Turmoil, Personal Piety: 1300–1500

The two hundred years covered in this chapter were filled with calamities both for Europe and for the Church. One war lasted for a century; plague killed almost one-third of the people of Europe; and, at one time, there were three men claiming the title of pope. Calls for reform were generated by a few brave souls, but these were mostly suppressed. Even so, a "rebirth" was beginning in Europe that would spur on great advances in science, literature, and the arts. These advances, partly created by the Church, would in turn influence the Church profoundly. And despite the turmoil and corruption, great saints worked faithfully amidst these conditions for reform and peace in the Church. Finally popular piety flourished in towns and villages, and Christian faith was carried to far-off lands.

The Popes Move to Avignon

During the 1300s the stable center of European life, the Church, was teetering. The Christians of Europe suffered from a decline in the power and prestige of their religious leaders, the popes. Older people remembered hearing their parents talking about the power of Pope Innocent III in ruling the Church—not allowing kings to do what they wanted with regard to the Church. Yet now, almost a century later, King Philip IV of France felt so secure in his power that he sent troops to Italy and put Pope Boniface VIII under arrest. Although the people of Rome rescued the pope and drove out the French soldiers, Boniface died a month later in October 1303. This manhandling of the pope signaled a radical change in the prestige of the papacy.

Two issues had caused this kind of violent action. First, the pope had objected when Philip decided to tax the French clergy, though he later consented to the tax. Second, the pope protested that a French bishop, who was accused of being a traitor to the French government, should have been tried in a church court rather than in a civil court as he had been. Unmistakably relations between the pope and the kings of Europe had changed footing; the kings wanted to control the pope. This desire became more clear in what Philip was able to do with the successors of Pope Boniface.

Two years after Boniface died, a French bishop who was a personal friend of the king, was elected pope. He decided to live in the south of France, at the town of Avignon (a-veen-*yohn*), where there was a huge castle built like a fortress. This first Avignon pope, **Clement V**, appointed new cardinals—all of them French. He changed some church policies that the French king had not liked, especially those concerning money—thus calming the king.

Suffering from cancer, living in France, and subject to the French king, Clement was in no position to oppose royal wishes.

Clement's successor, **John XXII**, also French, decided to make Avignon his permanent city by moving there all the officials needed to run the church government. In a few years, as succeeding popes continued to appoint Frenchmen as cardinals, there were only two or three who were not French. In all, seven French popes lived at Avignon from 1309 to 1377.

Christians all over Europe were disturbed that the pope was living away from Rome. They felt that the pope as the successor of Saint Peter should, like Peter, stay at Rome. The English were especially distressed that the French kings would have too much to say about how the Church should be governed. And the beginning of the Hundred Years' War (1338–1453), in which the English fought the French, increased their worry. They wondered if the French popes would rally other Europeans to the side of the French. In addition, the Church could hardly be accepted as an impartial mediator between France and England when the pope was French.

This situation was aggravated by the fact that the Avignon popes asked for more and more money—far more than previous popes. This was in the form of taxes, as well as donations for indulgences and for spiritual services. Living far away from their Papal States the popes could not collect the usual revenues from their own area and so had to find money in other ways in order to run the church government. Also, the popes wanted to strengthen the defenses of Avignon—which took lots of money. Further, a couple of the popes lived extravagantly—entertaining large parties of nobility and visiting church officials, which again was very costly.

The Black Death

Adding to the disruption in the stability of Europe was the arrival of the Black Death—bubonic plague. It attacked individuals suddenly. Parts of the body would swell up, and black and white splotches would form on the skin. Usually by the third day, the victim died in agony. No one was safe from the contagion, for even the clothes worn by a sick person could carry the plague.

The bacteria of the plague was brought to Italy and North Africa in 1347 by merchant ships of Genoa that had been trading with the East—most likely by fleas that infected the rats that seemed to be part of every cargo. The plague spread rapidly for about four years until it reached the northern areas of Scandinavia and Russia. Whole towns were wiped out. Monasteries were decimated. Cemeteries filled up, and in many places corpses were left unburied because gravediggers had died. In a few years, one-third of Europe's entire population had become victims. Over a thousand ghost towns dotted the map. In the country sheep died, crops were not harvested, and cattle wandered away because there was no one to tend them. A shortage of workers caused both prices and wages to soar, increasing the misery of families who had lost a father or husband.

Priests suffered in great numbers from the Black Death because they were constantly exposed to it while ministering to the sick. Indeed, when the plague died down, many towns were left without priests. Consequently new priests were often ordained without adequate training, and frequently the selection of priestly candidates was hasty and ill-advised, thus adding to the low esteem people began to have for the Church headquartered in Avignon.

Somehow the memory of Roman popes stayed alive, and the impetus for the popes to return to Rome increased. Several of the later Avignon popes thought of returning to the city of Peter—but this was a threatening idea to many people, especially the Frenchmen in key church positions. **Gregory XI**, the seventh Avignon pope, had been thinking about Rome for five years or more when unexpectedly a visitor came to see him. She was a thirty-year-old nun from Siena, Italy—**Sister Catherine.** Few of the French clergy were impressed by her; she seemed naive. Her message was indeed simple: while in prayer, she perceived that the Lord wanted the pope back in Rome; the people of Europe, still recovering from the devastation of the Black Death, needed to be reassured by a pope in Rome; moreover, only there could the pope bring peace between France and England and among the warring Italian city-states.

Gauging the impact of Saint Catherine's words on the pope is impossible, but in 1377 Pope Gregory brought the papacy back to Rome. He died a year later.

Catherine of Siena

Saint Catherine was born Caterina di Giacomo di Benincasa in 1347. It seems she was the twenty-fourth of twenty-five children. While her father was prosperous, the life of the people of Siena was never free from wars with other city-states. Early in her life Catherine decided to become a member of the *Mantellate*—an order of laywomen who wore the Dominican habit but who lived at home, serving the poor and sick under the guidance of a sister superior. The *Mantelate* was different from most of the other religious orders of women because at this time nuns, by definition, lived in cloistered convents. Catherine lived alone for some years but at age twenty-one became active in service to Siena's many poor people.

In the midst of her activities, she managed to learn how to read, something unusual for women of her time. Gradually she became recognized as an uncommonly holy person. As a consequence, she was asked to mediate disputes between city-states. In 1375 she persuaded Pisa and Lucca not to war on the Papal States. In 1376 she was asked to mediate a conflict between Florence and the pope—quite remarkable, for she was still only in her twenties. What is equally amazing is that, in an era when few women had any real rights, she was being looked to by nobles and generals for advice.

Catherine's main concerns were three: bringing about a general reform in the Church, encouraging the pope to return to Rome, and starting a crusade that would unite Christians and convert the Muslims. In 1376 she began to push the pope to return to Rome; and, partly due to her influence, he did return. Some church reforms did take place, but the crusade Catherine envisioned never materialized.

Her letters tell us much about the force of her personality and convictions. She started her correspondence first using secretaries, but at the age of thirty she learned how to write herself. Catherine established a monastic convent for sisters and eventually, at the urging of the pope, moved to Rome so that she could advise him. But at age thirty-three she died, the result perhaps of too strenuous a life. To Pope Gregory XI at Avignon, Saint Catherine wrote:

Alas, what confusion is this, to see those who ought to be a mirror of voluntary poverty, meek as lambs, distributing the possessions of Holy Church to the poor: and they appear in such luxury and state and pomp and worldly vanity, more than if they had turned them to the world a thousand times. Nay, many seculars put them to shame who live a good and holy life. . . . Holy Church should return to her first condition, poor, humble, and meek as she was in that holy time when men took note of nothing but the honor of God and the salvation of souls. . . . For since she [the Church] has aimed more at temporal than at spiritual, things have gone from bad to worse. . . .

Return to Rome. . . . Let not your holy desire fail on account of any scandal or rebellion of cities which you might see or hear. . . . Be manly in my sight, and not timorous.

And to King Charles of France, she wrote:

Maintain holy and true justice; let it not be ruined, either for self-love or for flatteries, or for any pleasing of men. And do not connive at your officials doing injustice for money, and denying right to the poor: but be to the poor a father, a distributor of what God has given you. And seek to have the faults that are found in your kingdom punished and virtue exalted.

Who Is the Real Pope?

Gregory was succeeded by **Urban VI**. He was a compromise candidate: the cardinals would likely have elected another Frenchman, but the people of Rome were demanding a Roman. Urban was an Italian, though not a Roman; he was chosen as second choice of both parties. The new pope saw that the top level of church government needed to be cleaned up, especially in places where the clergy were greedy for money. However, Urban had a hot temper, and he went about making changes in a way that turned people against him. The French cardinals slipped quietly out of the city and met in the coastal town of Naples to see what could be done. They claimed that Urban was not a real pope because they had elected him in fear of the Roman mob howling outside during the election. Accordingly they elected a French cardinal as pope. Naturally the French pope went to live at Avignon. Now there were two popes. There were two governments in the Church with duplicate officials, even two staffs for collecting taxes.

Who was the real pope? Christians had to make choices, and often these were based primarily on national loyalties and personal prejudices. England, Scandinavia, and parts of northern France chose to support the pope at Rome; France, Spain, and southern Italy obeyed the pope at Avignon; Germany and northern Italy were divided. This situation continued for about thirty years, with popes succeeding one another in Rome and Avignon. Shortly after 1400 some cardinals from each party met at Pisa in Italy to try to solve the problem; however, they only made it worse.

The council at Pisa elected a new pope in the hope that he would be accepted by everyone. As might have been expected, neither of the other two popes would agree to be pushed out of office by a newcomer. Now there were three popes.

The Hundred Years' War dragged on and on; recovery from the Black Death was painfully slow; taxes that were needed to pay governments and three rival popes were oppressive. The situation was intolerable. In 1414 the new Holy Roman emperor Sigismund decided that his first task was to put an end to this disunity in the Christian Church. He called for a meeting of clergy and laymen at Constance, a beautiful town on the lake at the German-Swiss border where the Rhine River has its source. At the opening of the **Council of Constance** (1414–18), the Pisa pope came in person, the other two sent their representatives. Realizing that the council would begin investigating his past life, the Pisa pope fled in the disguise of a soldier. The Roman pope decided to resign, but before doing that he agreed to declare the council a legal assembly according to the laws of the Church. The Avignon pope stubbornly held to his position; the council deposed him. After years of debate, at long last the council elected a Roman, Martin V, as the one and only pope.

As seems inevitable, another burning issue was raised at the council: Who is the top authority of the Church—a pope or a general council? For a number of years now the governments of leading nations in Europe included some kind of assembly or parliament to help the king rule properly—and sometimes to keep the king in line. Of course, the cardinals and many laypersons asked the same question about the council's power. The issue remained unsettled at this time. Martin V's election regained stability for the Church—that was enough.

More Wars and Intrigues

After the Hundred Years' War, France and England became separate, independent countries. In nearby Spain the Moorish Muslims were gradually being driven out. Royal power was greatly strengthened when Ferdinand, king of Aragon, and Isabella, queen of Castile, were married. They united Spain—partly by stamping out all possible sources of opposition. Thus, the infamous Spanish Inquisition began under the control of these two forceful monarchs. Its chief targets were the converted Jews and Muslims who, though baptized as Christians, were suspected of practicing their original faiths. The pope protested the cruelty of the Spanish Inquisition, but to no avail. Forgotten was the fact that these persecuted people for many years had brought to Spain economic prosperity as well as many cultural treasures—such as the beautiful buildings that people still admire today.

Unlike Spain, Italy was being torn apart by small wars among various city-states. Most of these were ruled by dictators who had to fight for the office and were killed by other power seekers. Among the most important of the Italian city-states were Milan, Venice, and Florence—the latter being a center of banking and also the center of the wood industry. The powerful Medici (*med*-eh-chee) family controlled Florence, having learned how to run a political machine with a boss, as well as how to rig elections so that they looked legal. During the reign of **Lorenzo de Medici** (called "Lorenzo the Magnificent") a Dominican friar named **Savonarola** (sav-uh-neh-*roh*-luh) began preaching publicly against injustice and against the dirty Florentine politics. Working people rallied behind him. Many people did penance for their sins. Savonarola was so popular that for a few months after Lorenzo's death he ruled the city. However, he went too far in what he said. The pope, an ally of the Medici family, commanded him to stop preaching. Savonarola continued, becoming more forceful all the time. At last he called for a council to depose the pope. When Savonarola refused to go to Rome to answer charges against him, the pope threatened to put Florence under interdict. An **interdict** would have meant that priests would be forbidden to administer the sacraments to anyone in Florence until the interdict was lifted.

Even though Savonarola had reformed the taxes for the people of Florence and had served the poor, they all turned against him. They were afraid that their enemies from other cities would attack them. A mob broke into the friar's monastery and arrested him. After a trial, held by the government of Florence, Savonarola was burned at the stake in the center of the city. The Medici family now returned to power; in effect, the pope, instead of supporting reform, supported the continuation of corruption and power.

During this time Germany was not as united as were England and France. The ruler of German lands still considered himself the Holy Roman emperor rather than just king of Germany. He ruled over as many as three hundred local counts who were more or less independent of him. Besides, a new emperor was not automatically his father's successor: there were seven electors who chose a new ruler either from the family of the dead emperor or from another family. Three of these electors were bishops who held the rank of princes, all from the Cologne area. The empire in the 1400s included, besides Germany, a loose league of such small states as Luxemburg, Bohemia, Carniola, and Tyrol. Switzerland's small states, called cantons, successfully preserved their independence. The autonomy of these many small German states was going to have a great influence on the movement of reform that began in the 1500s. But considerable tension and intrigue existed between these states, and sometimes the Church was caught up in these problems.

During the 1400s the nations north and east of Germany continued to grow. To the east Poland became stronger when its neighbor Lithuania became Christian and joined forces with it against the Prussians from northeast Germany. Universities were founded in Copenhagen and Uppsala. Farther south, Christian Hungary gathered strength too.

The Renaissance Begins

Some time after the Black Death, the educated people in Europe began studying the works of the pagan Greeks and Romans—especially their literature and art. This movement began in Italy, the center of the old pagan world. Naturally the popes of the later 1400s took interest in what was going on all around them. Most of the popes of the period encouraged the writers and artists in their work. Indeed, some popes became patrons—those who paid artists to do projects for them. **Pope Nicholas V** started the renowned Vatican

The facade of Saint Peter's Basilica (left) exhibits some of the design ideas that were adopted by Renaissance builders from classical architecture— as seen in the Roman temple below.

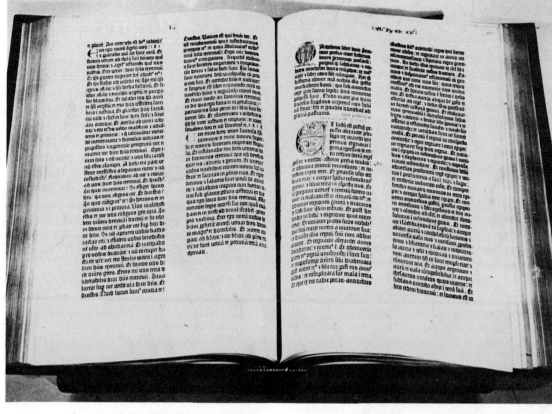

A copy of the first Bible printed by Johannes Gutenberg

library, where thousands of priceless manuscripts could be stored, catalogued, and studied. He also began plans for rebuilding the basilica of Saint Peter's at Rome—in the new style inspired by the ancient Greek and Roman temples. This movement in art, literature, and culture came to be named the **Renaissance**—which means "rebirth."

A tremendous boost was given to the rebirth in literature by the work of a printer living in Mainz, Germany. **Johannes Gutenberg** (*goot-uhn-buhrg*) cast letters of the alphabet in lead, making it possible to arrange them into words. This movable lead type could be used many times. Gutenberg then invented the printing press, modeling it on the presses used by winemakers and papermakers. The first large book issued from the printing press was the Bible—around 1456. Within a few years, there

were printing presses in most of the larger cities of Europe. Literature of the past, as well as new writings, could be multiplied quickly and easily. Soon almost everyone could own books.

The printing press contributed to the spread of literature; it also enabled any literate person to read the Bible. The popular possession of Bibles would be one of the catalysts in the Reformation of the 1500s. The new literature was mostly in Italian, French, Spanish, English, or other national languages—not Latin. This change increased the demand for Bibles in different languages as well.

In the midst of the Renaissance, in many ways a revival of the past, some scholars concentrated on the future—that is, on practical scientific inventions. Mathematics was used to help sailors navigate the Mediterranean as well as to make more accurate cannons. Merchants used mathematics to develop bookkeeping methods. The clock was invented around 1400, making use of the system of dividing the hour into minutes and seconds. Glasses for reading came into being with the invention of ground lenses. The horrible experience of the Black Death helped doctors learn something about the spread of infection. And all of this knowledge was quickly spread by the use of printing.

The personal lives of educated people were affected too. A taste for beautiful things became a way of life. Those who stressed making human life more tolerable and fulfilling by surrounding themselves with the beauty found in art, science, and literature were called **humanists**. Admittedly humanism sometimes became distorted and led to exaggerated forms of pleasure seeking. In admiring the Greek or Roman way of life, some Renaissance humanists adopted a pagan lifestyle. Even some popes, who are remembered today for sponsoring the work of great artists, did not succeed in putting the Christian way of life—serving the poor and homeless, living simply—ahead of the pagan lifestyle of pleasure and enjoyment. Because the popes were leaders in their time, this failure seems all the worse to us—as it did to people under their authority in the Church.

Of the ten men who are usually called Renaissance popes, all but two or three lived double lives. Some of them, ambitious for power, became popes through bribery and buying votes. Once in power they appointed loyal followers to important positions in the Church, very often their own relatives. Like many people who have money and power, most of them were surrounded by pleasure and ease. For two of these popes this meant openly violating their celibacy. **Alexander VI**, the most notorious of the Renaissance popes, had six children —although they were born before he became pope. Further, Alexander did not hesitate to publicly give his children high positions in the Church. Such horrible examples became excuses for other clergy and religious to sin against their own vocations.

On the other side of their double lives these popes patronized the arts (sponsoring great artists like Michelangelo and Botticelli), science (supporting the universities), and literature (giving allowances to writers). Most of the popes knew that reform was necessary. They just did nothing about it. The leadership of the Church was teetering on a point of crisis.

Christian Life for the Common People

Considering the many catastrophes of these centuries it is no wonder that people turned to God for relief. And neither the events of Avignon nor the corruption of the papal court at Rome destroyed the people's faith. They believed in God; they worshiped in the cathedrals; they prayed fervently for God's protection from more outbreaks of the plague; and they found comfort in belief in heaven. While many of the higher ranks of clergymen were not the examples of Christian service and love that they should have been, there were many simple priests who cared for their parishioners with patience and trust. Many of them lost their lives ministering during the plague; these were not forgotten by the common folk.

Life in the countryside had changed little for the serfs—primarily they hoped for just treatment and enough to eat. At noon and 6:00 P.M. they said special prayers when the cathedral bells rang out. They walked to Mass every Sunday, and like everyone else they enjoyed the celebrations of feasts.

The towns grew larger, with a new banking class now able to make loans to people in business. In each town a rich family or two had most of the money. The guilds of merchants and of craftsmen grew stronger, not only protecting their members but also becoming prominent organizations in the towns. Some of the crafts guilds, for example, put on religious plays in front of the churches or in

A Poor Parish Priest

Geoffrey Chaucer (c. 1340–1400) wrote *The Canterbury Tales,* a collection of stories told by fictitious pilgrims on their way to the shrine of Saint Thomas à Becket, the martyred archbishop of Canterbury, England. Becket's tomb was a holy place and drew pilgrims for many centuries in the Middle Ages. Supposedly the stories were told by the pilgrims to entertain themselves as they traveled together. On the trip were representatives of most levels of medieval society: a noble knight, a crude miller, a pampered prioress, a rotund friar, a lusty wife from the city of Bath, a pardoner, a pious parson, and several other typical characters. The church people described by Chaucer reflect the prevailing criticisms of them: the monk "loved hunting . . . had many excellent horses in his stable. . . . He didn't give a plucked hen for that text which says that hunters are not holy"; the friar was "a licensed beggar" and "no member of all four orders knew so much of gossip and flattering talk." But Chaucer pictures the poor parish priest as a genuinely good, although slightly boring, person—probably typical of common ministers of the Church of the day:

There was a good man of the church, a poor parish Priest, but rich in holy thoughts and works. He was also a learned man, a cleric, who wished to preach Christ's gospel truly and to teach his parishioners devoutly. He was benign, wonderfully diligent and extremely patient in adversity. . . . He did not at all like to have anyone excommunicated for non-payment of tithes; rather, he would give, without doubt, a portion of the offering and also of his salary to his poor parishioners. He needed little to fill his own needs. His parish was wide and the houses far apart, but he never failed, rain or shine, sick or well, to visit the farthest in his parish, be he rich or poor, traveling on foot with a staff in his hand. To his congregation he gave this noble example: first he practiced good deeds, and afterward he preached them. . . . For if a priest whom we trust is not worthy, it is no wonder that an ignorant man sins. . . . This Priest did not hire out his benefice* and leave his people in difficulties while he ran off to St. Paul's in London to look for an endowment singing masses for the dead, or to be retained by a guild. He stayed at home and guarded his parish well so that evil did not corrupt it. He was a pastor and not a mercenary. . . . His business was to draw folk to heaven by fairness and by setting a good example. But if any sinner, whether of high or low birth was obstinate, this Parson would at once rebuke him for it sharply. . . . He cared nothing for pomp and reverence; . . . he taught the lore of Christ and His twelve Apostles, but first he followed it himself.

---

*A benefice was the appointment to the local parish by the lord of the area; Chaucer is pointing to a big problem—that is, many parish priests hired younger clerics to take their parishes and went to the cities to be paid fat fees for performing church services for the rich. Saint Paul's is a major cathedral in London.

Devotion to Saints and Indulgences

Among the developments in the faith life of the common people was an increased devotion to saints. Some people began believing that Jesus was too inaccessible and that saints would intercede for them. Mary was particularly honored with devotion. This kind of devotion to the saints led to the collecting of **relics**—things such as small pieces of bone from a saint's body or clothing the saint wore. Nothing was or is wrong with devotion to saints. However, in the 1400s and 1500s devotion to the relics became a kind of hobby so interesting in itself that the collectors forgot their original intentions—to think of what the saints' lives meant as an expression of their love for God.

Another exaggerated element of the faith of the times was the interest in **indulgences,** which offered a release from the punishment due in the next life for sins done in the present life. The practice of granting indulgences for sin began several centuries before when people were allowed to build a chapel or contribute a stained-glass window instead of doing some other sort of penance for their sins. It was also connected to the idea that going on a crusade or praying at a certain church on particular days was meritorious in the eyes of God, and that merit gained from such actions could be stored up. Thus, when a person sinned, he or she used accumulated deeds of merits to counteract the punishment for the sins.

Seeking indulgences had a positive side; that is, it required a person to be sincerely sorry for his or her sins. However, this sincerity was often forgotten in a person's anxiety to avoid God's punishment, and eventually true penance gave way to buying and selling of indulgences—as though God could be bribed into forgiving sins.

What people seemed to overlook was that Jesus died for all humankind and has already forgiven sins; people's repentance is mostly a recognition of the forgiveness given freely. In

the village squares. They also took part in the liturgy, standing out as special groups with their banners and uniforms. At times there were strikes and violence in the towns as the craftsmen demanded more money for their work. A merchant class was developing in Europe. This rising class would pose many challenges for the corrupt officials in the Church in the next century.

error, too many people in these centuries believed that they could buy their way into heaven. Some church officials, including a couple of popes, did little to discourage this error. Popes endorsed the selling of indulgences to support the artworks that they commissioned for the Vatican and, eventually, to build Saint Peter's in Rome. Unscrupulous sellers of indulgences scattered throughout Europe. They used all sorts of pious threats and arguments to sell the indulgences to the simple people—and usually raised the prices so they could take an additional cut of the profits.

In contrast to the corruption in parts of the Church, a revival of meditation and prayer was going on in pockets all over Europe. Several of the great works of the spiritual life were written during this period by people like Nicholas of Cusa, Erasmus, and Gabriel Biel. Maybe the most famous of all these spiritual writings was the *Imitation of Christ* by **Thomas à Kempis** (1380–1471). In the works of these people and others, many found the necessary inspiration and support to be Christian—an inspiration and support that Rome did not always provide.

The Ottoman Turks

Christians in the East and West had another chance to be reunited. The Ottoman Turks had for a long time been advancing westward through Asia Minor, steadily breaking off pieces of Byzantine territory. By about 1400 they had captured most of Greece and were advancing northward into Serbia and Bulgaria. The Turks had strong military organization and were inspired and unified by their Islamic faith. They also had a steadily increasing supply of manpower—for they systematically took one boy away from each Christian family in Asia Minor, educated him in Muslim beliefs, and trained him to be a fearless fighter, called

a **janissary** (*jan*-eh-ser-ee). By 1400 the Turks had conquered almost the entire Byzantine Empire; Constantinople stood alone, a capital without a country.

Realizing that Constantinople could not survive a direct attack by the Turks, the Byzantine emperor John VIII asked the Christians of the West for help. In 1439 he traveled with a large number of Greek bishops and theologians to the council held at Florence. There the Greek Christian leaders signed an agreement accepting the pope as head of the Church. Officially all Christians were again united under the pope at Rome; however, the rest of the Eastern clergy and the common people would not accept the pope. Nevertheless, the pope called for a crusade against the Turks. The call was answered by the Hungarians, who were most likely to be attacked by the Turks, and by some French knights who had been fighting in the Hundred Years' War. After initial success, the crusaders were soundly defeated near the Black Sea, and the Turkish sultan began a two-year preparation to take Constantinople.

The sultan gathered eighty thousand men for the final assault on Constantinople. He also was aided by new weapons: muskets that used gunpowder and cannons mounted on ships for blowing holes in the massive city walls. The assault lasted many weeks. Before beginning his final attack, the sultan offered terms to the people of Constantinople. He would spare the city if they paid him a large bribe or if they surrendered and left. The people refused. The final battle lasted twenty-four hours. The last Byzantine emperor was killed in battle, and for three days the Turks looted the rich city. Christians who had crowded into Hagia Sophia were massacred. The church itself was turned into a mosque—that is, a Moslem place of worship. People spared were sold into slavery. Thus, in 1453 the "second Rome" and capital of a once great empire fell after a thousand years.

After the fall of Constantinople to the Turks, the city was renamed **Istanbul**. Many Greek scholars escaped to the north, especially to the new town of Moscow in Russia. While Islam was destroying the Byzantine Empire, the Russians were regaining their independence from the Mongols who had conquered them almost two hundred years earlier. The Mongols were fierce nomadic people who had migrated from the north of China—in the process conquering all of China and most of what is now the Soviet Union. Gradually they were losing their grip on Russian lands, and by the mid-1400s Ivan the Great, a Muscovite prince, was able to start building a united country.

The Russians were Christianized centuries before by missionaries coming from Greece. Thus, along with Constantinople, the Russians had rejected papal authority. With the fall of Constantinople, Ivan saw himself as the successor to the Byzantine emperor and considered Moscow as the "third Rome." Ivan ruled the Russian Church through his patriarchs just as the emperors at Constantinople had ruled the Greek Church. In the city of Istanbul, the sultan appointed a new patriarch to govern the Greek Church and allowed a certain amount of religious freedom to Christians.

At this point the Christian Church was divided into two parts: the Roman Catholic Church in the West and the Orthodox Church in Russia, Bulgaria, Greece, and Asia Minor. The Orthodox Church and the Roman Catholic Church remain separated to this day.

The Lure of Adventure

In the middle of the 1400s, the son of the Portuguese king was spending his days and nights making maps and ocean charts, sending out small boats to see if anything could be found in all that water. Prince Henry the Navigator had Portuguese ships exploring the west coast of Africa. This was worlds beyond the Mediterranean where the Italian merchant ships still had a monopoly of trade as far east as India—where they could get spices like pepper and cinnamon. The market for these spices was brisk as was the market for the jewels from the Orient. Not only were the Portuguese interested in getting some of this profitable trade—especially in the islands off India that were called the "Spice Islands" or the "East Indies"—but their spirit of adventure propelled them forward. By 1486 the Portuguese navigator Bartolomeu Dias sailed around the southern tip of Africa, called the Cape of Good Hope. Within a few years another Portuguese explorer Vasco da Gama went farther, sailing on into the Indian Ocean. On hand during all of these explorations were some hardy missionary friars ready to spread the Word of God. Franciscans began preaching in the Congo, or modern-day Zaire (*zeye*-uhr), as early as 1484. To the Church, exploration meant new fields for conversions.

In 1492, the year when they finally drove out the Muslims and united Spain, Ferdinand and Isabella sponsored the first voyage of a young Italian man who wanted to find a short route to India. Instead Christopher Columbus discovered a group of islands: San Salvador, Cuba, and Santo Domingo. His next three voyages, especially the discovery of the northern coast of South America, made it clear that this was a new land for Europeans. While he did not bring back masses of gold and rich treasure, Columbus's unplanned discovery inspired other explorations around the world.

In the year 1497 John Cabot, another Italian sea captain from Columbus's town of Genoa, sailed across the Atlantic under the English flag and landed at Newfoundland. With his exploration in the north and Columbus's in the south, a whole new world was opened up to missionary activity. Corruption in church and state, fear of the Black Death, poverty, and high taxes gave these adventures added appeal. New worlds to conquer for king or church were sources of hope in a Europe beset by so many problems.

Focus on the Models

For the common people of Europe, the Church remained the sacrament of Christ present in the world, despite the Avignon papacy and three popes claiming the chair of Peter. Yet a movement was afoot among serious believers based on the need to reform the Church. Much of the clamor for reform came from the new literate classes of merchants and skilled craftsmen who could now read the Bible and other religious books coming off printing presses all over the continent. Many monks and nuns were also calling for renewal.

The institutional Church carried on despite major problems. Most of the popes at this time were effective at collecting church taxes, sponsoring artists and writers, entertaining a large household, and plotting with different European families. On the other hand, dioceses and most religious orders carried on the work of the Church: that is, preaching the Good News, administering the sacraments, and serving the people. With such poor example given by some of the popes, it is a wonder that so many saints lived holy lives during this period.

The printing press was a great advance for the mission of heralding the Word of God. And with the new explorations, missionaries found people who had not heard the gospel message. As Servant, many of the services of the monasteries continued. In addition, orders like the one Saint Catherine of Siena belonged to enabled laywomen to devote their lives to aiding the poor. Another Catherine, Saint Catherine of Genoa, ran a hospital for the poor while living patiently with a brutal husband. In short, in the fourteenth and fifteenth centuries, many generous people were living the commandment to love their neighbors as themselves. They carried on the real life of the Church of Jesus even though highly visible church officials seemed to have lost their sense of purpose.

Review Questions and Activities

1) How did the popes' removal to Avignon signal a change in the status of the papacy?

2) The Hundred Years' War had implications for the Church. What were some of these?

3) In what ways was the Avignon papacy difficult for the whole Church at this time?

4) The Black Death killed one-third of Europe's population. What effect did this have on religious practice?

5) Explain why Saint Catherine of Siena was such an unusual person for her era—maybe for any era. Why was the religious order to which she belonged different from most of the other religious orders for women?

6) What were the causes and effects of the elections of two and then three popes at the same time? How was the situation resolved?

7) What was the political situation of Italy at this time, and how did it influence the Church?

8) After his death, Savonarola became somewhat of a hero to people trying to reform the Church. Why might this be so?

9) What is an interdict? Could it be used today by the pope? What would be the results if he tried to use it?

10) How did the political situation in Germany pose problems for the Church?

11) What was the Renaissance, and how was the Church a patron of this movement?

12) In 1456 the Bible was printed by Gutenberg. How did this event hasten the demands for reform in the Church?

13) The popes of the Renaissance seemed to lead double lives. What does this mean?

14) What were some of the ordinary religious practices of the common people during the fourteenth and fifteenth centuries? Particularly, how did the practice of granting indulgences begin, and what distortions resulted?

15) How did Moscow come to be called the "third Rome"? What relationship became established between the Roman Catholic Church and the Orthodox Church?

16) Why would people of this period look with such hope at the explorations of da Gama, Columbus, and Cabot? How did the Church view these discoveries?

17) During the fourteenth and fifteenth centuries, how did the Church act as Sacrament? Herald? Servant?

Personal Reflection Exercise

The events of this chapter may seem surprising to some people. However, most institutions go through periods when they need to be reformed; the Church is no exception. Many of the popes led double lives—at one level as leaders of the Church while on another level as greedy, pleasure-seeking men. Before all of this causes us to be too discouraged or critical of the institutional Church, maybe it would be useful to reflect on how we all sometimes live double lives. Here are some questions to guide your reflections:

- Have I ever knowingly done something that I knew was wrong?
- Have I ever disapproved of something that others did—but that I have done myself?
- Have there been times when I wanted to do one thing but ended up doing the opposite?
- How do I feel when I have been forgiven for my wrongdoing?
- If I have a hard time changing my ways, can I condemn the Church for not being perfect?
- Have I ever tried to make something good happen when I knew the way I was doing it was wrong?
- How can I help the Church strive to be what it is really intended to be?

12
A Reforming Church: 1500–1600

The changes brought about during the years 1500–1600 were some of the most radical that the Western world has ever seen. In less than a century, the cultural and religious unity of Europe was shattered. The one Roman Catholic Church was broken into many offshoots. Common people began exerting their rights. The intellectual and emotional ferment of these years would lead to revolutions and to the overthrow of monarchies in Europe.

As we saw in the last chapter, the demands for reform in the Church had been growing steadily. Suddenly they grew into a volcano that blew the top off religious conformity. At the center of this Reformation was one man, Martin Luther, about whom more has been written than about anyone except Jesus Christ. Certainly other people had significant roles to play, but Luther was the key actor in a drama of immense proportions.

The second great event of this century was the spread of Christianity in Asia, Africa, and the Americas. Missionaries were preaching, opening schools and clinics, and celebrating sacraments in areas still uncharted and unnamed by Europeans. The Church was becoming a worldwide religion.

Martin Luther's Call for Reform

The Reformation began on a cloudy, chilly 31 October 1517, when Father Martin Luther, thirty-four years old, hurried over from his monastery and stopped in front of the huge doors of the castle church of Wittenberg, Germany. The church doors often served as bulletin board, so Father Martin unrolled a large poster and fastened it to the door.

The poster is identified today as the **Ninety-five Theses.** These were statements about sin and its forgiveness, the meaning of indulgences, and the pope's power to grant indulgences. It was also an invitation to all who were interested in the topic to meet and discuss these theses with him in public. In addition, Father Martin sent printed copies of his Ninety-five Theses to friends in other towns, mostly teachers and preachers. In at least two of these places someone made a translation of them from the original Latin into the German so that everyone could read them. Before Christmas it seemed that everyone in the state of Saxony was talking about Luther's ideas. He seemed to be challenging church practices, and they began to want more information about the author who had signed himself, "the Reverend Father Martin Luther, monk of the Order of Saint Augustine, Master of Arts and of Sacred Theology."

Martin Luther (1483–1546) was a serious monk who held an important position in his order. His monastery was known for its strict religious life, much different from many other religious houses in Europe at the time. Martin himself kept the monastery rules faithfully. He was also a scholar who had studied the church fathers and, more importantly, the Bible. Luther recognized that a profound faith and trust in God was necessary for all Christians. And, as the practice of selling indulgences became more and more corrupt, he became critical of the value of indulgences. The indulgence preachers seemed to be offering a cheap way to heaven, a way that did not demand faith—that is, a complete change of heart and complete reliance on Christ. In short, some people thought they could buy their way into heaven.

Indulgences Corrupted

Why did medieval people believe in indulgences? It seems they were not so afraid of hell, but purgatory worried them. God was kind, but just too. To medieval people, God was like some lord or king who might not have them executed (put in hell) but who would certainly demand some sort of temporary purifying punishment as restitution for wrongdoing (in purgatory). Thus they believed that indulgences obtained by contributing to the Church would be reparation for sins. Consequently they would not have to suffer in purgatory. Unfortunately most people saw indulgences as a kind of magic cleanser that purified them without really requiring them to convert to a more Christian way of life.

Luther was convinced that people relied too heavily on all kinds of external practices to guarantee salvation. Long prayers in Church were common, accompanied by hymns and processions for which indulgences were granted. People visited shrines that had relics of the saints—Duke Frederick of Saxony himself had thousands of such relics in his palace right there in Wittenberg. On the other hand, Confession and Communion were rare, even among religious. Somehow priorities had gotten mixed up; people had forgotten the message of Jesus in the Bible, the sacraments, faith, and charity.

As people began to discuss the Ninety-five Theses, they naturally began to take sides. While many people were concerned about the theological issues involved, more than a few were concerned about the money. Why, they asked, should their German money go to Italy to build a church for the pope in Rome? Money, of course, had been a recurring issue between other countries and Rome for a long time. In Saxony, it was complicated because

An artist's rendering of Martin Luther
posting his Ninety-five Theses

the young archbishop had approved the indulgence campaign partly to receive a cut of the proceeds for his personal expenses. There was a second problem besides the outflow of money. Some even wondered whether the pope actually could grant indulgences. Did he have the authority to do such a thing? In any case, wasn't faith enough for salvation?

The man who was pope at this time, Leo X, did not take the Ninety-five Theses seriously. He saw it as an argument among monks. He was too busy with other pursuits (including his hobbies of horses and hunting dogs) to worry about what went on in a small German town. On the other hand, Duke Frederick of Saxony was on Luther's side; he was proud of his young university in Wittenberg and happy about the publicity one of his professors was giving the area.

Luther himself invited the Dominican preacher of the indulgences to debate publicly with him. The preacher turned down the invitation and instead wrote a booklet as an answer to Luther's points. Some Wittenberg students openly burned the booklets—the issue was literally heating up. Luther had a large following in Saxony and his support was spreading. However, others accused him of heresy for supposedly denying the pope's authority. Such accusations disturbed Luther, who decided to write directly to Pope Leo X.

Dated 30 May 1518, his letter begins: "Martin Luther, Augustinian monk, wishes eternal salvation for the most Holy Father, Pope Leo X." In the letter he denies any heresy, saying that he merely wanted what all other theology professors were always allowed to do—to discuss Christian teachings. Luther says that some misunderstood his theses: "These are theses that can be discussed, not doctrines." He ends the letter by assuring the pope of his loyalty: "I acknowledge your voice as the voice of Christ, who reigns and speaks through you."

Luther's Defense

The pope seemed rather unconcerned at this point, but the cardinals and bishops around him who ran the daily business of the Church were less satisfied. Three months after he wrote the pope, Luther was summoned to Rome to answer the charges of heresy. He was afraid to go to Rome for the hearing because, as everyone knew, a suspected heretic could be put into prison or even burned at the stake.

To make matters worse, the emperor of the German people, an old man expected to die any day, publicly said that Luther should be excommunicated. Luther appealed to Duke Frederick for protection. Then, instead of going to Rome, Luther wrote an answer to the charges against him.

Luther's theses were hardening into convictions. In his response he concluded that the pope and his councils were not the final authorities—only the Scripture was infallible, that is, entirely free of error. Moreover, people were saved by the grace of Jesus Christ, not through their own efforts. On the contrary, good works were the products of grace.

About this time, Duke Frederick arranged to have a special meeting in Augsburg between Luther and the pope's representative, **Cardinal Cajetan** (*kaj*-eh-tan). The meeting failed to bring about any reconciliation. Neither Cajetan nor Luther could change the other's mind.

A woodcut depicting the selling of indulgences in a German marketplace

Since Luther was now in an area controlled by those hostile to him, he decided to flee Augsburg for Wittenberg. Cajetan recommended that Luther be tried for heresy in Rome. One positive result of the meeting was that the cardinal wrote a position paper condemning the abuses of indulgence sellers and explaining the original purpose of the practice. The document was later sent out in the pope's name, with the result that the selling of indulgences gradually declined, even stopped in some areas.

Living in Wittenberg under Duke Frederick's protection, Luther continued to write, preach, and teach at the university. More and more, he came to the conclusion that the Bible is the sole authority in the life of a Christian. Traditions might be useful, but the individual had to follow the dictates of his or her conscience as informed by the Bible. This stood in direct opposition to the usually accepted position that a Christian must recognize the authority of both the Bible and tradition as interpreted by the Church—especially the pope and councils. Tradition includes beliefs and teachings that the Church has acknowledged as being inspired by the Holy Spirit and the Bible, but that may not have been spelled out exactly in sacred Scripture.

While Martin Luther was wrestling with religious questions, Charles V of Spain, who also held lands in Germany and in the Netherlands, was elected to succeed to the throne of the Holy Roman Empire. Sure of the new emperor's support, the Roman curia began work on a document excommunicating Luther. Cardinal Cajetan, who now knew Luther's works well, tried to get the officials in Rome to study his writings more fully. However, the curia demanded Luther's excommunication. Pope Leo X signed the document, giving Luther sixty days to reverse his teaching or be excommunicated. Clearly Luther was not given a fair hearing.

Luther Excommunicated

In the 1500s, excommunication orders were posted in public squares of as many towns as possible. The officials from Rome had a difficult time doing this in the case of Luther; most of the people were on Luther's side. In a few towns, however, his writings were burned in accordance with the instructions of the excommunication notice. Luther gave no signs of changing his stand; the excommunication became final on 3 January 1521.

According to European law of the time, Christian rulers had to arrest and punish heretics. Charles V called Luther to an assembly of nobles and church officials in the town of Worms, and upon hearing Luther maintain his position, gave him three weeks to reverse himself. Of course, the emperor did not hand down this ruling in public because he knew that most of the local dukes supported Luther. He waited until the sessions of the assembly were over and then got the approval of a small, handpicked group of electors (electors were nobles who ruled over small states in Germany).

With only three weeks before he had to recant or be arrested, Luther knew he had to find a protective ally. On his way home, a 300-mile trip, a "kidnapping" was staged by a group of knights. Luther was taken prisoner and hidden in a castle at Wartburg by his friend Duke Frederick. The duke arranged the kidnapping but could deny any knowledge of it. Thus he would not be in open opposition to the emperor.

An artist's conception of Martin Luther
before the assembly called by Charles V
at Worms (above)

The title page of the papal decree
directed against Luther (next page)

Luther lived for nearly a year at the castle; most of his time was spent writing. He was able to complete a translation of the Bible from Latin into German. This enabled more people to read the Bible—which was to Luther and his followers the sole authority for Christians. After about ten months, he returned to Wittenberg on the invitation of the town council. While he had been gone, many of the reforms that he suggested had been put into effect. In some instances, Luther was shocked by the zeal of his followers.

Luther still considered himself to be a Catholic. His original intent was to reform the Church, not to divide it or replace it. He believed in the sacraments but said that only two were justified from Scripture: Baptism and Eucharist. Luther believed in Christ's presence in the Eucharist, but he downplayed the idea of the Mass as a sacrifice. Emphasizing that people did not need intermediaries with God, Luther discredited relics, indulgences, praying to saints, rosaries, and other religious customs not biblically inspired. Preaching was given greater emphasis because people had to hear the Word to believe.

Finally, Luther stressed the priesthood of all believers; he taught that we all serve God and communicate directly without priests. Therefore, all Christians, not just specially ordained ministers, are responsible for the growth of the Christian Church. Consequently, Luther did not require that pastors remain unmarried. Luther saw these beliefs as reforms, not as innovations. Yet, as far as the church authorities

Bulla contra Erro res Martini Lutheri et sequarium.

were concerned, Luther was no longer a member of the Catholic faith. By 1525, Luther was married and still professor at the university; he preached and wrote vigorously.

Luther's Reforms and the Political Scene

Luther's ideas were also having widespread effects on German society. During this period, the German peasants were growing restless, tired of their hard lives. The peasants wanted freedom from lords who used and abused them without paying a living wage. At first, Luther took their side, urging nobles to reform the condition of Germany's working people. Little changed, and as a result, the Peasants' Revolt (1524–25) erupted. Luther condemned the ensuing violence. In the battles that raged between the peasants and the nobles' armies, thousands of peasants were killed. Luther never expected such consequences and was deeply disturbed by them. If peasants can communicate directly with God and if the Bible says that all people have dignity and are priests, why should a class structure exist that oppresses certain groups in society? Luther's theology led to results about which he had never dreamed.

Gradually, Lutheranism was growing into a popular movement in northern Germany—proceeding to take over Catholic churches and to hold new religious services. By 1526 the German national assembly was divided into two parties: Roman Catholic and Reformers. The assembly agreed to the principle that local rulers could choose the religion of their domains. Nevertheless there were armed conflicts between religions. Charles V agreed with the German assembly's decision in 1525 that gave Catholicism freedom to be practiced everywhere while restricting the new religion to places where it was already in existence. Because the Lutherans protested this decision, they became known as **Protestants**.

Divisions developed among educated people about the way reform was developing. The most famous scholar in Europe during the 1500s, **Erasmus**, criticized the Catholic clergy at least as much as Luther did, if not more. However, Erasmus did not agree with all of Luther's ideas of reform. He remained a Catholic. On the other hand, another theologian and good friend of Luther, **Melanchthon** (meh-*lang*-thuhn), composed a document for the Augsburg assembly in 1530 to show that Catholics and Lutherans agreed on the most important truths of faith and that there was a basis for compromise by the two groups.

"Military Affairs"—A Dialogue by Erasmus of Rotterdam

As was mentioned earlier, Erasmus was one of the great Catholic thinkers of the sixteenth century. While he remained part of the Catholic Church, he called for reforms too; he made these calls in public lectures and in his many writings. "Military Affairs" is a dialogue between Hanno, a Carthaginian commander, and Thrasymachus (meaning "swaggerer"), a foot soldier returning from battle.

In this dialogue, published in 1522, Erasmus makes foolish the reasons for war and also gets in some criticisms about selling indulgences. Thrasymachus thinks that simply by purchasing some indulgences he will not have to worry about any of the terrible crimes he committed during war. Clearly Erasmus wanted to challenge the consciences of his readers.

Hanno and Thrasymachus

Hanno: How is it you come back a Vulcan when you left here a Mercury?

Thrasymachus: What Vulcans or Mercuries are you talking about?

Hanno: You left as though wing-footed; now you're limping.

Thras: The usual way to come back from war.

Hanno: What have *you* to do with war? You're more timid than a deer.

Thras: Hope of booty made me brave.

Hanno: Then you come back rich with plunder?

Thras: No, with an empty purse.

Hanno: So much the less luggage to weigh you down!

Thras: But I return laden with sins.

Hanno: A heavy burden indeed, if the prophet speaks truth when he calls sin lead.

Thras: I saw and did more wickedness there than ever before in my whole life.

Hanno: Has a soldier's life any attraction at all?

Thras: Nothing's more wicked or more ruinous.

Hanno: Then what possesses those men—some hired for pay, others for nothing—who run off to war as if they were going to a party?

Thras: I can only suppose they're driven by devils and have given themselves over wholly to an evil spirit and to misery in such a way as to go to hell before their time.

Hanno: Apparently, since they can scarcely be hired at any price for honest purposes. But tell me how the battle was fought, and which side won.

Thras: So great was the tumult and the shouting, blasts of trumpets, thunder of horns, neighing of horses, and clamor of men that I couldn't see what was going on; I scarcely knew where I myself was.

Hanno: Then why do others who come back from war describe particular things—what each man did or said—as if they had been neutral observers who missed nothing?

Thras: For my part I think they're awful liars. What went on in my own tent, I know; as to what happened in the battle, I'm completely ignorant.

Hanno: Well, do you know how you got this lameness?

Thras: Damned if I know for sure. I think my knee was hurt by a stone or a horse's hoof.

Hanno: But I know.

Thras: You know? Did someone tell you?

Hanno: No, but I can guess.

Thras: Tell me, then.

Hanno: When you were scared and running away you fell down and knocked it on a stone.

Thras: Damned if you haven't hit the nail on the head! You've guessed right.

Hanno: Go home and tell your wife about your victories.

Thras: A sour song of victory she'll sing me for coming home empty-handed!

Hanno: But how will you make good what you've taken as plunder?

Thras: I made it good long ago.

Hanno: To whom?

Thras: Whores, wine merchants, and men who beat me at dice.

Hanno: The old army spirit! It's fitting that ill-gotten gains should be lost in a worse way. But you did refrain from sacrileges, I suppose?

Thras: On the contrary. Nothing was sacred there; no building spared, sacred or profane.

Hanno: How will you make amends for that?

Thras: They say you don't have to make amends for what's done in war; whatever it is, it's right.

Hanno: The law of war, perhaps.

Thras: Exactly.

Hanno: Yet that law is the greatest wrong. It wasn't devotion to your country but hope of spoils that drew you to war.

Thras: Granted; and in my opinion few men go there from any loftier motive.

Hanno: To be mad with many is something!

Thras: A preacher declared from the pulpit that war is just.

Hanno: The pulpit doesn't often lie. But war might be just for a prince, not necessarily for you.

Thras: I heard from professors that everyone has a right to live by his trade.

Hanno: A splendid trade—burning houses, looting churches, . . . robbing poor people, murdering harmless ones!

Thras: Butchers are paid to slaughter beef. Why is our trade denounced when we're hired to slaughter men?

Hanno: Weren't you worried about the destination of your soul if you fell in battle?

Thras: Oh, no, I was confident, because I had commended myself once for all to St. Barbara.

Hanno: Did she undertake to protect you?

Thras: Yes, she seemed to nod her head a little.

Hanno: When did this happen—in the morning?

Thras: No, after dinner.

Hanno: But then, I dare say, even the trees seemed to walk.

Thras: How he guesses everything! But I relied mainly on St. Christopher, whose picture I looked at every day.

Hanno: In tents? How came saints to be there?

Thras: We drew a charcoal picture of him on the tentflap.

Hanno: As protection that charcoal Christopher surely wasn't worth a fig, as they say. But, joking aside, I don't see how you can be absolved from such outrageous sins unless you betake yourself to Rome.

Thras: No, I know a shorter way.

Hanno: What is it?

Thras: I'll go to the Dominicans and strike a bargain there with the commissaries.

Hanno: Even for sacrileges?

Thras: Even if I had robbed Christ himself, yes even if I had beheaded him, such liberal indulgences have they and such authority to arrange matters.

Hanno: Very well—if God endorses your arrangement.

Thras: What I'm more afraid of is that the devil may not agree to it. God is forgiving by nature.

Hanno: What priest will you choose?

Thras: One I know to be as shameless and easygoing as possible.

Hanno: To be sure of finding like for like! When you're absolved you'll go straight from him to Communion?

Thras: Of course. After I once unload my sins into his cowl, I'll be free of the burden; let him who absolves me see to that.

Hanno: How do you know he absolves you?

Thras: I know.

Hanno: By what mark?

Thras: Because he places his hand on my head, mumbling something or other.

Hanno: What if he restores all your sins to you when placing his hand upon you, muttering these words: "I absolve you of all good deeds (of which I find none in you) and I restore your character to you and send you away just as I received you"?

Thras: Let *him* look to what he says. Enough for me that I believe myself absolved.

Hanno: But to believe that is risky. It may not satisfy God, to whom you're in debt.

Thras: How did I happen to run into you? You'd change my conscience from clear to cloudy.

Hanno: A lucky accident. It's a good sign if a friend you chance to meet gives you a timely warning.

Thras: I don't know how good it is, but it's certainly disagreeable.

The first part of Melanchthon's document, known as the **Augsburg Confession,** summarizes the teachings of the Reformers. It emphasizes the need for faith and the grace of God as a gift that we cannot earn by our actions. As editor of the Confession, Melanchthon wrote that "nothing in it is opposed to Scripture or the teaching of the Catholic Church. . . . We are therefore judged unfairly if we are called heretics." The second part of the Confession outlines the reforms implemented by Luther to correct the abuses in the Church: these included rejection of indulgences, allowing pastors to marry, stopping the veneration of relics and elaborate feasts, and so on. Luther was not present at the assembly at Augsburg, but he approved the Confession in a general way. This Augsburg Confession is still used by Lutherans today as the statement of their faith.

After 1530 the religious situation in German lands did not change much. The various provinces generally followed the religion of the local duke. Luther spent his time visiting parishes in order to preach his reforms. He also insisted that the Protestant theologians become well trained, especially in Scripture study. A major cause of problems in the Catholic Church was the poor education of most clergymen. For the ordinary people in his churches Luther translated works into and wrote in German: first the Bible, then two versions of a catechism, a hymnal, and the German Mass that stressed preaching from the Scriptures and receiving Communion.

From Luther's Germany the Protestant movement spread to other parts of Europe. People in various countries heard of the religious renovations from articles printed in booklets and from preachers who traveled from one region to another. Political authorities were usually the ones to decide what religion they would allow in their area—whether these authorities were local town councils, regional princes, or even the emperor himself. For some rulers, accepting the new reformed religion meant independence from Roman church taxes and from the Holy Roman emperor. For certain other rulers, staying with the Church secured their thrones by ensuring uniformity of belief. In short, whether a leader chose to stay in the Roman Catholic tradition or to join in the Lutheran movement was often dependent more on political than on religious motives.

In one way or another Protestantism moved into various European countries. Sweden joined Luther in 1527; Denmark, in 1536. By 1540 the New Testament had been translated into Icelandic for the Lutherans there. Holland, which was under Spain's rule, revolted and by 1584 had thrown off Spanish rule and Spanish Catholicism. Luther's ideas were taking hold in Scotland, Finland, Switzerland, and Moravia. Italy, France, Spain, southern Germany, and Poland maintained their ties to Rome. Russia, Greece, and some other Eastern European areas remained firmly in the Orthodox tradition.

John Calvin

As is the case with most periods of change, one change leads to another. Luther demanded reforms that were not too far from traditional Catholic thought and practice. The second most powerful reformer took Luther's ideas even further. **John Calvin** (1509–64) was a brilliant student of theology and law at the University of Paris. Reading Luther's works moved Calvin to challenge Catholic beliefs and eventually to reject many of them. Knowing that Protestants were being persecuted by King Francis I, Calvin left France for Switzerland. There he wrote *The Institutes of the Christian Religion,* very clearly outlining Protestant faith and religious practices. Unlike Luther, he rejected the Catholic form of the Mass as well as the belief in the presence of Christ in the Eucharist. Protestants in Geneva asked him to help them implement his reforms. As it turned out, he spent all but three years of the rest of his life in Geneva.

Calvin was an able administrator. He founded a university at Geneva to train the ministers of his churches. Calvin encouraged the work of hospitals and favored laws that promoted the economy, especially through the wool and silk industries. He preached almost daily and wrote approximately six thousand letters in his lifetime. Protestants came from all over to consult with him. He worked constantly in spite of chronically poor health.

Calvin wanted to build what Augustine would have called the "City of God." That the Church should dominate all civil affairs was clear to Calvin. Thus the Geneva council, under Calvin's influence, passed very strict laws for the city. For example, a woman who wore a fancy hairdo could be fined. Jail sentences were given for activities such as dancing in public, drinking in taverns, card playing, or even reading certain books. A strict adherence to moral principles was the duty of every citizen. In 1553, when Michael Servetus strongly criticized Calvin's directives and tried to organize opposition, Servetus was burned at the stake in Geneva. Calvin's churches worshiped simply, with little of the elaborate ritual of the Catholic tradition. Churches were stripped of their statues and ornamentation.

Predestination was a belief that was central for Calvin. Because God knows everything at all times, Calvin believed that God has marked certain people for heaven and the rest for hell. According to Calvin, our fates have been predetermined or predestined: "We declare that by God's providence, not only heaven and earth and inanimate creatures, but also the counsels and wills of men are governed so as to move precisely to that end destined by him." Clearly, Calvin's predestination stood in opposition to the traditional Catholic belief in free will. Thus Calvin carried the reform movement further than Luther.

Melanchthon (top), author
of the Augsburg Confession

John Calvin (bottom), author
of *The Institutes of the Christian
Religion*

The Church of England

About the time when Lutheranism was becoming well established and Calvinism was just beginning, another religious revolt was occurring in Catholic England. **King Henry VIII,** when he heard of Luther's attacks on the Mass and the sacraments, wrote a small book defending the teachings of the Catholic Church. For this the pope proclaimed him "Defender of the Faith," a title still held today by the rulers of England. Despite this defense of the Church, King Henry faced a serious problem: he had no son to succeed him on the English throne. In fact, the English considered this a crisis of major proportions. Each time that the succession was unclear, wars between contenders for the throne took place, and England became a battleground. As a responsible king, Henry saw it as his duty to England to have a son. Since his wife, Queen Catherine of Aragon (Spain), had not given him this son, he wanted to divorce her. He asked the pope for a divorce, citing the fact that a previous pope had given him a dispensation to marry Catherine even though she was his sister-in-law, the widow of his brother Arthur.

The request was poorly timed. The pope was under pressure from Emperor Charles V of the Holy Roman Empire, who was also King of Spain—and a nephew of Catherine of Aragon. When Henry's request arrived in Rome, in fact, the city was surrounded by Charles' troops. Charles did not want England's power to grow; a civil war of succession would prevent this. At the same time, a divorce would be a loss of face for Catherine and thus for Spain. In addition to these political considerations, the marriage was valid in the eyes of Rome.

When the pope refused the king's request for divorce, Henry ordered the archbishop of Canterbury to rule his marriage invalid. Henry then married Anne Boleyn. For various reasons, including the fact that their child was not a boy, Henry ordered Anne beheaded a few years later. He married six times in all: one wife died a natural death (at childbirth), two wife died a natural death (at childbirth), two were divorced, two were beheaded, and the last was scheduled for execution when Henry himself died in 1547.

By the time of Henry VIII the Catholic Church had been in England for more than twelve hundred years. The people of Britain were known for their loyalty to the Church; missionaries like Boniface had come from England. The barbarians who had invaded the island were all eventually converted. Even though King William the Conqueror (ruled 1066–87) strengthened the position of the English kings, he maintained his ties to the Church. But the popes' residence in Avignon during the war between France and England had strained the relationship between the Roman Church and its English members. Now the conflict over King Henry's divorce severed England from the Catholic Church.

Henry VIII managed the most complete takeover of spiritual authority yet seen in the West—more complete even than in Germany. Henry dissolved the monasteries and gave their lands to helpful nobles. In 1534, parliament passed the **Act of Supremacy,** which declared English monarchs the heads of the Church in England. Naturally Henry appointed bishops who were loyal to him. Every important person in public life was required to take an oath acknowledging the king's supremacy. Those who refused the oath were imprisoned and frequently executed. Among those executed were Bishop John Fisher and Sir Thomas More.

Bishop Fisher was a learned man, the head of Cambridge University for many years. He opposed Henry's attempts to divorce Catherine. **Sir Thomas More** held the post of chancellor of England—the highest official in the government—until he resigned in protest over the king's actions. More was a lawyer and writer; his novel *Utopia* is still studied. Over the years he held many government posts, and at one time he was young Henry's tutor. Arrested and imprisoned in the Tower of London,

Sir Thomas More (left) and Bishop John Fisher (right) were executed for opposing King Henry VIII's (facing page) attempts to divorce his first wife.

More refused to take the oath that negated the pope's authority—although he did not renounce the king. After a long prison stay during which Henry tried to change More's mind, More stood trial in parliament. He openly proclaimed his support of the pope. Soon after, he was beheaded.

It must be remembered that to reject Henry's claim to being head of the Church of England was considered an act of treason. Traitors were usually executed. Henry's methods, in fact, were not terribly different from those used in Spain by Ferdinand and Isabella when they persecuted the Jews. In Spain, not being Catholic was considered disruptive of social order and thus treasonous. While we do not burn heretics as traitors today, this was common practice in the religious quarrels of the sixteenth century.

Ironically the statements of faith and practice approved by Henry for the English Church were very Catholic. He rejected Lutheran teachings and never considered himself a Protestant. When Luther heard of the collection

of articles of faith called the "King's Book," he said: "This king wants to be God. He forms new articles of faith, which even the pope never did." Henry persecuted both Catholics and Protestant reformers. Edward VI, the son for whom Henry had sacrificed so much, solidified the status of the Church of England during his short reign (1547–53).

Council of Trent: Reform and Reaction

About the time Henry VIII was making himself head of the Church in England, a new pope, **Paul III**, took office. He was committed to making changes. First he appointed a commission to recommend reforms. In 1536 he sent a delegate to Wittenberg to discuss plans for a council. Generally the Protestant leadership was skeptical about the value of a council at this stage. Nevertheless, about five years later, a meeting of Lutherans and Catholics was held in southern Germany. The meetings began cordially enough but broke off over the issue of the meaning of the Eucharist.

Still, Paul III persisted in his commitment to having a council in any case. Emperor Charles V and King Francis I of France had finally ended their war, thus making travel possible. The pope wanted the council in Rome; the emperor, in Germany—which was, of course, unacceptable to the French. Ultimately they agreed to hold the council at Trent in the southern Alps, but under the emperor's rule.

There were to be two purposes of the council: to bring Protestants and Catholics back together again and to state very clearly the principal teachings of the Catholic Church. This program had to be changed when the Lutherans declined to attend. The meetings at Trent then concentrated on defining Catholic teachings and on setting up new rules for establishing order in the Church. **The Council of Trent** was responsible for what is called the **Catholic Restoration**: no essentials of faith were rejected, but the emphasis was to restore traditional Catholic faith and practice.

The Council of Trent met in three sessions over a period of eighteen years, from 1545 to 1563, each session running for approximately two years. The first session (1545–47) reaffirmed important Catholic teachings: that the faith of Christians is based in the Bible but also on the traditions that have come down from the Apostles; that the Church is the final interpreter of the Bible for Christians; and that salvation comes both from faith and from good works inspired by that faith. All seven sacraments were upheld as being valid. Bishops who lived outside the boundaries of their diocese were ordered to live within their dioceses (one problem had been that bishops of rural dioceses sometimes lived in big cities where life was more pleasant).

At the second session (1551–52) only fifty-nine participants came. The Holy Roman emperor and the French king were at war again.

And since the meeting was in German territory, only a couple of French churchmen were present. Some Lutheran representatives attended. After some debate about their views—especially their rejection of strong papal authority—the Lutheran delegation left. In the time remaining, the council discussed the "real presence" of Christ in the Eucharist and the validity of Confession and Anointing of the Sick. Then, since the duke of Saxony, who was fighting the emperor, was marching toward Trent, the second session disbanded in a hurry.

The final session of the Council of Trent (1562–63) was the best attended, with over two hundred representatives present. Besides supporting the traditional views that the Mass was a sacrifice and that Holy Orders and Matrimony were sacraments, this session set down new guidelines in several areas. Despite the emperor's opposition, celibacy for priests was upheld, and each diocese in which there was no university had to set up a seminary. The pope was asked to follow up the council meetings with the publication of a number of new books: a catechism or summary of church teaching, a breviary for the daily prayer of priests, a missal for use at the Mass, and an index or list of books that contradicted the faith or morals of Catholic people and therefore that Catholics were forbidden to read.

The Council of Trent had mixed results. For the most part, followers of Luther, Calvin, or Henry VIII were not swayed by the reforms. The decisions came too late and most supported traditional teachings. On the other hand, the council did reform many of the abuses that had scandalized serious Christians. The Church clarified its positions on many matters—this sort of discussion and clarification is always helpful. Religious orders returned to their rules, and new orders were founded to undertake the reforms started by the council. Thus there were positive outcomes. In fact, the decisions of the Council of Trent guided the Church steadily up until Vatican Council II.

The Society of Jesus

Among the new religious orders of this time was the **Society of Jesus,** or the Jesuits. This new order was founded by **Saint Ignatius** (ig-*nay*-shee-uhs) **of Loyola** (1491–1556), a nobleman who had to give up his military career when he was crippled by a leg wound. While Pope Paul III was struggling to make the council possible, Ignatius organized six of his fellow students at the University of Paris into a kind of religious club. In a chapel on a hill overlooking the city they made a vow to go to Palestine to convert the Turks to Christianity. When war prevented them from going to Palestine, they offered their services to the pope. Their main purpose was to spread the faith by teaching and preaching. They even took a fourth vow pledging absolute obedience to the pope. The order grew very rapidly.

Ignatius placed great emphasis on the training of his men; most went through at least fifteen years of study. Soon Jesuits were on the faculties of most of the major European uni-

Saint Ignatius of Loyola

versities in Catholic areas. In addition, they opened colleges and schools wherever they went. The Jesuits were convinced that a good Catholic education would ensure loyalty to the Church. Many of the seminaries were run by Jesuits, and so the level of education among the clergy increased. Through the peaceful means of study and teaching the Jesuits helped to stop the spread of Protestantism in Europe.

Jesuits spearheaded other religious activities for the Church. Many of the important theological works of the Church's restoration were written by Jesuits. In addition, Jesuit missionaries spread out to work all over the world. **Saint Francis Xavier** (*zay*-vee-uhr) traveled throughout Asia, preaching and converting in India, Sri Lanka, Malaysia, and Japan. Xavier was intending to move on to China; however he died in 1552 before completing that mission. The list of Jesuits known for their holiness is long; some of them are Francis Borgia, Aloysius Gonzaga, Peter Canisius, Robert Bellarmine.

Today there are about twenty-six thousand Jesuit brothers and priests worldwide—running universities, high schools, seminaries, missions, social service projects, retreat houses, information agencies, and religious education institutes. They are the largest order of religious men in the Church.

Holiness in an Unholy Time

Somehow good people manage to thrive in times of trouble. The early Christians became stronger the more they were persecuted. Augustine, Francis, and Catherine of Siena all emerged from times of turmoil. Perhaps the saints of this period of reformation and restoration stand out all the more because the times were so bad for the Church.

Saint Charles Borromeo, as archbishop of Milan, gave an excellent example of what a pastor should be like, reforming and educating the priests, setting up hospitals and services for the poor—even giving up his own home to shelter needy people.

An unusual kind of saint was **Philip Neri,** nicknamed "Pepo," who talked to everyone on the street corners of Rome about the love of God. People used to meet with him in the basement of a church to read the Bible, to pray, and to sing. When things got dull Pepo was known to do a clown routine—always speaking about God's love. He lived in the streets with the poor; later, holy men like Francis de Sales and Vincent de Paul would use his personable approach.

Saint Teresa of Ávila

In Ávila, Spain, **Sister Teresa** (1515–82) was aiding in the reform of monastic life. Originally named Teresa de Cepeda y Ahumada, she had entered a Carmelite convent at age twenty. The huge Incarnation convent was a busy place filled with activity—too much activity for Teresa. The monastic life was supposed to provide an atmosphere of prayer, study, work, and meditation. The Incarnation convent, like many in the pre-Reformation days, had lost the spirit of a quiet turning to God. In 1562, after over twenty-five years as a Carmelite, Teresa established a small convent called Saint Joseph's in Ávila. The Saint Joseph's community of thirteen nuns wanted to live very simply, pray regularly, and concentrate on meditation. To do so, they gave up the material comforts of the larger convent. The Carmelite order objected strongly and tried to close down the new convent. But Teresa was not naive; she managed to have her convent placed under the direct protection of the king, Philip II. Her group of Carmelites was called Discalced, that is, "without shoes."

After five years, Teresa was requested to open Discalced Carmelite convents all over Spain. She was in her late forties and early fifties when she traveled throughout the country founding new houses. Most of the trips were made on foot, or maybe bouncing in a

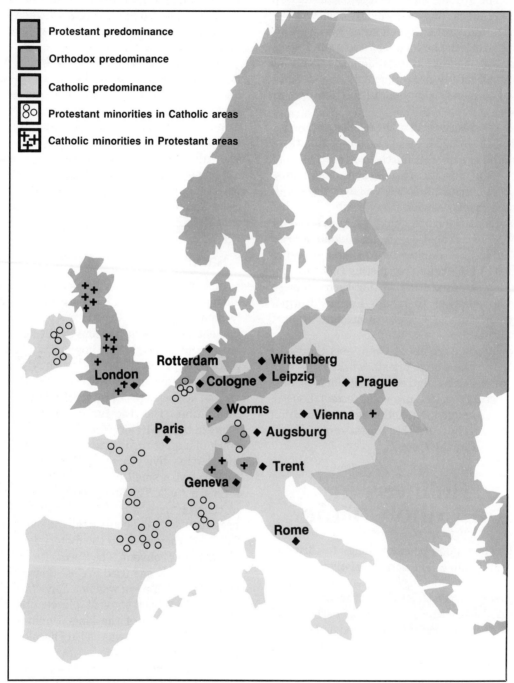

cart with no springs. What was especially hard was that all these travels kept her away from the silent life she desired. Nevertheless, convinced that convents would help restore the spiritual life of the Church, she carried on. In each town in which she was invited to begin a convent, she had to take care of the paperwork, raise the money to buy land and build the house, supervise construction, and recruit new members for the community. For several years, Teresa was opening two new houses each year. Her zeal and energy were immense. Soon there were Discalced Carmelites in Málagon, Valladolid, Toledo, Pastrana, Salamanca, and Alba de Tormes. Even more convents followed until the end of her life.

In the midst of all this, the main order of Carmelites was challenging Sister Teresa. They did not approve of what she was doing and did not like being confronted with their own lack of serious commitment. Finally, after several years of dispute, the king made Teresa's Discalced Carmelites a different order.

Saint Teresa of Ávila

Another major commitment of Teresa's time and energy was the correspondence she kept up. She wrote thousands of letters in her lifetime—some to instruct and inspire, others to discharge business. And she wrote several books. Her most famous book, one still read avidly today, is *The Interior Castle.* In it she describes how one can come to God through prayer and love. This classic book was written by Teresa in about two months.

Teresa of Ávila died on 4 October 1582. She was so famous that many different towns wanted her to be buried in their cemeteries or churches. First, she was buried in Alba de Tormes; then in 1585, the Discalced Carmelites had her body reburied in Ávila. Finally the Duke of Alba, wanting her body in his city, obtained an order from Rome designating Alba de Tormes as the final resting place of this saint who had traveled so far carrying out the work of reform started at Trent.

The Church Spreads to Asia

Some tough missionaries had preached to the Mongols in Peking as early as the fourteenth century. But when these missionaries died, the Gospel was not heard again in China until the 1500s. The voyages of Spanish and Portuguese explorers had opened up trade with India, Sri Lanka, Indonesia, and Malaysia. Traveling with the European traders to these Eastern countries were Catholic missionaries. Francis Xavier preached in all these lands. He even began a Catholic community in Nagasaki, Japan, which lasted up to the present—despite persecution and the executions of Jesuits and Japanese Christians in 1597.

Although Xavier died before he was able to enter China, his fellow Jesuit **Matteo Ricci** (1552–1610) worked in the Imperial court of China for years. Ricci gained entry through his knowledge of astronomy and other sciences. Once he became well known in royal circles, Ricci began slowly to talk about his religion. Gradually some converts were made, although the emperors of China never converted. Ricci spoke fluent Chinese and dressed as Chinese people did; he respected Chinese civilization and traditions and tried to show how Christianity complemented these traditions.

The difficulties of working in China and Japan were immense. Both countries had highly sophisticated cultures, in many ways far advanced of any in Europe. Accepting Christianity seemed to these Far Eastern people to be an acceptance of Western culture, which they looked upon as inferior to their own. And since the missionaries were involved with foreign governments that were clamoring for favorable trade agreements, the missionaries were seen as foreign agents. Indeed, the Spanish and Portuguese governments wanted the missionaries to be agents for them, in effect agents of colonial power. Thus in the early 1600s the Japanese, under the Tokugawa dynastic reign, closed Japan to foreign trade and began persecuting Japanese converts who were considered disloyal to Japan. Japan was virtually closed to the world until 1851.

Conversions in the parts of Asia not ruled by a colonial power were very limited. On the other hand, when the explorer Magellan (muh-*jel*-uhn) landed on Cebu (say-*boo*) Island in the Philippines, the Spanish friars began converting what is still the only Christian country in Asia. Magellan landed in 1521 but was killed in a war with the island's people. In 1565, Miguel López de Legazpi brought a larger force of Spanish explorers and, along with them, Augustinian friars. Having established Manila as the capital city of the colony, the

Spanish brought in more missionaries: the Franciscans (1577), the Jesuits (1581), and the Dominicans (1587). The Philippine Islands were split into regions with different religious orders in charge of different sections. In 1581, Domingo de Salazar, a Dominican, was named the first bishop of the Philippines. Thus the Church was established in these Asian islands long before it was in North America.

Even though the Church was allied with the Spanish colonial powers, who came to Asia to conquer and exploit the people there, the Church was often the only protection the people had from their oppressors. The Spaniards, soon after they had built Manila, began sending out parties of troops into the countryside. Soldiers would pacify an area and help a Spanish landlord organize his plantation—using Filipinos as virtual slaves. This practice was opposed by the friars. In fact, the friars objected to the ownership of the land by the Spaniards. In the late 1500s, Augustinian friar **Martin de Rada** wrote the Spanish officials: "I have asked the opinion of all the Fathers who were here, and all unanimously affirm that no part of all these islands has come under the power of the Spaniards by a just title." The friars were also responsible for convincing King Philip II in 1574 to prohibit slavery in the Philippines.

With the friars came Spanish culture, and the Philippines began taking on the religious practices of Spain, including fiestas and religious dramas. As the friars moved further and further into the villages and towns, they frequently became the presence of Spain in the countryside. Yet the friars preached and taught in the native languages of the country—Tagalog, Cebuano, Ilongo, or one of the eighty other languages. As a matter of fact, Spanish missionaries were the first ones to write grammars for these languages. In addition, the friars often helped with new agricultural techniques; some also opened small parish schools and clinics. Naturally they were still foreigners, still Spaniards, and thus still part of the colonial establishment. It would be three hundred years before Filipinos would have Filipino priests serving them and Filipino bishops leading them.

Spaniards in Central and South America

The amount of missionary activity in Africa was minimal during the 1500s, but the missionaries came in force to the New World during these years. As was the case in Asia, they came with Spanish soldiers. Columbus claimed many of the Caribbean Islands for Spain and touched land on northern South America. If he had explored further into the continent itself and into Mexico, he would have found three sophisticated cultures: the Mayas on the southeast coast of Mexico and Guatemala, the Aztecs in the central valley of Mexico, and the Incas on the western coast of South America, largely in Peru.

The Mayas built enormous temples at the same time that the Roman Empire was at its greatest power. They grew corn, cotton, squash, and beans—crops unknown in Europe. Their knowledge of astronomy enabled them to design a calendar more accurate than the ones used in Europe. In short, they were a knowledgeable people. By Spanish colonial times, however, the Mayas were overshadowed by a far more powerful group, the Aztecs.

The Aztecs ruled over an empire including many other Mexican tribes. Their temples were amazing feats of design and construction. Their governmental structure was complex, although ultimately one person ruled as both king and high priest. When the first white men appeared on the coast of Panama, the Aztec ruler was Montezuma II. Very soon he found himself facing **Hernando Cortés**, a crafty Spanish adventurer sent by the governor of Cuba to open this central Mexican territory to Spain.

The Spanish conquistador Hernando Cortés

Cortés had only a small group of soldiers called **conquistadores**. Yet they were armed with weapons more powerful than the Aztecs', and they had horses. These creatures awed the Aztecs, particularly when armored conquistadores were astride them. Cortés and his troops were supposed to barter for gold. Instead, Cortés decided to take the gold and Mexico with it.

Montezuma hesitated to fight the Spaniards because of an ancient Aztec belief that one of their gods who had a white skin would come back to rule them. The Aztecs wondered if the invaders might not be friends of their god; they even called the Spaniards "people of heaven." They soon found out otherwise. Cortés talked the king into giving up the gold and then took Montezuma hostage. Montezuma was killed; Cortés fled but came back with an army. After three months of siege and fierce fighting Cortés's army stormed the city, killing everyone and looting anything of value. All this was going on while Luther was publicizing his criticisms of the Church.

Further south, another treasure seeker, **Francisco Pizarro**, landed in Panama. Following the western coast of South America, he found the empire of the Incas in the Andes mountains—eleven thousand feet above the sea. In the Incan mountain cities, the Spaniards saw magnificent pyramid temples where sacrifices were offered to the sun. Of most interest to the Spaniards, though, were the gold and silver ornaments in these temples. Incan artistry was very advanced in jewelry, masonry, and weaving. And since usable land was scarce in the high Andes, the Incas had cut terraces on the mountain slopes, making narrow strips of flat level land for planting. The crops they grew would later be brought back to Europe as new foods: potatoes, tomatoes, corn, and chocolate. But first, Pizarro wanted gold, silver, and gems.

The Incas led a highly organized communal existence. Their laws were simple but effective; they kept extremely accurate statistics about population, crops, and taxes. Unfortunately, when Pizarro was marching toward Incan territory, the Incas were divided over who should succeed as ruler. Consequently social order was at a low point. After three expeditions against them, Pizarro managed to kill most of the Incas, steal all their treasures, and ruin their empire. Soon Peru was a destroyed land. The Indians who were not killed were made slaves of the Spaniards and set to work in the silver mines or on plantations. By 1550 there were two Spanish colonial empires in the new world, one centered in Mexico and the other in Peru.

The term *empire* may be an exaggeration. The Spanish killed a large portion of the populations of these areas, either by the sword or by the many new diseases they carried with them—especially smallpox or measles. By the end of the 1500s the native populations of Mexico and Central America were reduced to 10 percent of what they had been when Columbus first came west—90 percent had died. To make matters worse, the Spanish who came as colonizers were generally poor, uneducated men who could never rise in society in their homeland. They wanted wealth, no matter what the cost to the Indians—whom they considered to be subhuman anyway.

Missionaries in Central and South America

The missionaries who came to the colonies were usually powerless to stop the exploitation of the people. Nevertheless they preached the Gospel to the Indian peoples. The earliest missionaries were the Franciscans who began work on Santo Domingo in the Caribbean in 1500. In 1524 the Franciscans came to Mexico, later joined by the Dominicans and then the Augustinians. Generally they tried to learn the local languages, construct an alphabet, and then write catechisms. Mexico had its first bishop in 1530. Soon there were missionaries in Panama, Colombia, Ecuador, Guatemala, and Honduras. By 1549 the first Jesuits arrived in the jungles of Brazil, the colony owned by Portugal. Soon they fanned out into other parts of the continent, including Paraguay, Peru, and Mexico.

The Indians became Christians for a number of reasons. First, some of the missionaries were good to them. Some believed that the Christian god must be stronger than their gods because the Spaniards conquered them. Therefore, if they converted, they would be on the winning side—or at least they would have something in common with the Spaniards. No doubt others genuinely believed in the new faith. These reasons were similar to the ones the early Goths, Vandals, and Franks had for converting not too many centuries before.

Inevitably, as in Asia, "Christian" became equivalent to "Spanish." In this very confusing situation the missionaries themselves ran into split loyalties. They were loyal Spaniards, but they wanted to serve the people. Thus odd practices occurred. For example, in most places the Christian Indians were not given Communion for many years; they were allowed only the sacraments of Baptism, Penance, and Matrimony—sacraments that they could understand more easily than Eucharist. By the same token, no Indians were ordained as priests for almost three hundred years because the king of Spain forbade it.

As in Asia, the Indians were also victims of abuses—the worst one being slavery. Again, the friars were their main defenders. Especially famous for confronting the abuses was **Bishop de Las Casas;** he was the main power that finally caused the king to prohibit slavery. He went to Colombia in 1545 and worked for Indian rights there—eventually being forced out by plantation owners. In Guatemala the Spaniards tried to capture him, but he managed to escape. Conditions were much the same in Honduras and Panama. Las Casas had many allies among the friars and the Jesuits.

In the 1600s in places such as Paraguay, the Jesuits set up towns and areas like reservations for Indians. Here the Indians could live together under Indian authority. The Jesuits set up schools, weaving projects, and communal farming. These settlements were so successful that the Jesuits made enemies among greedy colonizers. Eventually these enemies forced the Jesuits out of South America.

Focus on the Models

This century was undoubtedly one of the most important in Christian history. The People of God, who were supposed to be the sign of Christ's presence and unified as the Body of Christ, were split into factions. The old saying from the times of the early Christians, "see how these Christians love one another," could be replaced now by "see how these Christians fight among themselves." Reforms were needed in the Church. The Council of Trent did begin the process of bringing the Christian community back together by clarifying beliefs, setting up seminaries, disciplining the clergy, and defining other issues. Tragically any dialogue with the Protestant groups and the Church in England was impossible because of antagonisms on both sides. The Christian Church was now divided into many parts: Orthodox, Catholic, Lutherans, Calvinists, Anglicans (Church of England), and some smaller groups. These divisions still remain today, and it is part of the duty of Christians to heal them if we are to be the Body of Christ.

Institutionally the Church was reorganized to more efficiently regulate church affairs. Some new offices were set up in Rome to guide the Church in more conscientious ways and, in many instances, keep the Church out of politics, when possible. The Church as Sacrament is seen in the Church worshiping as one; during this century, the Council of Trent prescribed each of the rituals so that the celebrations of the sacraments would be the same everywhere. As Servant, Christians continued to help the poor, even though the divided Church could do little in an organized way.

Finally, through the missionary activities of hundreds of rugged friars, many people in Asia, Africa, and the Americas heard the Good News—even if under less than ideal conditions. The often close relationship between Christian missionary work and colonial governments would, in the later centuries, cause crises of conscience for people who wanted to throw off the colonial powers yet remain faithful Catholics.

Another great advance for the spreading of the Good News was the distribution of printed translations of the Bible. Although the Council of Trent discouraged Bible reading for the average Catholic, in time these translations made the Gospel available to people of many languages.

Review Questions and Activities

1) What were the Ninety-five Theses and why were they so important?

2) What were the main reforms that Luther thought the Church should make?

3) Why were people so concerned about gaining indulgences? How did this lead to a corruption of the original meaning associated with indulgences?

4) Why was Luther excommunicated? Why was the situation more complicated due to political factors? What made excommunication such a terrible penalty?

5) What rather unexpected effects did Luther's teaching have on German society? Was he pleased with the results?

6) What were the three main emphases that Luther made in religious belief that differed from Catholic tradition?

7) Why are followers of Luther called Protestants?

8) How did Erasmus criticize both war and the selling of indulgences? How was his criticism different from that of Luther?

9) How was the religion of a region of Germany decided? Do you think this process would be acceptable today?

10) On a map, trace the movement of the Reformation through Europe.

11) How did Calvin take the Reformation many steps further than Luther? What relationship did Calvin see between church and state?

12) What is predestination? Why is this notion so different from Catholic belief?

13) Why did Henry VIII break from the Catholic Church? Why would the people of England generally understand, if not support, this separation?

14) The results of the Council of Trent were mixed. Why? Give examples of successes and failures of the council.

15) How were politics involved even in the Council of Trent? Is it possible to completely separate religion and politics?

16) Who are the Jesuits? Why did they play an important role in the Catholic Restoration?

17) Teresa of Ávila was very influential in monastic reform in Spain. Why was she such an influential person? Why did the Carmelites oppose her?

18) On a map, trace the spread of Christianity through Asia and South America. What problems arose because of the relationship between missionaries and Western governments?

19) Why did the missionaries experience so little success in China and Japan?

20) How did the friars often have to protect the local people from the Spaniards?

21) Why did the Indians of Central and South America become Christian? Would these motives cause problems for the missionaries?

22) How were the Indians really second-class members of the Church for many years?

23) Why is the division that splits Christians into many groups such a scandal to non-Christians?

Personal Reflection Exercise

Loyalty to one's country is certainly a value that is important. But how far can one go in loyalty to one's country? In this chapter, whole countries left the Catholic Church because of their leaders' commands. Would this be the proper motivation for a change in religious belief? List as many ways as possible in which government policy or power does or might conflict with personal moral choice. How do governmental decisions influence morality? Describe the dilemmas created for Christians. When religious convictions and governmental demands conflict, which should take precedence?

13
The Liberation of the Church: 1600–1900

Whereas the sixteenth century was a period of religious revolution, the next three centuries (1600–1900) were filled with scientific, industrial, political, and intellectual revolutions that challenged the very bases of faith and the structures of life.

The religious lines had been drawn rather sharply throughout Europe; countries were either Catholic or Protestant. This division of people by religion persisted throughout the three centuries; but, in the eighteenth century, called the Age of Reason, thinkers tried to use reason to criticize formal religion and even to deny God. Science, it was thought, would show the way to truth. At the same time, the Industrial Revolution completely altered the whole pattern of life for a previously agrarian Europe. Politically, calls for freedom and equality rocked the thrones of monarchs who, in turn, believed they ruled by "divine right."

The Reformation period pushed the Church to restore itself; these three centuries caused the Church in Europe to defend itself. Despite all the disruption in Europe, missionary activity went on all over the world, and the Church in North America was developing a life of its own, as we will see in the next chapter.

Religious Lines Are Fixed

By 1650, Europe was divided along religious lines. Scandinavia, Prussia, and parts of southern Germany were Lutheran. Switzerland, much of Holland, and Scotland were Calvinist. England had its own church. The rest of Europe was predominantly Catholic. These boundaries were established in 1648 at the Peace of Westphalia after thirty bloody years of war.

Naturally religion was not the only, not even the chief, reason for the Thirty Years' War, as it came to be known. However, religion made a noble-sounding excuse for the European powers to fight. At the start, the Catholic emperor Ferdinand II of Austria looked like he would beat the Protestant Prussians and their allies. When King Gustavus of Sweden came to the Protestants' aid in 1631, the tide of victory swung against the Catholics. Ironically, Cardinal Richelieu, the real power behind the French throne, allied his country with the Protestants. He was afraid that if Austria won it would unite Germany against France. In any case, when the treaty was signed in 1648, religious wars connected with the Protestant Reformation were largely over.

On the other hand, religious persecution was not over. For example, the Huguenots (French Calvinists) were hounded by Catholic officials. Campaigns were mounted to destroy Calvinist strongholds. In England, Catholicism was considered treason. All Catholic priests were thrown out of the country, and a harsh penal code was enforced against Catholics, or "papists." When the **Gunpowder Plot**—an attempt by Catholic fanatics to blow up the king and parliament—was uncovered on 5 November 1605, the reaction was swift and brutal.

Some Catholics were executed and others fled England for their lives. Catholics who stayed had to take an oath renouncing the pope. Nevertheless, Catholic priests were smuggled back into England; they lived in "safe houses" equipped with hiding places behind false walls, which offered protection during the police searches.

As the 1600s were ending, the harsh acts of government officials against dissenting religions declined, but restrictive laws stayed on the books. Catholics were denied certain rights in Protestant countries, and Protestants were second-class citizens in Catholic countries.

The Baroque Cathedral

During the Renaissance a new type of architecture had supplanted the Gothic style of the Middle Ages. This new style, called **baroque** (ba-*rohk*), featured columns patterned after those found in Greek and Roman temples; these columns supported triangular roofs and magnificent domes. The most outstanding example of the baroque churches is Saint Peter's in Rome, finished in the early 1600s.

The aim of the baroque architect was to overwhelm the churchgoer with the power and splendor of the building. The ornate and elaborate decorations, which usually covered every part of the church, were designed to demonstrate the many means of grace—that is, the Madonna, the saints, relics, the Mass, and the Eucharist. During this period, famous artists like Rubens painted huge murals of the Madonna and the Trinity, saints in prayer, and mystics in ecstasies of meditation. These pictures were meant to give examples to the devout Catholic. They also stressed those religious practices to which Protestants most objected. For instance, baroque churches featured tabernacles richly decorated so that the worshiper would focus his or her attention on the presence of Christ in the Eucharist.

Executions of Catholics in England

After the Gunpowder Plot was uncovered and the plotters executed, England became unsafe for any other Catholics—especially priests. The following is part of an account given by Father John Gerard, SJ, about his flight from persecution and about the executions of fellow Catholics. The events narrated took place from 5 November 1605 to 3 May 1606.

As my principal friends were involved in the catastrophe of the Powder Plot, the council was thorough and relentless in its hunt for me. They sent justices of the peace to the house. They were to search it scrupulously and if they failed to find me, stay on until they were recalled. Day and night guards were to encircle the house, and at night special watches set at a distance of three miles round, with orders to arrest any passing stranger. All this was carried out to the letter.

As soon as news reached us that a plot had been discovered and that some of our friends had been killed and others captured, we knew that we would have to suffer. However, we had prepared, and although the search lasted many days nothing was discovered till my hostess revealed to the chief pursuivant a hiding-place which had only a few books in it. Her hope was that they would think that, if a priest was in the house, he would be hiding there, and that they would then call off the search. But they went on till the end of the ninth day.

I was in my hiding-place. I could sit down all right but there was hardly room to stand. However, I did not go hungry, for every night food was brought to me secretly. And at the end of four or five days, when the rigor of the search had relaxed slightly, my friends came at night and took me out and warmed me by a fire. It was winter time, just before the season of Christmas. After nine days the search party withdrew. They thought I could not possibly have been there all that time without being discovered.

After the plot had been discovered and made public, the superior and Father Oldcorne were captured at the latter's house. They were discovered after a long search—they were twelve days in a hiding-hole. With them were taken two servants or, as I have since heard and believe, two brothers of our Society. Both were condemned to death and suffered martyrdom. One, Ralph, died with Father Oldcorne, whose companion and servant he had been. As the father mounted the ladder to the scaffold, Ralph clasped his feet and kissed them and thanked him for his kindness and for all he had done for him. Then he blessed God for granting him such a happy end to his life in such good company. The other was "Little John." For nearly twenty years he had been Father Garnet's companion and I have had occasion to mention him frequently in the course of this story. He was well known as the chief designer and builder of hiding-places in England, and was, therefore, a man who could hand over more priests and injure and betray more Catholics than any other single person. They tortured him long and mercilessly and in the end, unable to get any information out of him, they killed him, but they had been unable to break his constancy.

Also in that book I have told how Father Garnet and Father Oldcorne were brought to London. There they were examined time and again, particularly Father Garnet, and both were tortured, Father Oldcorne more often. Father Oldcorne was taken back to Worcester. Though nothing could be proved against him, he was condemned, hanged and quartered. It was a saintly martyr's death.

Baroque churches sprang up throughout Italy, Spain, Bavaria, and Austria. The quiet simplicity of the Gothic cathedrals, characterized by slender spires pointing to heaven, had been replaced by dramatic, vibrant sculptures and rounded domes meant to overpower.

New Styles of Religious Life

Even while these extravagant baroque churches were being built, women and men were fashioning a new style of religious life that sought to be of service to the human needs of the poor, sick, ignorant, and homeless—while at the same time instructing them in the Word of God. One innovative founder was **Saint Vincent de Paul** (1581–1660). Although born of peasant parents in France, he was sent by a rich patron to the seminary and ordained at age twenty. On a boat trip to Marseilles he was captured by pirates and sold as a slave to a farmer in Algeria. After converting his master to Christianity, he made his way back to France.

His rich patron helped him to finish his studies in Rome and to gain an appointment as chaplain to Queen Margaret of Navarre. The time at the French court was dazzling to the young peasant priest, but soon Vincent removed himself to become priest for a small country parish, for this is where his heart was. Yet Vincent was frustrated that he could not meet all the needs of the large population of poor people in seventeenth-century France. So he organized the Ladies of Charity who, among other things, volunteered to feed the hungry and care for the sick. By 1627, confraternities of the Ladies of Charity were set up in one hundred parishes in France.

Realizing that rural people were often ignored by dioceses that had their headquarters in large cities, Vincent also established the Congregation of the Mission—a band of priests and brothers who walked through the countryside preaching to and teaching simple folk. In 1625 his congregation took over an abandoned leprosarium, called Saint Lazare, as a head-

The baroque era of art and architecture is represented by Melk Church in Austria (facing page) and by the Throne of Saint Peter (above) in Saint Peter's Basilica.

quarters. By 1660 there were twenty-three houses of the Congregation with 131 priests and 52 brothers. So successful were Vincent's missionaries that the bishops asked him to open a seminary to train diocesan priests; soon many French seminaries were run by the Congregation of the Mission.

Vincent's most important innovation in religious life was his cofounding of the **Daughters of Charity.** Supervising the work of the Ladies of Charity was too big a job for Vincent to do alone. Fortunately a widow and mother of one son, **Louise de Marillac,** at age thirty-four began helping Vincent direct the activities of the Ladies. Quickly she took direction of the spreading movement. Realizing that service to the poor was part of the mission of the Church and that volunteers like the Ladies of Charity needed support from full-time sisters, Louise began establishing the group we know as the Daughters of Charity. In 1633 she took several women into her home and formed a community. Vincent de Paul wrote a rule for them to follow.

What made this group so revolutionary? Remember that up to this time all women religious were required to live in cloistered or closed convents, hidden from the world. Women religious were not supposed to be nurses, welfare workers, or teachers. In fact, the Daughters of Charity did not intend to be considered a religious order and were not recognized as such by the Vatican. This congregation of women took private religious vows for one year at a time. They wore the same style of dress as the French peasants of the time. Soon the Daughters of Charity ran hospitals, hospices, orphanages, and schools. Some of the Daughters even ministered to galley slaves. By the time of Vincent's death in 1660, there were fifty-one houses of the Daughters of Charity. Today they are the largest institute of religious women in the Church, with approximately forty-five thousand members.

The spirit of the Daughters of Charity was summarized in this comment by Vincent de Paul: "The love of the Daughters of Charity is not only tender; it is effective, because they serve effectively the poor, corporally and spiritually . . . [giving] oneself to God in order to serve Him in the person of the poor." The Daughters of Charity charted a new course of service for women in the Church; eventually many new congregations were founded on this model.

Another major development in religious life was the founding of the first teaching order composed completely of religious brothers. **John Baptist de La Salle** (1651–1719) was raised in a wealthy family in Rheims, France. After a brilliant scholastic career, he was established as a priest at the cathedral of Rheims. Gradually La Salle became involved in the educational work being done by two zealous friends of his. Like Louise de Marillac, La Salle realized that if the educational work among the poor were to continue, a group of religious men with a common rule of life and proper training was needed. Like Marillac, La Salle invited a group of young men to live in his house and form a community of schoolmasters.

La Salle's prominent family was horrified because schoolmasters were considered unsavory characters. Indeed, many tutors of the time could barely read or write themselves and could have made more money at just about anything else—if they had been capable of doing anything else. In the 1600s only the very rich could afford to educate their children. What La Salle was proposing—to teach the children of the poor—was revolutionary. His belief was that if children of the poor were given a practical education, they could support themselves and their families better and climb out of the poverty that spawned so much crime and despair. While receiving this education, they could also learn religion.

To that end, La Salle established the Brothers of the Christian Schools. He also developed much of the methodology that has since become standard in schools worldwide. For instance, the classroom, filled with rows of students, was created by La Salle; before his time students were taught, for the most part, one at a time by tutors. A fixed daily schedule of a variety of courses was required, and all subjects were now taught in the language of the students; before La Salle students had learned only classical literature and some mathematics—all in Latin. La Salle also created commercial or business courses not offered before. The brothers taught in the prisons of Paris and opened schools for orphans and homeless boys. In short, La Salle is considered the founder of modern education.

When La Salle died in 1719, there were 274 La Salle Brothers or **Christian Brothers.** The number was growing quickly and soon the brothers operated schools all over France. Today the Brothers of the Christian Schools are the largest order of brothers—and one of the largest men's orders—in the Church.

With the founding of these new religious orders, the revival of the Church took a giant step forward. The Church began serving the People of God, especially the poor. While there were many high church officials still heavily involved in the political intrigues of the courts of Europe, hundreds of devoted laypeople as well as women and men religious renewed the Church's commitment to service.

The Missions in the Seventeenth Century

The missionary activity begun in the 1500s took on new life in the 1600s. In 1622, Pope Gregory XV founded the Congregation for the Propagation of the Faith. This Vatican office coordinated the efforts of all missionary groups. In 1627 the College of Urban was set up in Rome to train missionaries. The Vatican also created a new position called the **vicar-apostolic;** a vicar-apostolic had the authority of a bishop, was responsible to Rome, but was not tied to one specific territory.

Finding God in Other People

Whereas the monks lived silent lives of prayer far away from the world, the new active religious orders plunged into serving people in a complex society. They had to learn to find the presence of God in the people with whom they worked—rather than in long periods of silence. Saint John Baptist de La Salle, founder of the Christian Brothers, describes in *Meditations for the Time of Retreat* how the brothers were to consider their students and their work. Every year the following thoughts from La Salle's work, written between 1707 and 1719, were the source of reflection for the brothers:

> Consider that it is only too common for the working class and the poor to allow their children to live on their own, roaming all over as if they had no home, until they are able to be put to some work. These parents have no concern to send their children to school because they are too poor to pay teachers, or else they have to go out to look for work and leave their children to fend for themselves.

> The results of this condition are regrettable. These unfortunate children, accustomed to an idle life for many years, have great difficulty when it comes time for them to go to work. In addition, through association with bad companions they learn to commit many sins which later on are very difficult to stop, the bad habits having been contracted over so long a period of time.

> God has had the goodness to remedy so great a misfortune by the establishment of the Christian schools, where the teaching is offered free of charge and entirely for the glory of God, where children are kept all day and learn reading, writing, and their religion. In these schools the children are always kept busy, so that when their parents want them to go to work, they are prepared for employment.

> Since you are ambassadors and ministers of Jesus Christ in the work that you do, you must act as representing Jesus Christ himself. He wants your disciples to see him in you and receive your teaching as if he were teaching them. They must be convinced that the truth of Jesus Christ comes from your mouth, that it is only in his name that you teach, that he has given you authority over them.

> They are a letter which Christ dictates to you, which you write each day in their hearts, not with ink, but by the Spirit of the living God. For the Spirit acts in you and by you through the power of Jesus Christ. He helps you overcome all the obstacles to their salvation, enlightening them in the person of Jesus Christ and helping them avoid all that could be displeasing to him.

One such vicar-apostolic, **Matthew de Castro,** a convert from Hinduism, went back home to India after training in Rome. He educated Indian clergy and handed over his work to two Indian successors. By the mid-1700s the Church was well established in the Kerala state of India. In Ceylon (modern-day Sri Lanka) a native priest, **Joseph Vaz,** opened scores of churches and converted large numbers of his countrymen. The French Jesuit **Alexander de Rhodes** worked in Asia from 1623 to 1645. His greatest successes were in Vietnam. De Rhodes put the Vietnamese language into a written form, translated religious materials into Vietnamese, and trained catechists. His catechists also learned simple medical treatments. Thus they spread the Word of God and also served God's people. By 1650, thirty thousand Vietnamese were Catholic. De Rhodes and other Jesuits worked in Macau (muh-*kow*), China, and established the first Asian seminary in Ayutthaya (ah-yoo-*teye*-eh), Thailand, in 1665.

In Africa, the Capuchins had been working in Zaire and Angola for years. By 1700 an estimated five hundred thousand converts had been made. However, the slave trade and the instability brought about by fighting among colonizers harmed the missionary efforts. Nevertheless, French missionaries began work in Senegal in 1626 and in Madagascar in 1686.

During the 1600s, Spanish missionaries continued their efforts throughout the Americas and the Philippines. Because of the agreement between the Spanish king and the pope that allowed the king to appoint missionaries and oversee their work, Spanish missionaries were seen as both preachers and colonizers. Also, since the Spanish king forbade the training of native priests, the Church was seen as a foreign institution in which the local people would always be second-class members. Despite this problem, converts were drawn to the Church, and the faith took root.

The Spanish methods of missionary work conflicted sharply with the approaches taken by the Jesuits. The Spanish friars—Dominicans, Franciscans, and Augustinians—tried to get the local people to accept Western culture and language, and to reject native customs and language. They believed that Western, especially Spanish, culture was best and more Christian. The Jesuit missionaries, on the other hand, tried to live as the local people did, to use the language of those with whom they worked. The Jesuit brand of missionary work was typified by Matteo Ricci (see page 224) and others who worked in China. Because Chinese culture was ancient and very sophisticated, Ricci tried to make his way into Chinese society by adapting to Chinese culture. For instance, by 1660 the Mass was being said in Chinese, not Latin.

At first the Congregation for the Propagation of the Faith endorsed the Jesuits' approach. However, the Spanish friars could not accept the practice of saying the Mass in any language other than Latin and they raised objections with various popes. Finally, in 1704, Pope Clement XI banned the Chinese Mass and approved of the notion that people in missionary lands should adopt Western customs along with Christianity. This decision had far-reaching effects, as we will see later. One immediate effect was that Emperor K'ang-hsi outlawed all Christian missionary work and threw almost all the Jesuits out of China. Understandably he found Clement's decision an insult to Chinese culture and to himself. Chinese Catholics felt abandoned; they were persecuted, and some who did not renounce their faith were executed as being traitors to China.

The Age of Reason

As Europe entered the 1700s, few startling events occurred within the Church. The popes of this century carried on the reforms begun at Trent but exerted little influence. Most of them were compromise candidates acceptable to the kings of France and the emperors of Austria. Several were very old men who occupied the chair of Peter for only a few months. Clearly the influence of the papacy on secular matters weakened considerably.

At the same time, a new attitude toward life was beginning to take shape. Philosophers like Descartes, Spinoza, and Leibniz were claiming that reason alone could help humankind arrive at truth. To these **rationalists**, the universe was ordered completely and reasonably. The laws that governed the universe could be explained clearly with the help of science. These laws could, in turn, be applied to human behavior. God was eased out of the picture. Even the philosophers who reasoned to the existence of God said that God had created and started the world but abandoned the universe to follow the course of these universal laws. Some philosophers discounted as ridiculous the notion of a personal God who was revealed in Jesus because it would be an interference in the natural order of the universe. The rationalist philosophers who believed in a God were called **deists** (*dee*-ists). Among their number were Benjamin Franklin and Jean-Jacques Rousseau.

Another group of philosophers who challenged religions were the **empiricists** (em-*pihr*-uh-suhsts). They were convinced that all knowledge must come through the senses or experience. That is, what we see, hear, taste, touch, and smell provides the basis for all knowledge. **John Locke,** a British empiricist, tried to show that certain Christian teachings were correct because they could be based on people's experience of them. So, for example, Locke thought that God must exist because the world around us that we can experience must have been made by some all-knowing intelligence. Because the miracles of Jesus go beyond the power of normal people and show his power over nature, he must be God. Thus, Locke applied empiricism to matters of religion. Other philosophers used the same method to try to show that God could not exist.

One such skeptical philosopher was **David Hume.** He said that it was impossible to prove from data of the senses that a soul existed. When we look at ourselves we just see matter—flesh, hair, teeth—not anything beyond the senses. Therefore, the soul does not exist. He dismissed the miracles of Jesus because they went against the laws of nature; to Hume, these laws were fixed and could not be changed. Hume and other empiricists were very influential during their time. They raised serious issues about religion that caused a new mood of doubt. What gave the empiricists even more force were the advances being made in science by people like Isaac Newton. While Newton himself did not believe that science

Voltaire (facing page), French writer
David Hume (left), Scottish philosopher
Sir Isaac Newton (right), English
mathematician and theorist

could be at odds with religion, the scientific laws at which he arrived seemed to show philosophers like Hume that the universe was guided by laws that stood outside a divine being.

Naturally an emphasis on reason and proof through the senses also affected the way people thought about government. If all persons could reason to the truth, then people were capable of directing their own destinies. Accordingly a government should reflect the will of the people. In this same vein, the philosopher **Jean-Jacques Rousseau** (roo-*soh*) declared that society is based on a social contract to which all the members of the society agree. This social contract treats everyone as a reasonable person, and thus gives the proper dignity deserved by each person.

Also, if one denies the existence of God, kings and queens cannot claim that they hold power through a right given by God. These notions were revolutionary—especially in countries ruled by absolute monarchs. Similar writings on democratic politics by Locke and Voltaire were read avidly and eventually ignited the American and French revolutions.

The rationalists and empiricists placed human beings—not God—at the center of the universe. To Immanuel Kant, another philosopher, Jesus was an enlightened teacher of excellent moral principles. To Georg Hegel, Jesus was the greatest and most complete manifestation of the divine spirit that ever existed. Unfortunately the God of the rationalists and empiricists was not the God of the Bible. But then, even the Bible was coming under serious criticism.

One result of rationalism and empiricism was the founding of the movement called **Freemasonry**. Responding to the thought of Locke, Rousseau, and others, many deists banded together in this secret brotherhood. They believed in doing good works out of purely human motives. They opposed monarchies and the Catholic Church. As time went on, these secret Freemason groups became a powerful force in the reshaping of Europe and the Americas.

Religious Nationalism

By the eighteenth century the popes had lost much of their political power. Even so, the French king wanted to strip the popes of even more authority. King Louis XIV tried to force Innocent XI, pope from 1676 to 1689, to install bishops that the king had appointed. Innocent refused, attempting to maintain the Church's autonomy. In retaliation, Louis seized the papal lands in Avignon and threatened to invade Italy. If the kings had control over dioceses, they could demand more loyalty from bishops—and more taxes.

This attempt by the French kings to dominate the Church in France is called **Gallicanism**. The kings wanted church and state to be in partnership, although the Church would be a subordinate partner. If the Church could be controlled, the French king could use bishops and priests to rally the people to do the royal will—even though this will might not be particularly in line with Christian principles. Louis XIV also promoted the notion that the council of bishops should have more power than the pope. Gallicanism amounted to **religious nationalism**—the French Church should rule itself. The popes successfully resisted Louis's scheme. Nevertheless, Gallicanism signaled a more independent attitude on the part of national churches.

In Germany there was also agitation for more independence from Rome for the German Catholic Church. Nicholas von Hontheim, also known as Febronius, spoke against the authority of the pope. Four German archbishops wrote a kind of "declaration of independence" from Rome. Since the majority of the bishops disagreed with this act, the movement called **Febronianism** never gained much momentum.

Gallicanism and Febronianism, rationalism and empiricism were movements that illustrate the position of the Church between the 1600s and 1700s. A trend of increased secularization—that is, separation of church and state, or the Church being put in a subservient position to the state—had begun.

One evidence of the control over the Church exercised by both France and Spain was the forced suppression of the Jesuits in 1773. The French and Spanish rulers did not like the influence that the Jesuits had over the students in their many schools or over the many people with whom the Jesuits worked through missions or retreats. Worse yet, since the Jesuits took a special vow to be obedient to the popes, they opposed religious nationalism.

In South America, for example, the Jesuits had run into conflict with the Spanish and Portuguese government officials because the Jesuits had supported the Indians' rights. In addition, the French king looked covetously at the property owned by the Society of Jesus. Thus the kings of France and Spain pressured Pope Clement XIV to disband the Jesuits. The thirty thousand members of the society were removed from their posts in schools, colleges, missions, and retreat houses all over the world. The Jesuit superior general died in prison; many of the priests became diocesan clergy. Others left the service of the Church entirely.

Ironically some Jesuits carried on the society's work in Prussia and in Russia—both of them non-Catholic countries. Frederick II of Prussia and Catherine the Great of Russia actually recruited Jesuits to run schools in their countries. Consequently a small band of Jesuits survived until the order was reinstated in 1814. The tragic suppression of the Jesuits dramatically illustrated the seeming helplessness of the popes during the eighteenth century.

The French Revolution

The Age of Reason—an era that developed notions like the social contract and that recognized the rights of the individual—evolved into the Age of Revolution. The most drastic change in government and national character occurred in France. For centuries the French peasants had lived teetering between poverty and outright destitution. Meanwhile, the small minority of nobles had lived in almost unimaginable wealth. And while there were poor parish priests like Vincent de Paul and servants of the poor and ignorant like John Baptist de La Salle, the majority of the French clergy were loyal to the monarchy. They depended on the nobles for positions and gifts. Furthermore, the belief in the divine right of the kings to rule had not died.

In effect, the Church was seen by many people as part of the old regime—the monarchy that had kept them in submission and poverty. By the 1780s, discontent among the masses of French common people had come to the boiling point. Louis XVI was an inept, extravagant king. The demands for change could not be denied.

In June 1789 a National Constituent Assembly was called to propose reforms. The country was reorganized so that there were eighty-three "departments" or states. Church lands became publicly owned, with the profits going toward financing the new social system. The assembly further decreed that priests and bishops were to be elected by the people and had to swear allegiance to the new French government in matters unrelated to religion.

For the most part, the clergy attending as delegates supported the assembly. They drew the line, however, at the election of bishops and clergy and at the appointment of clergy—as if they were government civil servants. Eighty percent of the clergy also refused the loyalty oath that, in effect, was a renunciation of the pope. Yet, even as the assembly argued over reforms, the storm of violent revolution was gathering.

In July 1789 a mob attacked the Bastille (ba-*steel*) Prison in Paris and freed the prisoners—many of whom were the king's political opponents or just poor people who could not pay their taxes. The Bastille was a symbol of all that was evil in the monarchy. This incident is looked upon as the real beginning of the French Revolution; the executions and exile of the nobility did not begin in earnest until later.

The national assembly continued to meet and became more radical. Along with the aristocrats, priests who refused to pledge their support to the Revolution—especially the part that renounced the pope's authority—were declared to be disloyal to the people of France.

In 1792 any unpledged priest who was denounced by twenty citizens was to be deported out of the country. Thirty thousand to forty thousand priests were hounded into exile. The death penalty was given to any priest who tried to return to France. In September 1792, French revolutionaries killed between eleven hundred and fifteen hundred priests in what is now called the September Massacre. Finally, on 21 January 1793, King Louis XVI was beheaded. The Reign of Terror, which would last for two years, had begun.

The Reign of Terror

The Reign of Terror was designed to wipe out all opposition to the radical revolutionaries. The "Committee for Public Safety" executed nearly thirty thousand people as counterrevolutionaries—in this group were many priests, sisters, and brothers. The leaders of the Reign of Terror were Jean-Paul Marat, George Danton, and Maximilian Robespierre. At one point, following a procession through the streets of Paris, these leaders chose a dancer with a shady reputation to be the "Goddess of Reason." She was enthroned in the Notre Dame Cathedral of Paris, where the kings of France had always been crowned. In the thinking of the revolutionaries, "reason" replaced God.

A new calendar was implemented in 1793 that removed all saints' feast days and any reference to Christmas and Easter. References to Christian religion of any kind were forbidden, books were banned, and penalties for Christian practices were enacted. Going further, in 1794, Robespierre declared a new religion for France; he proclaimed that there was one Supreme Being, one dogma (the immortality of the soul), and one moral principle (to do one's duty).

As often happens in violent revolutions, the bloodiest leaders eliminated themselves. Robespierre, Danton, and Marat fought among themselves, and eventually all three were killed. France fell into further chaos. Armies from neighboring countries who were worried about the revolution spreading marched on France, at one point entering Paris itself.

Out of the turmoil, one man emerged to lead France—**Napoleon Bonaparte**. When he took over in 1795, Napoleon restored order in the country using his army. But France, reunited under military rule, soon turned its gaze outward. Thus began Napoleon's campaigns against the powers of Europe. In a few short years, France had conquered western Europe and was threatening Russia.

One of the prizes Napoleon took was Rome. Pope Pius VI died while being shuttled in a carriage by Napoleon's troops between Italian cities. **Pope Pius VII** fared little better. In 1801, Napoleon signed a concordat—that is, a formal agreement—with the pope. In it, the pope officially recognized the French revolutionary government and allowed the government to veto any appointments of bishops or priests. In turn, the government granted salaries to priests. Napoleon immediately began going back on his word.

In 1804, Pius was ordered to come to Paris to crown Napoleon as emperor; when he got there, he was held virtual prisoner. At the ceremony Napoleon crowned himself as a public insult to the pope. By 1808, Napoleon declared the Papal States the property of France and exiled the pope to Fontainebleau near Paris. Pius was imprisoned—mostly in solitary confinement—for an entire six years. He was allowed no conversation with anyone, little food, and no writing paper, pens, or books. The Church was without its leader, but Pius's dogged courage and survival gained new respect for him and for the papacy.

Napoleon was finally defeated by the combined forces of the other European nations. Pius VII—sick, emaciated, and broken in body—was returned to Rome in 1814. His remaining life was short, but in one of his final, most important acts Pius restored the Jesuits to their status as a religious order.

A drawing of a procession in Paris celebrating the "Goddess of Reason"

After Napoleon's defeat, monarchy was reestablished in France, although the power of the king was somewhat limited. Priests returned to their posts, and other religious institutions tried to begin anew. Brothers of the Christian Schools—many of whom continued to teach during the revolution but in secular garb—soon were recruiting new members. Because the work of education was so important, other religious orders began, such as the Society of Mary founded by Father Chaminade and the Marists founded by Fathers Champagnat and Colin.

Even when the king was overthrown and Louis Napoleon Bonaparte was elected president of the Second Republic in 1848, the Church carried on its work in France. Yet the wealth and power of the Church was gone. France was now a secular society allowing

A drawing portraying King Louis XVI
as a prisoner of the national
assembly (above)

A painting showing Napoleon
about to crown himself as emperor

freedom of religion, although antireligious sentiment arose occasionally during the remainder of the nineteenth century. Nevertheless, the country's religious institutions multiplied, and thousands of French missionaries traveled throughout the world.

The Italian Revolution

For centuries Italy had been divided into small duchies ruled by rival families. The Austrians or the French continually crushed any efforts at unification in Italy. For instance, in 1820 a group of revolutionaries led by Giuseppe Mazzini tried to unify the country; they were swiftly suppressed by Austrian troops. These **Carbonari** ("Charcoal Burners") were motivated by the democratic movements in America and France, and even though they failed in 1820, their desire for one Italy stayed alive, and they did cause some reforms to be made in the Papal States.

Another movement for a united Italy wanted a constitutional monarchy to be established. This group gained momentum and formed an army with Giuseppe Garibaldi at its head. In 1848, Pope Pius IX had to escape from Rome, where a republic had been declared. The rulers of Sardinia, The Two Sicilies, and Tuscany had granted the people a constitution. Pius called on the Spanish, French, and Austrians to put down the revolution. This may surprise the modern reader, but it is important to remember that most of the calls for reform and democracy in Europe were strongly anti-Church and even antireligious. Many of the leaders were Freemasons. In addition, traditions die hard deaths; the popes had been rulers of the Papal States for twelve centuries. Many of the expenses of church administration were paid by the profits from these lands. Besides, the popes feared that they would become virtual prisoners of the Italian governments.

A unified Italy, however, was an ideal whose time had come. In 1859, with the support of the British and French, rebellion broke out throughout Italy and the Papal States. Garibaldi took Sicily and Naples. By 1861, Victor Emmanuel II was declared king of Italy. The pope was left with only Rome and its vicinity under his control. Pius called himself a "prisoner of the Vatican." Through the Law of Guarantees, he had to relinquish title to the Papal States that had been given to the Church in 755 by the Frankish king Pepin. Out of protest, from 1870 to 1929 no pope set foot on Italian soil.

The year 1870 marks the end of the worldly power of the Church of Rome. Pius lived on until 1878, but so strong was the feeling against the pope that a group of Freemasons tried to throw his body into the Tiber River during his funeral. Italy was unified; nationalism had triumphed.

More National Movements

Just as France and Italy demanded freedom from monarchies and church influence in secular matters, some of Spain's colonies in South America began breaking away. During the 1820s, Simon Bolívar led the overthrow of Spain's rule in Colombia, Ecuador, and Bolivia; and Bernardo O'Higgins and José de San Martín established a new Chilean republic. Not only were the colonies in revolution, but Spain was changing too.

Off and on throughout the nineteenth century, monarchies were replaced by anticlerical republics. Napoleon had conquered Spain and put his brother Joseph Bonaparte at the head of a French-style republic. When Napoleon fell, the monarchy was restored. The Spanish rulers repressed any reforms. Subsequently, during the periods 1820–23 and 1868–74, republics were established and led by Freemasons. Thus the Church was suppressed, and there were even some executions of priests. Following Joseph Bonaparte's practice, when republics were instituted seminaries were closed, monasteries and convents were confiscated as state property, and churches were harassed.

Why was republicanism so anti-Church in Spain? As in the cases of Italy and France, the Church was too often seen as rich and powerful, protected and courted by the kings and queens. In addition, bitter memories remained of the Spanish Inquisition when the nobility used the Church for political oppression. The pope was looked upon more as a foreign ruler, less as a spiritual leader. In order to separate church and state, the republics took harsh actions.

The Church ran into difficulty in Germany too. Prior to the mid-1800s, Germany was divided into smaller states. **Otto von Bismarck** (1815–98) changed all that. When he became chancellor of Prussia, his main goal was to unite Germany and make it a world power. First, he persuaded Austria to withdraw from the German Federation. As a result, Prussia became the strongest state in the group. When Prussia defeated France in the Franco–Prussian War, the other German states decided to join with Prussia. At the signing of the peace treaty in Versailles, Bismarck announced the beginning of the Hohenzollern Reich—with King William of Prussia now Kaiser William of the German Empire.

Most of the German states were Protestant. In order to unite Germany further, Bismarck promoted the **Kulturkampf**—the campaign to take pride in all that is German. Bismarck saw the Church as foreign and non-German. Consequently in 1873 the May Laws were passed. These laws were meant to restrict the power of bishops. For example, candidates for ordination had to study at state universities and to pass exams there. Also, the Jesuits were expelled, and all education came under state control. The May Laws stayed in effect for nearly fifteen years.

The Church in England and Ireland

Through the Emancipation Act of 1829, Catholics were finally freed to practice their religion and were given complete civil rights in England. Rapidly the Church reemerged and became active, especially with the arrival of immigrants from Ireland. Occasional outbreaks of anti-Catholic violence would occur, as they did, for example, in 1840 when the British parliament approved of funds to build an Irish seminary. Catholicism was seen as un-English since the Church was ruled by a foreign pope.

One group that took Catholicism seriously was a band of Oxford students known as the Oxford Movement. Among them was **John Newman** (1801–90). The Church of England had lost its appeal for these men; Catholicism attracted them because it had historical roots leading back to the Apostles. Newman first became an Anglican (Church of England) priest in 1824, but as time wore on, he became convinced that the Roman Catholic Church was more in line with the traditions of the early Church. In 1845, Newman became a Catholic. He wrote numerous articles and books explaining his decision. Newman was made a cardinal in 1877 partly because he was a profound influence in making Catholicism respectable again in England.

Another member of the Oxford Movement, **Henry Manning**, also converted, became a Catholic priest, and was named cardinal archbishop of Westminster. Newman helped non-Catholics in England understand the Church. Manning was more of an activist; he gained great respect when he helped Protestants set up a trade union. Later, he helped to settle a dock strike at great personal peril. Cardinal Manning also influenced social welfare policies for the poor as part of the royal commission on the poor. Oddly, while the Church was suffering in countries that had remained Catholic after the Reformation, in England the Church was gaining some measure of respect.

The Catholic Church had always been the mainstay of the Irish people. The English rulers of Ireland had tried to supplant the Catholic Church with the Church of England. The Irish had even been forced to pay taxes to support Anglican ministers, while priests were forced to subsist on the little money they collected in the baskets on Sunday. In the early part of the nineteenth century there were twenty-two bishops and eighteen hundred priests to serve 6.5 million Catholics in Ireland. With the emancipation of Catholics in England, the British government eased the pressure on the Irish to convert. By 1869 the Church of England ceased being the official church in Ireland.

Vatican Council I

Pope Pius IX led the Church from 1846 to 1878, the longest papacy in history. While he witnessed the loss of papal lands, he helped to solidify the spiritual authority of the popes. In 1854, Pius issued a papal document, *Ineffabilis Deus,* which proclaimed that Mary was free of original sin; she was given the title Immaculate Conception. He also encouraged all countries to build seminaries in Rome. Subsequently many countries sent their brightest seminarians to the Vatican. In this way, the Vatican could recruit the most capable young priests for its work, as well as influence and gain the loyalty of clergy throughout the world.

Pius was also concerned about many philosophic and social movements that seemed to threaten the Church. He published a list of errors Catholics should reject. Among the errors were rationalism, naturalism, socialism, and liberal capitalism. Clearly illustrating that traditions die hard, error number 77 was "It is no longer expedient that the Catholic religion should be treated as the only religion of the state, all other worships whatsoever being excluded." Pius and most religious thinkers of his time still believed that the state should be the protector and promoter of the Church. It would be another hundred years before the Church blessed the rights of individuals to follow their consciences in matters of religion.

Finally, to further cement the spiritual powers of the popes, Pius called all the bishops to Rome for Vatican Council I (1869–70). The 276 Italian bishops and 265 bishops from other countries gathered to discuss many issues that had come up since the Council of Trent three hundred years earlier. Yet the main issue was the question of the **infallibility** of the pope. Was the pope infallible? That is, could the pope make a mistake when speaking officially—as the successor of Saint Peter on matters of faith and morals—without the approval of a council? In 1870 the bishops accepted and published the doctrine of papal infallibility.

New Missions in the Nineteenth Century

With the revolutions of the late eighteenth and early nineteenth centuries, missionary activity slowed down. However, during the papacy of **Gregory XVI** (1831–46) many new missions were inaugurated under the direction of such new orders as the White Fathers, Congregation of the Holy Spirit, Society of the Divine Word, the Mill Hill Missionaries, and the Congregation of the Immaculate Heart of Mary.

The strongest emphases were given to Asia and Africa. Ninety percent of Filipinos were Catholic. And now the numbers of Catholics increased in other countries as well: Hong Kong, Sri Lanka, Malaysia, Burma, Thailand, and India. By 1890 there were five hundred thousand baptized Catholics in China and over three hundred and fifty Chinese priests. Unfortunately, China was being torn apart by the various Western powers who were taking over areas of the country for their own use. The Western powers controlled the coastal regions, forcing harsh trade agreements on the Chinese

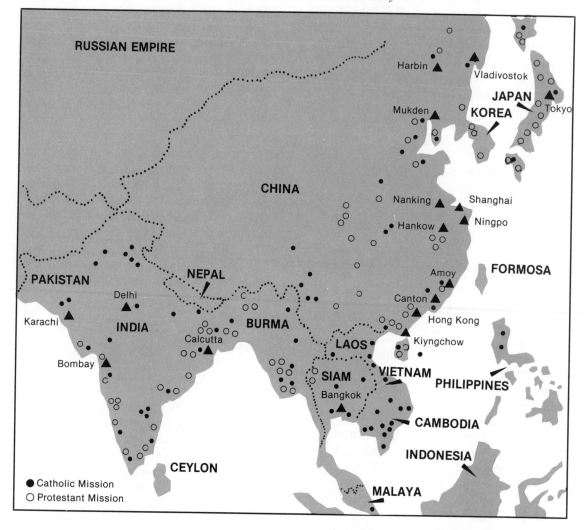

emperors. Although there were devoted Christian converts, many of the Chinese people saw the missionaries as part of the colonial exploitation of their country—as indeed some were. Many priests had not learned the lessons of Matteo Ricci—that is, they did not adapt their European ways to those of the people they were serving. As a consequence, in the Boxer Rebellion and the Communist Revolution, Christian Churches were expelled as foreign and oppressive influences.

Much success was found in Africa, although again missionaries were sometimes seen as agents of foreign colonizers. Missionary activities met with notable gains in Tanzania, Uganda, Zaire, Zambia, Kenya, and Malawi. By the turn of the century, there were one hundred and fifty thousand Catholics in Uganda alone. The Church had spread to all parts of the world—Catholics were now Oriental, African, and South American, as well as Caucasian.

The Industrial Revolution

The nineteenth century is frequently thought of as the age of the Industrial Revolution. Overseas trade began flourishing; machines produced far more goods than ever before, thus causing a need for more markets; people were flocking to the cities for industrial jobs; cities grew enormously. Clearly such a dramatic change from the traditionally rural, farming way of life caused problems. Cities became crowded slums; factories exploited workers with low wages and dangerous working conditions. The Industrial Revolution called for new approaches from the Church.

Bishops called for social reforms when they could. Welfare societies began in dioceses and parishes. Religious orders opened schools and hospitals specifically for the working classes in cities. Leaders like Cardinal Manning in England supported legitimate strikes and the formation of labor groups. In some countries, the Church formed Christian democratic parties that represented the workers in parliaments; especially strong were the parties in Belgium, Italy, Germany, and Holland.

In response to the ills of industrial society of the nineteenth century, **Karl Marx,** father of modern Communism, wrote *Das Kapital* and, with Friedrich Engels, *The Communist Manifesto.* These two works seemed to hold out hope for many oppressed workers; they were read widely in Europe. As a consequence, socialist parties formed in many places and began agitating for change. Marx blamed the capitalistic system for the poor conditions of workers. In a capitalistic economic system all or most means of production and distribution—land, factories, railroads—are privately owned and operated for profit. A concentration of profit in the hands of the owners, Marx felt, set up a class system with the majority of people being oppressed. Therefore, class struggle was inevitable. The consequence of this struggle would be a workers' state, and eventually, there would emerge a classless society. Marx discarded religion as just one more means of keeping people from rebelling against an unjust system. Clearly, Marx began a movement in the nineteenth century that has had profound results on the Church and on human society, although most of the results were not seen until the twentieth century.

One other revolutionary development of the nineteenth century was the theory of evolution as formulated by the scientist **Charles Darwin.** When his *The Origin of Species* was published in 1859, it ushered in a period of doubt about God. Did God really create the world? Did the human species simply evolve from a lower species without the work of a Supreme Being? If species survive because they are fit, strong, and adaptable, then wouldn't helping the weak, old, or handicapped be against the natural law? Furthermore, those who believed that the Bible must be read literally could not accept the idea that Adam and Eve did not exist just as the creation story described. In short, Darwin's book was scorned by many but caused most people to reevaluate their religious beliefs.

Pope Leo XIII, who was elected in 1878, tried to deal with the Industrial Revolution,

Pope Leo XIII (left)
Karl Marx (right)

socialism, and the questions posed by Darwin's studies. His papal letter *Rerum Novarum* (1891) encouraged gradual social reform, the establishment of trade unions, and the granting of just wages for workers. Leo criticized both extreme socialism and capitalism. As a result of his support, Christian trade unions were formed in many countries: the German Worker's Welfare Association (1879), Belgian Democratic League (1891) and the Christian Worker's Movement. Leo argued that workers had a right to organize, but that their attitude should be "collaboration [with employers] through conflict."

In answer to questions about the Bible, Leo instituted the Vatican biblical commission, whose duty it was to apply new methods of archaeology and linguistics to the study of the Bible. The Vatican archives were opened to scholars from all over the world too. This encouragement of scholarship would culminate in many of the decisions of Vatican Council II, over seventy years later.

Selections from *Rerum Novarum: On the Rights of Laboring People*

Religion teaches the rich man and the employer that their work-people are not their slaves; that they must respect in every man his dignity as a man and as a Christian; that labor is nothing to be ashamed of, if we listen to right reason and to Christian philosophy, but is an honorable employment, enabling a man to sustain his life in an upright and creditable way; and that it is shameful and inhuman to treat men like chattels to make money by, or to look upon them merely as so much muscle or physical power.

When work-people have recourse to a strike, it is frequently because the hours of labor are too long, or the work too hard, or because they consider their wages insufficient.

The grave inconvenience of this not uncommon occurrence should be obviated by public remedial measures; for such paralysis of labor not only affects the masters and their work-people, but is extremely injurious to trade, and to the general interests of the public; moreover, on such occasions, violence and disorder are generally not far off, and thus it frequently happens that the public peace is threatened. The laws should be beforehand, and prevent these troubles from arising; they should lend their influence and authority to the removal in good time of the causes which lead to conflicts between masters and those whom they employ. No man may outrage with impunity that human dignity which God Himself treats with reverence, nor stand in the way of that higher life which is the preparation for the eternal life of Heaven. Nay, more; a man has here no power over himself. To consent to any treatment which is calculated to defeat the end and purpose of his being is beyond his right; he cannot give up his soul to servitude; for it is not man's own rights which are here in question, but the rights of God, most sacred and inviolable. Particular societies, then, although they exist within the State, and are each a part of the State, nevertheless cannot be prohibited by the State absolutely and as such.

For to enter into a "society" of this kind is the natural right of man; and the State must protect natural rights, not destroy them; and if it forbids its citizens to form associations, it contradicts the very principle of its own existence; for both they and it exist in virtue of the same principle, viz., the natural propensity of man to live in society.

Focus on the Models

Having been stripped of its worldly power, the Church became, once again, primarily a spiritual force. While the loss of the Papal States was traumatic at the time, the Church was more able to go about the work that Jesus gave it to do without as many political concerns. In addition, as the Church was forcibly separated from the state, the Church was able to associate itself more and more with the common people, not merely the rich and powerful. Moreover, while governments became more secular, the institutional Church became more oriented to spiritual concerns.

The Good News spread throughout all parts of the globe. Mission stations were established in all continents; these were supported by Catholic schools and hospitals. Many new missionary orders were founded during these centuries. With the emergence of active women's orders, like the Daughters of Charity, the Church became more visibly Servant. Orders of brothers and sisters dedicated to Christian education started a tradition of Catholic schools that still flourishes.

As a People of God the Church returned to the tradition of the martyrs. In the face of the persecutions of the French Revolution and of the Spanish and Italian republics, Catholics had to stand up and be counted; many were executed for not renouncing their faith. So, in spite of revolutions, both political and industrial, and in spite of challenges, philosophical and scientific, the Church emerged from these three centuries much stronger and more authentic to the mandate given by Jesus to be the People of God.

Review Questions and Activities

1) What was the religious alignment of Europe by the mid-1600s? Had peace really been achieved?

2) How did the baroque cathedrals symbolize the status of the Church during the seventeenth century?

3) What revolutionary changes were begun by Vincent de Paul, Louise de Marillac, and John Baptist de La Salle? How are their works continuing today?

4) On a map, trace the spread of missionaries throughout the world during the 1600s. What conflict between the Jesuits and the Spanish friars caused a change in missionary policy?

5) How did the Age of Reason challenge traditional thinking about God? Who were the deists, and how did they lead the way for the formation of the Freemasons? How did the rationalists and empiricists give an intellectual basis for the French (and American) Revolution?

6) What were Gallicanism and Febronianism? Why did these movements begin?

7) During the French Revolution the Catholic Church was persecuted and replaced by a philosophy of reason. Why was the Revolution directed against the Church as well as the monarchy?

8) What was Napoleon's attitude toward the Church? How was this attitude demonstrated?

9) How did the Italian Revolution, in effect, free the Church from worldly power? What was the initial reaction (by church officials) to Italy's unification? How has the loss of the Papal States actually been a positive thing?

10) Describe the changing status of the Church in Spain, Germany, England, and Ireland.

11) What were the important declarations made by Pius IX before Vatican Council I? by the council itself?

12) What problems did Marx and Darwin raise for the Church?

13) How was the Industrial Revolution a challenge to the Church and all Christian people? Why was it truly a revolution?

14) What were Pope Leo XIII's attitudes toward unions, the rights of laborers, and Christian political parties?

Personal Reflection Exercise

Sometimes God does indeed work in strange ways. In this chapter, the Church was stripped of the Papal States—land it had ruled for twelve hundred years. And yet, this loss actually freed the Church from governmental power and allowed the Church to be the spiritual community that Jesus called it to be. In other words, God does act in history—that is, in the life of the Church and the lives of persons. Have you ever had something happen to you that at first seemed bad but turned out to be quite good? Think about this for a while. Think about yourself between the ages of one and six, then seven and thirteen, and finally during the years since then: Were there bad events that turned out well? How much of "being happy" is really a matter of the way we see and understand events and not just the events themselves?

14
The Church in North America

By the end of the nineteenth century the Catholic Church was the largest religious denomination in North America. However, the beginnings of the Church's mission on this continent were hesitant and filled with danger. In fact, the Church became a real force in North American life only when floods of immigrants came from European Catholic countries in the middle of the 1800s.

The first Catholic missionaries were Spanish friars who accompanied the explorers on their quests into the southwestern portions of the United States during the 1560s. Seventy years later French Jesuits sailed into the waters just off of Nova Scotia (then called Acadie). These missionaries played a large role in opening up the whole of North America. Not only were they missionaries, but they were explorers who helped chart the new territories' rivers, lakes, mountains, and valleys. Like the Spanish friars in the Southwest, the French priests worked among the Native Americans—preaching to them, educating them in Western customs, and sometimes protecting them from exploitation. But progress among Native Americans was very gradual.

For around 150 years the only significant growth in the Church took place in Canada with the influx of settlers from France. There were very few Catholics in the British colony now called the United States. What few Catholics there were practiced their religion under cover because Catholicism was illegal in England. Once independent from England, Catholics in the United States could freely worship, but their numbers remained insignificant until waves of immigrants began seeking refuge in the New World. First came the Irish, then the Germans. By the end of the nineteenth century, people from every continent had made North America the "melting pot" that it is today.

The great majority of these immigrants were Catholics. And while Catholicism flourished in the New World, it was practiced in forms so divergent that, for instance, German Catholics demanded parishes and schools that used German as the medium of communication; they would not accept Irish pastors. Living in the "melting pot" also meant living with people from countries that may have been ancient enemies. Sometimes prejudices from the Old World extended into the New. Coping with this new multiethnic Catholic Church was a tremendous challenge for church leaders.

Such internal difficulties were coupled with resentment from those who could trace their roots in North America to pre-Revolutionary times. These "native-born Americans" resented the immigrants because they crowded the cities, spoke foreign languages, and had strange, un-English customs. And they resented the Catholic Church because it was composed mostly of these foreigners. Nevertheless, the Catholic Church grew and adapted itself to the North American way of life.

Spanish Missionaries in North America

As early as 1513, the governor of Puerto Rico, **Ponce de León**, discovered the neck of land sticking out from the southeastern part of the present United States and named it Florida (meaning "feast of flowers"). In the years following, half a dozen Spanish colonies were started in Florida, but all eventually failed. About thirty years later **Hernando de Soto** landed on the western coast of Florida at Tampa Bay with more than six hundred men, including missionaries. The local inhabitants, mostly Creek and Cherokee Indians, gave them little or no trouble as they searched the peninsula for gold, which they never found.

De Soto and his men worked their way into parts of what are now Georgia, the Carolinas, Alabama, Mississippi, and Tennessee—where they found the wide Mississippi River flowing past the present location of Memphis. Villages of Natchez Indians thrived along the river—growing crops, fishing, and hunting buffalo, bear, and deer. The Natchez Indians worshiped a sun god from altars built on mounds sometimes a hundred feet high. Though a few Indians became Christians, most of them were hostile to the Spaniards. Attacks from the Indians forced the Spaniards to go down the Mississippi in hastily built boats. De Soto died during this part of the exploration, but somehow his troops crossed the Gulf and reached safety in Mexico.

In spite of these early failures, the Spaniards sought to establish their rule in Florida. In 1565, while Central America was being colonized, a Spanish settlement was built on the eastern coast of Florida and named Saint Augustine. Though they served both Spaniards and Native Americans, missionaries made very little progress with the local tribes because these bands were nomadic, never settling in one place for very long. Only when Saint Augustine was firmly established and Native American tribes settled around it did the Franciscans' efforts begin to bear fruit.

By the mid-1600s there were more than twenty-five thousand Christian Indians in Florida. The missionaries not only learned the native languages but also composed books for the Indians. Shortly after 1700 most of the Spanish missionaries' work was destroyed when England's conflict with Spain overflowed into the New World, and the English colonists in Carolina invaded Florida. The Indians were either killed or taken to Carolina as slaves. The Spanish lost their colony in Florida.

Santa Barbara Mission (facing page)

Besides the Spanish explorations in Florida, there were others in the American Southwest —including New Mexico, Texas, Arizona, and California. A few years after the conquest of Peru, around 1540, some Spaniards under **Vásquez de Coronado** came north out of Mexico looking for gold. They found no gold, but they did find several nations of Pueblo Indians. **Pueblos** were cities built against walls of canyons and laid out somewhat like apartment buildings. Some pueblos had as many as five stories with nearly eight hundred rooms. The Navajos, Hopi, and Apache who lived in the pueblos farmed the flatlands from Nevada to Texas. They were hardworking and peaceloving. Their skill in using medicinal herbs was very advanced. Their brilliant weaving and intricate pottery is preserved today in museums.

Shortly before 1600 a Spanish colony of men, women, and children crossed the Rio Grande into present New Mexico. They brought livestock with them. When a pueblo of Indians stood in the way of these colonists, the Spanish governor made slaves of some of the Indians and mutilated others, cutting off a hand or a foot. This kind of treatment made missionary work almost impossible, and the colony itself failed because the Spaniards did not adapt to the arid conditions. After about a year most of the Spaniards returned south into Mexico, though the missionaries stayed to teach the Native Americans. In 1609 the town of Santa Fe was founded—the second permanent Catholic settlement within the area of the United States. By 1630 there were roughly thirty-five thousand Christian Indians in the pueblo region.

In spite of this success the missionaries were sometimes hampered by the colonists who came there to get rich, such as the Spanish traders who raided Apache territory for slaves. After some years of this kind of oppression, a Pueblo chief named Popé organized several tribes in a revolt. They killed about a fifth of the Spaniards and tried to destroy everything that the foreigners had brought in. Since Christianity and the Spanish were so closely associated, the Pueblo Indians burned churches and returned to their traditional religious practices. Nevertheless, twelve years after the revolt, missionary work began all over again. But by this time many Indians had left the territory in an attempt to escape the Spanish.

Junípero Serra: The California Missions

In 1769 the Spanish friars began a period of successful missionary activity north of the Rio Grande River, in California. The person who started this work was the Franciscan **Junípero Serra** (*ser*-uh), already more than fifty years old and half-crippled with pain in his legs. Because walking turned out to be less painful than riding a horse, he limped along the trails of California, teaching and baptizing thousands of Native Americans. Serra established nine missions on the Pacific coast; among them were San Diego, Santa Clara, and San Francisco. Eventually twenty-one missions were built.

At the California missions the Indians found places to live and soon began to learn not only the Catholic religion but practical things as well. They learned to grow various grains brought from Europe, as well as to run looms and to make their own metal tools. Eventually the Indians owned herds of cattle, and also hogs, sheep, goats, and horses.

The California missions were free from some of the problems in other places where the Indians were caught in the conflicts between government officials and missionaries. In the time of Father Serra the government of Spain

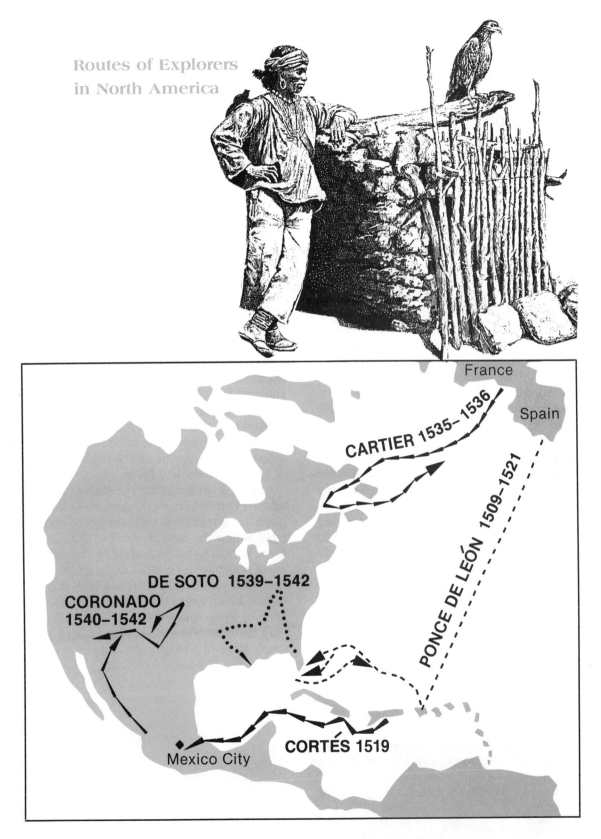

Routes of Explorers in North America

CARTIER 1535–1536

PONCE DE LEÓN 1509–1521

DE SOTO 1539–1542

CORONADO 1540–1542

CORTÉS 1519

Mexico City

France

Spain

was not as strong as it had been, and though a handful of soldiers carried out routine matters at the missions, the missionaries themselves were in charge. The California mission churches, most of which are still standing today, remind us of the best successes of the Spanish Catholics in the early history of North America.

The French Missions to Canada

France's exploration of the New World began in 1534 when **Jacques Cartier** (kahr-*tyay*) landed on the shores of America just north of the state of Maine. He found a land teaming with deer, bear, moose, rabbits, and beaver; and waters filled with cod, herring, scallops, oysters, and lobster. Cartier was immediately struck by the beauty of the beaver furs that the Hurons, an Iroquois nation living there, brought back from their hunting trips. On his next voyage Cartier sailed five hundred miles south on the Saint Lawrence River until he came to a Huron village at the future site of Montreal. Cartier's expeditions inspired other Frenchmen to come for fish and furs, but only a small number stayed to live there. By the time that the greatest of the early French explorers, **Samuel de Champlain,** arrived, the settlers of Cartier's time were all dead, and their sons were old men.

Champlain made a dozen trips to the New World during his thirty years of explorations. A good mapmaker, he accurately outlined the North Atlantic coast for future adventurers. He built a trading post and a small fort at Quebec in 1608—this was the beginning of New France. In his curiosity about this new country, Champlain investigated the lake between the present states of Vermont and New York, which still carries his name. He charted two of the Great Lakes, Ontario and Huron. Though he kept encouraging his countrymen to come to New France, it was only in 1634, a hundred years after Cartier, that Champlain was able to organize a colony that became permanent. This was on the Atlantic coast near Maine, in Acadie—that is, present-day Nova Scotia.

Champlain's New France was known to the Indians as Canada, meaning "a village" or "community." The country was filled with natural resources, but many of the first French explorers were primarily interested in beaver fur. In the 1600s beaver fur was used to make the felt hats worn at the time in Europe by both men and women. The pelts were used for other items of clothing as well. In order to continue trade in beaver pelts the French maintained good relations with the Indians.

Generally the Frenchmen lived among the Native Americans without disturbance. They paid by barter for what they wanted, instead of taking it at gunpoint. In return for beaver fur the Frenchmen gave the Indians iron kettles, axes, knives, cloth, guns, and—tragically—alcohol. The Indians helped the colonists learn how to survive in a wilderness that changed from humid summer heat with mosquitoes and black flies to bitter winter cold with snow and ice. The Indians also taught the French how to find their way through wilderness that had no roads and through hundreds of miles of rivers and lakes.

In their friendship with the Hurons of Canada the French became the enemies of the Iroquois League of Five Nations in the area of what is now the central region of the state of New York. Champlain, when exploring new areas with his Huron allies in the early years, once took part in their skirmish with the Mohawks, killing two of the Mohawks' chiefs with his gun. From that time on the Iroquois were enemies of the French, and one result was the martyrdom of French missionaries working among the Hurons.

When he started his trading posts, Champlain brought with him skilled workers to build houses and also missionaries to teach the Indians. In his colony at Acadie he started a school for both French and Indian children. In spite of this good start, not many Hurons were baptized in the next few years, though they were friendly to the missionaries. The French did not rush the Native Americans into Baptism until they were instructed sufficiently in the Catholic faith. But such instruction was almost impossible because the Indians were nomads, rarely settling down for long in a village. Of the various missionary orders the Jesuits had the best success under these conditions, especially those working in the mid-1600s in the Albany area of New York. Among these missionaries was **Saint Isaac Jogues** (*zhawg*).

After spending six years with the Hurons, Isaac Jogues was captured by a Mohawk war party and tortured during a year-long captivity. The Mohawks pulled out all of his fingernails and chopped off his index fingers; they beat him repeatedly and used him as a slave. Eventually a Dutch party that had sailed up the Hudson River from New Amsterdam rescued him. Jogues went back to France to recuperate but soon returned to Huron country. He helped his people make peace with the Iroquois, but trouble started again and Jogues was tomahawked by some rebel Mohawks. During these years on the frontier a total of eight French Jesuits were killed in the New York region.

A few years after the death of Jogues, in the same village where he had worked, a girl was born to Christian Huron parents. **Catherine Tekakwitha** (tek-uh-*kwith*-uh) became an orphan when her parents died of smallpox, a disease brought in by the Europeans. At the age of twenty she was captured by the Mohawks and forced to marry their chief. When she was found to be a Christian, the tribe turned against her. To save herself from their hatred Catherine walked two hundred miles through the wilderness until she came to a village of Christian Indians near the place where Montreal stands today. She devoted the rest of her short life to helping people in need. She died at age twenty-four. Pope John Paul II declared her to be Blessed Catherine Tekakwitha.

Saints like these—among both the Native Americans and the French—indicate that the great explorations of New France during the 1600s were not entirely for territory, wealth, or power. Usually the canoes on the lakes and rivers carried both explorers and missionaries. As early as 1639, five years after Champlain died, the Sulpician order was already working with the Chippewa Indians at Sault Sainte Marie, on the shore of the swift, rocky stream connecting Lake Superior and Lake Huron. At the same mission a few years later, Father Claude Allouez preached to both Indians and Frenchmen, claiming all the land westward for the king of France.

The French Push South and West

As the trappers, traders, and missionaries scouted new territories south and west of New France, mission posts were established. In 1672, **Father Jacques Marquette** (1637–75) opened the Saint Ignace mission—a settlement for Indians on the south shore of the upper peninsula of Michigan where Lake Michigan and Lake Huron meet. The next year Marquette was asked to go with **Louis Joliet**, a Quebec trader, to find the big river to the west that the Indians kept talking about.

With five French voyagers—hardy men who knew both waterways and forest trails and who could carry huge packs on their backs over long portages—Marquette and Joliet pushed their canoes into the water at Green Bay. They paddled down the Fox River into Wisconsin, portaged to the Wisconsin River, and then at Prairie du Chien (prer-eed-eh-*sheen*) floated onto the Mississippi. Going south as far as the Arkansas River, they proved that the Mississippi flowed into the Gulf of Mexico rather than into the Pacific Ocean. On the way back north Father Marquette taught the Illinois Indians for a short time at the mission at Kaskaskia, across the river from the present Saint Louis area. He spent the winter among the Illinois tribes on the south shore of Lake Michigan, on the site of Chicago. In addition, he made reports about his explorations, with maps to identify the places he had seen.

A second important explorer of the later 1600s was **Robert de La Salle,** a French trader appointed by the governor of New France to build up the fur trade around the Great Lakes. He had already explored the Ohio Valley, extending the area claimed by France. Now from the fort that he commanded on Lake Ontario, La Salle traveled four of the Great Lakes to Illinois country. From Lake Michigan he came to the Illinois River and reached the Mississippi, which he explored down to its mouth in the Gulf. He then went back to France to find enough people to start a colony on the lower Mississippi. However, sailing westward from Florida, his fleet could not find the Mississippi delta, and a landing had to be made on the Texas coast. La Salle's crew then mutinied, and he was murdered.

A few years later a French colony was started about a hundred miles upstream from the mouth of the Mississippi; they began growing crops such as rice and tobacco on their plantations. Earlier La Salle had named this region Louisiana in honor of the French king. Naturally missionaries also came to this new French territory. It gave them another base from which to supply missionary expeditions throughout the Mississippi Valley.

French pioneers also pushed westward. In 1680, Franciscan **Father Louis Hennepin,** who had been with La Salle on the Great Lakes, decided to paddle upstream on the Mississippi. After being captured and released by the Sioux Indians in Minnesota, he found the falls that are now within the present city limits of Minneapolis and named them Saint Anthony Falls.

Along the Ohio and Mississippi rivers and on the shores of the Great Lakes, French forts and villages sprouted up, built by a few soldiers and colonists. Among these was Detroit, built by Governor Cadillac between Lake Huron and Lake Erie. By 1710 the land west of the English colonies was dotted with French trading posts—with enormous distances between any two. New France was thus quite different from both New Spain and New England: it was primarily a trading empire, not a colonial one.

The government of France took care of the religious needs of their colonists and traders; virtually all of them were Catholics. In 1674, Father Francis Xavier de Montmorency Laval (luh-*val*) was appointed first bishop of Quebec. He was a good organizer, and soon there were parishes along the lakes and rivers for the people in the forts and surrounding villages. Priests educated in the Quebec seminary were appointed to these parishes, which stretched about three thousand miles from the Saint

Lawrence Valley down around the Great Lakes, along the Ohio and Mississippi rivers, down through Illinois and finally to the New Orleans region.

Usually the priests from the seminary took care of the French Catholics, while the missionaries—especially the Jesuits and Franciscans—taught the Indians; the number of Indian converts was never large. Somehow Laval managed to keep in touch with his continent-wide diocese, helped no doubt by the fact that the people were united in one faith. In his concern for the Indians, Bishop Laval did not hesitate to let the traders know that it was wrong for them to use liquor as a way of doing business with the Native Americans.

War Between France and England

New difficulties for the Church in New France came from the European wars fought at various times during a seventy-five-year period, mostly through the 1700s. Part of the hostility was due to the fact that France was Catholic while England was Anglican and Protestant. Eventually this conflict crossed the ocean. Then the Indians came into the dispute—the Hurons on the French side and the Iroquois with the English colonists south of Canada.

Outnumbering the French by as much as twenty to one, English settlers began to move northward in some places. In 1749 they took over the coastlands of Newfoundland and Nova Scotia. French Catholics in the colony they called Acadie refused to give allegiance to the king of England. As a result, many French Canadians were deported to various English colonies to the south, leaving behind their homes and farms. A large number who fled from English rule went all the way down to Louisiana where many of their descendants, known as Cajuns, still live today. The first English settlers who took over the North Atlantic area of Canada deprived those Catholics who remained of their rights: Catholics were not allowed to own land or to vote, nor could priests minister to them.

Within five years the outnumbered French lost their most important forts on the Great Lakes. By 1760 their largest towns, Quebec and Montreal, fell to the English colonists. The war between the French and English, called the Seven Years' War, ended with the Treaty of Paris in 1763. In it, France gave up all her posessions in North America, and Canada came under English rule.

In 1774 the British parliament passed the Quebec Act, giving back to French Canadians the freedom to practice their religion and to hold elected offices. This satisfied the French Catholics because they could then maintain their religious and ethnic identity. After the American Revolution a large number of colonists who had refused to fight against England, migrated to Canada, to the areas west of the Saint Lawrence Valley. These people, members of various Protestant churches and the Anglican church, were also given freedom of worship.

The Early English Colonies

While Champlain was opening Canada through the lure of the fur trade in the northern woods and lakes, three small ships sailed out of the London harbor carrying about 150 English people looking for adventure and profit. This was in early December of 1606. Having sailed the whole winter through high waves and stormy winds, they finally reached the western shores of the Atlantic. In the spring of 1607, as they sailed along a finger of land,

Letters of French Missionaries on the Frontier

These two letters from French missionaries indicate what life was like for these hardy men:

To Bishop Panet in Quebec; from Father J. N. Provencher in Red River Country [Minnesota], 1820:

I shall not allow a canoe bound for Montreal to leave without a letter from me.... I have no doubt that you will be glad to hear some news of the most distant missions of the diocese....

We have spent the winter without mishap; since every one from St. Boniface migrated to Pembina.... The buffaloes were numerous at all times and close to the settlement.... Everybody lived on the meat, there being nothing else.

Several tribes of Indians in this vicinity are threatening to make war. I am not sure upon which nation they will fall; some say upon the Sioux, which may prove disastrous to this colony, for we are expecting about a hundred cows to be sent from Prairie du Chien. Moreover, while the snow was still on the ground this spring, some men were sent to bring seed from that place, and they have not yet returned. In addition we are expecting Lord Selkirk ... to come from that place; they will all have to cross the territory inhabited by the Sioux, from whom there is little or nothing to fear; but there is a great deal to fear from the war parties who will go to attack them. These are in the habit of killing everyone they encounter.... The little seed we planted this year is looking fine; there are no grasshoppers.

Last week a dreadful thing happened at Pembina River; a young lad of fifteen years, who was still a catechumen, was killed and scalped; ... it was impossible to learn to which nation the enemy belonged....

I will elaborate no further, as news of this little settlement is not abundant.

To J. O. Plessis, Archbishop of Quebec; from Rev. Dumoulin, Priest, Red River, Feast of the Epiphany, 1821.

Is a man employed as a trader with the Indians unworthy of absolution on that account?

Can and ought we to baptize an interpreter who wishes to be legitimately married?

Some men once diluted the Indians' rum when they were drunk, or even robbed them; some of these Indians have died since then, others are ... far away. To whom should restitution be made? Can we have recourse to compensation, saying that they [French traders] were compelled to give them [Indians] a great deal of it [rum] for nothing?

they found a wide river, which they named the James in honor of the English king. They could hardly believe the beauty of this new world with its endless forests, unplowed meadows, and freshwater streams. These explorers were the Virginia colony, and the place where they encamped was named Jamestown.

Beautiful as this new land was, hardly anything went right for the Jamestown colony. Most of the people were "gentlemen" who came to find gold. They had no intention of getting their hands dirty with work. Ignorant of the wilderness, they chose a marsh full of infectious mosquitoes on which to build. Many fell victims to fevers. The food they brought with them ran out, and since they did not know how to fish, hunt, or grow crops, by summer half of the colonists had died of starvation and/or fever. Their Indian neighbors, when they saw what was happening, got the settlers through the winter by bringing them bread, corn, meat, and fish.

The next spring the new president of the colony's council, Captain John Smith, took charge. He insisted that the colonists till the land instead of prospecting for gold. Unfortunately, when Smith returned to England, having been hurt in a gunpowder explosion, bad times came to the colony again. Only about one out of ten colonists survived the winter of 1609–10, called the "Starving Time." Bad times in England, however, turned things around for this Virginia colony.

English farmers were being squeezed off their lands by sheep breeders. Because the English government favored sheep raising, many farmers decided to cross the ocean where there was plenty of land. The Virginia Company, an English trading company given rights by the king to settle this territory, offered fifty acres free to every man who could pay the boat fare to the colony. This generous offer was the result of the work of John Rolfe, a tobacco planter in Virginia. Tobacco soon became a very profitable cash crop—that is, a kind of money for the colony, accepted by everyone for any kind of trade or barter. Soon all kinds of people were coming to Virginia from England, not only skilled workers but also some that the mother country was eager to get rid of: orphans, paupers, vagrants, and petty criminals.

In 1619 two things happened that were to have significant effects on American life for a long time. Both events concerned a value that Americans hold most dear, that is, freedom.

In that year a Dutch warship dropped anchor just offshore from the Virginia settlement. On board were black people kidnapped from their West African homeland. Since the tobacco plantations were getting bigger and labor was scarce, the colonists purchased African slaves from the Dutch slave traders. This was the beginning of slavery in the future United States. In contrast to this utter denial of freedom, in that same year each of the little settlements among the plantations elected two representatives to the House of Burgesses. This was the beginning of the American system of self-government, and it illustrated the growing desire for autonomy present among the early colonists.

The next year, 1620, a shipload of determined settlers landed on the Massachusetts coast near Cape Cod. These were the Puritans from England who, before they left the *Mayflower,* signed a solemn promise, a covenant, to start a colony that would live according to the Bible; it would be a kind of New Israel. The Puritans had left their homes in England because they felt that the Reformation had not gone far enough; they felt that the Church of England still had too many practices and beliefs that it had inherited from the Catholics, especially the office of bishop. The Puritans got their name because they wanted to "purify" the Church of everything Catholic. The first village of the Puritans at Plymouth soon grew into a string of villages along the Atlantic coast, beginning around Boston and expanding into what are today New Hampshire and Connecticut.

The New England Puritans were a closed community, allowing no one to settle who did not accept their ideas about God and predestination—beliefs they had learned from the followers of John Calvin. There were dissenters like Roger Williams who refused to accept this religious tyranny. He was exiled from his home village in midwinter. Through the help of friendly Indians he was able to start life anew in Rhode Island. There he began a different religious group that eventually became associated with the Baptist churches.

There were no Catholic communities in Puritan New England, of course. Following the harsh treatment of Catholics in England by Queen Elizabeth, Henry VIII's daughter, many Catholics there had abandoned their faith. Laws forbade Catholics from owning property or from voting. Such anti-Catholic treatment followed English Catholics to the colonies. The situation improved somewhat when King James I gave Lord Baltimore, a Catholic, land for a settlement that was named Maryland.

The First English Catholic Settlers

The first settlers on Chesapeake Bay landed on Saint Mary's Island in 1634. Though the leaders of this colony of three hundred were Catholics, the majority of the colonists themselves were Protestants. The governor, Cecil Calvert, gave strict instructions that the Catholics were not to make any public displays of their religion. The British parliament was more and more dominated by staunch anti-Catholic members, and Catholicism was still illegal in England. Nevertheless, the Maryland colony welcomed anyone who wanted to live

there, and in 1649 a law was passed that was unusual for the times: this was the Act of Toleration, granting freedom of worship to all Christians. However, after some years non-Catholic settlers far outnumbered Catholics. In 1704 laws were passed against Catholics, depriving them of churches as well as of any political positions.

Fortunately, Catholic colonists found more freedom in the colony established in Pennsylvania by William Penn, leader of the Quakers—or Society of Friends. In Philadelphia, Catholics were able to build a church, Saint Joseph's, which at that time was the only Catholic church allowed in the British Empire. This is remarkable, especially because the Quakers themselves did not believe that an organized church with priests was necessary. They were convinced that God loves people and that each person should love all others.

During the 1600s, when French explorers were exploring the Great Lakes and the Mississippi, English colonists kept coming to the Atlantic shores, as far north as Maine and as far south as Georgia. The northern Puritan colonies seem to have had the most trouble with the Indians, who naturally objected to being pushed out of their forest homes. The Puritans looked on Indians as godless heathens who would have to accept Puritan Christianity in order to become even remotely equal. By the mid-century the Native Americans had lost the struggle with the colonists, who now greatly outnumbered them.

The middle colonies had less trouble with the Indians, partly because of the fairness of people such as William Penn, who bought land from the Indians instead of simply robbing them of it. Similarly the Quakers tried to live in peace with all people, and they respected the Native Americans as human beings. Nevertheless, from this point on, Native Americans were continually shoved off their lands, killed by the European settlers' diseases or bullets.

As time went on, the middle and southern colonies had richer families than those in the North, where most of the people were small farmers and craftsmen. As tobacco and cotton became the principal crops in the South, the plantations needed more workers and thus slavery increased. By the time of the American Revolution in 1776 almost half the population of Virginia consisted of slaves, and South Carolina was three-fourths slaves.

By the 1700s the colonies were prospering. They attracted Englishmen who were better educated than the first settlers. These people tried to build up in the colonies the kind of life they had in England, putting up fine homes and ordering furniture and silverware from England. At the same time, the English colonies began to realize their strength—they comprised almost four million people, with all kinds of land, and with seemingly unlimited natural resources. Yet they were still afraid of a minority among them: the Catholics, who were fewer than one in a hundred in 1700.

Independence from England

In 1774 the First Continental Congress displayed this fear of Catholics when it denounced the Quebec Act, by which the English government granted freedom of worship to the Catholics of Canada. Within two years, however, as the colonists became more and more determined to fight the mother country, bigotry against Catholics began to decrease. The colonists realized that they would need all the help they could get in a fight with powerful Britain, even the help of whatever Catholics were available.

In 1776 a three-man delegation was sent from Philadelphia to Quebec to ask French-Canadians to join the Americans in their fight with England. With Benjamin Franklin went two Catholics from a wealthy Maryland family—**Charles Carroll,** the only Catholic to sign the Declaration of Independence, and his cousin John Carroll, a Catholic priest. Remembering the harsh protest in Congress against the Quebec Act, the French Catholics of Canada refused to join the rebellion.

During the American Revolution, Catholic colonists wholeheartedly supported the war against England. Among the leaders were **Stephen Moylan,** a major general on George Washington's staff, and **John Barry,** a young sea captain from Philadelphia, known today as the father of the American navy. Among foreign Catholic noblemen fighting with the revolutionaries were **Kosciuszko,** an engineer, and **Pulaski,** a cavalry officer, who came from Poland to join the fight. The Frenchman **Lafayette** was one of the most popular of Washington's officers. His country's aid was most effective in the military success of the American colonies, especially in the key battle at Yorktown.

George Washington acknowledged the efforts of Catholics when he wrote to them after the Revolution: "I presume that your fellow citizens will not forget the patriotic part which you took in the accomplishment of their revolution and the establishment of its government; or the important assistance they received from a nation where the Roman Catholic religion is professed." Washington supported the Bill of Rights that gave to all U.S. citizens, among other rights, the freedom of worship. As a new country, the United States finally turned away from nearly two hundred years of religious bigotry and discrimination.

John Carroll: The First U.S. Bishop

Until the end of the Revolution there were only a handful of Catholic priests in the colonies, most of them in Maryland and Pennsylvania. They found it impossible to serve the roughly thirty thousand Catholics in the United States at the time. They had to ride circuit—going on horseback to the farms and small villages and encouraging the Catholics to pray in their homes. And during all this time, at least 150 years, there was no bishop for the Catholics in the colonies.

In the bigger towns the Catholic laypeople organized small parishes and tried to get the services of a priest whenever they could. The Church was poor too. Paying priests and building churches was extremely difficult. The Marylander **Father John Carroll** (1735–1815) was one of the first to take some action to build up a more complete U.S. Catholic Church.

One of Carroll's largest problems was that the priests and most of the people they served did not want a foreign Catholic bishop in the United States. Catholics of the United States were afraid that Americans would riot against a Catholic bishop as they had against an Anglican one a few years earlier—one who had been appointed by the Church in England. Since Catholics were now being accepted in the new country, they were anxious not to have the old bigotry revived. However, after much negotiating by Carroll, both in the United States and in Paris, and with the help of his friend Benjamin Franklin, arrangements were approved by the Vatican for the election of a bishop by the U.S. priests. Of the twenty-six priests available at the time, twenty-four voted for Carroll.

Bishop Carroll worked hard to establish order among the U.S. Catholic churches. One difficulty was that people who had had their own ways of doing things all their lives were not now eager to have a bishop tell them what to do. Many priestless congregations had been running their own churches. Also, from 1790 to 1860 the U.S. legislature mandated by law that every church had to have a lay board of trustees who were responsible for church temporalities—that is, debt payments, pastor's salaries, hiring and firing of church personnel.

In effect, many U.S. Catholics, in the fervor of the new democracy, wanted the Church to be run democratically too, with the "voice of the people" being the "voice of God." Bishop Carroll's task was to maintain the support of dedicated Catholics while at the same time to take firm control of church government.

Another major obstacle to church growth was the shortage of priests. Carroll established Saint Mary's, the first U.S. seminary, in Baltimore in 1791. Also, he was even expected to direct things out west, beyond the Alleghenies. He organized the territory into four huge dioceses. Seeing the pressing need for Catholic education, he helped start Georgetown College in 1789.

Finally a new problem arose from the fact that non-British colonists—particularly Germans—were coming to live in the new United States. He had to find priests who could communicate with these people. On the other hand, some of the French missionaries who worked on the frontiers could not speak English. Nevertheless, John Carroll succeeded in planting a Church that could grow in the United States. He was an excellent first bishop for the United States. He knew how to take care of the expanding U.S. Catholic Church, which grew from thirty thousand members at his ordination as bishop in 1790 to two hundred thousand at the end of his life in 1815.

The Movement West

When the revolution against England ended, the new United States of America claimed all land from the Atlantic Ocean to the Mississippi River. With President Jefferson's Louisiana Purchase from Napoleon in 1803, the area of the United States was almost doubled—extending all the way to the Rocky Mountains and north to what is now Oregon and Washington. With all this new territory, these were exciting years. By the year 1800, thousands of settlers were moving westward from the Appalachians on foot, on horseback, in wagons,

The clock tower at Georgetown University

and sometimes on flatboats. Where they settled later became the states of Kentucky, Ohio, Illinois, and Tennessee. After 1825 the new Erie Canal across the state of New York brought thousands of settlers into the Northwest Territory around the Great Lakes.

Since many of these frontier people were Catholic immigrants, especially German and Irish, missionaries came with them. Many of the priests were French, and from among them came the pioneer bishops. Their dioceses were wide open spaces, and so they practically lived in the saddle, riding from one settlement to another to give the sacraments and instruction to the people. **Bishop Flaget,** whose diocese at Bardstown, Kentucky, was the first west of the Alleghenies, had ten priests with whom he had to cover the area that later became Kentucky, Tennessee, Ohio, Indiana, Illinois, Wisconsin, and parts of Minnesota. **Bishop Edward Fenwick** started the first Catholic church in Ohio; as bishop of Cincinnati he eventually had twenty-two churches to look after. **Bishop Dubourg** of Saint Louis, a new town founded on the Mississippi in the 1820s, summed up his impoverished life in a remark he made to a generous parishioner who had given him a bed: the bishop asked if he could trade the gift for something he needed more—some food for himself.

The Development of Catholic Schools

No matter how devoted and tough these early bishops were, they had special help from the Catholic sisters who started schools, hospitals, and orphanages. The best known of these is **Elizabeth Ann Seton** (1774–1821), who was canonized in 1975 as the first saint born in the United States. The daughter of a well-educated Anglican father, she was the mother of five children and a widow before the age of thirty. She became a Catholic and started teaching children. At the encouragement of Bishop John Carroll she established a school and orphanage with a group of women who had gathered around her to help. Her group became the **Sisters of Charity,** and the schools of her sisters were the beginning of the Catholic parochial school system.

Other devoted leaders among the American sisters were **Philippine Duchesne,** of the Sacred Heart order; **Cornelia Connelly** of Philadelphia, founder of the Religious of the Holy Child; **Katharine Drexel,** who started more than fifty communities of sisters to care for poor blacks and Indians in the South and Southwest; and the daughter of Nathaniel Hawthorne, **Rose Hawthorne Lathrop,** who was specially devoted to caring for the sick and dying.

Fewer in number than the sisters were the religious brothers. Among the first brothers working in the United States were the Holy Cross Brothers, the Christian Brothers, and the Franciscans—all of whom began their work in the 1840s. Some of the men's universities founded during this period were Notre Dame by the Holy Cross Fathers in Indiana, Saint John's by the Benedictines in Minnesota, and Saint Mary's by the Society of Mary in Texas.

Until about the mid-1800s most Catholic children attended the public schools in their towns, if they went to any school at all. Since the school boards were composed almost entirely of Protestants and since separation of church and state was a constitutional law but

Elizabeth Ann Seton

not common practice, all children in public schools were required to read the King James version of the Bible and recite prayers. In 1844, Bishop Kenrick of Philadelphia asked the school authorities if Catholic pupils in the public schools could read their own version of the Bible rather than the King James version. The answer was a full-scale riot, including the burning of three Catholic churches and a number of private homes. During the rioting thirteen persons were killed.

In New York in the 1840s and 1850s about a third of the Catholic children were in schools run by the Catholic Church. Catholics there asked for a share of public school money, but the state legislature denied the request, saying that no financial help could be given to religious schools. This request also brought on heated reactions. However, Archbishop John Hughes promised that the Philadelphia violence would never take place in New York. He stationed armed guards around Catholic churches thus discouraging the opposition. Clearly public schools were Protestant schools and would stay that way up until the middle of the twentieth century.

Over the next forty years Catholics continued to struggle with the problem of education for their children. Even where a Protestant influence was not strong in the public schools, Catholic parents still wanted their children to have good instruction in their faith. As much as they were able, they built schools with hard-earned dollars, and many Catholic sisters and brothers gave their lives to teaching the children, getting only the necessities of life in return. Catholic families were proud of their schools, and these schools fulfilled a real need. Therefore, the Baltimore Council in 1884 ruled that within two years every parish should have a Catholic school.

In view of the many financial problems involved in setting up parish schools, **Archbishop John Ireland** of Saint Paul, Minnesota, at the 1890 convention of the National Education Association proposed that all schools, including parochial ones, should be run by the state and all students should be given special times for religious instruction. His plan was tried by several cities in Minnesota, but it came to an end within a few years because of non-Catholic opposition. Ever since then, Catholic families have continued to support their own schools, bearing a double burden through the taxes they pay to finance public schools.

Reactions to Immigrants

Anti-Catholic prejudice, though reduced by the bravery of Catholic patriots during the Revolution, surfaced again from about 1830 to the Civil War. As the number of Catholics in the United States increased, the English-speaking Protestant and Anglican majority became afraid of the Catholic immigrants coming into the country. Persons who called themselves **nativists** wanted the United States for "native-born Americans," that is, for themselves (they forgot that the original native-born Americans were the Indians). The Irish who came to the cities in the East took hard jobs, working on roads and on the Erie Canal. In time they moved west. With their knowledge of English they had an advantage over other newcomers and so were considered a real threat to the "native-born."

The nativists' fear of Catholics was so deep that some well-educated persons took their views. Among them was **Samuel Morse**, inventor of the telegraph, who wrote a book about the conspiracies between Rome and the Catholic immigrants to take over the United States.

Archbishop John Ireland

Building a Missionary School on the Colorado Frontier, June 1876

Sister of Charity, Sister Blandina Segale (1850–1941) was sent to Trinidad in the Colorado Territory to open a school in 1870. At first she was alone, but eventually she was joined by two other sisters, one of whom was Sister Eulalia Whitty. Sister Blandina had to be resourceful, and she certainly seems to have possessed a good sense of humor. Reputedly she even talked Billy the Kid into helping her in her work. What follows is part of a letter addressed to her sister, Sister Justina:

To-day I asked Sister Eulalia if, in her opinion, we did not need a new school building, which would contain a hall and stage for all school purposes. She said: "Just what we need, Sister. Do you want to build it?" I answered, "Yes, I do." She added, "We have not enough cash to pay interest on our indebtedness. Have you a plan by which you can build without money? If so, I say build."

"Here is my plan, Sister. Borrow a crowbar, get on the roof of the schoolhouse and begin to attack the adobes. The first good Mexican who sees me will ask, 'What are you doing, Sister?' I will answer, 'Tumbling down this structure to rebuild it before the opening of the fall term of school.'"

You should have seen Sister Eulalia laugh! It did me good. After three days' pondering how to get rid of low ceilings, poor ventilation, acrobats from log-rafters introducing themselves without notice, and now here is an opportunity to carry out a test on the good in human nature, so I took it. I borrowed a crowbar and went on the roof, detached some adobes and began throwing them down. The school building is only one story high.

The first person who came towards the schoolhouse was Dona Juanita Simpson. ...When she saw me at work, she exclaimed, "Por amor de Dios, Hermana que esta Vd. haciendo?" (For the love of God, Sister, what are you doing?)

I answered, "We need a schoolhouse that will a little resemble those we have in the United States, so I am demolishing this one in order to rebuild."

"How many men do you need, Sister?"

"We need not only men, but also straw, moulds, hods, shovels—everything it takes to build a house with a shingle roof. Our assets are good-will and energy."

Earnestly, Mrs. Simpson said: "I go to get what you need."

...On this day of my hod-carrying, the Rt. Rev. Bishop Machebeuf of Denver, Colorado, arrived on his visitation. The first place to which he was taken was the schoolhouse being built without money. Bishop and Pastor had just turned the kitchen corner when the three of us came face to face. Both gentlemen stood amazed. I rested my hod-bucket. Father Pinto looked puzzled. The Bishop remarked:

"I see how you manage to build without money." I laughed and explained the situation.

Father P. N. O'Brien Writes from Deadwood, South Dakota, During the Gold Rush

To Bishop O'Connor:

I would have announced to you my arrival before this. But I wanted to "prospect" some as the miners say.... The B[lack] Hills as a mining region is [sic] no fraud. There are thousands of dollars taken daily from the mines.... There are supposed to be about 1500 people within an area of twenty miles making Deadwood the center. This is a busy little town full of stores of every description. Saloons, however predominate. ... I have taken a little advantage of the outlook and secured five acres in a most desirable location for a cemetery and also a site for the hospital. The hospital is a growing necessity here. The place is most unhealthy. There are from five to seven deaths every day. The disease is most malignant and the stoutest and most robust struggles but a very short period when attacked. The disease is known as "mountain fever." I have already agitated the necessity of a hospital.... If I get $1500 I believe I ought to commence and when once begun the Sisters ought to be here. They can do better than any one else. Everything is most expensive. I pay $15 per week for board and lodging.... If you send another priest here I want him to be a strictly total abstainer and willing to work in unison with me for God's honor and the benefit of our holy religion. Priests need to be careful here, for the miners though rough are smart and watchful and are very easily given offence.

Though he lost his race for governor of New York on the nativist ticket, his nomination shows that nativism was a strong movement. In Boston, the Presbyterian clergyman Lyman Beecher preached several sermons against Catholics, and as a result, the nativists burned down an Ursuline convent there.

In 1840, when Governor William Seward of New York, a Protestant, tried to obtain financial aid for the Catholic schools of his state, nativists successfully opposed his plan. The Protestants feared that the increasing number of Catholics would result in their taking over the public schools. Undoubtedly nativists remembered that the Church in Catholic European countries had suppressed Protestants through laws, taxes, and even direct persecution.

Anti-Catholic feeling developed into a political party, usually called the Know-Nothing party because its members answered questions about their organization with, "I don't know." In 1855 the Know-Nothings controlled the legislatures in a half-dozen eastern states. However, in their national convention, where they had hoped to nominate a victorious presidential candidate, they split over the slavery question. Following the convention, the Know-Nothing party lost its strength and soon disappeared.

The Frontier Church

In the period just before the Civil War, the young United States continued to spread westward; the new states of Minnesota, Iowa, Missouri, and Arkansas formed a kind of western border. The areas that are now Texas, New Mexico, Arizona, and California were annexed to the United States after the Mexican-American War of 1846–48. This new territory was inhabited by Catholic Mexican-Americans. However, much of the new territory was unsettled, and the land north of these newly acquired territories was inhabited only sparsely by tribes of Native Americans. Since new immigrants were coming into the United States at the rate of two million every ten years, land and work were needed for them. Also, with the discovery of gold in California in 1849, poor immigrants had an extra incentive for "going west."

As the boundary of the United States gradually moved to the Rocky Mountains and down to Santa Fe from Oregon, Catholic missionaries went out to the new lands. **Father de Smet,** a Belgian, was among the first to work with the Plains Indians, whose land was being invaded. He was a true friend to the Indians, free to come and go in safety. The U.S. government asked him three times to represent it at important Indian councils. Unfortunately efforts at reaching just settlements failed because of the onslaught of settlers.

Another great missionary was **Jean Baptiste Lamy,** a French priest who eventually became archbishop of the whole southwestern area of the United States. He was such an interesting church leader that the American author Willa Cather wrote the novel *Death Comes to the Archbishop* about him. Lamy covered thousands of miles of dangerous territory alone on horseback. His thirty-eight years of hard work were successful, not only in expanding churches that had already been started by the Spanish friars but especially in inspiring the clergy already there with new enthusiasm.

Slavery

The western expansion of the United States sharpened a problem that had been growing each year—that is, the problem of black slavery. So strong were the feelings about slavery that in the mid-1800s it became the principal concern for the growing nation. Even nativists put aside their attacks on the Catholic immigrants to take sides on the prevailing slavery question: Should slavery be allowed in the new territories in the West?

Leaders in the fight against slavery were northern Protestant clergy, especially New Englanders. On the other hand, many northerners were not overly interested in seeing slavery abolished, particularly since they feared that the freed blacks would come north to take their jobs away. The immigrants, who themselves were poor people at the bottom of the social ladder, felt that they were as badly off as the slaves in the South. The decisive event came with the election of a Republican president, Abraham Lincoln. Before he was even inaugurated, seven slave states, beginning with South Carolina, seceded from the Union to form the Confederate States of America. Four years of terrible warfare claimed the lives of more than six hundred thousand men —totaling more than the number of casualties in World War II, which was fought in various parts of the world with modern weapons.

The hatred and evil of the Civil War tore apart several Protestant churches, separating northern and southern members. The effect on Catholics was not as severe since they were not divided along regional areas. In 1839 the Vatican had condemned the slave trade, but some Catholics felt that this did not condemn the holding of slaves already in the United States. They argued that there are no condemnations of slavery in the Bible.

In any case, at the time of the Civil War, there was no one, unified position in the U.S. Catholic Church regarding slavery. This is evident in the differing attitudes of two bishops at the time. **Archbishop John Hughes** of New York was sent by President Lincoln to France to explain the stance of the North and to help keep France out of the war. On the other side, **Bishop Patrick Lynch** of Charleston was asked to go to Rome to explain the southern view of the slave question to the Vatican. In spite of clearly different views on slavery, U.S. bishops were able to meet peacefully in the first Council of Baltimore to discuss Catholic issues.

The Civil War was not over when the shooting stopped: there was much suffering from the loss of family and property, more in the South than in the North. Southerners lived under military law for more than ten years.

The last third of the 1800s saw much industrial development in the United States. Steel, textile, lumber, and other kinds of mills were built at an incredible rate, especially in the northeastern states. A most important advance, also, was the transcontinental railroad. One of the results of this achievement was the expansion of cattle raising in the plains; another result was the final suppression of the American Indians who were now forced onto reservations.

The Immigrant Flood

The majority of the immigrants who flooded into the United States after 1850 were poor and uneducated, having suffered from bad times in their old countries. These immigrants were hopeful that they could build a new life. In the early years the immigrants were mostly Irish and German, later the majority came from Italy, central Slavic Europe, and Russia. Because they did not know English, most of them lived with their own countrymen.

Many got jobs as laborers and worked hard for little pay. Many women got jobs that they could do at home, being paid a few cents for each article they turned out. If workers tried to unite to bargain for better conditions, they were fired when their union was discovered. By 1886 a union known as the Knights of Labor had grown to seven hundred thousand members—many of whom were Catholics.

When the Knights were attacked, Cardinal Gibbons of Baltimore wrote to Pope Leo XIII in their defense. The pope responded in 1891 by writing *Rerum Novarum,* the first of his social encyclicals, in which he strongly asserted that all workers have a right to just wages and decent working conditions.

In other ways the Catholic Church tried to keep up with the needs of new U.S. Catholics. Sisters like **Mother Cabrini,** an Italian immigrant herself, organized people to teach in the parochial schools, to care for homeless children, and to nurse in hospitals. Such organizations as the Saint Vincent de Paul Society made it possible for Catholics to help one another with donations of clothes and furniture for distribution to the needy.

Because of the rapid increase in the number of quality schools, colleges, seminaries, and charitable institutions, Catholics and Catholicism gained the respect of Americans. Catholic leaders were recognized throughout the country. For example, **Cardinal Gibbons** was publicly praised by President Theodore Roosevelt as "the most venerated, respected, and useful citizen in our country."

The Ethnic Churches

While the Know-Nothings ceased to be a powerful anti-Catholic force and while the Catholic Church had certainly organized itself, the ethnic churches caused new difficulties. Since the Irish were the first wave of Catholic immigrants and since there were so many of them—4.5 million from 1820 to 1920—most of the priests and bishops were Irish. This created problems for the German Catholics who came to the United States in huge numbers during the last half of the 1800s. They wanted to practice their religion as they had learned it in Germany, and they wanted to preserve the German language. To do this, they established German parishes.

German churches were the centers of the German communities. While the Mass was said in Latin, like it was in other churches, and while most of the devotional practices were similar to those of other ethnic groups, German Catholicism did have its own emphases. For example, German parishes stressed excellence in church music. The parish choir was respected, and membership was considered an honor. In some cities German interparish Catholic choirs put on magnificent concerts. Also, German parishes loved processions through their neighborhoods on saints' feast days. Often German Catholics published their own newspapers, and German was taught in the parish schools. In effect, German parishes supplied a sense of continuity and tradition from the old country.

Three booming cities of the time—Cincinnati, Saint Louis, and Milwaukee—became known as the German Triangle. German Catholics naturally wanted pastors who spoke their language, and they especially resented Irish priests. Eventually, German parishes asked Rome to form German dioceses in the United States. Pope Leo XIII turned down their requests—he stressed that nationality should not be the basis of decisions in the Church, but the Church would take care of the needs of each ethnic church. Ethnic churches continued in the United States for many years, in some places into recent times. Most cities had German, Polish, Lithuanian, Italian, and Irish parishes—each serving their own ethnic constituency.

Cardinal Gibbons Defends the Knights of Labor, 1887

That there exist among us, as in the other countries of the world, grave and threatening social evils, public injustices, which call for strong resistance and legal remedy, is a fact which no one dares to deny, and the truth of which has been already acknowledged by the Congress and the President of the United States. Without entering into the sad details of these wrongs . . . it may suffice to mention only that monopolies on the part of the individuals and of corporations, have already called forth not only the complaints of our working classes, but also the opposition of our public men and legislators; . . . the heartless avarice which, through greed of gain, pitilessly grinds not only the men, but particularly the women and children in various employments, makes it clear to all who love humanity and justice that it is not only the right of the laboring classes to protect themselves, but the duty of the whole people to aid them in finding a remedy against the dangers which both civilization and the social order are menaced by avarice, oppression and corruption.

It would be vain to deny either the existence of the evils, the right of legitimate resistance, or the necessity of a remedy. . . . It can hardly be doubted that for the attainment of any public end, association—the organization of all interested persons—is the most efficacious means. . . .

Democratic Ideals and the Church

Along with the dilemmas associated with ethnic parishes, among some Catholics there was a question of the way U.S. democracy and freedom could mix with a faith that was not a matter of individual opinion. Some leaders felt that Catholics had to segregate themselves if they were to keep their faith in a land open to individual choices of all kinds. Some bishops were convinced that it was not possible to combine being an American with being a true Catholic, at least in matters concerning faith.

At the Council of Baltimore held in 1884 the bishops commissioned a catechism for all Catholics in the United States—a book that would guide them in what they were to believe. Although the final version was never ratified by the bishops, the Baltimore Catechism became the standard text for Catholic school children through the 1950s. The Council of Baltimore stressed that all children should attend Catholic schools where the content of religious instruction would be the same for all.

In the last few years before 1900 a number of priests in the United States thought that the Catholic Church should start using modern American ways of doing things, including the study of Scripture. Some thinkers believed that church government should be more democratic too—reflecting the spirit remaining from the days of lay trusteeship and the election of John Carroll as bishop. In 1907, Pope Pius X condemned what was called Modernism, insisting that the changes suggested were not consistent with church tradition. While Pius did not direct his condemnation directly at U.S. Catholics, his statement served to warn those who wanted to alter longstanding practices.

The Canadian Church in the Nineteenth Century

By the Quebec Act of 1774 the settlers of Quebec were allowed to keep their French culture and religion. In effect, Canada became divided into two parts: Quebec was French and Catholic while all the other provinces were

Newsboys sleeping in a church corner, about 1890

English-speaking and Protestant or Anglican for the most part. In 1867 the Dominion of Canada was formed. Canada thus grew by a union of British colonies—unlike the United States, which became an independent country through revolution.

There were Catholic-Protestant troubles in Canada as well as in the United States. And problems surfaced within Catholic congregations themselves. For example, three Catholic groups coexisted in the small area of the Atlantic provinces: the French-Canadians living on parts of three islands, the Irish in Halifax, and the Scottish in Nova Scotia. There was no bishop for the Atlantic provinces until 1847, and there had been a shortage of priests for years. Quebec was far away, and so the people had to do what they could, even though divided into three ethnic groups. By the time of Confederation there was no wall of separation between church and state as there was in the United States; rather the Canadian government gave help to each church to run its own schools without interference in religious matters.

The Canadian Church grew through the large influx of immigrants, especially the Irish. By 1900 Catholics in Canada were the largest single denomination, numbering about 40 percent of the population. After the turn of the century more and more immigrants were settling in the Canadian West, most of them English-speaking.

To care for the Catholics on these prairie lands and out to the mountains, English-speaking bishops were appointed to serve in Vancouver, Toronto, Calgary, and Winnipeg. The Church also helped establish the faculties for many of Canada's universities. After World War I the four largest churches in Canada were the Catholic (with 46 percent of the population) followed by the United, Anglican, and Presbyterian churches.

The Twentieth-Century U.S. Church

A stream of immigrants continued to pour into the United States up until World War I. When the United States entered the war, there were fifteen million Catholics in the country, about one in five or six U.S. citizens—a real contrast with the period of the American Revolution when there was one in a hundred. Because the world situation was desperate, the war tended to unite Americans, and it united Catholics among themselves as well. The German parishes, for instance, downplayed their German heritage and sought assimilation into the mainstream of U.S. life and the U.S. Catholic Church.

The 1920s was a time of great material progress in the country. Henry Ford made it possible for middle-class families to buy cars. More and more homes were equipped with electric lights. The first radios—crystal sets that needed constant tuning and tinkering—fascinated everybody. And of course, the movies lured crowds of people eager for entertainment. For the first time the majority of Americans lived in cities. Jazz blared out from dance halls and nightclubs.

The postwar period had a contrasting side, especially in some of the new laws. Almost immediately after the First World War, Congress passed the Prohibition Amendment making it illegal to sell alcoholic drinks. America's immigrant classes had not experienced this kind of prohibition in the old country. The pressure for prohibition came primarily from a few Protestant churches. Thus Catholics frequently resented what they saw as an intrusion into their rights.

In 1924, America's door began closing against great numbers of immigrants. Quotas were established to allow only a certain number to enter each year, with northern and western Europeans allowed the greatest freedom. Growth of the Catholic population because of immigration slowed considerably.

Despite the "mainstreaming" of immigrant U.S. Catholics, the old nativist prejudice that early Catholics suffered showed itself with bitterness in the presidential election of 1928. New York governor **Alfred E. Smith** was badly beaten on the presidential ballot amid loud attacks on the loyalty of Catholics to the country. Many Americans were still afraid, in spite of the sacrifices that Catholics made in the war, that a Catholic president would put his religion ahead of his patriotism—indeed that the pope would run the United States through a Catholic president. This same anti-Catholic rhetoric was used against John F. Kennedy when he ran for president over thirty years later. Fortunately Kennedy's election and his term of office dispelled fears surrounding a Catholic presidency.

In 1929, a year after Alfred E. Smith's defeat, the stock market crashed. A worldwide depression left millions of people without work,

homeless, and on the brink of starvation. Many Catholic social services increased their efforts to aid the needy. Some Catholic institutions had to close their doors when they ran out of funds. Nevertheless, the Church continued to grow in numbers through the Depression and World War II.

After the Second World War the Church went on an unprecedented building program. Many new Catholic colleges opened their doors in the 1950s. Most dioceses, whose only Catholic high schools had previously been owned and run by religious orders, now began funding the construction of schools owned and operated by the dioceses themselves. New Catholic newspapers came off the presses at a remarkable rate. All this activity reflects the fact that

between 1945 and 1960 the Catholic population in the United States doubled and was much more prosperous. The Catholic Church had arrived as an established part of religious life in the United States.

Focus on the Models

The Church modeled itself as Herald as it always had: through brave missionaries and teachers who preached and taught the message of the Gospels on the frontiers and in the cities, to Sioux Indians and Italian immigrants, in sod huts and in stone cathedrals. In the age of the radio, TV, and cheap newspapers, the Church adapted all these media to the cause of spreading the Good News. Clearly Catholics stood out in American society; and, despite pressures to give up their particular religious tradition, U.S. and Canadian Catholics were symbols of the Church as the People of God loyal to the traditions of the early Church. Even though there were adjustment problems between immigrant groups, North American Catholics shared in the common sacraments that formed a bond of unity with the universal Church.

As Institution, the Church expanded dramatically in a very short period. Presently there are 175 archdioceses and dioceses in the United States; all these have been created since John Carroll became the first U.S. bishop in 1790. With such phenomenal growth the Church has built other institutions to serve the Catholic community. Through Catholic hospitals, schools, charities, social service agencies, refugee programs, presses, and so on, the Church also fulfills its role as Servant.

Review Questions and Activities

1) On a map, locate the places where Spanish missionaries worked in what is now the United States. What problems did these missionaries encounter? Why were the efforts of Father Junípero Serra so remarkable?

2) Using a map showing Canada and the United States, locate the spots identified in this chapter as places where the French missionaries worked.

3) Why was the French approach to dealing with Native Americans so different from those of the English and Spanish settlers?

4) Why were the explorations of Marquette and La Salle not only important for France but for the Catholic Church?

5) What sort of moral problems confronted the French missionaries in their frontier congregations?

6) What was the Quebec Act of 1774, and why was it so important to Canadian Catholics?

7) The Puritans and many of the other religious groups who first came to America were escaping religious persecution in their homeland. Why then were they so intolerant of Catholicism?

8) Why would American Catholics support the Revolution so staunchly?

9) Describe the many difficulties facing Bishop John Carroll as he took office in 1790.

10) Why did U.S. Catholics establish their own school system? Why were these schools the source of such violent controversy?

11) Who were the nativists, and why did they object to immigrants and to Catholics in particular? Can you think of any examples of similar kinds of anti-Catholic groups active today?

12) What are ethnic parishes and why were they established?

13) In what ways was the development of the Church in Canada different from its development in the United States? In what ways was it similar?

14) How did the two world wars contribute to the unification of the U.S. Catholic Church?

Personal Reflection Exercise

After reading this chapter you have some idea of what life for Catholics was like in North America up until the present. To add to your impressions, try to interview your oldest relative, for example, your great-grandmother or your grandfather. Ask them to describe what it was like to be a Catholic when they were fourteen to seventeen years old. How did the Church fit into their lives when they were growing up? Record the impressions they share with you. Now imagine that, in fifty years, your grandchild comes to you with the same questions. How would you answer them?

15
War, Fascism, and Communism

The Catholic Church in the twentieth century has faced and is still facing enormous challenges: Fascism, Communism, irresponsible capitalism, globally destructive weapons, and extremes of poverty and wealth. Despite these threatening forces, the Catholic Church has grown in size and in its spiritual leadership. Perhaps, as was the case with the early Christians, persecution has led and will lead to further conversion. While the twentieth century has brought great changes, it should be apparent by now that every other period in history has also been filled with failures and triumphs, corruption and virtue, hate and love.

The First World War

From 1903 to 1914 the Catholic Church was led by **Pope Pius X.** Pius was a simple and a holy man. He encouraged **Catholic Action** groups—associations of Catholic laypersons involved mostly in charitable work among the poor. Many of the Catholic social service groups that are sponsored today in dioceses and parishes received their inspiration from these early Catholic Action associations. Pius promoted early Communion for children, more frequent attendance at Mass, and study of the Bible by capable scholars. In short, he was a pastor of a world Church, which is what Catholicism had become. He died on the eve of the First World War—a horrendous event that would change the face of Europe and even change the nature of war itself.

As we saw in chapter 13, Prussia had united all of Germany into a powerful country. Allied with Germany was Austria-Hungary—which was at this time one country that included much of Czechoslovakia. Germany was ambitious to exert its might. The other powers of Europe were just as concerned to protect their empires. As a result, most of the countries had been engaged in a furious arms race. The spark needed to set off the war was given when Archduke Francis Ferdinand of Austria was killed at Sarajevo (now in Yugoslavia) on 28 June 1914. Soon Europe was engulfed in war.

Many circumstances made this a new type of war. First, it was total war that was fought on air, sea, and land. Airplanes and blimps were employed for the first time; these could strike targets deep in enemy territory, including civilian targets. Submarines were used for the first time with deadly effect to block shipments of supplies and troops and to squeeze the economies of the enemy. Submarines could also knock out shipping from South and North America, Asia, and Africa. On land, new weapons, such as poisonous mustard gas and the machine gun, increased the slaughter. Finally, it was a world war—Japan, Australia, the United States, and Canada were drawn into a war that started in Europe. Also the winners

of the war (if there are ever real winners in war) would take control of new colonies and, thus, new sources of wealth. And so, for instance, if Germany conquered France, Germany would take control of France's colonies in Africa and in Asia—Vietnam, Laos, and Cambodia. At stake was global dominance.

Of course, millions of Catholics were caught up in the battle—on both sides. Trying to encourage a swift settlement to the conflict called on all of the diplomatic skills of **Pope Benedict XV** who served from 1914 to 1922. His calls for peace were ignored amidst the lust for power and the fervent nationalism on all sides. Benedict condemned the war as unjustified and gave away huge sums of Vatican money for relief work among the thousands of homeless, sick, and wounded people—most of whom were refugees. In fact, when Benedict died in 1922, the Vatican treasury was so empty that it could not cover the expenses of the conclave called to elect his successor.

Following the Germans' sinking of the British ship *Lusitania,* the United States

Pope Benedict XV (facing page)
Battlefield in World War I (above)

joined the war. The tide turned against Germany. In 1917, Russia withdrew from the war; the Communists had taken power in Russia. One of the pledges Lenin and other Communist leaders had made was that when they took power, Russia would withdraw. Actually, Russian forces were too busy fighting on both sides of the revolution at home to be very effective against the Germans. The war tended to overshadow the Russian Revolution, but the full weight of the Communist takeover would be felt very quickly after the war.

The Aftermath

On 11 November 1918 Germany surrendered. Millions of people had lost their lives in this war that was supposed to "end all wars." At Versailles, France, the Germans were forced to sign a treaty that demanded huge reparations to be paid to the Allied victors. Other harsh measures were taken to insure that Germany would become a second-class, powerless state. Six new eastern European countries were formed—Poland, Hungary, Yugoslavia, Czechoslovakia, Bulgaria, and Romania. A

Jewish homeland was guaranteed by the Versailles treaty; this land would be carved out of Palestine. Jordan, Syria, and Lebanon were created out of the Turkish Empire, which had lost the war on the side of Germany. The map of Europe changed dramatically, but the age-old hostilities did not end so easily. The harsh conditions placed on Germany were the seeds that would blossom into the Nazi party and World War II. Pope Benedict tried to warn the Allied powers not to totally humiliate Germany: "Remember that nations do not die; humbled and oppressed, they chafe under the yoke imposed upon them, preparing a renewal of the combat, and passing down from generation to generation a mournful heritage of revenge." Unfortunately his wisdom was ignored. After the war Germany's economy was in shambles; its citizens were bordering on starvation; and its young people, decimated by the war, were angry and humiliated.

Hundreds of thousands of people on the Allied side had died too. France had even drafted priests and religious into its army. Approximately thirty-three thousand French priests fought and forty-six hundred died defending French soil. Besides the casualties among priests and religious, churches, schools, and other church institutions were destroyed in the bombings, shelling, and house-to-house combat. Worse perhaps than the destruction of buildings was the bitter divisiveness that split the German Catholics from French, Belgian, Dutch, and Italian Catholics. Religious faith was overshadowed by national pride and national humiliations.

The balance of power in the world also underwent a change. Suddenly the United States and Japan were great powers. Without the U.S. entry into the war, the conflict would have lasted far longer, and the results might have been far different. On the other side of the world, Japan was rapidly industrializing and building its armed forces. Japan had soundly defeated Russia earlier in the century and had taken possession of Korea. With a fast growing population and a lack of natural resources to fuel its industry, Japan had to expand. The only way to expand was through conquest.

In addition, with the resources of France and Britain being funneled into the war and into the recovery afterward, their control over their colonies began to slip. India, Ireland, and the Middle Eastern colonies began agitating for independence from Britain. Vietnam, Algeria, and some of the African colonies became restless under French rule. European colonialism was threatened, and while it would be some decades before Britain and France finally relinquished control over their colonies, nationalism in the colonies placed the Church in a precarious position. The first missionaries to these colonies came with the colonizers. While many priests and religious recognized the rights to independence of, for example, India or the Philippines (a U.S. colony), at the same time they were loyal citizens of the colonial powers. And, as has been illustrated before, the Church was sometimes seen as part of the ruling power. Consequently the movements for independence were difficult for the Church.

The idea that World War I would end all wars was clearly an illusion. It had temporarily ended some conflicts, but it also caused new ones: that is, German bitterness against the Allies; Russian Communist hostility toward the West; national independence movements; Japanese determination to take new lands; disputes within the Middle East—especially between Jewish nationalists and Palestinians.

A Time of Disillusionment

Another result of the war was a feeling of disillusionment among people—especially writers, scholars, and those who had to face the full destructive force of the new military technology. As people were killed at long distances by bombs or artillery shells, the honor of fighting for one's country came into question. Gone were the days when a soldier looked his enemy in the eye, when wars were person-to-person struggles, when there was some

sense of respect for the enemy. Clearly this war illustrated that wars do not end war. Many people realized this and knew that it would only be a matter of time before there would be another and even greater catastrophe.

During the 1920s, or the Roaring Twenties, a live-and-let-live mood seemed to pervade many European countries, the United States, and Canada. The war had been won; people wanted to celebrate the good times before war came again. For many people the old values and standards no longer seemed to mean anything. War was no longer honorable; death came impersonally, often with no warning (mustard gas silently burned out the lungs); the forces of religion seemed to have little if any power to stop the madness.

As a result, people tended to grasp other, nonreligious answers to their situation. Especially as some people began to conceive of humankind as just another species of animal struggling to survive (Darwinism), as controlled by forces inside themselves over which they had no power (Freudianism), as deter-

mined by economic forces (Communism or Marxism), as members of races some of whom were meant to rule and others to be enslaved (Fascism), they began to turn to a cutthroat type of antireligious selfishness.

Capitalism

Many of the Western countries that had become industrialized operated with capitalist economies. Competition is the basis of **capitalism**. For example, two companies make shoes to sell to a certain number of buyers. To make a good profit, both companies compete by trying to sell more shoes than the other company. So if one can pay workers less than the other company, it can underprice the shoes and thus outsell the other company. Theoretically this sort of competition is good for the customer, keeping prices down and quality up. But generally in competition there are winners and losers: that is, some businesses make profits and others fold. Thus there are those who make money and those who go bankrupt and wipe out jobs. Taken to an extreme—as it was during the last part of the 1800s and even into this century—capitalism offered rich prospects but frequently resulted in dangerous working conditions, low wages, and frequent unemployment. Unbridled capitalism is clearly unchristian because it destroys trust, brotherhood-sisterhood, and hope.

One way of justifying irresponsible capitalism was to explain it using Darwin's theories. "Survival of the fittest" was the natural law of the universe in this view of the world. All species were in competition for survival—humankind was no exception. Competition in business merely reflected the way of nature: that is, the strong companies survived and prospered; the weak were eliminated. If the strong survived, humankind would be better off.

Psychology:
The New Science

While some people gave themselves to a search for meaning in gaining wealth through capitalism, others looked for answers in the new science called **psychology**, literally "the study of the mind." Enormously influential in this field was **Sigmund Freud** (1856–1939), who is considered the father of psychology. Freud concluded that the personality of human beings consisted of three elements. Simply put, one part of us—the **id**—consists of our natural, unconscious drives for reproduction, food, and survival. Another aspect of us—the **superego**—consists of our learned behavior: laws, rules, customs—all imposed on us by society to control the id. According to Freud, one of the forces of the superego is the moral code of religion. Finally our **ego**, the third aspect of our personalities, is the synthesis of the id and superego—that is, our conscious personality.

Freud taught that mental illness resulted from suppression of our natural drives by the superego—by the rules of society and religion. If we could free ourselves from the effect of these rules, we would be healthier. Religion, Freud said, causes guilt for wrongs committed against a code of behavior. Guilt causes anxiety and sometimes depression; in extreme cases, anxiety and depression become mental illness. If people could be free from guilt, they could probably overcome their illness. Of course, this explanation of Freud's work is overly simple; nevertheless, because of this line of thinking, Freud rejected religion. He saw God as a father figure who rules and controls, yet who supports and comforts those who keep the rules. Freud's view made God an oppressor and manipulator.

The contributions of Freud to the development of modern psychoanalysis should not be underestimated. Much of his thinking is valuable, and his work began the serious study of the mind that has had a positive effect on the treatment of mental illness. However, his rejection of religion, although largely ignored today, had a strong influence in the 1920s and 1930s. To some, it was a comfort to think that the disasters of war were really the results of man's nature being twisted, and that freedom from society's or religion's norms might bring back natural human goodness.

Totalitarianism

While some people sought a sense of purpose in capitalism and/or Freudian psychology, masses of people looked to two totalitarian ideologies to solve the problems facing them. **Totalitarianism** is a belief that one official ideology or theory will explain all aspects of human life and, if followed, will lead to a perfect state for humankind.

V. I. Lenin and Joseph Stalin (above), the first two leaders of the Russian Communist party

In totalitarian countries, a single party led by a dictator or a small group dedicated to the ideology controls all aspects of life for the people. Usually opposition is eliminated by a political police; media and education are controlled by the party and used to manipulate the populace. In very real ways, totalitarianism only became feasible in this century. Modern technology—the radio, movies, newspapers—spread ideas on a mass scale not possible in eras when people could not read or when there was no electricity.

Two totalitarian systems came to power in the twentieth century: Communism and Fascism. In both forms of totalitarianism, religion is only tolerated if it does not conflict in any way with the party ideology. Since the Gospels do conflict with party thought, Christian religion is often suppressed.

Communism

The major tenets of **Communism**, or **Marxism,** were spelled out in the nineteenth century by Karl Marx. In practice, Communism called for a **proletariat** or workers' revolution that would wipe out capitalism and private ownership of property. Afterward, a workers' state would emerge in which all workers would be treated equally and would control their own destinies. To bring this workers' state about, the Communist party would take the lead because the masses of people were ignorant of Marxist theory and methods. This centralized party would rule in the name of the people; control of the economy would be complete and rigid. Organized religion would be suppressed because the capitalist class uses it to keep people in bondage. Also, the Communists thought that the only reason people need religion is to offer them some hope in the next life because their present lives were so terrible. With the wonders of the classless, workers' state, life would be so much better that they would not need religion any longer.

Strong Marxist parties existed in Britain and Germany by the turn of the century, but Communism first manifested itself in the Russian Revolution of 1917. The Russian czar was overthrown; a workers' state was proclaimed with the Communist party in control. In 1919, **Lenin** began the Communist International (Comintern) to coordinate world revolutions. One of the earliest moves of the Communist party was to confiscate all church lands and disperse priests, brothers, and sisters. Most Russians belonged to the Russian Orthodox Church, but some Roman Catholics lived in the Soviet Union too. While the official constitution allowed freedom of religious belief, the Communist party systematically began suppressing the Christian churches. In 1925 the party organized the League of the Godless to harass churchgoers. When Joseph Stalin seized control of the party in 1927, religious freedom was limited even more.

Stalin set the first five-year plan for the Soviet economy (1928–33). He was determined to wipe out landowners and prosperous peasants, to turn private farms into communal operations, and to industrialize quickly. The plan was mostly a failure; people do not change rapidly. Many Russian peasants did not want communal farming; many did want religion. In 1929 the Law on Religious Associations was decreed, allowing people to worship in the churches that remained. However, they could not be instructed in the faith; nor could they gather for prayer or discussions. All congregations had to register with the government. Christians could not be party members, and so they were restricted in the jobs they could get. All these measures were part of Stalin's plan to end the religious life of the Russian people.

In 1930, **Pope Pius XI** called for a worldwide day of prayer for suffering Christians in Russia. His letter *Divini Redemptoris* condemned the errors of Communism. Pius realized that Communism, as it was practiced in the Soviet Union, was in opposition to Christianity—even though the motivation of Marxist thought was to help the poor reach a better standard of living. Indeed, Russian Communism was totalitarianism; only one ideology would be allowed in the Soviet Union. Christian churches—Russian Orthodox, Roman Catholic, Protestant—prevented ideological unity of the Soviet Union. Pope Pius knew what Christians could expect from Communism.

Fascism

The other major totalitarian form of government that thundered into the consciousness of people in the 1920s was **Fascism**. The Fascist philosophy stressed class or racial dominance; it glorified one class over another and a national unity based on racial purity. In Germany, this came to mean that the German people were superior to all other races and nations. In Italy, Benito Mussolini proclaimed that Italy must recover its proud heritage and become an empire once again. Religious ceremonies were replaced by civil ones—often in the form of mass rallies for the Fascist party. If they dared to oppose the party rules, oppressive measures would be used to discredit religious groups. Under a Fascist regime, private property and capitalism are controlled closely. The rise of Fascism in Europe in the 1920s caused

The signing of the Lateran Agreement by Mussolini

the deaths of millions of people, the realignment of national boundaries, and frightening dilemmas for the Church. Fascist governments dominated three countries: Italy, Spain, and Germany.

Fascism in Italy

In 1919, **Benito Mussolini** and his Fascist party took control of the Italian government. While the king still was legally the final authority, in fact, Mussolini reigned. He took power on a platform of reordering an eroding national economy and of opposing Communism. Quickly the Fascists began controlling all aspects of Italian life. While the trains in Italy did begin to run on time and the economy did show some signs of recovery, opposition politicians were hounded by the Fascist troops; some were jailed, some killed. Mussolini also began to rearm a weak military.

The harsh measures to control the country soon posed moral questions for the Church, but Mussolini's actions were not so extremely brutal as to clearly demand a Vatican condemnation—at least in the early days. Mussolini

certainly could not afford this condemnation. In an effort to calm fears that the Fascists would try to compromise the Church, talks were opened with the Vatican. The goal was to reach some new accord between Italy and the Vatican. Remember that since 1870 no pope had stepped on Italian soil; the popes still considered themselves prisoners of the Vatican.

After careful negotiations, the Lateran Agreement (1929) was signed. The papacy legally gave up any territorial claims in Italy and recognized the ruling dynasty—the king. The pope also agreed to stay out of Italian politics and to allow the government to approve the nominations of bishops. In turn, the government recognized the existence of Vatican City as an independent nation and compensated the Church for the loss of Rome and the Papal States in 1870. Religious orders gained legal standing along with other church institutions. The Catholic religion could be taught in all secondary schools, and marriage throughout Italy would follow canon law.

Mussolini saw the state as superior to the Church but could not push this notion into action without turning the people against him. At one point, he tried to suppress the activities of Catholic Action groups. Pope Pius XI publicly opposed this and in 1931 published his encyclical *Quadragesimo Anno,* which criticized an absolutist state that controlled all aspects of life. Mussolini backed away from his open crackdown on Catholic Action.

On the other hand, there was little that the pope could do to stop Mussolini from swaying the masses of Italians who backed him as the **Duce,** or "leader." The pope's criticisms of the Italian invasion of Ethiopia fell on deaf ears; most Italians thought that the victory was justified—indeed, even a source of national pride. Italy marched further and further along the road to Fascism, soon joining into alliance with Adolf Hitler.

Fascism in Spain

Spain's ruling party was Fascist by 1939, but before that time, the largely Catholic country was run by the Communists. During the 1920s, the leftist government actively persecuted the Church: church property was nationalized, education was thoroughly secularized, religious orders were suppressed and disbanded. In some places squads of extreme Communists burned churches and attacked and, in some cases, killed priests and religious. The government turned a blind eye to much of this anti-Church activity. However, a growing resistance to the Communists was being led by Fascist military men. In 1933 a moderate but ineffective government came into office, but fighting between the Communists and Fascists was inevitable. Between 1936 and 1939 civil war wracked Spain. The Church backed General Francisco Franco's Fascists

against the Communists even though they were armed and supported by Hitler and Mussolini. After all, in 1936 alone, ten bishops, six thousand priests, and sixteen thousand religious and lay leaders had been murdered by Communists.

By 1939, Franco was firmly in charge of Spain. Most of the army had sided with the Fascist Nationalists, and a majority of Spaniards supported them too. A state of military rule existed; Communists who had not been killed were locked away or fled into exile. Little opposition was tolerated, and gradually some semblance of order returned to Spain. Catholicism was given official recognition and protection by the Nationalist government.

Nazi Germany

The pope from 1922 to 1939 was Pius XI. For over thirty years he had been a librarian and scholar. In 1918, when Poland received independence from Russia and Germany, Pius was sent to Poland to help establish the Church there. His diplomatic skills were exceptional. Dealing with Mussolini, the Spanish Civil War, and the rising threat of Nazi aggression took all of his diplomatic skill and deep faith.

While dealing with Mussolini was no easy task, coping with Adolf Hitler's followers was a life-or-death matter for the German and, finally, the entire European Church. Nevertheless, Pius came to the point where he could not in conscience tolerate the pagan rituals, brutal persecutions, and crass suppression of the Church in Germany. In May 1937 the pope had his letter *Mit Brennender Sorge* smuggled into Germany. At Sunday Mass in every parish in Germany Catholics heard the words of the pope condemning Nazi brainwashing. In a rage Hitler closed the presses that printed the letter. He then threw priests and laypeople into prison on trumped-up charges in an attempt to threaten the pope so that he would not criticize German Fascism any further. Pius continued to try to lead German Catholics away from Hitler. When Pius died in 1939,

Nazi control of Germany was complete. Hitler seemed to offer Germans a path to greatness once again.

Why was Nazism such a potent force in Germany? How could people be swayed by someone like Hitler? Pope Benedict's predictions were correct about the crushing effects of the Versailles treaty on the German people. The treaty had robbed Germany of its self-esteem, economic solvency, military power, and national pride. To make matters far worse, an economic depression struck Germany after World War I; thousands were unemployed and hungry. Consequently most Germans were looking for a leader who promised them a return of national dignity and power. Out of bitterness came a desire for revenge.

Fascists led by Hitler vied with the Communists for authority in Germany. Many Germans feared Communism because of its ties with their age-old enemy Russia. **Nazism,** or National Socialism, stressed absolute unity of the German people under the **führer**—that is, the "leader." The Nazis guaranteed a "super community" in the state. German blood and soil were considered sacred; and the people of the soil, the Aryans, were claimed to be superior. To a nation humiliated by World War I and the Versailles treaty, the National Socialist banner was appealing.

The Nazis chose as their scapegoats the Jews, gypsies, and any other non-German people. The Jews were accused of being a culture-destroying race. In addition, the Nazis blamed the Jews for conspiring to take over German economy and industry—which was considered part of a plot to subjugate the world. Using scapegoats is common in history; the Roman emperors blamed the Christians for the collapse of the Roman Empire. Tragically, by their silence most Germans joined in the suppression, if not the mass murders themselves, of the Jews in Europe.

By 1933, Hitler had soared into power. Once he was chancellor, he became absolute ruler of Germany within two years. Most Christian leaders, including many of the Catholic bishops, endorsed the new Nazi regime. The Catholic Center party voluntarily voted to allow Hitler to rule by decree. The Catholic trade

Adolf Hitler at a reception with a papal representative

unions dissolved by their own will. Hitler agreed to allow Catholics the freedom to practice their religion, and he approved funding of the churches (although the funds were gradually eliminated). Catholic schools could operate but had to teach the Nazi party line. Clergy were forbidden to participate in political activities. In effect, the German Church let Hitler have his way. As the excesses of Nazi Fascism became more flagrant, some church leaders did protest. Most were quickly silenced.

The Nazis methodically destroyed all church organizations and clamped down on the Catholic press. Hitler occupied the Rhineland in 1936, annexed Austria, and took over Czechoslovakia in 1938. The rest of the world reacted in fear and bewilderment; European powers

Edith Stein (1891–1942): Scholar and Victim

Edith Stein was born to a Jewish family but lost her faith in Judaism in her youth. She was a brilliant student of philosophy at the University of Göttingen in Germany. Here she came into contact with many intelligent Catholics. Eventually she was baptized into the Catholic Church, being especially influenced by Saint Teresa of Ávila. Stein became a university professor, writer, and well-known philosopher.

When the Nazis took power in 1933, she was dismissed from her teaching post because she was non-Aryan, even if Catholic. Soon after this, she became a contemplative Carmelite nun in Cologne, Germany; her religious name was Teresa Benedicta of the Cross. She continued to write books of philosophy although they could not be published because she was considered Jewish.

As conditions worsened in Germany for all Jews, Sister Benedicta was sent to a convent in Echt, Holland. Soon, however the Nazis grabbed Holland too. When the Dutch bishops denounced Nazism, reprisals began with the deportation to concentration camps of all priests and religious who were converts from Judaism. Edith Stein—Sister Benedicta—was sent to Auschwitz concentration camp where she was tortured, then sent to the gas chambers to die on 9 August 1942.

The insanity of Fascism and genocide is well demonstrated in the death of this one intelligent, religious, selfless person. Her story was repeated in millions of cases. The following is the account of the arrest of Sister Benedicta by the Nazi S.S. (*Schutzstaffel*, or elite security corps of the Nazi party) as told by the prioress of the convent where Sister Benedicta lived:

Rosa [Edith Stein's sister] was already waiting in the outer part of the parlour. Speaking through the choir-window I said to the community, "Sister, please pray. I think it is the Gestapo!" Then I stationed myself beside the parlour door in order to follow the conversation. To my horror I discovered that it was something much worse. They were members of the "S.S." One of them, the spokesman, ordered Sister Benedicta to leave the convent within five minutes. She replied, "I cannot. We are strictly enclosed." "Get this out of the way [he meant the iron grille] and come out." "You must show me how to do it first." "Call your superior." Having heard it all myself I made a slight detour to go to the parlour while Sister Benedicta returned to the Choir.

She knelt imploringly in front of the Blessed Sacrament and then left the Choir with the whispered words, "Pray, please, sister!" She signed to Sister Pia, who hurried after her and asked anxiously, "What is it, Sister Benedicta?" "I must leave the house in ten minutes." "But where to?" "He didn't say."

Only then did Sister Pia realize that it must be the S.S. Mother Antonia meanwhile had been speaking to the S.S. man. He said, "Are you the Superior?" "Yes." "Sister Stein must leave the convent in five minutes." "That is impossible." "Then in ten minutes. We have no time!" "We have taken steps to have the two sisters received into Swiss convents and are only waiting for sanction from the Germans. On the Swiss side everything is arranged." "We'll see about that later, but now Sister Stein must come out. She can either dress up or come as she is. Give her a blanket, a mug, a spoon and three days' rations." Again the anguished Superior protested. The S.S. man replied, "You don't need me to tell you what will happen to you and your convent if you refuse to send Sister Stein out." Thinking that he was trying to frighten her the Prioress said, "Give us half an hour at least." "We will not. There's no time." Seeing that nothing would move him she said, "If we must give way to force, then we do so in the name of God." She left the parlour and went upstairs to Sister Benedicta's cell, where several of the Sisters were already helping her to pack. She was still convinced that the transfer to the Le Paquier Carmel was a hope. She scarcely spoke again, and her mind seemed to be far away.

signed the Munich Appeasement Act in which the Germans promised not to conquer any more territory. Within a few short months, the **blitzkrieg** (literally, "lightning war") had smashed the Polish armed forces and Hitler had claimed Poland for Germany.

With the conquest of Poland, extermination of the Jews became a consuming obsession with Hitler and his close circle of advisers. As more concentration camps sprang into operation in Germany, Austria, and Poland, news began leaking out about these death camps where millions of people were gassed, shot, hung, or worked to death.

With Nazi victories in Belgium, Holland, France, and Scandinavia, German pride was at a peak. Yet with the opening of the battle with the Russians and the stubborn resistance of Britain, many in Germany began to see that the Nazis were leading Germany to the same catastrophe that had happened in the First World War.

After the United States entered the war, German losses began to mount up. The **Wehrmacht** (the German army) was not invincible, the **Luftwaffe** (its air force) was losing in the air, and the German navy was being blown out of the water. Conditions at home became dangerous; the U.S. and British air forces were bombing German cities into rubble. In addition, some Germans were repelled morally by the existence of the concentration camps. Resistance to the Nazi regime within Germany increased.

Resistance took many forms, and most of the deeds by the German underground have gone unrecorded. Thousands of priests, religious, and laypeople were executed for church activity. The Nazis cleverly persecuted the lower ranks of the clergy and laypeople. The bishops who protested were left unmolested but knew that the more they protested, the more often their priests and lay Catholics would "disappear" or be executed on phony charges.

One of the more famous groups that formed to stop Hitler was called the Kreisau Circle. Included in its membership was Jesuit Father Alfred Delp. When the plot to assassinate Hitler on 20 July 1944 failed, the entire Kreisau group was executed. Count Klaus von Stauffenberg, who planted the bomb in the assassination attempt, was a Catholic. While the Church did not officially approve the plot, many Christians—Catholic and Protestant—knew that the madness must stop. The disaster of the war was not what the people of Germany had foreseen when they had elected Adolf Hitler in 1933.

Imperial Japan

Halfway around the world, Germany's ally Japan was becoming an empire. In the early 1600s, Christian missionaries and their converts had been executed by the Japanese and the borders of Japan were closed to the outside world. The Japanese felt threatened by the many changes brought by Westerners. In the middle of the nineteenth century, the United States used its navy to force Japan to reopen trade. The emperor at this time decided upon a course of modernization for Japan; industrialization followed.

As Japan became more prosperous, its population grew. As its industry expanded, so did the demand for raw materials. Japan decided to copy the lesson they had been taught by the Western powers—that is, if you want land, take it. Japanese students spread out throughout the world to learn modern methods of warfare. From the British they learned shipbuilding and naval tactics. From the Germans they learned to shape a modern army. In the twentieth century's early years Japan had defeated Russia and had taken Korea. By the 1930s Taiwan and Manchuria were theirs. All of southern Asia remained ripe for the picking.

Whereas Germany chose Hitler because they wanted to regain national pride, the Japanese backed the warlords because they needed land —and also because they saw it as their destiny to lead Asia. To become the most powerful force in Asia, the Japanese had to destroy the French control of Vietnam, Cambodia, Laos; the British rule in Hong Kong, Malaysia, Singapore, Burma, India; the American possession of the Philippines; and the Dutch ownership of Indonesia. The Japanese also cast their eyes on parts of their old enemy China.

After bombing Pearl Harbor, the Japanese quickly destroyed the European forces in Asia—forces that were already weakened by supplying manpower to fight in Europe. Sweeping down from their northern islands, the Japanese soon raised their flag with the rising sun over most of the Far East. Europeans, Americans, and those resisting the Japanese were either killed or put into hellish prisoner-of-war camps. Those imprisoned included almost all the missionaries in the area. Many priests, religious, and laypeople died from a combination of disease, starvation, or overwork. An entire generation of missionaries nearly perished in places like Changi Prison in Singapore or Los Banos in the Philippines. After the war, missionary efforts would be set back many years because of the losses.

Both Wars End

Germany's fall ended a period of the worst devastation in the history of humankind. Thirty million Russians were killed; six million Jews met death in concentration camps. Millions of other people lost their lives in a European war that made World War I look almost small by comparison. Most of the great cities of Europe and countless towns and villages were flattened. Millions of people returned from prison camps or battlelines to find their families dead and homes destroyed.

Would the Allies treat Germany in the same merciless manner they had at Versailles? At one of the Allied conferences late in the war, one of Stalin's first remarks to Churchill and Roosevelt was, "How are we going to divide Germany?" As the battle with Germany ended, it had already become apparent that an even larger conflict loomed ahead between the Soviet Union and the West.

As 1945 neared an end, the Japanese had been driven off or killed on battlefields throughout Asia. Japan itself had been bombed continually by the sophisticated new U.S. airplanes. Naval forces of the United States were steaming toward what would have been the invasion of Japan when news reached them of the obliteration of the cities of Hiroshima and Nagasaki by an "atomic" bomb more powerful than any bomb ever imagined.

As a result of World War II, humankind was confronted with a whole new array of problems. For perhaps the first time in history, huge civilian populations had been the direct

targets of attacks. Weapons were more lethal than ever before—the atomic bomb being the best example. Germany's missiles came into use late in the war, signaling another advance in destructive capability. The close relationship between the military and industry was something rather new too; a novel term emerged—**the military-industrial complex.** With all the high technology needed to fight modern wars, the military had to depend on the industrial sector. And, primarily since weapons cost a lot of money, the leaders of industry gladly cooperated.

In previous wars, religion was often used as an excuse to start hostilities—the Crusades or Muslim **jihad** (holy war) are examples. Even in World War I, people on both sides asked God's help to do their Christian duty by defeating their enemies. In World War II, the Nazis and Fascists systematically attempted to destroy religion; it became an enemy. And the resulting new level of **genocide**—the wiping out of an entire race or group of people—was unparalleled in history. Certainly there had been periods of religious or ethnic genocide, but nothing matched the Nazis' methodical extermination of non-Germans.

Once again, national boundaries were changed. In Europe, Russia annexed whole territories as client states. The cry for a Jewish homeland gave impetus for the formation of Israel. And colonies in Asia and Africa demanded freedom. France and Britain were so weakened by the war that by the 1950s most of their colonies were either independent or close to it; this included almost all of Africa. In global politics, the Soviet Union and the United States squared off as the two most powerful nations with two very different forms of government and national ideologies.

Pope Pius XII, the War, and Its Aftermath

Trying to lead a worldwide Church during world war is an impossible job. However, if there was anyone qualified to try to do so, it was **Pope Pius XII** (Eugenio Pacelli). For most of his career as a priest, Pius had served as a Vatican diplomat. Nine years of his work had been in Germany. Thus he had a deep appreciation for German people and culture. When Hitler began assuming power, the then Cardinal Pacelli was Vatican Secretary of State and had to negotiate diplomatic relations with Hitler. He distrusted the Nazis but feared the Communist threat even more.

As the real nature of the Nazi regime became clearer, Pacelli helped Pope Pius XI formulate his condemnation of German Fascism—*Mit Brennender Sorge,* already mentioned. When Pius XI died, Pacelli was the natural successor; he chose the name Pius XII. He was immediately caught in a dilemma. If he condemned the Nazis and used whatever power he had to stop them—diplomatic protests, excommunication of Catholic Nazis (limited power at best)—he would alienate German Catholics and the Nazis would step up persecution of the Church in Germany. Nazi police would shut down all communication between Germany and the Vatican, thus hampering its efforts at peacemaking.

Neutrality of the Vatican insured its survival. Without the Vatican the pope and the agencies of the Church would have had no base from which to do whatever good could be done. For instance, four hundred thousand Jews were saved from extermination by seeking help from the Vatican. Also, the Vatican sent out an enormous amount of relief supplies to destroyed towns. In addition, the pope had seen what happened when the Dutch bishops had condemned the deportation of Jews; Nazi reprisals crippled the Dutch Church. Finally the pope realized that the Church could not stop Hitler.

After the war, the Church tried to help the

Pope Pius XII

world rebuild. Papal prestige was high because the pope was seen as a hero by thousands who crowded into Saint Peter's Square to receive his blessing. He was awarded a medal from the Israeli government for saving Jews from death.

During the pontificate of Pius XII (1939–58), four hundred new dioceses were created worldwide. He appointed many non-Italian cardinals to reflect the fact that the Church extended everywhere. And, as the Communists strengthened their hold on more countries and persecutions of the Church increased, Pius used what persuasion he had to confront Communism. In 1949 he excommunicated Catholics involved in Communist activities, denounced the Communist persecution of the Church, and encouraged any efforts of resistance to Communism. Nevertheless, the "cold war" between Western and Communist governments had begun.

The Church and Communism: Postwar

Just as they had done in Russia after the revolution, the new Communist regimes in eastern European countries suppressed religion. Countries dominated by Russia included Hungary, Czechoslovakia, Yugoslavia, Poland, Bulgaria, and Romania. East Germany was also under Soviet rule. Millions of Catholics lived in these countries, and they were progressively denied their right to worship.

Hungary was a kingdom from 1920 until the Nazi takeover. After the Germans had been pushed out by the Russians, a Communist government was installed. Cardinal Mindszenty was imprisoned in 1949. By 1951, Archbishop Grosz was sentenced to fifteen years at hard labor; fourteen hundred priests were either exiled, jailed, or forced to leave their ministries for work in factories, farms, or civil service; and one hundred thousand were deported to labor camps. Catholic schools were confiscated by the government. Religious activity continued underground but at great risk. In 1956 the Hungarian people rebelled against their Communist overlords, but Russian troops crushed the uprising. The poorly armed Hungarians were no match for Soviet tanks and well-armed troops. Harsh repressive measures stamped out the resistance and inevitably any church activity.

Czechoslovakia was three-quarters Roman Catholic. The Nazis had imprisoned and executed many priests and Christian people; the Communist regime tried to complete the task. Yugoslavia suffered a similar fate. Four hundred priests had been killed in the war or immediately afterward by the Communists; five hundred other priests had been forced into exile. Cardinal Stepinac survived six years at hard labor and was then confined under house arrest.

At the beginning of the war, Poland had been divided by Russia and Germany, who had been allies when the fighting started. The Soviets killed 1.5 million Poles; among these were four thousand priests. The Germans deported twenty-eight hundred priests to the Dachau concentration camp, where less than nine hundred survived. Instead of being freed at the end of the war, Poland came under the

Czechoslovakian Communist Instructions About the Church, to Party Members, 1942

The Vatican: You are to undermine the authority of the Vatican by all means, especially by attacks in the press, compromising articles and news items.

To break down unity among the clergy, separate higher from the lower clergy, drive a wedge between bishops and clergy, also between the priests and their parishes.

Attack the Catholic Church with all the usual weapons: unreasonableness of celibacy, economic power and wealth of the Church, the Church as a capitalist institution, moral delinquents. . . .

Archbishops and bishops should be prevented from communicating with the Vatican otherwise than through the Government.

Pastoral letters must always have previous Government authorization.

Sermons of priests and all addresses to church associations should be censored and kept under rigid control.

The Czechoslovak Church and the Church of the Evangelical Brethren should be made state churches. The Catholic Church's property should be seized and distributed among national churches.

The Catholic clergy should be forced to join the National Church.

The Catholic clergy should be morally compromised, if necessary by means of woman agents.

iron hand of the Soviet Union. Despite repeated attempts to stifle the Catholic Church, it grew stronger and more important as the symbol of freedom and hope, and as a rallying point for resistance to the Communist's rejection of God.

Communism also gained adherents in Italy and France. In 1946, Italy was declared a republic. Since then the Communist party has become a strong factor in Italian politics. The French Communists also built a political party but have never yet seriously threatened to take over the government. The Church in France was concerned that the working people would be attracted to Communism and leave the Church. Consequently priests began taking jobs on the docks and in the factories to toil alongside the working people. In this way Catholicism could penetrate all aspects of French society.

Focus on the Models

During the first half of the twentieth century, there were few changes in the Church as Institution. As Servant, the Church taxed all of its resources to help the millions of refugees from the two wars. The Servant Church also tried to act as peacemaker. The Church has never ceased acting as Herald—now using media such as radio and television to broadcast the Good News even into Communist countries. Despite Fascist and Communist persecutions Catholics stood firm in their religious convictions. Cardinals Stepinac and Mindszenty and thousands of unacknowledged Christians who continue to practice their faith under oppressive governments are Sacraments of Jesus' continuing presence in the world. For instance, in Poland Catholics are clearly witnessing to the reality of the Church as the People of God. Through public displays of devotion and through active promotion of human rights, the Church in Poland has shown that it is the Body of Christ. Since Fascism and Communism are still spreading in the world, the Church will continually be confronted with ways to remain true to its mission of being the community that Jesus calls it to be.

Review Questions and Activities

1) What tremendous problems did World War I create for the Church? How did the Church deal with these problems?

2) How were the seeds of World War II planted at the Treaty of Versailles?

3) How did the First and Second World Wars influence the colonies of the European powers? And, how did they influence the Church in these colonies?

4) Why did the First World War cause a search for meaning among people? Why was religion unsatisfactory for some people? To what did people turn for their sense of meaning?

5) Describe the differences between Fascism and Communism. How are they both considered totalitarian systems? What is the place of religion in both of these types of totalitarianism?

6) Why did Fascism appeal to the Italian and German peoples?

7) How did Mussolini and Hitler treat religion—especially the Catholic Church?

8) Under what difficult circumstances did the Church in Spain work? Why did the Church side with Franco and the Nationalists?

9) Why did Pius XI condemn the Nazi practices in Germany?

10) How did Hitler use the Jews as scapegoats? What was the Church's response? Why did the Church respond as it did?

11) How did Japan's conquest of most of Asia influence the Church?

12) What new problems faced humankind and the Church after World War II?

13) What attitudes did Pope Pius XI and Pope Pius XII have about Communism? What did they say to Catholics about Communism?

14) Describe the relationship that has existed between Communism and the Church since World War II. Have there been any signs of change in this relationship?

Personal Reflection Exercise

Pointing out ways in which Communism and Fascism oppress religion is quite easy. Perhaps it would be useful for us to consider ways in which capitalism can be oppressive to religion as well. Take some time to think about ways in which capitalism influences people's morals. If a person were really committed to capitalism, how would this commitment influence his or her relationship to the parish community? Capitalism is based on there being corporate winners and losers. Pushed to an extreme, what effect would capitalism have on the Church's being the People of God?

16
The Church Now and in the Future

The twentieth century has seen unprecedented growth in the Catholic Church. The faith has spread throughout the globe. Indeed, by the year 2000, almost 70 percent of all Catholics will live in Asia, Africa, and South America. Gone are the days when the Church was primarily European. Besides the dynamic growth of the Church, it has also renewed itself in dramatic ways. The particular source of this renewal was the Second Vatican Council opened by Pope John XXIII. The complete picture of the future of the Catholic Church is unknown, but even with changes in externals, the Church will continue to fulfill its mission as Herald, Sacrament, People of God, Institution, and Servant. And this mission will be fulfilled through people: sometimes through well-known people like Dorothy Day and Mother Teresa, but also by people like us.

The Young Churches

The expression "young churches" came to be used to signify the fact that former "missionary" areas were now independent from direct control of foreign church leaders. For example, the Philippines is considered one of the young churches even though Spanish priests began converting Filipinos back in the 1500s. It is a young church because only within the last one hundred years have Filipino bishops and priests taken charge of the Church there. Often the change in status from a missionary church to a young church occurred simultaneously with national independence.

Ironically much of the growth of the Catholic Church in Asia and Africa occurred despite delayed training of native clergy, appointments of native bishops, and many other serious difficulties. Up until the 1950s most countries were largely served by foreign missionaries. In many cases these devoted people still insisted that Africans and Asians adapt to Western culture and language. When independence came in some of the countries, it meant rejection of Christianity too.

The two world wars, as has already been mentioned, hastened the end of colonial rule. People in Asia and Africa realized that Western superiority and enlightenment were myths. Nations that could invent mustard gas, machine guns, incendiary bombs, concentration camps, gas chambers, and the atomic bomb could not claim to be more civilized, more humane, or more enlightened. Since the Christian religion was an integral part of Western culture and since this religion that preached love did not prevent the cataclysms of the two world wars, how could Christianity be superior to local religions?

Another obstacle in the missionary effort was competition among Christian sects. Catholics claimed that they had the true faith—but so did Methodists, Baptists, Anglicans, and Presbyterians. And all of these groups claimed to follow Jesus Christ and the Bible. The missionary rivalries caused great confusion.

Finally, Western religion seemed to stress an individual morality that did not address the many injustices that were part of the everyday life of people living in developing countries. Rich Catholics often perpetrated crimes against poor Catholics. And, if religion did not mean anything by way of helping people lead more just lives and lives of service, then why believe?

Yet, to repeat, the growth of the Church in the Third World countries has been enormous. (Third World countries are those that are preindustrial and agrarian—and where human energy is mostly used to provide the necessities of life.) New orders were founded to do missionary work. For example, the Maryknoll Missioners started only in 1911, and yet Maryknoll is now almost synonymous with missionary work. In the United States, the Catholic Extension Society was inaugurated in 1905 to supply funds and other aid to missionary efforts.

The popes of this century have also prodded non-native bishops in the young churches to recruit and train native clergy. In 1926 six Chinese bishops were ordained. In 1927 the first Japanese bishop was consecrated, and finally, the first African bishop became head of a diocese in 1939.

The Asian Church

Many factors have curtailed missionary efforts in Asia. For instance, in 1965 in Burma a socialist government closed all Catholic schools and restricted church work. Despite this, brothers, sisters, and priests have adapted to the new conditions, and the Church has expanded. In Indonesia, Malaysia, Bangladesh, and Pakistan, restrictions have been placed on Christian activities because these countries are officially Islamic. Indeed, it is against the law to convert from Islam to Christianity in Malaysia. India also restricts foreign missionaries. Nonetheless the Indian Church is well led and very strong with over fourteen million Christians.

Asia contains 54 percent of the world's population; only 2.3 percent of Asians are Catholic—most of whom are Filipinos. In Japan, Catholicism has made very gradual progress; the foreign roots of Christianity remain a hindrance to acceptance by the Japanese people. Some accommodations have been made to Japanese customs. For instance, in 1936 participation in Shinto Shrine rites (Japanese rituals that honor ancestors and the Imperial family) was allowed by the Vatican. While Catholic schools and other services are admired by the Japanese, formal religion generally is not a part of Japanese life.

The spread of the Church in Korea was virtually stopped by the Japanese occupation until 1945, and since then by the partition of Korea between north and south, by the Korean War itself, and by the recovery afterward. However, in recent years, the Church has added members at a surprising rate. The Korean bishops and many priests, religious, and laypeople have taken active roles in defending human rights. Catholic schools, hospitals, and orphanages have provided services that have been greatly appreciated and respected by the Korean people.

Active missionary work occurred throughout the seventeenth and eighteenth centuries in Vietnam. When the French took over the governance of the country in 1886, five hundred thousand Vietnamese already shared in the Catholic tradition. Yet most of Vietnam is Buddhist. As agitation for independence grew, some Vietnamese associated Catholicism with the French—this was especially true of the growing Communist party. Then, after years of guerilla warfare, Vietnamese revolutionaries defeated the French army in 1954.

In the treaty negotiations, the Western powers decided to divide Vietnam into the Communist north and the republican south. Thousands of North Vietnamese Catholics fled to the south. As happened in the division of North and South Korea, a civil war broke out, during which the forces of the north led by the revolutionary leader Ho Chi Minh tried to unite the country.

Despite the huge commitment of U.S. money, armaments, and troops, the South Vietnamese could not resist the onslaught of a determined North Vietnam. By the mid-1970s Vietnam was at last unified by a Communist government. Catholic schools were confiscated; lay leaders, religious, and priests were either arrested and sent to "re-education camps" or were assigned jobs in industry or agriculture. Today some church worship is allowed, but Catholic life is hampered by legal restrictions and by the fear of reprisal. Nevertheless, devoted Catholics carry on the faith in Vietnam.

The Church's history in China continued to be stormy in the twentieth century. In 1900 the Boxer Rebellion raged through China. The Boxers were fierce nationalists who wanted to rid China of all foreigners and foreign influences.

Indeed, for nearly a century China had been dominated by the French, British, Japanese, German, and American businesses that were backed up by the armed forces of these countries. These foreign powers were stripping China of its natural resources, giving little in return. The British supplied China with opium in return for products the British got at extremely low prices.

Missionaries accompanied the foreign powers, and in some cases created "rice Christians"—that is, people who converted because the missionaries supplied them with rice, the staple food in Asia. The Boxers wanted to end the abuse of China. In the violent rebellion, five bishops, 130 priests and religious, and thirty thousand Catholics were killed. The rebellion was eventually crushed by troops from the foreign governments that took Peking and overran pockets of resistance. Tragically, not having learned their lesson, the foreign powers imposed even harsher terms on China.

In 1912 a republic was declared in China; the emperor had been overthrown. Yet old patterns and customs die hard. Soon the president of the republic was acting like an emperor, with few improvements for the masses of peasant farmers. Unrest seethed in the countryside. Wealthy landowners still extorted huge taxes from the peasants; and in famines, hundreds of thousands of peasants died of starvation or diseases related to it.

In the midst of this turmoil the Church continued to open schools and hospitals. By 1926 there were six Chinese bishops and nearly two thousand Chinese priests. Nevertheless, the Communist party under Mao Tse-tung (*mow-zeh-dung*) had begun organizing the peasants to rebel.

There were brief periods of peace between the republic's armies and the Communist Red Army, so that they could fight the Japanese invaders. Even so, President Chiang Kai-shek directed most of his energy in combating Mao. As a result, many Chinese sided with the Communist party—at least they seemed to be fighting the foes of China. When the war with Japan ended, civil war began. In 1949, Mao Tse-tung declared the creation of the People's Republic of China.

At the time, there were four million Chinese Catholics. As was true in the Soviet takeovers in Europe, the Chinese imprisoned or expelled all foreign missionaries. The Churches were liquidated. Mao stressed the need for Chinese nationalism and the destruction of all that was foreign and corrupt. Catholics lost their lives or had to go underground. Today worship is permitted, but a bishop appointed by Rome would be rejected. The Chinese government wants to control the Catholic Church in China and to do so government officials appoint church leaders.

Africa

In fifty years the Catholic population of Africa grew 600 percent—from two million in 1900 to twelve million in 1952. Then from 1952 to 1972, the Catholic Church grew to a membership of thirty-six million.

The phenomenal growth of Catholicism in Africa can be traced to many factors. First, thousands of Africans were trained in mission schools. Naturally these schools were vehicles for teaching the Catholic religion. In many regions even now, Catholic schools are the only sources of education. Second, there is a deeply religious spirit among African people that has been nurtured by their culture. Unlike much of Western culture, African culture has not destroyed a sense of the mysteriousness of life, and of God's presence in the world.

During the 1950s and 1960s most African nations gained independence. In some cases missionaries were expelled, schools were confiscated, and hospitals were nationalized. However, in more recent years, there has been a deep appreciation for the services sponsored by the Church. There has been a return of expelled missionaries to countries like Zaire. Most importantly, a strong African clergy and lay leadership has emerged.

Significant problems remain for the African Church. Illiteracy ranges from 50 percent to 95 percent in the sub-Saharan countries. Thus, access to the Bible and religious instruction is limited. However, the Bible is avidly appreciated and studied.

Another problem facing Catholicism is the practice of polygamy—allowing a spouse, the man usually, to have more than one mate at a time. Polygamy has been a longstanding African tradition, but it presents an obstacle to admission to the Church.

Finally many African nations have experienced governmental instability. Whenever a new regime takes power in one of these countries, that country is thrown into turmoil. This kind of instability deepens the massive economic problems facing African nations, most of which have few valuable natural resources and are generally overpopulated.

Pope John Paul II on a visit
to the African nations in 1980

South and Central America

The Catholic Church in South and Central America had for centuries depended on Spanish help—including both missionaries and money. Even when countries gained independence in the nineteenth and early twentieth centuries, many of the clergy who remained were Spanish. Or, in cases where missionaries were asked to leave, the native clergy was so small that Catholics were left unattended. While the situation has gradually improved—in part due to replacement missionaries from Canada, the United States, and other European countries—South and Central America are still badly understaffed by priests, religious, and lay ministers.

The Catholic Church is also hindered by the oppressive regimes that govern many South and Central American countries. In Spanish times, certain families were given huge land grants. The **Indios** were made to work the land for the rich **haciendos**. Over the years, these wealthy families came to rule most aspects of life—the governments, industry, agriculture, and politics. The common people were considered expendable and had few real rights. In El Salvador and Guatemala, these elite families still hold power.

Frequently the military works in collaboration with the rich families or with multinational corporations to insure that these groups can continue to exploit the common people. As a consequence of these oppressive regimes, Communist parties have begun organizing guerilla rebellions in many countries. Poor people may not be completely convinced of Communist ideology, but they are so desperate to create a better life for their families that guerilla warfare seems the only answer.

During the last twenty years, the Church in South and Central America has more and more become the voice of the poor and oppressed. Leaders like **Bishop Dom Helder Camara** in Brazil and **Bishop Oscar Romero** in El Salvador have spoken out for justice from military rulers. Bishop Romero lost his life because of his vigorous stand against the slaughter of women, men, and children by death squads hired by those who want to stay in power; he was assassinated while saying Mass in his cathedral.

The Vicariate of Solidarity in Chile was formed by the Chilean bishops in order to challenge the dictatorship of General Augusto Pinochet—a military ruler whose troops had executed thousands of people without trials for crimes such as having once belonged to a union. Government harassment of the vicariate is constant, but the Church in Chile continues to call for justice and human rights.

South and Central America contain the largest concentration of Catholics in the world. The Church is faced with monumental difficulties —shortages of lay leaders, priests, and religious; wholesale poverty; and congregations divided between Catholics who are rich and powerful and those who are poor and oppressed by these powerful fellow Catholics. Coupled with this is the dilemma of how far to collaborate with underground resistance groups—many of whom are composed of Catholics who lean toward Communism. As is often the case in complex matters, there are no easy answers for Catholics.

Some national churches have chosen to treat the government with "critical collaboration," that is, they support what is moral in government activity and criticize injustices. As would be expected, "critical collaboration" is easier said than done.

Bishop Dom Helder Camara (above)
A church in San Mateo, Guatemala
(next page)

The Church Now and in the Future   313

Another exciting development is the formation of Basic Christian Communities. These are communities formed in neighborhoods by church workers to supply spiritual, financial, and moral support for all the members. These communities center their lives on reading the Bible and trying to apply its message to their present circumstances. They are modeled after the early Christian communities described in the Acts of the Apostles. Basic Christian Communities are helping thousands of Catholics—especially the poor—face life with support from fellow Christians, and with the hope that comes from that mutual concern and from the Word of God.

By the year 2000, almost 70 percent of all Catholics will live in Third World countries. This means that on the whole Catholics will be poor and extremely young. The Third World Church is creating new ways of ministering to meet the needs of its people. In all of these places, Jesus Christ is the source of faith and hope. In South and Central America, Jesus is often pictured as a liberator. In Africa, Jesus is the source of love, and to many Asians, the image of Jesus as risen from the dead is most appealing. Indeed, Jesus is all of these images and will remain the life-spring of the young churches.

Pope John XXIII and Vatican Council II

Pope Pius XII had a long and difficult papacy. He led the Church through World War II and through some of the worst days of the Cold War. Nevertheless, when he died in 1958, the Church was deeply rooted all over the world. His successor was, in many ways, his opposite. Pius XII was born in a wealthy family; **John XXIII** came from Italian peasantry. Pius seemed more distant and cultured; John was approachable, warm, and humorous. On the other hand, both were competent diplomats and had brilliant minds.

John XXIII (Angelo Roncalli) was a sergeant in the Italian medical corps in World War I; later he was made a lieutenant and chaplain. After the war, he moved into the Vatican diplomatic corps, spending nineteen years in the Near East. Finally he became **nuncio** (Vatican representative or ambassador) to Paris. His diplomatic career ended when he was named archbishop of Venice.

Then, in 1958, at age seventy-six, he was elected pope. John was a compromise candidate. Few observers expected much from him, and most thought he would last only a short time. They were wrong on both counts. John's style was very different; he invited various people to dinner with him, sometimes wandered the streets of Rome, visited hospitals and prisons, and told jokes.

The greatest surprise Pope John gave the Church was calling for an ecumenical council on 25 January 1959. Certainly councils had been called before, but usually in times of great crises for the Church. Most Catholics in 1959 could not perceive the problems that John saw clearly confronting the Catholic community. The Second Vatican Council had many purposes, but two major ones were (a) to promote the unity of all Christians, and (b) to study how the Church could adapt itself to the rapidly changing world.

In effect, John opened up the Church to dialogue with the world. John understood all too well that the Church was no longer a European institution, but a worldwide community, made up of women and men with extremely diverse cultures, values, needs, and contributions to offer. The Church could no longer ignore that developments in technology, politics, economics, and science would demand new perspectives.

Despite resistance from many sources, John's council began in 1962 and closed in 1965. Important adaptations were made in five major areas of Church life: the liturgy, the Church's understanding of itself, the Church's attitude toward other Christians, a renewal of a sense of history, and increased dialogue with the modern world.

Liturgical Renewal

Since the Council of Trent in the 1500s, the form for all liturgical worship had been fixed and followed universally. For instance, the entire Mass was said in Latin; the priest faced the tabernacle not the people. Participation was limited to trying to follow the Mass prayers using a missal (although these became common only in the early twentieth century). Even the Gospel and Epistles were read in Latin. Communion was received only in the form of the bread— and that was placed on the tongue by the priest. There were no lay lectors, ministers of communion, or permanent deacons. The focus of the Mass was on worshiping Jesus as God present in the Eucharist.

Vatican Council II altered the focus of the Mass and the celebration of all the sacraments. Clearly, the Mass today is different: English is used; the priest communicates directly with the congregation; the readings of the Gospels and Epistles are given great importance; the congregation participates through spoken responses and singing; Communion is sometimes in the forms of both bread and wine; and so on. The primary focus of the liturgy is to celebrate Jesus present among the community of believers, and to support the faith and growth of the community.

Because of the Church's increased understanding of the Scriptures and the life of the early Church, many of the changes in sacramental practice were patterned after the rituals of the early Christian communities. To many Catholics the changes seemed drastic; in reality, they were rooted in the earliest traditions of the Church.

The Church's Understanding of Itself

Throughout this text, the expressions "the People of God" and "the Body of Christ" have been used to describe the Church. These two ways of describing the Church indicate that all Catholics share in the presence of Christ on earth today. Thus, all of us have important roles to play in the Church. While this may seem ordinary to us now, Vatican Council II was responsible for changing the emphasis away from Church as a hierarchical institution —one in which the pope ruled, priests exercised authority under him, and everyone else followed along.

What this change has meant is, in part, much more consultation within the Church. Parishes now have councils that help manage the life of the community. Parochial schools are run by boards, not just by the local pastor. Catholic high schools and colleges are often led by laypersons and are not so dependent on members of religious orders. In short, the life of the Church is in the hands of all church members, not just the clergy.

Again, the emphasis on the Church as the Body of Christ or People of God is a return to the tradition of the early Church. Perhaps symbolic of this return to early practice was the reinstitution of the permanent diaconate. Remember that very soon after the Church formed itself into a community, deacons were appointed to look after the welfare of its poor, widowed, and sick members. In the Church's history, the diaconate predated the formation of the priesthood. Today, permanent deacons, married and single, fulfill many service roles in the Church and provide leadership. They are a sign that the Church is open to different forms of ministry.

Ecumenism

Certainly one of the most welcome movements brought about by Vatican Council II was the movement to reunite all Christians. Vatican II opened up dialogue with other Christian denominations, seeking common ground for mutual cooperation. As a result, theological commissions from the Catholic Church and from other churches have studied points of similarity and sought to understand areas of difference. In local communities, common prayer services have broken down some of the barriers separating Christians. The Catholic Church and other Christian churches now cooperate more fully in confronting social problems.

Indispensable in beginning efforts toward healing the divisions among Christians were the personal examples given by John XXIII, Paul VI, and John Paul II. Pope Paul VI surprised the world when he embraced Greek Orthodox patriarch Athenagoras in Jerusalem. While neither the pope nor the leader of the Greek Orthodox Church would underestimate the existing differences, their personal meeting broke the ice that had formed by over nine centuries of separation. All three of the popes mentioned above have encouraged shared worship, shared ministerial training, common Bible translation projects, and further theological dialogue.

In its *Declaration on Religious Freedom,* the Second Vatican Council affirmed the value of religious freedom for all people in all nations. The dignity of all persons was proclaimed by Jesus. People must be free to choose or reject Christianity. The proclamation on religious freedom departed from the centuries-old custom in which the Church mandated that Catholicism is best served when it is the only religion allowed by the state. The recognition of freedom of religion echoes the Gospels and Epistles and writings of the early church teachers.

Adopting a Historical Perspective

The Church, just like human beings and human institutions, is shaped constantly by the culture in which it exists. In many of its discussions the council took a historical perspective —that is, instead of looking only at the most recent ways of doing things, the council tried to look at the full range of historical considerations before formulating positions.

For instance, taking the historical perspective, the bishops realized that for various reasons the celebration of the Mass had become less and less a community celebration. Having lost this dimension, the Mass was inconsistent with the practice handed down by the Apostles. Thus, the bishops altered the practice of the Mass to make it more like the original celebration in the early Church. Consequently by taking a historical perspective the Mass is a fuller experience of community.

Scripture is another area where the bishops took a more historical approach. As translations from the original languages were completed, fuller understanding of the original meanings became more clear. New study guides were written to help Catholics read the Bible.

Increased Dialogue with the Modern World

The Second Vatican Council opened avenues of discussion with all sectors of the modern world. Two brief examples illustrate this. First, the Vatican began talks with Communist governments. While Christianity and Communism stand largely at odds with each other, discussion should still go on. In fact, communication between the Vatican and some of the eastern European nations has reduced pressure on Christians living in those countries.

Second, in 1965 the Index of Forbidden Books was eliminated. The Index had been established by the Council of Trent to protect Catholics from materials considered dangerous to their faith. Unfortunately some books of the Index were works of great thought. To open up dialogue, people first have to understand what those with differing views believe. Thus, all viewpoints must be open to study. Just these two examples show that Vatican II did in fact open windows onto the world.

The full impact of the Second Vatican Council will not be felt for many years to come. The man who began the council died in 1963; but his successor, **Pope Paul VI,** continued the work of renewal that he had begun. Besides his meeting with Patriarch Athenagoras, Paul traveled to many places in the world to which popes had never gone. One of the most dramatic instances of the pope reaching out to the world at large was Paul's speech before the United Nations in which he pleaded for peace. Vatican II made the Church truly a church for all peoples in all lands.

At the final session of the council, 2,399 bishops were present. They had produced sixteen important documents setting the course of the Church for decades and maybe even centuries to come. This was the first council of the twenty-one councils held by the Church that was not heavily influenced by secular governments, and the first to be attended by official delegates from other denominations. Whereas the work of the council ended in 1965, the work of the People of God to renew the Church had just begun.

Our Future in the Church

As is undoubtedly apparent by now, Christians throughout the centuries have made the Church what it is today. The Church of the future, in turn, will be made by us. We are the Church; we will be the Church.

But we are not alone in this process of building. Equally clear in our study of the Church's history is the presence of the Holy Spirit. The Church has always been maintained in truth, by individual Christians who listened to the Spirit: Paul listening on the road to Damascus, Augustine sitting in his garden reading the Scriptures, Teresa of Ávila listening to God telling her to reform her order, Francis of Assisi hearing the call to the simple life, Louise de Marillac listening to the voice of God through the cries of the poor in France. Even when awful corruption seemed to tear the Church apart, the Spirit of God through people in the Church called the People of God to renewal.

Pope Paul VI

Each individual has his or her special role in the life of the Church—the Body of Christ. Just as the body suffers when any part of it suffers, so the Church suffers when any one member suffers; the health of the whole body rests in the health of all the parts. Therefore, to build the Church, the Christian is called to be his or her best self. The Church will be compassionate, concerned, and caring, when individuals like us are compassionate, concerned, and caring.

Somehow it seems fitting to end this story of the Church with the words of two great twentieth-century Christians: Dorothy Day and Mother Teresa of Calcutta. They are models of what Christianity has been, is, and will be. They speak and live the faith, hope, and love that are the cornerstones of the Church.

Dorothy Day

Dorothy Day was born in 1897 in Brooklyn, New York, but her sportswriter father moved the family around. After living in Chicago for a while, Dorothy went to the University of Illinois for two years. She became impatient with academic life because it did not seem to be helping to change the many injustices she saw in the world. Moving to New York, Dorothy Day wrote for radical papers and joined in demonstrations—protesting the entry of the United States in World War I, supporting the rights of workers to unionize, and calling for women's right to vote.

Along with many other "radicals" of the time, she lived in Greenwich Village in New York. Among her friends were Eugene O'Neill, the great playwright, and John Reed, an American socialist and journalist, who is the only U.S. citizen buried in the Kremlin with Soviet presidents and Russian heroes. Even a life among such active friends was not satisfying to Dorothy. Somewhere along the way, she began reading the Bible, and soon after she gave birth to her daughter Tamar Teresa, Dorothy wanted her baptized as a Catholic. Breaking with her socialist, atheist, and Communist friends, Dorothy received the sacraments of the Church in 1927.

To support herself and her daughter, Dorothy Day wrote as a freelance reporter. Tugging at her heart and mind were the visions of the hundreds of poor, lonely, hungry men and women who were victims of the Depression.

Then she met Peter Maurin, a sort of wandering Christian philosopher. Together they began the *Catholic Worker,* a monthly newspaper that explained Catholic social thought and that sold for a penny a copy. To help the poor directly, they opened the first House of Hospitality, which provided food and shelter for homeless, hungry people from the streets of New York. (There are now about thirty Houses of Hospitality all over the United States.) The rest of Dorothy Day's life was spent publishing the *Catholic Worker;* managing the House of Hospitality; and demonstrating for civil rights, against war, and for social justice.

Three years before her death in 1980, Dorothy Day published the following letter, which summarizes rather well her views on the Christian life and the way she lived her own life:

Dear Friends,

We are all poor in one way or another, in soul, mind, and body, in exterior or interior goods. Yet even the widow gave her mite and the little boy his loaves and fishes, and the Lord will see to it that they are multiplied to cover our needs.

All through the year, we take what comes to us from day to day, to keep our three houses going in this area, and sometimes clothes come in, sometimes bread, and, last week, a whole carton of frozen ice cream sticks! It is only once a year that we imitate most truly the poverty of Christ and come to you to beg, saying, playfully, "I have shown you honor by giving honor to a greater Lord in your home, for the Lord takes great pleasure in poverty, especially in the form of voluntary begging."

Individually, in our houses, we beg from the one who holds the purse, and that purse is only filled by you, our readers. In return, we give what we have, the *Catholic Worker,* its articles and reviews, to you, and our services, as your stewards, to the destitute who come to our doors.

Sometimes, I think the purpose of the *Catholic Worker,* quite aside from all our social aims, is to show the providence of God, how God loves us. We are a family, not an institution, in atmosphere, and so we address ourselves especially to families, who have all the woes of insecurity, sickness, and death, side by side with all the joys of family. We talk about what we are doing, because we constantly wonder at the miracle of our continuance.

Dorothy Day

This work came about because we started writing of the love we should have for each other, in order to show our love of God. It's the only way we can know we love God.

For forty-four years we have maintained St. Joseph House of Hospitality in the city. The daily soup line still goes on there. Now, seventy-five people share St. Joseph House on First Street and Maryhouse on Third Street, and about fifty are at the farm in Tivoli. Just the heating bill for these places is appalling. No use trying to be businesslike. None of us has that talent. The paper sells for a cent a copy, and the printing bill is big. But no salaries are paid to anyone, so there is not that overhead. Besides, we want far more than a weekly wage. We want God to teach us love. Without it, we are sounding brass and a tinkling cymbal.

The main thing, of course, is to love, even to the folly of the Cross. In the Book of Hosea in the Old Testament, the picture of God's love is the picture of the prophet loving his harlot wife, and supporting not only her but her lovers. What foolish love, what unjudging love! And the picture of God's love in the New Testament is of Christ, our Brother, dying for us on the Cross, for us who are ungrateful, undeserving. Let us love God, since He first loved us. And let us show our love for God by our love for our neighbor.

Our Lord said, "To him who asks of thee, give, and from him who would borrow of thee, do not turn away." And so again we beg, in the name of St. Francis, and in the name of St. Therese, whose desire was to make Love loved.

Gratefully yours in Christ,
Dorothy Day

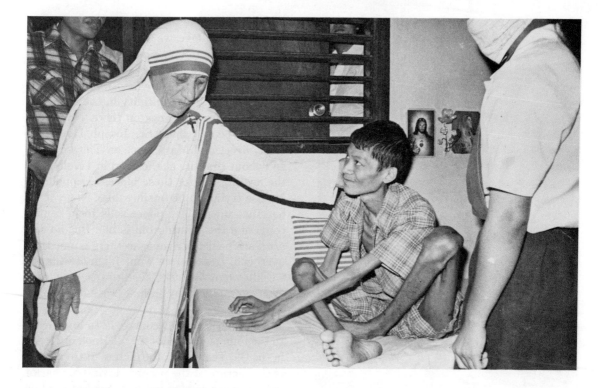

Mother Teresa of Calcutta

Mother Teresa was born in Yugoslavia in 1910. While attending a government school, she belonged to a Catholic youth group. Her life changed when she met a missionary recruiting volunteers to work in the missions in India. In 1928 she joined the Loreto sisters in their work in India. From 1929 to 1948 she taught and administered Saint Mary's High School in Calcutta.

But in 1946 she felt a strong call to work directly with the poor of her adopted city. After having received permission to open a school, she dressed in the white sari (a long dress worn by Indian women) with a blue border and a cross pin and began teaching the children of Calcutta's slums—in a courtyard surrounded by crowded, dirty dwellings.

Soon women began requesting to join her. By 1950 the **Missionaries of Charity** had been approved by Rome and were spreading their charitable work throughout India. The **Missionary Brothers of Charity** were approved in 1963. Today, there are Missionaries of Charity in Venezuela, Rome, New York, Manila— and in many other places where there are poor people. Mother Teresa has received the Nobel Peace Prize and many other awards. Nevertheless, she always returns to the poor, the dying, and the starving.

A British journalist, Malcolm Muggeridge, interviewed Mother Teresa at length. Through Mother Teresa's own words, it is easy to understand what makes her one of the great Christians of our times:

Malcolm: **Mother, how did it happen, the second vocation?**
Mother Teresa: **In 1946 I was going to Darjeeling, to make my retreat. It was in that train, I heard the call to give up all and follow him into the slums to serve him among the poorest of the poor.**

Malcolm: What did you do then?

Mother Teresa: I left the Loreto convent and I went first to the Sisters in Patna to get a little training in medical work so that I could enter the houses of the poor; up till then I was only a teacher and I could not start on work with teaching. First I had to go into the homes and see the children and the sick. At the first little school I started on the first day there were five children. Slowly after that we had more and more children. At present in that place we have got over five hundred children who come daily to school.

Malcolm: In the place where you started?

Mother Teresa: Yes, where I started, out in the compound of a family in the slums.

Malcolm: When I think of Calcutta and of the appallingness of so much of it, it seems extraordinary that one person could just walk out and decide to tackle this thing.

Mother Teresa: I was so sure then, and I'm still convinced, that it is he and not I. That's why I was not afraid; I knew that if the work was mine it would die with me. But I knew it was his work, that it will live and bring much good.

Malcolm: You presumably just taught kids off the streets. What did you teach them?

Mother Teresa: I began with teaching them their alphabet because, though they were all big children they had never been to school and no school wanted them. Then we had practical lessons on hygiene; told them how to wash themselves. Next day two or three girls came from the school where I had taught, they helped me with the children. Gradually the work started to grow and some ladies from Calcutta who had been teachers in the school where I had been teaching also came. And so the work started growing.

Malcolm: I suppose you must have had some money; where did that come from?

Mother Teresa: At first I had only five rupees, but gradually, as people came to know what I was doing, they brought things and money. It was all divine providence because right from the very first I didn't ask for money.

Malcolm: The money had to be voluntary contributions.

Mother Teresa: It was all a gift. I wanted to serve the poor purely for the love of God. I wanted to give the poor what the rich get with money.

Malcolm: You've got your school going, and it's growing; you've got a few helpers, and you've got a bit of money and gifts coming in. What happened then?

Mother Teresa: The Sisters started coming in 1949; the first Sister who joined our congregation was Sister Agnes. She is my assistant now.

Malcolm: She was a schoolgirl in Loreto, wasn't she?

Mother Teresa: Yes, and the first ten girls who came were all students that I had taught in the school. One by one, they surrendered themselves to God to serve the poorest of the poor. They wanted to give their all to God. Then other helpers came; doctors and nurses came on a voluntary basis to help us. In 1952 we opened the first Home for the Dying.

Malcolm: When you say Home for the Dying, you mean that these are people on the streets who have been abandoned and are dying.

Mother Teresa: Yes, the first woman I saw I myself picked up from the street. She had been half eaten by the rats and ants. I took her to the hospital but they could not do anything for her. They only took her in because I refused to move until they accepted her. From there I went to the municipality and I asked them to give me a place where I could bring these people because on the same day I had found other people dying in the streets. The health officer of the municipality took me to the temple, the Kali Temple, and showed me the dormashalah where the people used to rest after they had done their worship of Kali goddess.

I was very happy to have that place for many reasons, but especially knowing that it was a centre of worship and devotion of the Hindus. Within twenty-four hours we had our patients there and we started the work of the home for the sick and dying who are destitutes. Since then we have picked up over twenty-three thousand people from the streets of Calcutta of which about fifty percent have died.

Malcolm: What exactly are you doing for these dying people? I know you bring them in to die there. What is it you are doing for them or seeking to do for them?

Mother Teresa: First of all we want to make them feel they are wanted. We want them to know that there are people who really love them, who really want them, at least for the few hours that they have to live, to know human and divine love. That they too may know that they are the children of God, and that they are not forgotten and that they are loved and cared about and there are young lives ready to give themselves in their service.

Malcolm: How are people to have this faith that is lacking in the world today?

Mother Teresa: It is lacking because there is so much selfishness and so much gain only for self. But faith to be true has to be a giving love. Love and faith go together. They complete each other.

Malcolm: How are people to find this? Our fellow men, or many of them, perhaps including myself, have lost their way. You have found the way. How do you help them to find the way?

Mother Teresa: By getting them in touch with the people, for in the people they will find God.

Focus on the Models

Perhaps in this century more than in previous centuries it is easy to watch the Church operate in its different models. As Herald, the Church has sent out more missionaries than ever before. There are few people on the globe who have not heard at least part of the Word of God preached. Even in Communist countries there are active underground groups of Christians who circulate smuggled Bibles, and radio programs beam into the farthest corners of the world. In developed countries, TV programs teach the Christian message. Perhaps most importantly, Catholics are reading and valuing the Scriptures and are finding them a source of strength.

As Sacrament, especially with the renewal started by Vatican Council II, the Church is gradually becoming more a visible sign of Jesus present in the world. Clearly the emphasis on community celebration of the sacraments has made Catholics more aware of their role in building the church community as this sign of Jesus working among humankind. More and more members of the Catholic Christian community are becoming more involved in ministering to one another and are taking responsibility for church life. Consequently the Body of Christ is becoming more alive.

Even the institutional Church has changed dramatically. The offices and congregations, on both the diocesan and Vatican levels, reflect better today the worldwide nature of the Church and the new sense of mission that the Church has to all people. More authority and leadership is in the hands of people on the local levels—for instance, in parishes and dioceses. Thus the Church can be more sensitive to the situations of people from different cultures.

Finally the Church is seen as Servant everywhere—whether through soup kitchens in New York's Bowery, clinics in the Papua–New Guinea rain forest, counseling services on Chicago's West Side, a Catholic university in Peru, or a crisis center in Toronto. The ways in which the Church serves humankind are as varied as the needs that humans have. Jesus came to serve people's real needs; the Church continues his work.

Each chapter in this text has concluded with a section entitled "Focus on the Models." Why? Because while many outward aspects of the Church have changed drastically, and while the Church has gone through many times of difficulty, corruption, and persecution, it has always remained faithful to its mission to be Herald, Sacrament, Institution, Servant, and People of God.

The Church has fulfilled its mission always through people. There are outstanding people —the saints, for instance. But most of the people who have kept the mission of Jesus alive, those who have have kept the Church alive, are common people like us. People who in their own ways have had faith, hope, and love; who have shared their talents in service to others; who have raised their children in the religion of their ancestors; who try to do good in small ways; who share in the life of worship of their local parish.

What the Church will be in the future will depend on the people who make up the Church today; it will depend on us.

Review Questions and Activities

1) What problems affected the missionary work in the young churches? Why is the term *young churches* used?

2) The missionary effort in Asia has been hampered by certain factors unique to Asia. What are some of those factors?

3) The conversions in Africa have been very encouraging. Why have the missionaries had such success there? What problems are unique to Africa?

4) South and Central America are the most Catholic regions in the world. However, significant difficulties plague the Church in this region. What are some of these? How has the Church's role in South and Central America changed over the years?

5) Explain the major areas of renewal promoted by the Second Vatican Council. Think of some examples of how the council has influenced members of your family. Perhaps interview your parents or some adult friends and relatives. Ask them how Vatican II changed many of the practices of Catholicism. Try to gather as many opinions and feelings as you can about the effects of the council.

6) In many ways, the Church reflects the models of Herald, Servant, Institution, People of God, and Sacrament as well today as it ever did. How so? List some examples of how the Church models itself in the world today.

Personal Reflection Exercise

Reflect back over the whole history of the Church as presented in this book. What images, events, and people did you find most inspiring, most worthy of imitation? In what ways has the Church remained the same throughout history? Has the Church played a vital role in the development of humankind? Will the Church play an important part in the future? List ways in which you see yourself being part of the Church in the future.

Index

Pronunciation Key

A syllable with primary
stress is in italic

uh or **eh**	the, was, puff
ay	fade, day
ee	key, feed
eye	fine, ice
oh	boat
oo	flu
a	mat, air, apple
e	bet
ih or **i**	tip
u	foot, curl
ah	farther, hot, arm
ow	now
aw	raw, dog

Acknowledgments (*continued*)

Scriptural excerpts used in this work are from *The Jerusalem Bible*. Copyrighted by Darton, Longman & Todd, Ltd., London, and Doubleday & Company, Inc., New York, 1966.

Drawing on pages 40–41 is from *Jesus and the Four Gospels* by John Drane. Copyrighted by John W. Drane, 1979.

Excerpts on page 44 are from *The Catholic Almanac* 1981, 1982, and 1983. Used by permission of Our Sunday Visitor.

Excerpt on page 59 is from translation of Pope John XXIII's address in *The Documents of Vatican II*. Published by America Press, 1966. Used by permission of publisher.

Excerpts from Tacitus, Justin, Saint Francis, and the anonymous letter to Diognetus, on pages 76, 82, 176, and 71 respectively, are from *The Lion Handbook: The History of Christianity*. Copyrighted by Lion Publishing, Tring, Herts, England, 1977.

Excerpt on pages 102–103 is from *A Treasury of Early Christianity*, ed. Anne Fremantle. Published by Viking Press, 1953. Used by permission of the editor.

Excerpts on pages 114–116 are from *The Confessions* by Saint Augustine. Copyrighted by Andrews McMeel & Parker, 1943. Reprinted with permission. All rights reserved.

Excerpts on pages 114–116 are from *The Seven Storey Mountain* by Thomas Merton. Copyrighted by Harcourt Brace Jovanovich, Inc., 1948; renewed by The Trustees of the Merton Legacy Trust, 1976. Reprinted by permission of Harcourt Brace Jovanovich, Inc. and Sheldon Press.

Illustration on page 136 is Plate IV from *Gregorian Chant* by Willi Apel. Copyrighted by Indiana University Press, 1958. Used by permission.

Music on page 137 is from *Liber Usalis*, ed. by Benedictines of Solesmes. Published by the Desclee Company, New York, 1959.

Excerpt on page 147 is from *A History of the English Church and People* by Bede. Copyrighted by Penguin Books Ltd., 1955. Reprinted by permission of Penguin Books Ltd.

Selection by Bertran de Born on page 184 is from *Feudal Society* by Marc Bloch, as quoted by Barbara Tuchman in *Distant Mirror*. Copyrighted by Alfred A. Knopf, publisher, 1975. Used by permission of University of Chicago Press and Routledge & Kegan Paul Ltd.

Excerpt on pages 184–185 is from *Summa Theologica* by Thomas Aquinas, Part II–II, Q. 40, Art. 1, which appears in vol. 19 of *Great Books of the Western World*. Published by Encyclopedia Britannica. Copyrighted 1952. Used by permission of Benziger, Bruce & Glencoe.

Excerpts on page 192 are from *Saint Catherine of Siena, As Seen in Her Letters*, ed. and trans. by Vida D. Scudder. Copyrighted 1911. Used by permission of J. M. Dent & Sons Ltd.

Excerpt on page 198 is from *The Canterbury Tales of Geoffrey Chaucer* by R. M. Lumiansky. Copyrighted by Simon & Schuster, Inc., 1947, 1975. Reprinted by permission of Simon & Schuster, Inc.

Excerpt on pages 212–213 is from *The Colloquies of Erasmus*, trans. Craig R. Thompson. Copyrighted by University of Chicago, 1965. Published by University of Chicago Press. Used by permission of publisher.

Excerpt on page 233 is from *The Autobiography of a Hunted Priest*. Copyrighted by Newman Press, 1967.

Excerpt on page 238 is from *Meditations for the Time of Retreat* by John Baptist de La Salle, trans. Brother Augustine Loes, FSC. Copyrighted by the Christian Brothers Conference, 1975. Used by permission.

Excerpt on page 253 is from *Rerum Novarum*, by Pope Leo XIII, 1891. Used by permission of Paulist Press.

Excerpts on page 266 are from *Documents Relating to Northwest Missions, 1815–1827*, ed. Grace Lee Nute. Copyrighted by the Minnesota Historical Society, 1941. Used by permission.

Excerpt on page 274 is from *At the End of the Santa Fe Trail* by Sister Blandina Segale. Bruce Publishing Company. Copyrighted 1948. Used by permission of Sisters of Charity of Cincinnati, Ohio.

Excerpt on page 275 is from *History of the Catholic Church in Nebraska*, vol. 1, by Henry W. Casper. Published by True Voice Publishing Company, 1960.

Excerpt on page 279 is from Cardinal Gibbons' Defense of the Knights of Labor, 20 February 1887, as quoted in *The Catholic Church and the Knights of Labor* by Henry J. Browne. Published by Catholic University of America. Copyrighted by Henry J. Browne, 1949. Used by permission.

Excerpt on page 298 is from *Edith Stein* by Sister Teresia. Copyrighted by Sheed and Ward, Inc., 1952. Reprinted with permission of Andrews McMeel & Parker. All rights reserved.

Excerpt on page 304 is from *Readings in Church History*, vol. 3. Published by Newman Press, 1965. Permission granted by Christian Classics, Inc.

Excerpt on pages 318–319 is from *By Little and by Little: The Selected Writings of Dorothy Day*, ed. Robert Ellsberg. Copyrighted by Alfred A. Knopf, Inc., 1983. Used by permission.

Abridged selection on pages 320–321 is from *Something Beautiful for God* by Malcolm Muggeridge. Copyrighted by The Mother Teresa Committee, 1971. Reprinted by permission of Harper & Row, Publishers, Inc., and Collins Publishers.

Photos: Art Resource, cover and pages 11, 17, 34, 48, 50, 55, 62, 65, 72, 81, 95, 99, 106, 109, 110, 122, 144, 170, 176, 195, 212, 293, 311; The Bettmann Archive, Inc., pages 9, 36, 39, 43, 44, 57, 64, 66, 68, 71, 76, 79, 85, 88, 104, 115 (left), 119, 124, 129, 132, 133, 142, 149, 151, 154, 159, 166, 174, 182, 185, 191, 196, 208, 216, 218, 219, 221, 225, 234, 235, 241 (right), 245, 246, 252 (left), 262, 263, 271, 272, 279, 280, 281, 283, 288, 291, 292, 295, 297, 301, 303; Christian Brothers Conference, page 237; EKM-Nepenthe, pages 53, 260; Frost Publishing, pages 15, 60, 83, 84, 91, 111, 121, 126, 130, 141, 157 (upper), 164, 168, 169, 186, 188, 199, 202, 204, 207, 210, 230, 240, 241 (left), 254, 256, 284, 286, 289, 313; Mimi Forsyth, page 323; Jack Hamilton, pages 6, 12 (lower), 18; Albert Moldvay (Illustrated Stock Photos), pages 20, 22, 32, 317; Religious News Service, pages 115 (right), 252 (right), 300; Nicholas Sapieha (Art Resource), page 312; James Schaffer, pages 12 (upper), 28, 30, 157 (lower), 183, 266, 273, 275; UPI/Bettmann Archive, pages 25, 319, 320